Society and Culture in
Early Modern France

Society and Culture in Early Modern France

EIGHT ESSAYS BY

Natalie Zemon Davis

Stanford University Press

STANFORD, CALIFORNIA

1975

Stanford University Press
Stanford, California
© 1965, 1968, 1973, 1975 by Natalie Zemon Davis
Printed in the United States of America
ISBN 0-8047-0868-1   LC 74-82777

Contents

Illustrations

(between pp. 188 and 189)

PLATE 1: Title page of *Les plaisans devis, recitez par les supposts du Seigneur de la Coquille, Le Dimanche 6. Mars, 1594. A Lyon, Par le Seigneur de la Coquille.* Copy at the Bibliothèque municipale de Lyon.

PLATE 2: Emblem of the Aumône-Générale of Lyon from *La Police de L'Aulmosne de Lyon* (Lyon: Sébastien Gryphius, 1539). Copy in the Archives municipales de Lyon, GG140.

PLATE 3: Float of the Abbé des Conards of Rouen from *Les Triomphes de l'Abbaye des Conards, sous le Resveur en Decimes Fagot Abbé des Conards, contenant les criees et proclamations faites, depuis son advenement iusques à l'An present* (Rouen: Nicolas Dugord, 1587). Copy at the Houghton Library, Harvard University.

PLATE 4: Distribution of bread and money by the Aumône-Générale of Lyon, 1539, in *La Police de L'Aulmosne de Lyon* (see Plate 2 above).

PLATE 5: Mock coin of the Baron of the rue Neuve, Lyon, 1596, with the device *"Nostre iustice regnera en tous temps."* Numismatic Collection, Musée de Lyon.

PLATE 6: Chariot of Mère Folle of Dijon, about 1610, from M. du Tilliot, *Mémoires pour servir à l'histoire de la fête des Foux* (2d ed.; Lausanne and Geneva, 1751). Copy in the author's collection.

PLATE 7: Parade on an ass of a husband beaten by his wife from Claude Noirot, *L'Origine des masques, mommeries, bernez, et revennez es iours gras de Caresme prenant, menez sur l'asne à rebours et charivary* (Langres: Jean Chauveau, ca. 1609). Copy at the Réserve, Bibliothèque Nationale.

PLATE 8: A charivari from a manuscript of the *Roman de Fauvel,* early fourteenth century. Bibliothèque Nationale, Mss. fr. 146.

PLATE 9: *a.* Wife beats her husband with a fagot, from a German playing card by Peter Floetner, about 1520. Reproduced in Eduard Fuchs and Alfred Kind, *Die Wieberherrschaft in der Geschichte der Menschheit* (Munich, 1913), 1: 2, plate 2 (Bancroft Library, University of California, Berkeley). *b.* Wife wearing a codpiece beats her husband. Engraved by Martin Treu, ca. 1540-43, working perhaps in Bavaria (G. K. Nagler, *Die monogrammisten*, 4, no. 2180; Adam Bartsch, *Le peintre graveur* [Leipzig, 1854-76], 9: 77; prints in the Dep't of Prints and Drawings, British Museum, and the Albertina, Vienna). Reproduced in Julia O'Faolain and Lauro Martines, eds., *Not in God's Image* (New York, 1973), plate 17. *c.* "LECOLE DES MARY" [*sic*], French broadsheet printed at Orléans in 1650 and reproduced in Fuchs and Kind, *Die Wieberherrschaft*, 1: 272-73. *d.* Struggle for the breeches, a French engraving of 1690, reproduced in Fuchs and Kind, *Die Wieberherrschaft*, 1: 430, plate 393.

PLATE 10: Woman shakes male fools from a tree, a drawing of about 1526 by the Petrarch-Master of Augsburg. Art Collection, Veste Coburg, reproduced in *Erasmus en zijn tijd* (Catalogue of the Exhibition at the Museum Boymans-van Beuningen, Rotterdam, October-November 1969), no. 150.

PLATE 11: Phyllis riding Aristotle, a woodcut done in 1513 by Hans Baldung, alias Grien. Reproduced in Hermann Schmitz, *Hans Baldung gen. Grien* (Bielefeld and Leipzig, 1922), plate 66.

PLATE 12: Dialogue of Solomon and Marcolf, woodcut, late fifteenth century, from *Solomon et Marcolphus collocutores* (n.p., n.d.). Copy at the Réserve, Bibliothèque Nationale.

PLATE 13: Skimmington Ride, engraved about 1726 by William Hogarth as an illustration for Samuel Butler's *Hudibras*. Reproduced in R. Paulson, *Hogarth's Graphic Works* (New Haven, Conn., 1965), 2, no. 83.

PLATE 14: Interior of the Reformed Temple de Paradis at Lyon between 1564 and 1567. Anonymous painting, perhaps by the Protestant painter and engraver Jean Perrissin, at the Musée de Genève.

PLATE 15: Author portrait of the midwife Louise Bourgeois at age 45, 1608, in *Observations diverses sur la sterilité, perte de fruict, foecondité, accouchements et maladies des Femmes et Enfants nouveaux naix ... par L. Bourgeois dite Boursier, sage femme de Royne* (2d ed.; Rouen: widow of Thomas Daré, 1626). Copy at the Medical Library, University of California, San Francisco.

PLATE 16: Author portrait of the reckonmaster Milles de Norry at age 42 from *Larithmetique de Milles Denorry gentilhomme chartrain, contenant ... la forme de l'achat, vente et distribution de toute sorte de marchandise* (Paris: Gilles Gorbin, 1574). Copy in Special Collections, Columbia University Libraries.

PLATE 17: "*Horribilia scelera ab Huguenotis in Gallijs perpetrata,*" from Richard Verstegen, *Theatrum crudelitatum haereticorum nostri temporis* (Antwerp: A. Hubert, 1588). Copy at the Thomas Fisher Rare Book Library, University of Toronto.

PLATE 18: "Le massacre fait à Sens en Bourgogne par la populace au mois d'Avril 1562" by Jean Perrissin, 1570. Reproduced in A. Franklin, ed., *Les grandes scènes historiques du XVIe siècle. Reproduction facsimile du Recueil de J. Tortorel et J. Perrissin* (Paris, 1886), no. 15 (copy at the University of California, San Diego).

Acknowledgments

Of the eight essays in this volume, five have been published before in slightly different form. Chapter 1 first appeared as "Strikes and Salvation at Lyons" in *Archiv für Reformationsgeschichte*, vol. LVI (1965). Chapter 2 was published as "Poor Relief, Humanism, and Heresy: The Case of Lyon" in *Studies in Medieval and Renaissance History, Vol. V* (1968). Chapter 3 was initially published by the University of Michigan Center for Continuing Education of Women in *A Sampler of Women's Studies* (1973), edited by Dorothy McGuigan. Chapter 4, originally entitled "The Reasons of Misrule: Youth Groups and Charivaris in Sixteenth-Century France," appeared in *Past & Present*, no. 50 (February 1971), © 1971 The Past and Present Society; Chapter 6, originally entitled "The Rites of Violence: Religious Riot in Sixteenth-Century France," appeared in *Past & Present*, no. 59 (May 1973), © 1973 The Past and Present Society. I am indebted to Mr. T. H. Aston, Editor of *Past & Present*, for permission to reprint these essays.

Minor revisions have been made in these five essays for the present collection. Where there was some overlap in example or argument among them, I have altered or shortened the text a little, though not so much as to destroy the independence of each essay. I have corrected errors where I knew of them, sharpened a few fuzzy formulations (much aided here by the careful reading of Peter J. Kahn of Stanford University Press), and added new bibliographic references here and there in the notes.

In preparing these essays for publication, I have been assisted by research grants from the University of Toronto; the University of California, Berkeley; the American Philosophical Society; and the American

Council of Learned Societies. I am grateful to these institutions and organizations for their financial aid. My thanks also go to Helen Thompson and Julie Hess for their services in typing and typesetting the Notes, respectively.

My research has taken me to several archival collections abroad and numerous libraries on this continent and in Europe. The excitement of discovery is always associated for me with one of these settings—Mère Folle, for instance, with the beautiful eighteenth-century library at Dijon; the varied signatures of sixteenth-century artisans with the quiet reading room of the Archives du Rhône, high above the city of Lyon and once the home of its Carmes-Déchaussés. For the assistance of the archivists and staff at the splendid collections in Lyon (the Archives municipales, the Archives Départementales du Rhône, and the Archives de la Charité) and at the Archives d'Etat de Genève I am ever appreciative. I especially value the gracious and generous help of Mme Jeanne Veyrin-Forrer, *conservateur en chef* of the Réserve of the Bibliothèque Nationale, and of Me Jean Tricou of Lyon, a master of its archives and curator of the Numismatic Collection of the Musée de Lyon. So, too, I want to thank those who brought stacks of books to an American scholar, always more pressed for time than she wished, in the municipal libraries of Lyon and Dijon, in the Bibliothèque Méjanes in Aix-en-Provence, and at the Réserve of the Bibliothèque Nationale. What can I say of the personnel in the rare-book room of the Jagiellonian Library in Cracow, still cheerfully supplying volumes from the great Bernstein Collection of proverbs at 8:30 P.M. on a Saturday night?

And finally, there have been riches closer to home—sometimes even books that I could not find in France—in the Houghton Library of Harvard University; the Newberry Library in Chicago; the Folger Library in Washington, D.C.; the Thomas Fisher Rare Book Library at the University of Toronto; the Drake Collection at the Academy of Medicine in Toronto; the Bancroft Library and Kofoid Collection at the University of California, Berkeley; and the medical libraries of the University of California, San Francisco, and of Stanford University.

Ideas, criticisms, and bibliographical suggestions from friends, colleagues, and students have contributed to these essays in fundamental ways. I have acknowledged the specific aid of some of them in the notes; to many others with whom I remain in continuing scholarly dialogue I here express my gratitude. With one friend that conversation is silenced —the late Rosalie L. Colie. Her support came when it was needed, her criticism when it was deserved. She first urged me to publish a collection of my essays, and I wish she could read them.

Last, I must pay tribute to my best general reader, my husband Chandler Davis, mathematician and writer. With unflagging interest or at least patience, he has listened to, read, and reacted to many versions of these essays. Upon an author with a natural Talmudic cast of mind, he has urged economy of expression and the art of persuasion. He has never let me get away without asking myself the central question of my goals as a historian.

N.Z.D.

ENVOI

Born abroad, she longs for you, compagnons.
She longs to shake your hand, to share your wine.
She longs for home, four hundred years away.
Through the pane she hears you but is not heard.
She deserves your pity but will not have it.

The songs you think are vanished once they're sung,
The pleas you think are wasted if turned down,
Jokes you dismiss if no one laughs or winces,
She listens for. You speak sometimes too soft.

And since there is no God she notes your prayers.
And since there is no God she marks your fall.

—Ch.D.

Introduction

These essays are about peasants and even more about artisans and the *menu peuple* of the cities. The very rich, the powerful, the learned, and the priestly are described primarily in relation to the lives of the "modest"—as they reacted to them, conflicted with them, or shared their activities and beliefs. The interaction between Society and Culture and the balance between tradition and innovation are thus explored only for certain segments of the social order, and then through a set of case studies rather than systematically.

The cases are linked, however, by a ramifying chain of historical concerns. Sometimes a question in one essay leads directly to the next essay. So Chapter 1 considers what sorts of social experience might help form Protestant consciousness among male artisans, and how or whether their fight against the Catholic clergy might connect with economic conflict. What, then, prompted Protestant allegiance among some groups of urban women—the subject of Chapter 3—with their different patterns of geographical mobility, literacy, skill, and employ? If, under certain circumstances, economic enemies could be religious allies within the printing industry, what would one find if one looked anew, as in Chapter 2, at the relation of religious sensibility to the treatment of poverty in the sixteenth century? Under certain circumstances, could religious opponents be political allies in the reform of urban welfare institutions?

So too, Chapter 4 examines a wide range of political and social uses for both carnivalesque topsy-turvy and festive organization, including their relation to the socialization of youth; but it stops short of analyzing the meaning of symbols in cultural play. This then becomes the issue in Chapter 5, at least for the complex case of sex-role reversal in rite and festivity. And if one can make such sense of popular recreations, which are sometimes dismissed merely as means of blowing off steam, can one go on to discover some order even in the extreme popular violence with which sixteenth-century crowds defended their religion? Chapter 6, "The Rites of Violence," suggests that this is so.

Next, "Printing and the People" returns to the interaction between literate and oral culture, now conceived more broadly than in the initial chapters on the Reformation. In the course of reviewing the impact of printing on villagers and city folk in the sixteenth century, one comes upon two genres that put the relation between the learned and the people in unusual perspective: collections of common proverbs and collections of "popular errors" in regard to medicine. These are examined in the last chapter from the end of the Middle Ages through the French Revolution. They turn out to generate some interesting questions about our own role as scholarly interpreters of the historical past.

Indeed, throughout the essays I have had a continuing concern about the sources for the lives of people most of whom were illiterate—not only where these sources were, but what they were. Thus, research became not simply a matter of scouring libraries for popular playlets, poems, and pamphlets and of sifting criminal and judicial records, welfare rolls, notarial contracts, and militia and financial lists for mentions of artisans and the poor. It was also a matter of recognizing that forms of associational life and collective behavior are cultural artifacts, not just items in the history of the Reformation or of political centralization. A journeymen's initiation rite, a village festive organization, an informal gathering of women for a lying-in or of men and women for story-telling, or a street disturbance could be "read" as fruitfully as a diary, a political tract, a sermon, or a body of laws. Further, I began to understand that a book or a proverb not only could speak for its author or reader, but could be a clue to relationships among groups of people and among cultural traditions.

In interpreting this material and in accounting for the direction of change in early modern France, I have been guided by a few rules. First, I have tried to be especially attentive to the context of a change, an occurrence, or a decision. For example, the existence during the first half of the sixteenth century of some spheres of urban activity in which the boundary between the secular and the sacred was quite clearly delimited seems to me an essential condition for the events described in Chapters 1 and 2. Alter those boundaries, and journeymen and magistrates would have acted quite differently. But second, I have not assumed that either context or any single attribute of these peasants and city people—whether their sex, or their relation to property and production—in itself determined their behavior. Rather I have imagined these features of their lives as shaping their condition and their goals, as limiting or expanding their options; but I have seen them as actors, making use of what physical, social, and cultural resources they had in order to survive, to cope, or sometimes to change things.

It may also be helpful to readers if I here make explicit certain views about social structure in early modern Europe that I have developed in the course of writing these essays. I do not think only of persons or families mapped onto a one- or two-dimensional chart according to their property, power, prestige, or what have you. I picture a many-dimensional chart in which the axes of measurement represent qualitatively different kinds of power, property, and control, as well as other variables—such as sex and age—that can determine social organization. Different hierarchies may connect in various ways but are not reducible one to the other without some important social transformation.

To give an illustration, a beneficed cleric in Catholic Europe differs from a poor layman not only along the same axis as a merchant differs from a journeyman, but also along another axis in which control over expressive and emotional resources is the criterion. The Protestant Reformation erases this axis in some regions and makes "clergy" roughly equivalent to other professions. It also leads to a simplification of the criteria used to relate male and female, while sharpening the boundary between the superior and the subject sex.

Readers will catch sight of a like process several times in the pages that follow. Social hierarchies are simplified, or the "low" raised up a little to be more like the "high," but the remaining boundaries are more firmly drawn and an effort is made at tighter control over the whole social order. (A friend and I have joked about a possible "law of conservation of boundaries." Let us hope it is not universal.) The simplifiers and raisers-up are sometimes Calvinist leaders, sometimes city fathers dealing with the starving, sometimes humanists writing in the vernacular for the uneducated. Of the ways in which traditional Catholicism, more at home with the inflections and complexities of a multiform social order, also institutes tighter forms of control, I have said only a little in these essays. But I do not intend to suggest that only Protestant societies provide a pathway to the "modern."* Nor, indeed, do I intend to suggest that new techniques of enlightenment and control had no support from the lower orders or always led to the results anticipated by their betters. But let the reader hear what the Lord of Misprint and Ghostly Sally have to say about that.

* I have discussed this matter also in a recent essay "Some Tasks and Themes in the Study of Popular Religion," in Charles Trinkaus and Heiko A. Oberman, eds., *The Pursuit of Holiness in Late Medieval and Renaissance Religion* (Leiden, 1974), pp. 307-36.

Society and Culture in
Early Modern France

ONE

Strikes and Salvation at Lyon

Lyon was large and it was prosperous. Its population grew to up to 60,000 by the mid-sixteenth century; its wholesale industries expanded; its annual fairs became a center for the European money market. Not unexpectedly, these rapid changes brought some unhappiness in their wake, and the inhabitants made no secret of their discontent. Protests ranged from the violent grain riots of unskilled laborers and their wives to the well-organized pressure of master craftsmen and merchants for tax reform and a less exclusive town Consulate. During the same period Protestantism grew in the city. Approximately one-third of the inhabitants were converted to its doctrine and then, after a successful Calvinist uprising in 1562, the rest were compelled to attend its services. After a year, the Catholics were back and a decline in Protestant numbers began—gradual at first, accelerated in the late 1560's, and sealed by the blood of the Vespers' massacre of 1572.[1]

The printing industry of Lyon provides an excellent case study by which to examine the interrelations between "social forces" and Reformation in the city. Its personnel of about 600 included men of most social levels: the great merchant-publishers, who were on the town Consulate; the independent publisher-printers, who were among the "notables" of the town; the lesser master craftsmen and printers' journeymen, who were lumped together with other artisans as *menu peuple*—the little people. All that is missing is the unskilled day-laborer. There was much economic discontent in the industry, masters siding with publishers against the journeymen in the period up to 1572. There were coalitions, conspiracies, court fights, strikes.[2] But also, as is well known, printing supplied many supporters to the Protestant cause in Lyon as in other printing centers.

A natural guess, in anticipation of the evidence, is that most of the Lyon Protestants in the printing industry were lined up on one side of the economic battle. But this turns out not to be the case. I have examined evidence of group behavior and of books printed, as well as the lives of a few hundred individual publishers, masters, and journeymen, and have found that Protestantism took hold early on all levels and by the mid-1550's had won the commitment of the large majority of men in the printing industry.[3] Economic opponents were ordinarily religious allies, even within a single printing shop. Only around 1565 does some correlation between religion and economic position appear, with publishers and masters more likely to stay in the Reformed Church than journeymen.

Let us concentrate on the journeymen printers. It was about groups like theirs, after all, that Henri Hauser said decades ago that the Reformation was a social revolution as well as a religious one; that the popular classes were rising not only against corrupt dogma and the clergy, but at the same time against poverty and injustice, and were seeking in the Bible not only salvation by faith but the original equality of men.[4] It is in urban groups like theirs —men new to the city and cut off from mastership—that some historians have found a social matrix for radical Protestantism and revolutionary millenarianism.[5] Are these assertions true for the printers' journeymen? What were they actually like? How can we account for their interest in Protestantism and their ability to differentiate between religious considerations and economic ones? What finally happened in the 1560's to make economic and religious choices impinge upon each other? In answering these questions, we will see that "social forces" is a broad and slippery term.

It can refer to circumstances or events that shape a man's attitude toward many things—his wife, his wealth, his chances for wisdom. But it can also refer to certain specific goals a man consciously adopts in regard to his job or his superiors and to specific steps he takes to achieve these goals.

The printers' journeymen were men who spent several years and often all their adult lives working for wages as pressmen, typesetters, and proofreaders. They came to Lyon from all over—from rural villages, from other cities, even from outside France. Almost all of them were doing something different from their fathers before them, and they were doing it in a trade that was relatively new and without traditions.

It is not surprising that they tried to create traditions for themselves and did what they could to feel less lost and lonely. Their life in the shop helped somewhat. They worked together, three and four to a press; and pressmen coordinated their labor with typesetter and proofreader. As the journeymen themselves said, "[we] can't be compared to other artisans who work independently."[6] Unmarried workers often lived together. They all ate together at the master's table. They spent their free time together, drinking and talking at taverns, roaming the streets, planning recreations of one kind or another. But their appetite for belonging to and participating in a meaningful collectivity was not sated. They were bothered by the gulf between them and their masters. Not only was there an economic gulf, but they were being cut off from administrative responsibility. There was even a threat of personal separation when the masters, to save money, tried to force the journeymen to eat out. The journeymen fought this and began to suspect their masters of "conspiring" to "ruin and destroy" them. How wrong this was, the workers said, in the printing industry where "above all other Arts, the Masters and Journeymen are or ought to be only one body together, like a family and fraternity."[7]

Yet the gulf was there, and nostalgia could not hide the fact that a conflict of economic interests was widening it. Thus the journeymen lost their enthusiasm for the Confraternity of the Printers, in which they had participated *with* their masters at the Carmelite monastery in the opening years of the sixteenth century. Instead they formed a secular brotherhood of their own and called it a Company[8]—the Company of the Griffarins.*

Their situation with regard to the Catholic clergy in Lyon was similar. The parish churches serving the printing quarter were dominated either by the "nonchalant" sons of nobles from nearby provinces or by canons who belonged to the Consular families of Lyon. This might have made less difference if there had been more men like the Dominican Santo Pagnini around (see p. 30). He preached eloquently for Catholic orthodoxy and for a new system of urban poor relief. He squeezed money for a new hospital out of his rich friends and relatives, yet was also familiar to men in several printing ateliers. As it was, hardly any of the Lyon clergy followed his example until it was too late.[9]

It is small wonder that when the possibility appeared of a new style of worship with congregational participation and a liturgy in the vernacular, printers' journeymen responded. A poor weaponmaker who risked his life to proselytize among them in the 1530's did not seem at all nonchalant. He told them he was as much a priest as any man, that Heaven was God's church and the earth His carpet, that one could say sacramental words anywhere.[10] The kind of religious experience that printing workers sought afterward is expressed in the public processions they organized in 1551. They acted independently of the clandestine pastors who were meeting with less obstreperous Protestants in small conventicles. A few hundred armed journeymen led other artisans and their wives up the streets singing the Psalms in French and

---

* The title was variously pronounced Golfarin, Gorfarin, Gourfarin, and Griffarin. Golfarin is an old French word for "glutton." This was an accusation often thrown at the journeymen by their masters, who resented their demands for a higher food-salary. From Golfarin, the name became most frequently Griffarin, a neologism suggesting claws or talons, and thus the power of the Company. See N. Z. Davis, "A Trade Union in Sixteenth-Century France," *Economic History Review* 19 (1966): 48-69.

even interspersing their Psalms with insults shouted at the noble canon-counts at the Cathedral of Saint Jean.[11] Their numbers and the activistic fellowship of their singing not only helped them brave arrest, but also allayed more profound fears of death and human isolation.

Printers' journeymen had a second trait, which all the authorities called "impudence," but which we can describe as confidence or pride. Partly they were proud of their skills; about two-thirds of them could read and write. Their learning may not have gone very deep—"lightly tinted with letters" is how one disgusted editor described them—but then the journeymen were comparing themselves with their fathers or other artisans, not with scholars. They even boasted about how hard it was to work at the press.[12] In addition, their pride was rooted in a conviction shared by masters, publishers, and many others that printing was of enormous value to Christian society. Minerva, "the Mother of Printing and Goddess of Knowledge," was the central figure in a festival they organized, and the journeymen proclaimed themselves to be the men who made her honor shine (see Plate 1).[13] Nor were they embarrassed by the fact that others had the capital while they did the work. Rather, they said, "the name Printer should truly be reserved for [us, since we] perform the greatest part of printing." Royal authorities might prescribe corporal punishment for them as they would for persons doing physical labor, but the printers' journeymen believed that they labored not out of coercion, as slaves, but "as free men working voluntarily at an excellent and noble calling."[14]

Such self-confidence had important consequences for their attitudes and actions both in the printing shop and in regard to religious matters. They might be among the highest paid workers in Lyon (along with carpenters' journeymen and painters' journeymen), but no matter, they thought they deserved better, especially when, as they put it, the publishers and master printers were "daily acquiring great and honorable wealth at the price of [our] sweat and marvelous toil—yea even at the price of [our] blood."[15] They showed no guilt about their militant disobedience in setting up their journeymen's organization, in arranging work stoppages or industrywide strikes, in taking days off when they needed them, in appealing the king's edicts to the Parlement of Paris in the face of specific royal prohibitions. Indeed, among the oaths sworn by initiates into the Company of the Griffarins was one "to maintain the right order of the Printing Industry."[16] *They* were the ones who knew what that order was and they were prepared to fight for it.

During the same years, Protestant preachers and booklets in Lyon were saying again and again that the Catholic clergy treated laymen below their worth. Already in 1524 a Protestant preacher had proclaimed with Paul the message of the New Testament— only God has authority over our hearts. "Must we always have over us a schoolmaster with a whip in his hand?" he asked, "as if we didn't have enough sense to conduct ourselves? Must we always be apprentices?"[17] Others went on to urge all Christians to test the lies of the clergy themselves against the Scripture which they could read in the vernacular.[18] If a few Protestant worries began to be voiced in the 1550's about whether the simple and untutored could understand the Bible without help, nevertheless in the same years a Protestant play, probably performed on a Lyon street corner, made fun of a stupid Catholic priest who frets over the heretics. "Why you will see an artisan, a shoemaker or a locksmith, a goldsmith or a dressmaker who knows the Testament of Jesus Christ by heart. Oh, what error! Oh, what poison!"[19]

The printers' journeymen were very ready to believe the Protestant argument. But did they actually study the Scripture with care in those years when few of them were involved in organized conventicles? It is hard to know. Certainly some of the pastors with whom they were to have dealings doubted their seriousness and their understanding of doctrine. But that they had the right to such "celestial bread" (as one printer called his publications of the Gospel in French), the proud printers' journeymen were sure.[20]

The connection found here—between confidence bred from

pride of calling and confidence in one's worth relative to the Catholic clergy—may go far toward explaining the social and vocational distribution of the Lyon Protestants in the period up to 1567 or so. The Calvinist movement as a whole drew from rich and poor—from Consular families, notable families, and families of the *menu peuple*—in numbers roughly proportional to their distribution in the population at large. If there is no significant correlation between socioeconomic position and religion in those years, there is one, however, between vocation and religion. Certain occupations were overrepresented in the Protestant movement relative to their distribution in the population. These were métiers in which skills were involved, and often in which there was some novelty—e.g. new technology (as in printing), new claims for prestige (as in painting and jewelry and goldsmith's work), and even recent arrival in Lyon (as in the manufacture and finishing of silk cloth). In contrast, very few grain merchants, vintners, butchers, bakers, or ropemakers of *any* status became Protestants.[21]

Sharing an interest in Protestantism within a craft did not preclude fighting on economic matters. Protestant barber-surgeons—masters and journeymen—had their conflicts, as did Protestants in the silk industry. But the battles that seem most paradoxical are those in printing. There journeymen, masters, and publishers cooperated under the very nose of the Inquisition to produce quantities of heretical editions. Nevertheless these conspirators were clashing with each other about, for instance, the masters' using unpaid apprentice labor to take the place of journeymen at the press and the composing table.[22] I think we can explain this phenomenon for the printers' journeymen by the existence of secularistic* attitudes that made them *not* unreligious, but rather skillful at differentiating between the specific goals of their economic agi-

---

* By "secularistic" I mean to suggest a wide but interrelated group of phenomena: the explaining, planning, and justifying of events in this-worldly terms; the use of nonreligious sanctions and techniques to influence social action; and the assumption by laymen of increasing responsibility in directing social activities formerly directed by the clerical estate.

tation and those of their religious agitation. They were not trying to get higher wages when they sang Psalms publicly in the streets of Lyon. For *this* purpose they had established the Company of the Griffarins and a whole set of practical techniques. Nor did they imagine that their strikes were going to end "the eight or nine hundred years of tyranny of the canon-counts of Saint Jean."[23] To *that* end they printed certain books with their masters and ultimately used their knives, swords, and guns in an armed uprising. They did not even employ the apparatus of the Griffarins as such—its oaths and punishments—to enforce religious conformity within the Company. In the 1540's, when more and more of its members became Protestant sympathizers, the Company stopped paying for a common mass. During the next decades it remained a secularistic organization.[24] This had the practical advantage of maintaining labor unity between the large majority of Protestant Griffarins and the small number of Griffarins who remained Catholic in the late 1550's.

The sources for this secularistic attitude are several. The printing workers were men of quite wide experience. Many of them had moved from city to city, and their own circle in Lyon was cosmopolitan. Their literacy and other distinctive skills facilitated accurate observation and differentiation. And then they were living in a city that had a laic tradition of its own—one bred of centuries of conflict between town Consulate and ecclesiastical seigneurs, and reinforced in the 1520's and 1530's when the Consulate had taken over responsibility for secondary education and poor relief in the city.[25] Even the *menu peuple* of Lyon had inherited from the early days of the commune a vague but secularistic notion of their right to rebellion in times of oppression.*

* The tradition of rebellion is suggested by the special term used for such popular revolts in Lyon: *rebeine*. On *rebeines* in Lyon, see, for instance, Claude Bellièvre, *Souvenirs*, ed. C. Perrat (Geneva, 1956), pp. 45, 72, 81-101; Guillaume Paradin, *Memoires de l'histoire de Lyon* (Lyon, 1573), pp. 234-35; Claude de Rubys, *Histoire veritable de la ville de Lyon* (Lyon, 1604), pp. 332, 502; and René Fédou, "Une révolte populaire à Lyon au XVe siècle: La Rebeyne de 1436," *Cahiers d'histoire* 4 (1959): 129-49. This old tradition of

In this secularistic context *and* with their ability to observe daily affairs realistically, the printers' journeymen did not conclude that a change in religious institutions and practices was essential for change in relations between them and their masters.* To be sure, they blamed their difficulties on "the immoderate and excessive desire" of their masters for gain. And they must also have thought that "avarice" was susceptible to religious controls. But that would take a long time, "human nature being more inclined to evil than to good," as they said soberly in another connection.[26] Meanwhile, they set the wage scale that they wanted and would work for no master who paid less; they refused to work for a master who had unjustly fired a Griffarin; they walked out of a shop if a master refused to accede to a request made three times; they beat up apprentices whom the master put on their jobs; and for those journeymen who would not join the Company of the Griffarins they reserved a vile name (Forfant) and a painful punishment—hamstringing.[27] They were rewarded for their organization and insight by some small success. They kept their wages at a level that made masters and publishers complain to the king and

rebeine is only one of several factors undermining Henri Hauser's claim that the grain riot of 1529 involved expressions of Protestant heresy ("Etude critique sur la 'Rebeine' de Lyon," *Revue historique* 61 [1896]: 265-307). Henri Hours has challenged Hauser's view in his "Procès d'hérésie contre Aimé Meigret," *Bibliothèque d'humanisme et renaissance* 19 (1957): 20-21. Furthermore, none of the 113 known rioters can be connected with Protestant heresy, and their vocational distribution (many were unskilled workers) differs markedly from the vocational distribution of the Protestant movement.

* My analysis of differentiation and secularization is related to that of Robert N. Bellah in his "Religious Aspects of Modernization in Turkey and Japan," *The American Journal of Sociology* 64 (1958): 1-2, where he distinguishes between prescriptive and principial societies. Lyon is clearly the latter. Charles Glock's discussion of this problem in "The Role of Deprivation in the Origin and Evolution of Religious Groups" (R. Lee and M. Marty, eds., *Religion and Social Conflict* [New York, 1964]) is also relevant. He distinguishes between circumstances that encourage a secular response and those that encourage a religious response to social and economic deprivation (p. 29). I differ from his analysis, however, in viewing the journeymen's attempt to change the form of the Catholic Church as a realistic response (not a compensatory one) to what they perceived as unjust treatment by the clerical estate.

look for cheap labor elsewhere, and up to 1572 their briefs won for them royal approval of the food-salary their employers were trying to end. Of course, their demands did go well beyond this and the masters did win on many other issues. Still, the journeymen did not suffer the constant frustration that can deflect such a movement into diffuse revolutionary action.

For revolutionary in the full sense the printers' journeymen were not. Radical though their notion was about the relative importance of labor to capital, they still thought of their industry in terms of right ordering and allowed something of an elite to grow up within the Company of the Griffarins itself.[28] Slightly fantastic though their image was of the golden age of printing, when they said gentlemen had worked as printers' journeymen,[29] no egalitarian or communistic millennium in the future danced before their eyes. They did not draw upon the Bible to justify their secular demands—either in public statements before king and Consulate or in frank sworn testimony by individual Griffarins. They justified their claims only in terms of the kind of work they did, and they "sanctified" them by an awe-inspiring but profane initiation rite of their own creation. And, finally, they did not have the revolutionary's sustained concern for secular problems beyond his own métier. It is true that in the early 1530's they led popular demonstrations for urban poor relief. From time to time they also beat up scabs for the dyers' journeymen in return for similar services toward their own Forfants.[30] Ordinarily, the Griffarins focused on concrete problems in printing. It was only in regard to changing the religious life in Lyon that they habitually felt themselves part of a larger movement.

Then, in the 1560's, the religious movement in which they had long been popular leaders was transformed into the Reformed Church of Lyon. Despite the jubilant enthusiasm in 1562 when Lyon was "reduced to the Gospel" or in 1564 when psalm-singing men, women, and children dug the foundations for a Reformed temple, the religious expectations of the printers' journeymen were disappointed. First of all, they had no chance to participate in the administration of the Church. The Consistory of Lyon was set up in early 1560. Out of 95 men who served as *surveillants* (or monitors, as they called their elders) and deacons of the Church up to 1565, seven were publishers, one was a paper merchant, two were master printers, and none was a printers' journeyman.[31] Pierre Viret, the city's leading pastor, explained that "special vocation" in the Church could not disturb too much "rank and order" in society.[32] The noble and Catholic canon-counts of Saint Jean were shocked by the extent to which artisans and foreigners did play a role in the Consistory;[33] but the proud printers' journeymen, with somewhat different standards of rank and order, were surely sorry to be thus cut off from special vocation.

Another source of trouble was the Consistory's standards of moral behavior. No one, whether banker or shoemaker, liked being haled before the Consistory and denied the Holy Supper for drunkenness, gourmandism, wifebeating, flirting, and the like. But at least many members of the Church felt guilty about what they had done; with the printers' journeymen this was often not the case. Though they could discipline themselves around the press or in organizing a strike, there were many sensual impulses they saw no harm in indulging. The hearty appetites of the pressmen were notorious, for instance. We can already see this difference in religious sensibility in the 1550's, when the printers' journeymen were out singing Psalms in the streets while more introspective Protestants in the conventicles were striving for "the witness of good life and conversation."[34] The workers learned only in the 1560's that their pastors classed them with the "epicureans," who "seek carnal liberty under the false title of Gospel."[35] Even then many printers' journeymen saw nothing wrong in the old custom of rousing sleepyheads on the Feast of the Innocents with a spanking—and maybe a kiss for the girls—even though the Consistory of Geneva called this "lewdness."[36]

Perhaps some of these tensions could have been resolved if the preaching of the pastors and the discipline of the Consistory had had some years to work. But before that could happen, the Griffarins were to hear themselves talked about by Protestant pastors in the following terms: "The Griffarins have conceived a mortal hatred for other printers' journeymen whom they call Forfants . . . because they work for lower wages. . . . They have plotted to exterminate them. . . . This is in itself atrocious, enormous, barbarous—thus to take away the means by which these poor journeymen [i.e. the Forfants] can earn their living at moderate and reasonable wages. But in addition this leads to monopolies, which are pernicious to the public. It holds the master printers in subjection and raises the cost of books whose use is very necessary."[37]

What is significant about these remarks is *not* the assumptions upon which they rest. The traditional dutiful servant turns up as regularly in Catholic writing of the time as he does in Pastor Viret's books. And, as Raymond de Roover has shown, the evil nature of "monopolies" had been discussed by Catholic theorists since the fourteenth century.[38] The difference lies not in how Catholic and Protestant clerics thought, but in what they *did*. The Catholic clergy of Lyon did nothing about strikes in the printing industry.* It did not say anything on the subject; it did not urge any particular government action; it certainly invoked no spiritual penalties against striking journeymen. Ultimately, in the late 1560's and after, it even half-tolerated the Company of the Griffarins in hopes

---

* Etienne Dolet's claim in 1543 that he had been turned over to the Inquisition by master craftsmen getting revenge for his support of the journeymen is hard to believe. First, most members of the masters' committee were strongly sympathetic to Protestantism and were printing or were shortly to print the very same works that had incriminated Dolet. Second, Dolet's views of journeymen (as expressed in his *Avantnaissance*, written the year of the first strike) show him not sympathetic to the journeymen. It *is* very likely that he offered good terms to the workers he hired in 1538-40, or how else would he have been able to set up shop and print so many works right in the midst of serious labor trouble? That his fellow masters were irritated by this, there is no doubt; but that they turned him over to the Inquisition is incredible. Rather, this statement of Dolet's is either attributable to his paranoia (see Lucien Febvre, *Le problème de l'incroyance au XVIe siècle* [Paris, 1947], pp. 34, 54) or a clever maneuver to divert the attention of the Inquisition from his many evangelical publications.

that, like other, more respectable craft groupings, the Company could be enticed into Catholic support. Nothing can better illustrate the free play that the Lyon Catholic Church allowed to secular forces at this date than the strike that occurred within its own bosom—that of the perpetual chaplains at the Cathedral of Saint Jean. The chaplains struck against the canon-counts for an increase in the distributions given them after daily masses—that is, they refused to say their responses at the great annual festival in June. As there were no Forfants, the canon-counts had to chant responses themselves with the simple priests, a scandal unheard of in the long history of this eminent chapter. Although the canon-counts thundered that these upstarts were really conducting a "monopoly" against God, no spiritual punishment was used against any of them. None of the rebels was unfrocked, demoted, or removed from the cathedral. They won their increase, too.[39]

Such laxity* was not at all the style of the energetic Protestant ministers and members of the Consistory, who were trying to impart to all relationships at least the outward character of the holy community. The matter of "good police" in the Lyon printing industry was discussed both in the Consistory of Lyon and in that of Geneva, since there was so much movement of Lyon workers back and forth between the two cities in the 1560's. Consistories did not always take the masters' side, of course.[40] What was im-

---

* Only in its brief and losing battle with the Consulate over the Collège de la Trinité did the Church threaten excommunication, here against fathers who sent their children to the school. It is true that in the mid-seventeenth century the Faculty of Theology of the University of Paris conducted an investigation into the heterodox practices of certain *compagnonnages*. It is also true that in the early sixteenth century the abuses and debauchery of craft confraternities had been *generally* condemned by the French Church; E. Levasseur, *Histoire des classes ouvrières . . . avant 1787* (2d ed., Paris, 1900), 1: 703-4; 2: 131. But in the late sixteenth century the Lyon Church wanted first and foremost to win back heretics and had neither the desire nor the apparatus to probe into the details of journeymen's organizations. For similar clerical tolerance, see H. Hauser, "Les compagnonnages . . . à Dijon aux XVIIe et XVIIIe siècles," *Revue bourguignonne* 17 (1907): 24-32.

portant for the decisions of the printers' journeymen, however, was that the secular context in which their economic agitation had previously been carried on was now altered.

Before 1560, at least three views on the printing strikes were prevalent in Protestant circles—one pro-journeymen, one pro-masters and publishers, and one urging compromise.[41] Now in the mid-1560's there was a detailed official view that could be associated with the Consistory. Earlier the Griffarins had had only royal lieutenants and urban sergeants from whom to conceal their doings. Now *surveillants* and pastors were investigating them as well. Before 1560 the only punishments that members of the Griffarins anticipated if they were caught were imprisonment and whipping. Now there was the danger of being denied the Lord's Supper.[42] This was a serious penalty in those years, for it put the soul in jeopardy. It was much easier for Satan to torment people cut off from the sacrament, Lyon Protestants were being told, and those who remained unreconciled to God and His Church would ultimately be cut off not only from the Lord's Supper and the company of the faithful, but also from eternal life.[43] In short, strikes had become relevant to salvation.

The story of the Company of the Griffarins was unearthed by the Consistories mostly in the course of two inquiries—one following the death of a Protestant Forfant after a fight with a group of Protestant Griffarins, the other following the unsuccessful attempt of several refugee Griffarins to maintain their organization in Geneva. There was much to be shocked at: the economic "monopolies," of course; but also the initiation ceremonies in which godfathers poured water and wine on the journeyman's head and gave him a new and usually coarse name, and the profane song in which the name of the Lord began and the name of the Holy Ghost ended each verse (in a version some Griffarins imagined to be more proper, the words "fat Margot" were substituted for the Holy Ghost).[44] But also, the Consistories were extremely uneasy about the "sect"-like qualities of the Company of the Griffarins, by which they meant the way it divided men from other loyalties. For instance, an oath was taken putting loyalty to one's fellow Griffarin above loyalty to a father or brother who happened to be a Forfant. The Reformed Church was jealous, and with reason, of any special group in a Reformed society that tried to possess too exclusively the loyalty of its members.[45]

Thus a conflict was set up for the Protestant Griffarins in the mid-1560's. They had to choose between their Company and their Consistory, which was insisting that all members renounce their oaths. Were they to abandon the organization they had created to achieve their secular goals? But, indeed, the organization was much more than that, as the Consistories had rightly guessed. The Company was the one group to which they belonged that had given them traditions and identity; a sense of fellowship, of participation, and of some control over their worldly destiny; and even material aid when they were sick or out of work. They had created among themselves the kind of communal relationships that sociologists consider a sensible response to big-city life.[46]

Of course, the Company of the Griffarins could hardly give them any identity in an absolute sense. Its ceremonies could help them cope with fears about life, but not with fears about death. And the "order of the printing industry" was hardly a sufficient guide for dealing with the many other problems that make this world a place of danger or of grace. But as we have just seen, religious troubles with the Reformed Church had been making it hard for them to get answers there. What other religious choices were there for them? Anabaptism was out, not only because the loyalty it exacted from its members was even more exclusive than that of the Reformed Church,[47] but also because the printers' journeymen were not in sympathy with Anabaptist views of society. Anyway there was virtually no Anabaptist proselytizing in Lyon. What about Spiritual Libertinism? Possibly, if it had had some organization and had been more than a stirring among eccentric editors and professional men in the city.[48]

The only real alternative was the Mother Church. They returned to her somewhat lukewarmly, since even her most effective champion, the great Jesuit preacher Emond Auger, would not agree that "low and ignorant artisans" should read and judge the Gospels.[49] Henceforth their pride would be expressed only through Minerva, the Mother of Printing, who presided over their secular festivals. One could at least be a Griffarin and a Catholic without too much discomfort. The movement away from the Reformed Church began in 1566. By 1572 it was almost complete. The psalm-singing printers' journeymen became in the late sixteenth century Catholic *politiques* who regretted that France should tear herself to pieces for the sake of religion.[50]

Poor Relief, Humanism, and Heresy

"The vicar of the Bishop of Tournai is abusing my little book on the poor [*De subventione pauperum*]," the great Spanish humanist Juan Luis Vives wrote to a friend in 1527; "he rules that it is heretical and Lutheran."[1] A few years later the mendicant orders of Ypres were saying the same thing about the poor-relief system which the magistrates of that Flemish city had recently established: "Forbidding [anyone] to ask for alms . . . is evil, vicious, and in conformity with a principle of Luther which has been condemned." The eminent theologians at the Sorbonne thought the Ypres scheme was at least "salutary and pious," but they went on to warn in 1531 that the magistrates must not prohibit public begging and alms-giving in the streets; any attempt to appropriate ecclesiastical revenues for poor relief "would be the part not of good Catholics, but of impious heretics, Waldensians, Wycliffites or Lutherans."[2] Not long after, the Dominican prior and Inquisitor of Lyon, one Nicolas Morin, raised the same issue there. In 1532 he wrote an attack on a passionate sermon[3] in which the French cleric and humanist Jean de Vauzelles had urged the notables of Lyon to introduce sweeping new welfare measures. The book was filled with errors, Morin said, "and pernicious to Catholic piety." Lyon had much more to fear from a host of heretics and unfaithful than it did from an abundance of poor strangers.[4]

Blaming Protestantism for new poor-relief measures did not, of course, end with the sixteenth century. R. H. Tawney, while admitting that indiscriminate charity had had its critics before the Reformation, thought it had been undermined only by the Protestant attack on monasticism and hypocritical works. "The new medicine for poverty" (to use his famous phrase)—that is, harsh discipline or deprivation to uproot the poor from idleness—may have been prompted by political and economic changes, but it was prescribed by Puritan self-righteousness.[5] More recently Christopher Hill has argued in a study of the influential Puritan divine William Perkins that it was the Calvinist view of church polity that convinced the rich not to give alms indiscriminately and the poor not to expect them. The undeserving poor were "outcasts, outside the law and outside the church," and thus, says Hill, fit only for being a large cheap labor supply for developing capitalism.[6]

In the sixteenth century the magistrates of Ypres said they were astonished to be called Lutherans when all they cared about was helping the poor.[7] And several modern scholars would agree with them that poor-relief reform was not necessarily connected with heresy. Brian Tierney, for instance, has proved that canon lawyers had always perceived the spiritual dangers of involuntary poverty and had also worked out some bases for discriminating among those asking alms.[8] Other historians have said that by the fourteenth and fifteenth centuries even voluntary poverty was losing its extraordinary allure for the morally sensitive: some Florentine humanists were preferring the civic uses of wealth to voluntary poverty, while northern thinkers like Jean Gerson were valuing inner detachment from material goods over literal abandonment of one's possessions.[9]

Just as some scholars have shown that attitudes toward poverty were clearly changing before the sixteenth century, others have shown that poor-relief measures of the seventeenth century were not always the result of Protestantism either. The employment of children, says one economic historian, owed more to an "awareness, however crude, of basic demographic circumstances" than to Puritan doctrine.[10] And Emanuel Chill has demonstrated for seventeenth-century France[11] that the movement to enclose the poor in disciplinarian "hospitals" was led not by Huguenots or even by government bureaucrats, but by the pious members of the Company of the Holy Sacrament.*

Finally, comparative studies of poor-relief institutions during the sixteenth century have uncovered striking similarities. Already in the 1880's, when German industrialization was prompting comparative economic history, Georg Ratzinger and Franz Ehrle pointed this out.[12] Building on their work, W. J. Ashley told English readers that reforms in poor relief had as intellectual sources both the continental reformers and the Catholic humanist Juan Luis Vives, while the magistrates of Ypres had cited in their support an argument from the late Conciliarist John Major. Sidney and Beatrice Webb followed Ashley's view in their well-known *English Poor Law*.[13]

Yet the ghosts of the mendicant orders of Ypres and the theologians of the Sorbonne, and now of the Inquisitor Nicolas Morin, live on to worry us with their accusations. They haunted the Belgian scholar Pierre Bonenfant when he described welfare reform in Catholic Mons and Ypres as "a curious and without doubt generally *unconscious* introduction of Lutheran principles."[14] They haunted G. R. Elton when he was trying to identify the anonymous author of an impressive draft proposal for poor-law reform in England in 1535. "Because of his opposition to indiscriminate alms," said Elton, he must be "a reformer in religion."[15]

Perhaps the trouble is that we have not sufficiently convinced ourselves of how and why European religious sensibility had changed in regard to begging and the charitable act even without the impact of Reformed teachings on these subjects. Perhaps we have not been sufficiently aware of the extent to which Christian

---

* Brian Pullan, in his important book *Rich and Poor in Renaissance Venice: The Social Institutions of a Catholic State, to 1620* (Cambridge, Mass., 1971), shows how the Catholic sensibility of the Counter-Reformation helped shape new welfare institutions in Venice.

humanists other than Vives played a role in reforming poor relief on the Continent. Perhaps also we have not inquired closely enough whether certain assumptions underlying the new poor laws do not flow as naturally from Erasmian views of education, order, and charity as they do from Protestant ones about works and church polity. And finally perhaps we must ask once again whether businessmen and lawyers on European town councils did not, irrespective of their religious convictions, bring their vocational experiences to bear on the difficulties of urban life.

I want now to make such an inquiry about the institution of the Aumône-Générale of Lyon during the early 1530's. This organization, of which the Lyonnais were very proud, is typical of the urban welfare projects of northern Europe and even of a few municipal experiments in Spain.[16] The problems of urban disorder, misery, and illness that Lyon faced were more acute than in less rapidly expanding cities, but they were no different in kind. But what makes Lyon especially useful for analysis is that during the 1530's she was a Catholic city, whose clergy ran the spectrum from the Catholic reformer through the nonchalant canon; that she had important circles of humanist activity; and that she already had a small but fairly identifiable Protestant movement. Thus we can sort out what religious variables, if any, were involved in the creation and support of the Aumône-Générale.

Let us begin then with an examination of poverty in Lyon and its impact on city life and feeling. Later on we can take a look at the men who brought about welfare reform and analyze the institutions they created.

[1]

Lyon's population was already growing by 1490, and it had very likely doubled by the mid-sixteenth century. In the 1530's between 40,000 and 45,000 people were living within its expanded city walls. New subdivisions were laid out in neat rectangles, new houses went up, and the Consulate began to talk of widening streets and squares.[17] Demographic recovery was of course gen-

TABLE I

Occupation of the Male in 93 Families Added to Relief Rolls,
May-December 1534 and January-July 1539*

Occupation	Husband living	Husband recently dead	Total
Unskilled day laborers	21	—	21
Urban winegrowers, gardeners	5	2	7
Boatmen, wagoners	6	1	7
Butchers	2	—	2
Millers	—	2	2
Bakers, pastrymakers	3	—	3
Candlemakers	—	1	1
Pouchmakers	2	1	3
Shoemakers, cobblers	6	—	6
Masons, stonecutters	3	1	4
Carpenters, cabinetmakers	5	2	7
Cutlers, pinmakers	4	—	4
Glassmakers	1	—	1
Weavers, embroiderers	6	2	8
Carders	1	—	1
Shearers	—	1	1
Dyers	5	1	6
Tailors, dressmakers	4	—	4
Printers, cardmakers	2	—	2
Schoolteachers	1	—	1
Archers	1	—	1
TOTAL	79	14	93

SOURCE: Archives de la Charité de Lyon, E4 and E5.
* About two hundred families are recorded in the Archives de la Charité de Lyon as being added to the rolls during this total of fifteen months, but occupations are given for the males in only 93 instances. In the case of artisans, the records rarely state whether the man was a master or a journeyman. In addition, the occupations of three women are given: a weaver, a wet nurse, and a glovemaker.

eral in Europe in the late fifteenth century as the death rate declined, but in Lyon, as in other cities, the population was swelled especially by immigration. Chances looked good in a city with four annual fairs—a city the Italian banking houses had already made a center for the European money market, and where new shops were opening in printing, in the metal trades, and in finishing textiles. So they came—the children of peasants from the Lyonnais, Burgundy, and Savoie; young artisans from Flanders, Germany, and Italy, from Dijon and Troyes and Paris.

They came poor, and most of them stayed that way. But poverty was not a condition peculiar to newcomers; natives suffered it as well. What accounts for this? We expect it in the men who have no skills, the *gagnedenier* who did odd jobs when they could find them for three sous a day. But poverty was also the plight of the skilled journeymen whose wages were two or three times that much, and poverty could sometimes grip their masters as well. For instance, 79 families in which the husband was still alive were added to the relief rolls of the Aumône-Générale in a fifteen-month period of the 1530's (see Table 1). Only 41 percent of these men were unskilled; the rest were artisans.[18] This was the case partly because the incomes of artisans had to stretch to feed so many mouths. "Poor householders and artisans heavily burdened with children," said the ordinances of the Aumône-Générale. The "heavy burden" was most likely to be three dependent children,[19] but some poor families had more (see Table 2). Is it surprising that the master weaver Pierre les Combes with his five children should need help even though he had two looms and a journeyman and one of his own sons to keep them busy? Or that the notary André Gouzebaud had sold most of his furniture to feed his seven children and pregnant wife?[20]

TABLE 2

*Number of Dependent Children in 41 Families Aided
by the Aumône-Générale, 1534 and 1539**

Children per family	No. of families with husband living (33)	No. of families headed by widows (8)	Total families (41)
1	5	2	7
2	9	4	13
3	8	1	9
4	4	—	4
5	3*a*	—	3
6	1	1	2
7	3*b*	—	3
Median no. of children	3	2	3
Average no. of children	3	2.3	3

SOURCE: Archives de la Charité de Lyon, E4, E5.
* Dependence is assumed because otherwise the records would not have mentioned the children.
a Includes two women pregnant with sixth child.
b Includes one woman pregnant with eighth child.

Even in families with one or two children, there were many emergencies in which savings were wiped out. Some trades, such as construction, just stopped during the damp, cold winters of Lyon; others were "reduced to nothing" by foreign competition. An expanding industry like printing had its troubles, too, for demand was not always translated promptly into orders, and the presses of small shops were quieted from time to time.

One might be laid off, or one might get sick. By the early 1530's citizens were claiming that plague was "sprouting" in Lyon every year.[21] Visitors noticed that the Lyonnais always suffered with colds and pleurisy. Printers' journeymen complained that presswork gave them arthritis.[22] During one year in the 1530's, 544 poor people, most of them males still working at their trades in Lyon, entered the Hôtel-Dieu for ailments other than plague (see Table 3). About 30 percent of them died there, and the families of the others suffered temporary loss of income. These figures do not take into account the poor people who were sick at home. The period of lying-in for poor mothers was costly, too,[23] since many of them worked or helped their husbands. Of course, the rich got sick and had babies as well, but on the poor the economic effects were devastating.

TABLE 3

*Entries and Deaths at the Hôtel-Dieu for
Selected Periods from 1530 to 1540*

Period	No. of entries	No. of deaths	Ratio of deaths to entries
March 1530	61	18	.30
December 1530	51	17	.33
June 1534	38	9	.24
December 1534	26	8	.30
March 1535	30	4	.13
March 1537	38	7	.18
October 1537	149	30	.20
March 1539	34	11	.32
June 1539	46	13	.28
October 1539	50	11	.22
December 1539	36	11	.31
March 1539– April 1540	544	162	.30

SOURCE: Archives de l'Hôtel–Dieu de Lyon, F 18, F 19, F 20.

Finally, there was the other great scourge of preindustrial society—famine. In normal years an unskilled worker in Lyon paid more than half a day's wage for a weekly supply of low-quality bread for himself alone; but there were several years between 1500 and 1531 when grain, and accordingly bread, cost three to six times that price. This was largely the fault of a primitive agriculture and inadequate transportation, but (as food rioters believed and recent research has confirmed) hoarding by grain speculators made matters worse.[24]

Urban poverty had had all these components to some degree since the fourteenth century, but in the first decades of the sixteenth century they intersected with a period of population growth to increase greatly the dangers of city living. Poverty was not usually shamefaced, did not remain quietly sick behind closed shutters; instead it poured into the streets with begging, noise, crime, threat of disease, and rioting. Who were the beggars? A small minority were adult males, skilled and unskilled, who were temporarily out of work. Some were new to the town, others were regular inhabitants. But what the poor craftsman or day laborer was much more likely to do when times were hard was send his children out to beg. Even the Consulate was turning out foundlings from the Hôtel-Dieu at the age of seven to ask alms in the street, with a sign explaining their plight.[25] So townsmen complained of "the great number of little children crying and hooting with hunger and cold day and night through the town, making a marvellous racket in the churches, disturbing the devotion of the people. . . . Oh, what confusion, heartbreak and scandal." The poor girls were getting pregnant and their futures were ruined. Seven out of thirteen cases of begging discussed by the rectors of the Aumône-Générale in its first months involved children.[26] The presence of many children among city beggars may well have been a new development, one associated with the population growth of the late fifteenth century. In any case, as we shall see, it was an important factor in welfare reform and in humanist interest in poor relief.[27]

Making noise and scandal in the streets along with the children were the professional beggars, men and women who rarely if ever worked for wages and who used all their skill to collect alms. Some were sick, old, or disabled, and made the most of their deficiencies. The rest were *"maraux,"* *"ribauds,"* *"belîtres,"* and *"coquins"*—these terms from Jean de Vauzelles' sermon give a glimpse of the rich vocabulary of opprobrium that the higher orders throughout Europe had evolved to describe its vagrants and vagabonds, its bums, tramps, and loafers. Legislation against them began in Europe even before the Black Death,[28] but by the fifteenth century the magistrates of Basel could detail 25 distinct categories of phony beggars, and they missed a few that were current in France.[29] There were those who pretended to have epilepsy and those who pretended to have been bitten by mad dogs; there were men who pretended to be hangmen on expiatory pilgrimages, and women who pretended to be penitents, begging by day as Mary Magdalene and then "moonlighting" later at Mary Magdalene's former trade. The beggars' art had its discomforts, too: some asked alms almost naked even in winter; others rubbed their skins with chemicals to give the impression of disease.

All of this behavior shaded off into confidence games, dishonest gambling, and other forms of petty crime—"the art of conny-catching," as it was called in England.[30] (Compare Hieronymus Bosch's painting of the conjurer playing the old shell game while his partner works the audience lifting purses.) To make matters worse, the numbers of beggars and vagabonds on the streets of Lyon were constantly being swelled by strangers seeking alms—vagrants passing through, beggars coming at fair time, and beggars following the royal court, which stayed in Lyon, for instance, in 1524-25. Every June there occurred the big religious festival of the year, the Pardon of Saint Jean Baptiste, and the cloister of the cathedral was jammed with mendicants from nearby provinces, "running, jumping, shouting and singing," to the annoyance of the canon-counts.[31] And finally, when famine hit surrounding areas, the city not only had to worry about provisioning its own inhabitants, but could always expect visitors from the countryside. Sometimes they came in orderly processions, all barefoot and dressed in white as penitents calling "rain, rain" in the country dialect of the Lyonnais. Sometimes, as in the terrible spring of 1531, they came from as far away as Burgundy "in great troops and boatloads without any government among them."[32]

Under these circumstances it is hardly surprising that ecclesiastical and lay sentiment had long since hardened against the professional beggar, but the point is that it was now turning against *all* beggars in the city. For one thing, crowds of beggars deserving and undeserving were thought to enhance the danger of plague. (In fact, rats and fleas do not need mendicants to thrive and migrate; but the spread of other diseases may well have been facilitated by crowds of beggars, and these in turn may have lowered the resistance of the population to plague.) In Lyon and elsewhere throughout Europe authorities had long made temporary prohibitions against begging whenever the Black Death struck.[33] Now that the Consulate had gone to the trouble of building a special hospital on the outskirts of Lyon to isolate plague victims, it is not surprising that it would think of taking permanent measures against begging. Later on the Aumône-Générale was to be presented to archbishop and king as in part a way to keep down contagion. For the humanist Vives, as well as for the Venetian Senate in its poor law of 1528 and the town council of Avignon later in the sixteenth century, welfare reform was also a health measure.[34] Thus, a revulsion against mendicancy could grow independently of any religious critique of the merits of charitable acts.

At the same time, however, events in Lyon were leading not only Protestant sympathizers but many Catholics as well to ask whether an act of charity could best occur within the traditional pattern of giving. No one remembered experiencing anything so horrible as the spring famine of 1531. More than 1,500 country folk and at least 4,500 inhabitants of the city were in desperate need.[35] The mobs looked, said Jean de Vauzelles, like bodies dug up from their graves. Like corpses used for anatomical dissections, said a witness a few years later. "I am dying of hunger, I am dying of hunger," they cried; and they did die, right there in the streets. "My heart broke," wrote the Inquisitor Nicolas Morin; "I will never forget it." At first the inhabitants tried to feed people in the old way—individual handouts outside their houses. But all that happened, said Vauzelles, was that some of the starving gorged themselves so suddenly that they suffocated and died, while others threw themselves upon the donors so violently that the food was lost and they became afraid to give. And all the while "the poor were overwhelming us . . . with their clamor and laments . . . outside our doors."[36]

Under these circumstances, for Vauzelles, compassion was transformed into fear and horror, and the fruits of compassion were death, not life. And indeed, the city of which Vauzelles was so proud—"the refuge of the Gauls . . . the emporium . . . of all the world"—had lost its identity, "so thickly sown with poverty that it resembled rather a hospital of the famished." It was only when the Consulate and notables had set up an organization, a precursor of the Aumône-Générale, with all food distributed regularly in specified places, with everyone off the streets in temporary log cabins—only then could Vauzelles talk of charity in the city, of Jesus "by a new rebirth . . . enveloped in the misery of these poor and receiving a greater welcome than in his town of Bethlehem." It was only then that Vauzelles could think of Lyon as a city again, now "a holy city of Jerusalem." And since people do such execrable things when they are starving, Vauzelles concluded that it was better to prevent people from ever falling into such hunger than to lift them out of it.[37]

Poverty was threatening not only physical and spiritual health, but also property and power. Despite a hint of violence,[38] the mobs of 1531 were too far gone to organize an uprising; but in the spring of 1529 there had been a serious food riot, or *rebeine* as the Lyonnais called it (see p. 8n). Blaming the rather high price of grain on speculators and conniving magistrates, about two thousand inhabitants, most of them unskilled laborers, women, and boys in their teens, looted the municipal granary, the Franciscan monastery nearby, and the homes of several wealthy men, including that of Lyon's earliest humanist, the physician and former Consul Symphorien Champier. The Consulate promised concessions to restore order, but a few weeks later it was busier with whipping and hanging the rebel leaders than with reducing the price of bread.[39]

That the Consulate at first put punishment above prevention is not surprising. For a day the rioters had been masters of the city. Meanwhile peasants in the Lyonnais were refusing to pay their tithes.[40] Nicolas Volcyr's hair-raising description of the Peasants' Revolt in Alsace was being read among the Consular families, and Champier was imagining that the same thing could happen in Lyon.[41] In addition, the people had become uppish and ungrateful. Champier was so insulted at the attack on his house that he wrote a book on the *rebeine* of 1529, reminding the poor how he had persuaded the Consulate, in speeches decked out with Hebrew, Greek, Egyptian, and Roman examples, to put a tariff on wine rather than on grain or flour.[42] If Champier stood alone among his contemporaries in believing that the rioters' disobedience was the result of heresy (and my own research has shown that what Protestant sympathizers there were among the poor were *not* in the mob, but in the special troops set up to restore order and requisition grain by force from private granaries),[43] nevertheless the burghers and merchants were nervous about the danger of *sédition* for a long time. Three years later the Consulate and royal officers were still tracking down and hanging the leaders of the *rebeine*.

But punishment was no answer—"a hungry people cannot fear the gibbet," said Jean de Vauzelles—and the autumn of 1530 was to see well-armed and disciplined artisans—printers' and dyers' journeymen—marching through the streets and posting placards about the cost of living.[44] Champier told the Consulate that these evildoers must be punished, but also that the bakers should be constrained to bake bread at a decent price "so there would be no cause for the people to get stirred up."[45] The next spring, of course, was the terrible famine, and not long after, the plague worsened. The temporary *aumône* of 1531 was repeated briefly in 1532. If the notables did not immediately make the *aumône* permanent, it was because they were considering at many a Consulate meeting how they would finance such a novel and large-scale venture and whom among the "great multitude of poor" they could afford to support. But all the conditions that were making life intolerable for the inhabitants of this expanding and cosmopolitan city had come to a head early in the 1530's and finally led in 1534 to the establishment of an organization "to nourish the poor forever."[46]

[11]

The new organization involved a dramatic shift of funds and power from ecclesiastical to lay hands, and a change in the act of charity. It was a *reformatio* of a kind, but one that was created not by a religious party but by a coalition of notables: Catholics and Protestant sympathizers, and all of them goaded on by Christian humanists, who like Vives believed that cities had been founded "for the increase of charity and human fellowship."[47]

Let us see who some of the members of this coalition were. Only two of them were clerics, and those two were the only important literary figures in the Lyonnais clergy of their day. One was the priest and doctor of laws Jean de Vauzelles,[48] now in his thirties, descended from an old communal family of notaries, holder of a priory and of an important judicial post under the noble canon-counts of Saint Jean, one of the many protégés of Marguerite de Navarre. Though he liked to find antique precedents for everything—poor relief included—and though the royal entry parade he directed in 1533 was sprinkled with learned references,[49] it was the Italian language and letters rather than the classical ones that he knew well and adored. Almost all his published works, however, were in French, inexpensive, and intended to communicate to a wide public the simple essentials of the Gospel and to move them by stylistic and pictorial devices to live according to the teachings and example of Christ. Thus his French translation of a concordance of the Gospels; his translation of Aretino's Bible stories; his edition with commentaries of Holbein's *Pictures of Death*, from which the artist had banished the gruesome touches of the earlier *danse macabre* as Vauzelles wanted to banish disgusting sores and wounds from the streets of Lyon.[50] An opponent of persecution and a literary friend of Protestant sympathizers such as Etienne Dolet, he nevertheless held with Erasmus to a Catholic view of the merit of true charity. And as for the Lutherans, he was shocked by their impetuous iconoclasm and destructiveness, and thought Luther a scourge sent to rid the church of hypocrisy.[51]

In Santo Pagnini of Lucca,[52] Vauzelles' colleague in welfare reform, we see a rather different blend of humanist interests with Catholic orthodoxy: a Dominican of the convent at Fiesole, a doctor of theology, master of Greek and Hebrew at the encouragement of Savonarola, celebrated and eloquent orator in Florence, and finally protégé of the Medici. He taught Greek and Hebrew in Rome until Leo X's death; then he made his way to France, settling in 1526 in Lyon, where he was told by Italian residents that there were "many people infected with heresy" against whom he must raise his voice.[53] Though already in his mid-fifties, Pagnini plunged actively into the life of his new city, preaching in Latin, French, and Italian; squeezing money for the plague hospital out of his rich Florentine relatives; making friends with French literary figures like Champier; and publishing Hebrew grammars and dictionaries, a new translation of the Bible from Hebrew sources, and a defense of Catholic doctrine drawing heavily on the early Church Fathers.[54] Though he himself had made unpublished translations of the *Odyssey* and part of the *Iliad*, he criticized people who were more ardent for the "fables of poets" than for the Scripture. Scholastic disputes about "instances, relations, quiddities and formalities" had nothing at all to do with salvation.[55]

What did Pagnini and Vauzelles do to help the Aumône-Générale get started? Vauzelles' sermon to the Consuls and notables in late May 1531[56] exhorted them by flattery, promises, and prophetic threats to continue the organized charity they had just begun and to extend its scope (don't stop now, don't look backward; remember what happened to Lot's wife). To those who argued that it was impossible to support such a big expense and that the poor should now be chased out of the city, he said this was like sending Jesus from Anne to Caiaphas. Furthermore, the new system would cost them less than handing out alms at their doors, especially since once the king had heard about it he would surely grant the city tax exemptions. To those who could think only of the danger of an uprising, he said they were washing their hands of the matter like Pilate. And besides, the only way to end the threat of riot was to end starvation. To his fellow humanists in the audience, he said that the new organization was even more important than their pet projects of a university and *parlement* for Lyon.[57] Not only would they clear the city streets of the clamorous poor, but they would also put themselves in mystic communion with the Church Triumphant. And finally, in words reminiscent of Erasmus' *Enchiridion*: "Charity is certainly much more agreeable to God than fasts, prayers, abstinence or austerity of life."[58]

A year later, with nothing permanent established, it was Pagnini's turn. The Consulate was demoralized by the low pledge made by the Church. Pagnini, who had acted as the Consulate's go-between in the affair, told the Consuls that "just because Messieurs the Archbishop and Canon-Counts won't give as much as last year is no reason to stop. Everyone must do his duty." Pagnini then did his, by putting his "splendid oratory"—the phrase is Champier's—to the service of the poor.[59]

This use of vernacular eloquence on behalf of welfare reform was an important contribution of the Christian humanists. Let us see how a scholastic would treat the subject. Brian Tierney has called attention to the astonishing lack of imagination with which canonists approached problems of poor relief at the end of the Middle Ages. "What was really needed by the fifteenth century

was a kind of scholastic critique of employability in able-bodied
vagrants." Instead the canonists repeated thirteenth-century arguments at three times the length.[60] In 1516, however, one nominal-
ist theologian did say something new—the Scotsman John Major,
a Conciliarist and distinguished professor at the University of
Paris.[61] He thought it would be a good idea for secular governments to provide for their impotent poor and prevent all begging.
This view was buried in a traditional discussion of alms-giving in
Major's "Fifteenth Distinction, Seventh, Eighth, and Ninth Questions on the Fourth Book of Peter Lombard's Sentences."[62] Few
if any town councilors had read this. If the magistrates of Ypres
referred to Major in their brief to the Sorbonne at the end of 1530,
it was because some scholar had just told them how to impress
that important body.[63] They were to be disappointed. Major himself had recently left the Sorbonne, and evidently he had been unable to convince even his fellow theologians of his point of view.
The Sorbonne disapproved of that part of the Ypres ordinances
which forbade all public begging.

Vauzelles and Pagnini in contrast were trying to *persuade* as
many people as they could to create a new social form. Furthermore, Vauzelles helped shape the final organization. In his sermon
he offered to write out a plan for it and gave right there some of
its essentials, such as training and education for poor children,
enforced work for healthy beggars, a central treasury, and administration by laymen.[64]

Administration by laymen. Let us stress that this is what these
two humanist clerics wanted; for in Ypres the mendicant orders
had objected to just this, as the Augustinian Lorenzo de Villavicenzo was to do years later.[65] In part, Vauzelles and Pagnini were
simply being realistic: however much they hoped to reform clerical mores and motivation, it was obvious that they were the only
clerics in Lyon taking initiative in regard to poor relief.* In fact,

* The lack of interest of the secular clergy in welfare reform is illustrated by
the provincial Council of the Church at Lyon, March 1527/28, which Vau-

the leaders of the Church were rarely there at all. In 1534 the arch-bishop of Lyon was to hear only by letter from the Consuls that "in his benign absence" (he had been living in Paris for many years), they had set up a new order for the poor, to which they hoped that he "as principal protector of the poor" and "guide for others" would contribute generously.[66] Nor had the Franciscans acted as a guide for others. They carried on their traditional dis-tribution of free medicine to the poor, but they made no move to introduce in Lyon the low-cost loans (or *mons pietatis*) that their Italian colleagues had championed some decades before and that a papal bull of 1515 had said were not usurious.[67]

Furthermore, Vauzelles and Pagnini shared with Erasmus and Vives a high evaluation of the Christian possibilities in the life of the laity. To the priest Vauzelles, lay administration of the *aumône* was a potential avenue of true charity. "Follow the apostles," he said; "do not disdain to be the commissioners and agents for the poor." "*Soyez charitables vigilateurs*," and you will appease the wrath of God, who has sent us of late so many scourges. Thus our city will be preserved and we will be pardoned in the celestial Jerusalem.[68]

The Consuls and notables responded, of course, and the plan-ning, worrying, and leg-work devolved on them. Among them were influential lawyers, with good laymen's memory for the long struggle that their commune had been carrying on against the jurisdictions of its medieval seigneurs—the archbishop and noble canon-counts of Saint Jean. Such a one was Mathieu de Vauzelles, Jean's brother and a doctor of laws from the University of Pavia. Already partially educated to the needs of the poor by his work reforming the Hôtel-Dieu, he was one of the few notables to urge prevention over repression even before the famine of 1531.

---

zelles attended in an uninfluential capacity. There was a little discussion of suppressing Lutheran heresy and reforming clerical morals and education; much talk about whether to help pay for the king's ransom; and no talk about hospitals or the poor. G. D. Mansi, ed., *Sacrorum conciliorum . . . collectio* (reprint; Paris and Leipzig, 1901-27), 32: cols. 1130ff.

Since he served the royal government in the Lyonnais as well as the Consulate, Mathieu de Vauzelles later helped win approval from the *"gens du roi"* for the new jurisdictions that the Aumône-Générale required over vagabonds, poor inhabitants, and orphans.[69]

The contribution of lawyers to welfare reform was based on more than influence and judicial insight. They were also building up libraries of classical and humanist works (as were their colleagues in other French cities), giving each other copies of Erasmus' works,[70] and frequenting the same literary milieu as Jean de Vauzelles. They may well have bought copies of the edition of Vives' *De subventione pauperum* that was printed in Lyon in 1532.[71]

Most of the notables whom Jean de Vauzelles and Pagnini harangued were merchants and industrial entrepreneurs, dealing in books, banking, textiles, and spices. With a few exceptions, these businessmen had had less exposure to humanist writings and ideas in the 1530's than the lawyers, or than their own sons were to have fifteen years later. What they did have was an understanding of accounting and of economic expansion that enabled them to see possibilities in the humanists' proposals that Vives and Vauzelles had not perceived. Some of these merchants came from well-established Lyonnais families. Others, like Jean Broquin, had made good marriages but had not yet reached the status of Consul. Indeed, Broquin might never have been elected to the Consulate at all in December 1533 had he not distinguished himself as a treasurer for the temporary *aumônes* of 1531 and 1532.[72] And finally there were men—like the remarkable capitalist Etienne Turquet from the Piedmont[73]—who were foreigners or recent arrivals. Thus from the beginning the Aumône-Générale involved all the nations upon which the developing economy of the city was based.

What of the religion of these lawyers and businessmen? The large majority of them were Catholic at the time, and most remained so all their lives (indeed, only about a third of Lyon's inhabitants were committed Protestants at the height of the movement in 1560). For instance, Mathieu de Vauzelles was later to say that if his Holiness the Pope would just see to it that more ecclesiastical property was reallocated for the relief of the poor, "all these new and damnable sects would be easily . . . appeased and reduced."[74] In some cases, we cannot categorize the notables according to religious belief. During the 1520's Jean Broquin had had for his stepfather a banker who was one of Lyon's earliest converts to the ideas of Guillaume Farel; years later Jean's own son was to become a Calvinist. Yet Broquin's mother remained a Catholic and he himself died in 1539, when religious lines were still fluid.[75] We know what this merchant thought about poor relief, but not about predestination.

Of the other welfare reformers of the 1530's, however, there are a few whose secret Protestant sympathies can be disclosed. Johann Kleberger of Nuremberg is a good example. He gave more money to the Aumône-Générale than any other individual in Lyon, including the archbishop. He could afford it, too, with the money he had amassed in commerce and banking. He had known Ulrich von Hutten, had his portrait painted by Dürer, corresponded with Erasmus, and quarreled with his former father-in-law, the humanist patrician Willibald Pirckheimer. He left Nuremberg for Lyon, but had the chance to see the new welfare organization that the German city had established in 1522. That his religious sentiments had finally settled in a Protestant mold is clear from his marriage in the mid-1530's to a woman who was a friend of Calvin and who had barely escaped the heretic's stake at which her first husband was burned in Paris in 1535. The Klebergers maintained their contacts with Geneva, but Johann, who had no taste for martyrdom, had a quiet Catholic burial in Lyon when he died in 1546.[76]

Thus we have the coalition for welfare reform in the 1530's. It was not a "united front" of clearly defined parties, but a cooperative effort of men who came from different places and whose personal religious views covered some range; they wanted to declare, if not a war against poverty, then at least one against begging and starvation, and to make of their common city, in Vauzelles' words, "a vision of peace."

[III]

They did not have to start from scratch, of course. Despite important innovations, in some respects they were continuing medieval developments. For purposes of discussion, let us divide all efforts to relieve poverty into, first, the redistribution of wealth and, second, the creation of new sources of wealth and economic opportunity. The *forms* in which wealth was redistributed to the poor during the later Middle Ages—such as giving away food, money, clothes, and fuel; free medical service; price-fixing; and tax policies that favored the poor—all persisted throughout the sixteenth century. New forms, such as subsidized housing,[77] were not tried except in a few local instances.

In both the Middle Ages and the sixteenth century clerical and secular authorities had no intention of using welfare services to change the social order. Communal ownership of property—the extreme case of redistribution of wealth—was practiced only in such places as monasteries, Anabaptist communities, and experimental communities (started by the Spanish cleric Quiroga under the influence of More's *Utopia*) among the Indians in the New World.[78] Even as a way of life for the saintly, communal ownership had little appeal to the laymen of the busy city from which the Waldensians had departed three hundred years before. As one old-timer among the Consuls said, "There are many poor now living [on Waldo's former street], but not voluntary ones as they were then." Rather than sharing poverty, the journeymen of Lyon were more likely to form *compagnonnages* to better their standard of living within the current framework of property ownership.[79]

If sixteenth-century poor laws did not spring from a new attitude toward property, their ambitious goal—to find practical means to eliminate all begging and death by starvation—did imply something new: now there are conditions of life that society should not and dare not tolerate *at all*, in Protestant Nuremberg and Norwich, in Catholic Ypres and Lyon. The suggestion is there, whether the urban welfare schemes succeeded or failed. And Vauzelles' sermon shows how this idea can be introduced into the old Catholic framework: "the poor are on the cross of adversity as much for the salvation of those who aid them charitably as for their own salvation," *but* they must not be so wretched that they fill the city with their complaints and their corpses.[80]

The other major difference between the medieval period and the sixteenth century in redistributing income to the poor is in administration. Medieval poor relief, though sometimes very generous, was even more fragmented and spotty than today's. At Lyon as elsewhere, there were random individual gifts in the streets and at doorways, handouts at funerals and other anniversaries, doles from monasteries and certain cathedral chapters, aid at hospitals (the Hôtel-Dieu was the only important one in Lyon), sporadic action by the Consulate, and aid from confraternities to their poor members in times of hardship. Parish assistance seems to have died out, parochial revenues probably having been appropriated by patrons. Only at the cathedral of Saint Jean was a weekly dole administered, and the elasticity of its funds was limited by old foundations that read, for instance, "provide a supper every Holy Thursday to thirteen poor people, who will then go pray at my tomb." Whether the small group of poor who gathered at the cloister for their handout were in fact the most needy according to canon law—one would have liked to know—was anyone's guess.[81]

In the thirteenth and fourteenth centuries, laymen in certain towns in Flanders and northern France (Louvain, Mons, Douai, Lille, Saint-Omer, Béthune, and others) had set up within each parish collection and distribution tables for the poor. However useful the work of these Tables des Pauvres, they did not centralize poor relief. The parishes' tables acted independently of each other, and ordinarily the *échevinage* had no supervision over them. Moreover, many other forms of charitable relief, including the handout to individual beggars, existed side by side with the tables.[82]

Tables des Pauvres did not develop in Lyon or in most parts of Europe; but by the end of the Middle Ages administrative initiative in redistributing income to the poor was already passing in one way or another into the hands of laymen—government bodies and lay confraternities. Newcomers to Lyon, such as the Germans, founded confraternities in the late fifteenth century, partly for mutual aid, and older lay confraternities expanded their activities. There were limits to what they could do, however, since some of the poor, such as the unskilled dayworkers, had no confraternity to join. In any case the lay confraternities could not supply overall administrative leadership for the city.* For instance, the Confraternity of the Trinity with its 1,700 members was unable to administer the school it had founded in 1519, so much in demand were its services; and in 1527 it turned the school over to the Consulate.[83]

Thus it was the lay government that was to build on its medieval activities—quarantining and other sanitary measures, taking care of the Rhône Bridge, provisioning the town with grain and wood, and fixing the weight or price of bread—and to gain control of all public welfare services.[84] The Consulate had already taken over administration of the Hôtel-Dieu from the church in the late fifteenth century, not long after Lyon's fairs had been instituted. The priest and the nuns were kept on, of course, along with the other personnel; but their activity was now supervised by the Consuls. No doubt the Consulate's experience in the 1520's

---

* Similarly, Brian Pullan has shown that the Scuole Grandi, the great lay confraternities of Venice, while expanding their charitable activities and developing new relations with the Venetian state, were unable to deal with the broadest problems of poverty in the sixteenth century. "The Scuole Grandi existed to serve the established, resident respectable poor. . . . They did not cater primarily to vagrants or displaced persons. . . . They provided for the pious, respectable poor, not for criminals and prostitutes. . . . They admitted many artisans, but did not plumb the lower depths of society." Dealing with this latter group was the task of new religious movements in collaboration with the state. *Rich and Poor in Renaissance Venice*, pp. 186-87.

in setting up new accounts for the Hôtel-Dieu and worrying over what to do about the foundlings lodged there helped it for the more difficult problem of establishing the Aumône-Générale.[85]

Henceforth, all charitable distributions in Lyon, and most charitable services, were to be performed by a new government body, the Aumône-Générale, or by the hospitals run by the Consulate. People could still give charitable bequests to their servants or acquaintances and might provide gifts of clothing and the like to poor men who carried their coffins.[86] Also, the funds used by Lyonnais confraternities for mutual aid were not at this time deflected to the municipal charity, as Charles V had ordered in the Netherlands in 1531. (Perhaps this was owing to the curious status of confraternities in Lyon in 1533. They had been declared illegal since the *rebeine* of 1529, but in fact were being tolerated.)[87] However, all the various alms given out at Saint Jean and other churches and monasteries during the year were now to be paid as a lump sum to the Aumône. No one was to give any handout of any kind in front of his house or in any public place (though no penalty was created for doing so), but contributions were to be given to an Aumône-Générale cannister or collector. All begging was prohibited[88] under pain of whipping and banishment.

For the first time in the history of Lyon a list was drawn up, based on house-to-house visits by officers of the Aumône, of all the poor inhabitants and the state of their need. Any sick people discovered in the survey were taken for free treatment to the Hôtel-Dieu. Fortunately, the Consulate had recently enlarged its staff (François Rabelais was physician there at the time the Aumône was formed). Most of the others—the impotent and the working men unable to support their families—were issued tickets entitling them to relief. The ticket was neatly printed, with blank spaces left so that all the officers of the Aumône had to do was fill out the name, the amount, and the length of time of the aid. The ticket-holders then went each Sunday morning to specified distribution centers and came up to receive their bread and money, "one by one."[89] Their numbers were constantly revised by further neighborhood visits and by hearings at which the poor could state their cases to the rectors.

These new arrangements, including the census,[90] were characteristic of sixteenth-century municipal charities. I suspect that the confiscation of ecclesiastical funds for the poor in Protestant areas would have made little difference to welfare services in those cities if it had not been accompanied by such administrative reform. The major economic advantage of centralization was that aid could flow to many more people and more equitably than before, and that greater or lesser expenditures could be made in different times and places as needs changed (more results for each sou given). Vauzelles himself had an imprecise understanding of this, for in 1531 he had claimed merely that a "premeditated system" would cost no more than spontaneous handouts in the street.[91] It was especially the businessmen like Jean Broquin and Etienne Turquet who appreciated the economic superiority of the new system.

Welfare reform in sixteenth-century towns thus extended accounting and measuring into an enlarged area of social life. If this had not happened, the premeditated systems would not have lasted a month. In the records of the chapter of Saint Jean, whose time and money had long been frozen into discrete blocks, the scanty data about charitable funds and their uses were scattered here and there. The records of the Hôtel-Dieu and Aumône-Générale reported in one place and in detail all income and expenditure. Admittedly, the accounting system was single- not double-entry, and in the early days there were some mistakes in addition. But many new or at least more precise measurements were made by the rectors. How much bread does a man eat in a day? Answer: a pound and a half.[92] How much bread and money is being given out at each distribution center each week? Is the number of people decreasing or increasing? Plans would be made accordingly.[93] How many people are entering, leaving, or dying at the Hôtel-Dieu each week, and who are they? The answers to these questions, compiled by 1529, provided the first systematic death records in

Lyon. Then in 1534, the rectors of the Aumône-Générale asked the vicars in each parish to keep a list of everyone they buried, thus anticipating the king's ordinance to this effect by almost thirty years.[94] Their reason? They wanted to be sure that no family was collecting for deceased persons.

If all this came from the businessmen, humanist sensibilities did contribute something distinctive to the orderliness of the new system, particularly in the distribution of alms. In 1539 the *règlements* of the Aumône-Générale were printed by Sébastien Gryphius, the celebrated publisher of humanist texts. Possibly Vauzelles was the editor.[95] The work included a woodcut of a typical Sunday distribution (see Plate 4). There in the office of the Aumône are the poor of Lyon, in queues as orderly as any could have been in the sixteenth century. One beadle has his long stick just in case, but he does not need to use it. Only one crutch is in evidence, no gaping wounds, only tattered clothes show poverty. A few hands are reaching out, but no one is crying or throwing himself on the donors. And one by one, just as the ordinances said, the men, women, and children are receiving their bread and money from the beadles. The rectors are seated behind a table, one of them checking the register of the poor, another quietly handing money to a beadle. This picture is unlike Pieter Cornelisz's *Acts of Mercy* or Bruegel's *Caritas* or any related northern European work of art of the late fifteenth or sixteenth century that I have seen, for such works, meant to depict only the virtue of charity, are picturesque genre studies, with the importunate and pathetic poor clustered around busy donors out in the street or in a temple. The Lyon distribution scene thus breaks with the traditional pattern to show the order and harmony that the humanist Vauzelles hoped would be achieved and that in part was being achieved in poor relief. It also illustrates what has been said earlier about the level of subsistence that welfare reformers hoped to guarantee: the poor of Lyon are shown as rather sturdy and not wholly unattractive human beings.[96]

In addition to redistributing wealth, a society can alleviate poverty by creating new sources of wealth and economic opportunity. The sixteenth century was to give much greater stress to these techniques of treating poverty than the centuries before it. It took the accelerated technological innovations and the geographical discoveries of the fifteenth century to lead authorities to think in terms of "new sources of wealth," though they were still a good way from the insights of Francis Bacon, not to speak of "production possibility curves." In Lyon, it was the successful introduction of printing in the 1470's that made the Consuls and notables finally aware of how employment and prosperity were connected with new industry. By 1528 the Consulate was telling the king that without new manufactures in woolen cloth or silk, the populace would have a hard time supporting itself.[97]

Likewise with education and rehabilitation of the poor. In the medieval period, prisoners' debts had been paid, poor girls had been dowered by bequests, and poor boys apprenticed, but at least in northern Europe* only a few individuals were helped each time. Free tuition in cathedral schools and other city schools provided for only those poor boys who were going toward a clerical career.[98] Lyon did not even have a municipal school until 1527, so strong had been the opposition of the archbishop and canoncounts to any limitation on their educational prerogative.[99]

With the Aumône-Générale, however, humanist views on education and training combined with economic interest to produce an important program for children.[100] Two hospitals were opened to receive poor orphans and foundlings leaving the Hôtel-Dieu at age seven. All the children, except those born out of wedlock, were legally adopted by the rectors—an unusual feature of the Aumône and one that symbolizes its aspirations. The boys were taught to read and write, and so were a few of the poor girls with ability and inclination.[101] Bright orphan boys were sent free of charge to the municipal Collège de la Trinité, where they might mix with the sons of the well-to-do and learn from the humanist

---

* Brian Pullan reports large contributions for dowries for poor girls beginning among the Venetian Scuole Grandi already in the fifteenth century.

schoolmasters the college was attracting to Lyon.[102] If the orphanage educational program had limited itself to this, however, it
would have gone no further than fellowships for the gifted Negro
to attend Yale and Princeton go in solving the problem of the
blacks in the slums of American cities. But it did go further. Most
of the male orphans were apprenticed to artisans at the expense
of the Aumône, sometimes in highly skilled trades—printing,
smelting, painting, sword gilding, embroidering, and the like. An
analysis of the apprenticeships of 31 boys in the first nine months
of the operation of the Aumône shows that the overwhelming
majority of them were placed in trades more remunerative or
skilled than those of their fathers (see Table 4). All the girls were
dowered when they married, which was a way of helping their
husbands get started. Before marriage, though, some of them were
put out as serving girls, and increasing numbers were trained to
work in two industries new to Lyon.

The establishment of the silk industry was proposed in 1535 by
the Piedmontese Etienne Turquet, who had been active in founding the municipal school as well as the Aumône-Générale. The
town instantly financed him to the sum of 500 écus, and Mathieu
de Vauzelles saw to it that various privileges were bestowed by
the king.[103] The Aumône-Générale, of which Turquet was now a
rector, then rented several buildings in Lyon and paid the wages
of Italian silk winders or spinners to teach their skill not only to
the orphan girls, but also to girls in the quarter and especially to
the daughters of families on the relief rolls.[104] Once trained, the
girls worked for artisans whom Turquet and his partners had
installed in Lyon. Thus Turquet rapidly increased his labor supply, and many poor girls learned a skill better paid than domestic
service. A similar arrangement was made for the "cotton" manufacture (presumably fustian) introduced by another Italian who
had had his hand in founding the Aumône.[105] Though no further
training centers were set up, the rectors went out of their way in
the next years to apprentice boys to Italian silk weavers, potters,
gold-thread drawers, and faience-makers who had recently come

TABLE 4

Analysis of 31 Apprenticeships of Orphan Boys by the Aumône-Générale, April-December 1534*

Boy apprenticed to more skilled or more remunerative trade than father (7 cases)

Father:	day laborer	Boy:	dyer
	day laborer		glover
	joiner		locksmith
	laboureur (well-off peasant from Dauphiné)		dyer
	packer		founder
	packer		joiner
	stocking maker (from Geneva)		grain merchant

Boy apprenticed to less remunerative trade than father (2 cases)

Father:	baker	Boy:	pinmaker
	butcher		pinmaker

Three cases difficult to determine

Father:	dressmaker	Boy:	weaver
	weaver		pinmaker
	weaver		pinmaker

Only geographical origin known; father probably of peasant background (13 cases)

Origin:	Beaurepaire (Dauphiné)	Boy's trade:	beltmaker
	Beaujeu (Beaujolais)		cutler
	La Buissière (Dauphiné)		furrier
	Chazelles (Forez)		furrier
	"Saint" (near Bourg en Bresse)		glover
	the Charolais		locksmith
	St.-Symphorien-d'Ozon (Dauphiné)		locksmith
	Bresse		mercer
	Quincieux (Beaujolais)		merchant
	Champier (Dauphiné)		playing-card maker
	Bray-sur-Somme (Picardie)		servant to physician
	Messimy (Lyonnais)		shoemaker
	Feurs (Forez)		weaver

Nothing known about father (6 cases)

Boy's trade: maker of pearls and scales, merchant, nailmaker,[a] pinmaker, dollmaker,[b] dollmaker

SOURCE: Archives de la Charité de Lyon, E4.
* There were also two boys adopted during this period, one by a publisher, the other by a carpenter.
[a] The boy is described in the records as "povre orphelin."
[b] The boy is described in the records as "povre enfant."

to Lyon. It would be interesting to know whether other European cities used their poor-relief systems to aid expansion of manufacture.

These features of the Aumône fulfilled quite well Jean de Vauzelles' prediction that "a great number of boys and girls would learn in their youth some art or skill which would keep them from becoming bums and beggars." Vauzelles had also promised in 1531 that the rogues and vagabonds would stop their mischief, because they would be forced to work or to leave town.[106] This is precisely what the Aumône-Générale tried to do. The work provided was digging ditches for the new fortification system and cleaning filth from the streets. It was often performed in chains and paid for only in food and drink. If the rogues were disobedient they were put for a while in a special "correction" tower maintained by the Aumône, and if they were caught begging they were whipped and run out of town.[107]

In evaluating this program and its relation to humanist assumptions, we must remember first of all that it could have been worse. In Rouen the healthy beggars worked in the shadow of the gallows, in Troyes under a strappado.[108] Moreover, in the seventeenth century the tower in Lyon became a so-called hospital—half prison, half workhouse—for permanently enclosing the healthy beggars. Feeling would deepen against the vagabonds at the end of the sixteenth century, partly because of the failure of the enforced public works to transform these men.[109] But in the 1530's, when the Lyonnais notables were deciding what to do about the healthy beggars, they seemed as concerned about saving money as they were about making the "rogues repent." While the "*maraux*" were working on the ditches they were supported by tax money already allocated for fortifications and not by the funds of the Aumône.[110]

Second, the widespread notion that the administrators of urban charities were unable to distinguish between the professional beggar and the temporarily unemployed worker is not borne out by the evidence. Such a distinction was made in Paris in an ordinance of 1551; and in 1534 a thoughtful lawyer in Rouen told authorities there that it was hard for a man accustomed to one craft to take just any job when he was unemployed. If he could not find work in his craft, he should not for that be considered "of evil nature and condition."[111] And consider this example from Lyon: the beadles evict two unknown men for begging in the streets; a relative comes to the rectors, explains that they are artisans who want to find work in their craft; the rectors let them return as long as they promise not to beg.[112] Also the families of temporarily unemployed artisans and laborers seem to have been included in the Sunday distribution, so long as the rectors believed there was sufficient need (or *"pitié,"* as the records often put it) and that the aid was not dissuading the men from working.[113]

Third, in no place in Europe were the laws on healthy beggars and vagabonds much better. It is true that in Paris the men on the public works projects were paid token wages in addition to food; perhaps that city could afford this largesse more easily than Lyon. But the punishments meted out were more severe and public works as disagreeable.[114] Even in Spain, where sympathy for the deserving beggar was quite widespread, whipping and even the galleys threatened the vagrant.[115]

Still when all allowances are made, we may ask why the humanist conscience, with its conviction that education can change character to some degree, did not envisage better rehabilitation for the healthy vagabond. A 1535 English proposal for poor relief offered essentially the same solution, even though the English humanist who drafted it clearly understood how a healthy working man might fall willy-nilly into permanent vagabondage.[116] The humanist could answer, of course, that education works best on the young: in Vauzelles' words, "once hooked by vile habits, one can not shake them."[117] The Aumône-Générale would eliminate the next generation of vagabonds; for now, it would stop the begging, and one might hope, as Sir Thomas More said of the unpleasant work of the bondsmen in Utopia, that the healthy beggars would "be tamed by the long hardship" of cleaning sewers and digging ditches.

I doubt that any of them were so tamed, but to have conceived a better program would have required *understanding* the beggars. It would have meant more than acquaintance with their picturesque customs and jargons, such as one finds in entertaining and satirical English rogue literature; it would have meant going beyond even the wonderful sympathy and irony of Spain's *Lazarillo de Tormes* to a relativistic social examination that could serve as a basis for policy. This was conceivable in the sixteenth century: Bernardino de Sahagún and Alonso de Zorita tried to do it for the Aztecs. For some reason France produced less rogue literature than England, and few French authorities bothered to consider with Montaigne how hard it was to deflect beggars from behavior to which they were accustomed and which they found gratifying.[118]

We can see in retrospect that many professional beggars and vagabonds had skills of a kind (we certainly reward the skills of persuasion well enough today!); they traveled together and stayed together; they had partnerships for their "business"; they had initiation ceremonies and status ranks and "courts of miracles."[119] In other words, they had ways to defend themselves against powerlessness and alienation. They were very poor, but no one was promising them a greater income from public works. In some ways they would be harder to "rehabilitate" than the isolated suspicious "unemployables" and semiemployed of our own cities, because they belonged to a subculture in which François Villon, for instance, had been glad to live.[120] Indeed, the professional beggars in Lyon thought the rectors of the Aumône were at fault, not themselves, and agreed with those who demonstrated the day that rector Jean Broquin was buried: "The poor can rejoice because now their enemy is dead. . . . The devils will take messeigneurs of the Aumône, and they've caught the first one now."[121]

Some of the deserving poor were also sorry to see begging outlawed, and were deterred from continuing to beg only by the threat of being stricken from the relief rolls when they were caught. Others simply did not like to see beggars beaten and raised tumults among the bystanders against the beadles who did so.[122] None of this means, however, that the majority of the *menu peuple* in Lyon really honored the status of beggar, deserving or undeserving. For instance, the printers' journeymen said contemptuously of the men who refused to join their trade union, "They'll work for beggar's pay." And when, during one of their strikes, they were classified in a public cry as "vagabonds," who must go back to work or leave town within twenty-four hours, they appealed the cry to the king as "ignominious and scandalous."[123]

The poor eligible for the relief rolls had more important things to worry about than whether they could beg or not. They could object to the rectors when their weekly distribution was too little to help them live, but the rectors always had the last word. If they kept on protesting, they might be led off to the tower. They did not like surprise visits from rectors who wanted to make certain that the children they were collecting for were really theirs and still alive, any more than present-day relief recipients like midnight raids from welfare agents. They were not happy about being forbidden to spend money at taverns or on cards and dice if they wanted to receive their dole, any more than today's recipients are happy to sell some of their belongings to qualify for relief. Journeymen who were out on strike could never collect from the Aumône and simply depended on the "common purse" of their *compagnonnage* to tide them over. Such groups had to accept as a fact of life the unwillingness of all authorities to view higher real wages as a possible solution to poverty.[124]

When all is said and done, though, the advantages of the Aumône for the poor probably outweighed its disappointments in its early decades. During the years 1534 to 1561, at any one time slightly more than five percent of the total population were receiving a weekly handout (see Appendix, p. 62). It was not lavish, and the rectors do not seem to have made sufficient adjustment for inflation in granting monetary alms. But there was enough wheat bread for the week and enough money to buy, say, a few pounds of beef.[125] About three hundred children were being cared for at any one time at the new children's hospitals, while the rectors were supervising the treatment of many more of their *"adoptifs"* as apprentices or servants. The reorganized Hôtel-Dieu, which had eighty patients in early 1524, was able to cope with three or four times that many in later decades without a significant rise in the death rate.[126] These services relieved the worst pressures of poverty a little and may have diminished the incidence of certain infectious diseases. Though adult beggars continued to be a problem, the number of children in the streets was reduced. And during the astonishing drought in the Lyonnais in 1556, Lyon was not reduced to "a hospital of the famished."[127]

To accomplish this, the financing of the Aumône had to become better organized and more predictable than during the famine of 1531.[128] Pledges of weekly or monthly contributions were obtained from individual inhabitants, from the archbishop and all the religious establishments except the mendicants, and from the foreign "nations" residing in Lyon. Whoever did not come through with his pledge might find himself being visited by a rector or even prosecuted.[129] By 1539, gifts of real estate and pensions had been made to the Aumône, and they were to increase enormously. Once the girls from Saint Catherine's had been trained to spin silk or fustian, their wages were paid to the Aumône until they were old enough to be dowered and leave the hospital. Finally, money came in from canisters all over town, from wills, from court fines, and even from lotteries, which were prohibited to relief recipients but permitted for donors.

All of the aid described above went to the poor people actually living in Lyon in 1534. But what about the many newcomers of the years that followed? And what about the hordes of poor who had descended upon Lyon at different times of year? Vauzelles assured his listeners during the 1531 famine that under the new plan "you will promptly see yourselves relieved of all the foreign poor with whom you are now so heavily burdened."[130] The In-

quisitor Morin pounced on this statement. Hadn't the Bible said
there was to be no distinction between Greek and Jew? Hadn't
the early bishops of Lyon sent messengers all the way to Burgundy to invite the poor to come to the city for alms?[181] The
mendicant orders of Ypres made similar objections and so did
Friar Domingo de Soto of Salamanca in regard to urban relief
experiments in Spain.[182] With cosmopolitanism a characteristic
of both humanism and the economy of Lyon, we may well ask
how the Aumône-Générale treated the foreigner.

And the answer is that a major purpose of the Aumône was to
hold the city together "even though," to quote its ordinances,
"its people be the most mixed with different nations of any in
France."[183] As foreigners—non-Lyonnais and non-Frenchmen
both—sat on the board of rectors and both collected for the Aumône and contributed heavily to it, so foreign inhabitants were
accepted on the relief rolls.[184] Even healthy beggars who were
not natives could stay in the city if they stopped begging and
went to work on the ditches. The distinctions made were between
residents and nonresidents, and were never intentionally used to
restrict the labor supply, a restriction which could have put some
of the industrial entrepreneurs among the rectors and Consuls
out of business. Rather the policy was intended to protect the
city from professional beggars and to prevent its treasury from
being exhausted immediately. Thus all poor travelers, pilgrims,
and hungry peasants were registered and given one and only one
distribution, a so-called *passade*. If they were ill, they were treated and fed at the Hôtel-Dieu as long as necessary; otherwise they
were ordered to leave.[185] Thus there were guards set up at the
docks and bridges to keep out professional beggars and other
poor, such as old women or widows with children, suspected of
coming to Lyon only to get on the relief rolls. Over the years,
however, thousands of unemployed artisans and young women
from the country came to Lyon, found jobs, maybe left and returned again—all without being molested.

Finally, and much more serious, by 1539 there was a residence requirement, not for medical care, or for the orphanage, or for emergency aid, but for weekly distributions. In the 1540's, it may have been as much as six years; by the end of the century it ranged from three to seven. With their limited finances and more primitive economy, of course, their law was less a violation of charity than the residence requirements (some almost as long as theirs) made for public relief today.[136]

Similar policies toward peasants, travelers, and newcomers are found in the many European cities in which welfare reform occurred, though the rapidity with which new residents were admitted to the rolls varied. Paris, for instance, had a residence requirement of three to four years (perhaps it had greater financial resources than Lyon); Geneva, the city of refugees, had to set up a special Bourse des Pauvres Étrangers to deal immediately with new inhabitants.[137] At any rate, no city had to feel that it was breaking completely with Christian precedent in helping residents ahead of nonresidents: the notion that "charity begins at home" had been long incorporated into the canonists' analysis of how to allocate scarce funds among numerous applicants.[138]

Moreover, the welfare reformers did not completely neglect the question that Domingo de Soto posed: where are the people whom you turn back going to go for help? Other towns would follow the example of reform and the burden could then be shared.[139] Thus the Lyonnais had learned from Vives and perhaps from Nuremberg and were to consult the Parisian ordinances for suggestions.[140] Thus Vauzelles had rushed his sermon into print in Lyon in 1531 and sent it to a Catholic friend in Toulouse, Jean Barril, who had it printed there.[141] And thus the ordinances of the Aumône-Générale were published in 1539 as "an exemplary work for other cities and communities." The work must have been sought after, because Gryphius made two impressions in the same year.[142] Indeed, can we not discern an international movement for welfare reform in Europe during the decades after 1520, when Vives' book is published in several countries and translated into German, Italian, and Flemish; when the Ypres statutes are printed and trans-

lated by William Marshall into English; when the statutes of Nuremberg, Lyon, Paris, Chartres, and Bruges appear in print; when
the Benedictine Juan de Medina describes the reform in Salamanca, Zamora, and Valladolid and pleads for others to follow?[143]
These books influenced not only town councils but also kings.
Urban models were behind the 1531 placard of Charles V for the
Netherlands and behind Charles IX's order in 1566 that all French
towns and parish organizations support their poor. For various
reasons national legislation did not succeed in France, and most
poor relief was to come for some time as it had in Lyon—from
the cities.

[IV]

The publication of Jean de Vauzelles' sermon also elicited a
hostile reaction. Nicolas Morin, native of Blois and doctor of
theology, had come to Lyon in 1529 as prior to the Dominicans.
He received his title of Inquisitor in 1532, and his maiden effort
in this capacity was *A Treatise of Catholic Erudition . . . confut-
ing a pernicious little book which uses as a cover a zealous plea
for alms for the poor of Lyon.*[144] Though never mentioning Vauzelles' name, Morin must have known he was the author. The
sermon was printed anonymously because Vauzelles never put
anything more than his device on any of his works,[145] but it had
been given publicly and Morin could not have failed to hear of it.

One would hardly know from Morin's 160-page Latin attack
on Vauzelles' short piece that the subject was poor relief. Though
evidently moved by the events of 1531, Morin in describing the
temporary *aumône* showed no awareness of its novelty or social
significance. His mechanical use of biblical formulas—"And they
gathered the people, sanctified the church, and assembled the elders"[146]—made the reality of reform dissolve into the distant past.
Nor did his brief comments on the foreign poor—"We must turn
our face from no one"—provide any guidance for the notables
who argued for hours about whom precisely they could feed (just
the inhabitants? peasants from nearby? sick strangers? anybody

willing to dig ditches?).[147] Morin did not even take up Vauzelles' concrete proposals. As he said himself, "I have neither the vocation nor the talent for this kind of examination." When Pagnini came to see the Consulate, it was to talk about poor relief; when Morin came, it was to tell the city it owed the convent some back rent.[148]

What bothered this correct doctor of theology about the exhortation was its "popular idiom," its freewheeling use of biblical examples, and especially its Erasmian sentiments. Morin is the closest one comes in Lyon to Noel Béda (whom he praised in the *Treatise*), to the hardcore Sorbonne opposition to Erasmus. He was undoubtedly unhappy about Pagnini, who continued to say, in the face of doubts from the august Faculty of Theology, that Greek and Hebrew letters helped in interpreting Scripture. As for the presumptuous Vauzelles, he would discredit him as an ignoramus whose ideas smacked of heresy.[149]

Thus Morin pedantically and humorlessly went through correcting Vauzelles' biblical metaphors. It was true that Vauzelles, carried away and composing in haste from his not very good memory, had called Hannah Elkanah; had forgotten that Simeon had never been to Egypt; and then had sent the work directly to the printer without checking his references (the printer did not check them either). For the sake of the alms given, said Vauzelles, "God had cured the sick, made the dumb to speak, the lame to walk," etc. No, said Morin, there was precisely one miracle. Morin also took very literally Vauzelles' ironic reference to the Waldensians, but ignored his genuine criticism of Luther.[150]

But Vauzelles had erred most perniciously in talking of charity and ceremonies. "The experience [of the new order for giving] will bring you prompt faith," Vauzelles had said. Now this idea of "faith formed by charity" had been developed earlier by the Franciscans and, as Lucien Febvre has shown, was currently "familiar to many a devoted reader of Erasmus." It was to reappear in Lyon the next year in Rabelais' *Pantagruel*, printed by the same man who had put out Vauzelles' sermons. Calvin was to call the view a Sorbonnic lie, but our Morin blunders along telling Vauzelles that faith comes from hearing the word of God.[151]

Morin returned to a more clearly traditional position when he defended ceremonies and masses for the dead against Vauzelles, who had cried, "It is to the living, to the living and not to the dead that are owed the alms which resurrect." Vauzelles surely knew he was sticking his neck out, for a provincial Church Council at Lyon, which he had attended a few years back, had prohibited anyone's speaking against masses for the dead. But the Christian humanist was not going to be deterred by people like Morin (who believed he was sneaking heretical frauds into a seemingly orthodox confession) any more than his great contemporary Erasmus was being deterred by Béda.[152]

Vauzelles won. He went about his business at the chapter of Saint Jean unmolested. And he made sarcastic remarks about the Pharisees and Jews who were always asking where a man had received his degree in theology.[153] Meantime one can imagine the fireworks between the two doctors, Pagnini and Morin, at the Dominican convent. Morin stayed on as prior for a while longer, but in 1534, when some real heretics were being questioned, another religious had replaced him.[154]

And the Aumône-Générale won. Morin's attack had been too irrelevant to excite support. Most of the clergy appear to have been rather glad to be relieved of their responsibility. Chapters and Benedictine houses calmly made over all their old foundations for alms and grain distributions to the Aumône-Générale and agreed to pay a further specified sum each week. The canon-counts turned over to the rectors the headache of administering the alms and stopping the begging at the great Pardon of Saint Jean—one of the special occasions when nonresident poor were allowed to flock to Lyon. The archbishopric was sued in 1537 for 250 livres arrears in its pledge, and when ordered by the seneschal to pay, it paid. Mendicants from outside Lyon got their *passade* along with other travelers and were forbidden to beg in the city. No one complained. The mendicant orders in Lyon itself got two donations each year from the Aumône. Every Lent the rectors sent them gifts so they would remember the charity in their sermons, and the mendicants received a further contribution during the Easter fair.[155]

By 1540 Jean de Vauzelles could rejoice at the extent to which the laity was involved in this great Christian work—from the would-be Consuls who served as rectors free of charge, to the women who passed the cup in church and the master craftsmen who went door-to-door collecting; from the storekeepers who kept canisters on their counters, to the notaries recommending the Aumône to those about to draw up their wills. Possibly Vauzelles' hope that money would be redirected from masses for the dead toward the Aumône was partially realized for a few decades in the wills of prosperous Catholics. This is a problem that needs further study.[156]

What is clear is that, despite tactics which made many donations virtually obligatory, the Aumône still invited spontaneous action and innovation. A merchant opens a theater for religious drama; he agrees to give a percentage of the receipts from every performance to the Aumône. The printer Sébastien Gryphius turns over all the profits from sale of the ordinances to the Aumône. He also donates the profits from a sermon by Gregory Nazianzen on helping the poor[157] (the first edition in French of that Church Father, with whom Pirckheimer and Erasmus had been occupied a few years before). The Aumône-Générale also had an impact on the physicians. Champier suggests a system of licensing for physicians, surgeons, and apothecaries to raise the level of medical practice in Lyon.[158] Two other humanist physicians publish French translations of medical and surgical works for the benefit of journeymen in surgery and pharmacy. If such work was partly motivated by literary and professional considerations, the decade of welfare reform inspired its social dimension.[159]

Vauzelles and Pagnini had another success. The mendicant orders of Ypres had argued that impersonal giving to a governmental body would harden hearts and lead to indifference.[160] But the laity of Lyon had come to believe that the Aumône-Générale was a genuine expression of charity. For the Catholic layman, this was facilitated by certain Catholic features of the institution. For instance, every year at Easter there was an enormous Procession of the Poor—not of the donors, as one was to see much later in Paris in the Counter-Reformation charitable confraternities, but of the recipients. All the orphans and the thousands of poor on the relief rolls, followed by the mendicant orders and the Consuls and the rectors, paraded through town to Saint Jean's, singing and praying and carrying a great cross. The procession was intended partly to show the public where their money was going, as the ordinances said, and partly to arouse their good will. Furthermore, Catholics could count on the poor praying for the souls of their benefactors.[161]

The emblem of the Aumône-Générale also reflects the attempt to infuse this governmental institution with charity (see Plate 2). It appeared by 1539, when the *règlements* were printed up, and characteristically was also placed on the very impersonal items—the canisters[162] and the printed tickets. A seated woman with three children pressed round her neck and body holds in her free hand a purse from which the money is pouring. On her head is perched a pelican which is striking its breast so that pelican children can drink its blood. The woman is, of course, a charity figure; the pelican, an old symbol both for Christ and for charity. And as natives and foreigners had worked together to form the Aumône, so its emblem amalgamates diverse artistic traditions. The seated charity with children was a recent Italian invention used by Michelangelo (whom Pagnini had known in Italy); the pelican on the head of a standing charity had first appeared in France toward the end of the fifteenth century.[163]

How would the Protestants have responded to the Aumône? To its Catholic trappings, unenthusiastically; but to its emblem they could respond freely from within their own doctrinal context. To quote one of the early clandestine proselytizers in Lyon, "charity is the mark by which one knows the true disciples of Jesus . . . the truest witness we have of our faith."[164] And evidence shows that individual Protestants contributed to the Aumône, collected for it, served as rectors, and received relief, in the years up to the First Religious War.[165] Its basic institutions and policies were sufficiently acceptable to them so that in 1562-63, when the Huguenots were masters of the town, they were to change the Aumône-Générale very little. (The ward officers or *quarteniers*, who helped the rectors check on the needs and morals of the poor, were replaced by the *surveillants* of the Consistory, but then they had to check on everybody's morals anyway.)[166]

The Protestant support for the Aumône-Générale in the 1530's is not hard to explain. They were all living in the same growing city and knew its hazards. Some Protestants, such as Kleberger, had a humanist background and had assimilated humanist views about social rehabilitation even though they were convinced that there was no training or job by which one could rehabilitate oneself in God's eyes. And they liked the elimination of begging. As Pastor Viret was to say from Switzerland: "Though still detained by Anti-Christ and living in the disorder of the papists, [the Lyonnais] have so well provided for their poor that mendicity is abolished. . . . Perhaps God will have pity on them and next they'll chase out the really great hypocrites and loafers [that is, the clergy]."[167]

Pastor Viret's words suggest once again the reasons why coalitions such as that which formed and sustained the Aumône-Générale did not grow into firm alliances to achieve reform of the church. Usually we talk about the breakup of alliances in terms of irreconcilable views on doctrine and the effects of persecution. Here we can see the failure in terms of priorities and organizational energy. The early Protestant militants, the proselytizers risking their lives, never saw the Aumône-Générale as more than a short step in the right direction. There was no time for the militants to play a role of *leadership* in welfare reform, and, though they might use social indignation to rouse sentiment against the clergy (as Antoine de Marcourt did in his *Livre des Marchants* of 1533),[168] there were more urgent issues for sermons than poor relief. They were eager to build the new Jerusalem as soon as possible, whereas the more patient Protestants who helped create the Aumône-Générale wanted to ameliorate Lyon even before the Lord saw fit to release her from the papists. Thus in the early 1550's, Protestant pastors were urging the conventicles to set up a secret charity of their own[169] while other Protestants were serving as rectors of the Aumône-Générale.

What is significant about the Aumône-Générale, however, is the extent to which it continued to remain "general" during the years when Catholics and Protestants were uncharitably burning and killing each other, or confiscating each other's property. In 1537, the rectors, most of them Catholic, included in their annual aid to prisoners five sous for "Francois' wife, who is a prisoner for heresy." In the tense months just before the First Religious War, some Protestants refused to give at all to the Aumône because there was discrimination against Huguenots at some distribution centers. Yet a rectorate half-Catholic and half-Protestant insisted that the *policy* of the Aumône was to give to people "indifferently, having regard only to whether there is need." The Calvinist regime of 1562-63 let ten months of warfare go by before the rectors made a concerted effort to remove secret papists from its rolls. Then in the summer of 1563, only a few weeks after the clergy and the mass had been restored, Catholic contributions resumed to the Aumône, even though it was still administered by Protestant rectors.[170] The next twenty years, with Lyon Catholic again, were to see the same pattern. Some of the dwindling number of Protestants were discriminated against; others were received for distributions. Some Protestants gave nothing to the Aumône; others gave both to it, or at least to the Hôtel-Dieu, and to the Charity of the Reformed Church.[171] This was not a pretty picture by any real standards of human solidarity, but that the principle of "indifferent" giving by the Aumône-Générale survived the Religious Wars at all is a tribute to the coalition that founded the Aumône. Unlike Nicolas Morin, they thought that misery was a greater danger than heresy to the life of Lyon.

I hope that the material in this paper will serve as a basis for further research on social and religious change during the sixteenth century.* The context for welfare reform, it seems to me, was urban crisis, brought about by a conjuncture of older problems of poverty with population growth and economic expansion. Trouble was caused by country-dwellers and others from outside the city who poured in at times of famine or war, but also by the men, women, and children who lived in the city all the time. Protestant cities and Catholic cities and cities of mixed religious composition initiated rather similar reforms, usually learning from each other's efforts. Lyon is an example of a religious coalition for welfare reform dominated by Catholics. Is Nuremberg an example of welfare reform by a religious coalition dominated by Protestants? The fact that reform in poor relief cut across religious boundaries and that Protestants and Catholics worked to-

---

* Among several valuable studies that have appeared since the original publication of this essay are Harold J. Grimm, "Luther's Contribution to Sixteenth-Century Organization of Poor Relief," *Archive for Reformation History* 61 (1970): 222-33; Robert M. Kingdon, "Social Welfare in Calvin's Geneva," *American Historical Review* 76 (1971): 50-69; Jean-Pierre Gutton, *La société et les pauvres. L'exemple de la généralité de Lyon, 1534-1789* (Bibliothèque de la Faculté des Lettres et Sciences Humaines de Lyon, XXVI; Paris, 1971); Marc Venard, "Les oeuvres de charité en Avignon à l'aube du XVIIe siècle," *XVIIe Siècle* 90-91 (1971): 127-43; Howard Solomon, *Public Welfare, Science and Propaganda in Seventeenth Century France. The Innovations of Théophraste Renaudot* (Princeton, N.J., 1972); Michel Mollat, ed., *Etudes sur l'histoire de la pauvreté (Moyen Age-XVIe siècle)* (Publications de la Sorbonne, Etudes, VIII; Paris, 1974); Brian Pullan, *Rich and Poor in Renaissance Venice*; Richard C. Trexler, "Charity and the Defense of Urban Elites in the Italian Communes," in F. Jaher, ed., *The Rich, the Well Born and the Powerful* (Urbana, Ill., 1974), pp. 64-109.

gether on it shows the extent to which it rested on values and insights common to both groups.[172] I have tried to show how the vocational experience of businessmen and lawyers and certain humanist concerns could provide these insights. And businessmen and lawyers are found throughout the town councils of Europe. Humanists, or at least their writings, have some impact on every European city. In addition, Protestant and Catholic religious sensibility and doctrine found their own paths to justify the elimination of begging and the establishment of centralized organizations to provide relief and rehabilitation. For the Catholics, I speculate that the path was often opened as it was in Lyon—by Christian humanists following an Erasmian program for reform.

There are certainly some differences between Catholic and Protestant welfare arrangements, if only in style, and they must be investigated systematically. But I am not at all sure that most of the differences in welfare systems can be explained by simple religious variables or will even break along religious lines. For instance, the poor laws of Catholic Lyon and Ypres prohibited all begging; the Elizabethan Poor Law allowed some licensed begging (Article X). Protestant Geneva insisted upon the principle of voluntary donation to welfare institutions; Catholic Lyon moved in the direction of obligation, whereas Catholic Paris instituted for a while a *"taxe des pauvres."* What explains the vigor of voluntary philanthropic institutions in Protestant England and Catholic Spain? And how do we account for the variation in lay or clerical control of welfare activities? In Venice the provisions of the poor law were carried out by both parish priests and laymen; in Calvin's Geneva, the General Hospital was administered by deacons of the Reformed Church. The rectors and agents of the Aumône-Générale of Lyon were all laymen until the Protestant period of 1562-63, when deacons and *surveillants* were used; only in 1575, in the spirit of Counter-Reformation, was one canon-count from Saint Jean added to the board of rectors.[173]

Also, I think we should remember how few attacks on welfare

reform were based on its association with Protestant heresy. For every Nicolas Morin or Lorenzo Villavicenzo, there were ten Catholic towns that instituted the new order without opposition from the friars. The reservations of the Sorbonne about begging in Ypres do not seem to have been taken seriously by French authorities, and I cannot see that the Sorbonne pressed the issue in later years. Later on, French authorities resisted strongly the Council of Trent's canons on ecclesiastical supervision of hospitals, and even the French bishops would not accept them undiluted. Moreover, the really meaningful criticism of welfare schemes, some of it made by the poor themselves, did not concern itself with heresy. The Dominican de Soto based his entire argument on principles of natural law and observations about the unequal distribution of wealth and poverty throughout Spain. Printers' journeymen in Lyon called the rectors incompetent to judge need fairly, not as laymen, but as friends or relatives of employers.[174]

Finally, I would like to sum up the implications of this study for the current debate on the *engagement* of humanists in civic affairs.[175] Humanist circles in Lyon were interested in welfare reform partly for self-preservation like everybody else: like Champier, one might get his house pillaged. They were interested in it partly because they had relatives in the Consulate or highly placed in the foreign community, or perhaps were on the Consulate themselves. But their tastes and intellectual concerns as humanists gave them a distinctive approach to the problem of urban poverty. Their aesthetic commitment to classical ideals of beauty, order, and harmony made them especially unable to tolerate the noise, disorder, and human "ugliness" on the city streets. Second, their interest in educational reform made them especially aware of what happened to children who were badly educated by their life as permanent or occasional beggars. They noticed the children and had the impulse to retrain them. And third, their devotion to eloquence and its uses made them speak and write for reform. If one wanted a city without "clamorous complaint," one had to speak. If one wanted a "vision of peace," one could not be silent.

The Lyonnais, moved by love and fear, tried to make of their growing city a place where strangers might live as brothers. Erasmus had asked, "What else is a city but a great monastery?" And so a humanist said of Lyon in 1539 that since the poor had been so cared for, the city seemed "compared to past times, almost a true monastery and congregation of good brothers, though it be the most mixed with diverse nations of any people in this kingdom."[176] Erasmus' question is still being asked of us, and we must find our way to that congregation of good brothers.

APPENDIX

Numbers of People Receiving Distributions from the Aumône-Générale

The distribution rolls of the Aumône-Générale have unfortunately disappeared, as have the censuses of the poor and their needs. Records of families or individuals asking to be *added* to the rolls have been preserved in the minutes of the Sunday meetings of the rectors, but for certain periods (such as the last half of 1551, Archives de la Charité, E7) even these data were not given in the scanty minutes. Thus to estimate the number of inhabitants given distributions by the Aumône, we must fall back upon the weekly accounts of how much bread and how much money were given at the five distribution points. We also have guesses from witnesses in 1534 and 1558 of how many poor people *"tant grands que petiz"* (E4, 79r) marched in the annual Procession of the Poor—3,000 in 1534 and more than 4,000 in 1559.[177]

From the accounts of the weekly distributions, we can at least see some trends. The weekly average of distribution to inhabitants in May 1534, 1550, and 1561 is given in Table 5. In evaluating the amounts of the 1561 distributions, we should remember that the Charity of the Reformed Church of Lyon had been set up recently and was helping perhaps 100 to 200 families. Even allowing for this, however, it is clear that the Aumône-Générale was unable to keep pace with the population increase in Lyon in those years (roughly from 45,000 to 60,000), and that the increased stress on aid in money, whatever freedom of choice it gave the poor, did not keep pace with inflation.

TABLE 5
Average Weekly Distribution of Bread and
Money by the Aumône-Générale for Three Periods
During the Sixteenth Century

	Average weekly distribution			
Period	Loaves of bread	Money £	s.	d.
May 1534	765	37	4	1
May 1550	605	37	11	—
May 1561	503.5	55	15	6

In trying to extrapolate from these accounts how many people were helped—men, women, and children—we face several problems. The basic *aumône* in the 1530's for an adult male was one twelve-pound loaf of bread and one sou. Heads of families and widows with children received in theory two or three times this much. There is no *certain* evidence that the basic *aumône* had been increased in 1561, despite the lower purchasing power of the sou. In fact throughout these years the rectors used their discretion in fixing the amount of aid, with a lone widow, for instance, receiving only half a loaf per week; or an old man receiving aid only in money because he could not chew bread; or a family *without* children receiving as much as 5 sous per week; or a family with seven children receiving as little as one loaf of bread and one sou. Despite all the variation in practice, it is worthwhile trying to estimate the number of inhabitants helped, if only to find the order of magnitude. Thus I am assuming that an average *aumône* for four people per week was one twelve-pound loaf of bread and one sou. We then arrive at the picture illustrated in Table 6.

On the basis of Table 6 we can say very roughly that slightly more than five percent of the inhabitants were being helped by the Aumône at any one time. Since many people were aided for only a few months in the year, the percentage of the population helped at all during one year was, of course, higher.

How does this compare with poor relief in other cities? J. F. Pound tells us that Norwich in the 1570's had about 13,200 Englishmen and about 6,000 foreigners (19,200 people in all) and that approximately five percent of the English population and 3.5 percent of the total population were "permanent pensioners." The town of Exeter, according to Wallace MacCaffrey's study, had about 7,687 people in the 1570's, with 160 individuals receiving help outside of almshouses in 1564-65.[178] If

TABLE 6

*Estimated Number of People Helped Each
Week by the Aumône-Générale for Five Periods
During the Sixteenth Century*

| Period | Average weekly distribution | | People helped each week | |
	Loaves of bread (× 4)	Sous (× 4)	Average number	Estimated pct. of total population
May 1534	3,060	2,976	3,018	7%
May 1550	2,419	3,004	2,712	5
March-December 1550	2,290	2,965	2,628	5
May 1561	2,014	4,462	3,238	5
January-December 1561	1,931	4,167	3,049	5

we assume that 110 of these people had spouses and an average of two children (Pound's average for Norwich), we find that five percent of the population was being aided there. Much comparative study needs to be done on this problem, but these estimates suggest the order of magnitude of assistance given by urban welfare organizations apart from hospitals, workhouses (or public works), and orphan training programs. Given the financial resources of sixteenth-century towns and their assumptions about poverty, how should we evaluate the figure of five percent?

City Women and Religious Change

Looking back on the birth and progress of the Calvinist heresy
in the course of his own lifetime, the Bordeaux jurist Florimond
de Raemond remarked on how much easier it was to entrap
women into heresies than men. The Church Fathers had warned
us of this long before. Women were weak and imbecile. They
could be as precious as pearls or as dangerous as venomous asps.
Very often in our religious quarrels, de Raemond went on, their
distaffs spun more evils than could ever be wrought by the parti-
san slash of seditious swords. He knew this from his own experience, for during a few misguided years in the 1560's he had been
part of the Huguenot movement himself.[1]

De Raemond was not the only Catholic male to try to discredit
the Protestant cause by associating it with the weak will and
feeble intellect of the female. Protestant polemicists returned the
compliment by characterizing Catholic women as at best ignorant and superstitious and at worst whorish and frenzied.[2] Most
modern historians of the Reformation go them one better: they
scarcely mention women at all.

Oh yes, there have been and are exceptions. In a tradition of
women's history that goes back to Plutarch and Boccaccio, portraits of individual women have been collected—of the wives of
Luther and Calvin, for instance, and of Protestant duchesses and
queens—which show that, after all, women had something to do

with the Reformation. More than a century ago the Scottish pastor James Anderson published his *Ladies of the Reformation, Memoirs of the Distinguished Female Characters Belonging to the Sixteenth Century*; and even today are appearing the charming and useful vignettes by Roland Bainton called *Women of the Reformation*. Furthermore, the great political and literary leaders have been given their due: Marguerite de Navarre, sister of King François Ier of France, whose poetry and patronage were so important in the early days of the French Reformation, and her militant daughter, the Huguenot Jeanne d'Albret, queen of Navarre.[3]

Few social studies exist, however, that try to look systematically at the role of women in religious change in the sixteenth century.[4] Did the Reformation have a distinctive appeal to women? If so, what was it and to what kinds of women? What did Protestant women do to bring about religious change? And what innovations did the Reformation effect in the lives of women of different social classes?

Some hypotheses have been offered. First, there are those that pick out features of a religious movement most likely to attract women. Max Weber has suggested in his *Sociology of Religion* that women are always especially receptive to nonmilitary and nonpolitical prophecy and to religious movements with orgiastic, emotional, or hysterical aspects to them. Weber's assumptions remind us uncomfortably of the Church Fathers and Florimond de Raemond, but in any case we will want to ask whether such criteria could apply to a religion as disciplined as Calvinism. A broader approach is found in Keith Thomas' study of women in the civil war sects of seventeenth-century England. He suggests that the spiritual status and scope of activity—emotional or nonemotional activity—offered to women are what drew them to new religions. The more spiritual equality of the sexes, the more women in the movement.[5]

A second set of hypotheses concerns the state of life of women before religious conversion. Some historians stress a prior sense of uselessness, of imprisonment, from which fresh religious commitment served as an escape. Speaking of the attraction of Protestantism for the women of the English aristocracy, Lawrence Stone comments, "Given the idle and frustrated lives these women lived in the man's world of a great country house, it is hardly surprising that they should have turned in desperation to the comforts of religion." Robert Mandrou attributes the same kind of motivation to the wives of traders, artisans, and unskilled workers in sixteenth-century France: "Stuck in their houses, wholly occupied by their little courtyards and inner world of family and children, these women no doubt found in religious movements a kind of liberation."[6]

Other historians, however, talk about this liberation as if it had begun to occur even before women were caught up in religious reform. Nancy Roelker sees the Huguenot noblewomen as strong-minded and already quite independent wives and widows who found in the Reformed cause a way to enhance their activities (by converting their relatives, protecting pastors, giving money and strategic advice to male leaders, and so on) while at the same time preserving their feminine identities. Similarly, Patrick Collinson thinks that it was the education and relative freedom of social life that prepared English gentlewomen and merchants' wives to respond positively to Puritanism in the sixteenth century. "The example of modern Islamic societies," Collinson writes, "leads one to expect the enthusiastic, even violent adoption of political causes by a partially emancipated womanhood. Translated into sixteenth-century categories, we are perhaps witnessing something of the same sort in the vigorous religious partisanship of the women of that time."[7]

Which of these hypotheses best fits the case of the Protestant women in French cities? We will answer this question in the course of this essay. We may note in passing, however, that both of them invoke psychological solutions but do not address themselves to the actual content and organization of the new religious movements. Indeed, Robert Mandrou says that his little housewives might be liberated either by Protestantism or by the transformed Catholicism of the Counter-Reformation; it did not matter which.

A third group of hypotheses has to do with the consequences of the Reformation for women. It is usually argued that it was life within the family that changed most for Protestant women, and for the better. Not only the elimination of clerical celibacy but also the definition of marriage as the school of character is supposed to have led to greater friendship and more equal partnership between Protestant spouses than was possible between Catholic spouses of the same period.[8] Less attention has been paid, however, to the changed roles of women within the life, liturgy, symbolism, and organization of the Reformed Church. Some speculation has been made about the social and psychological origins of Protestant opposition to Mariolatry,[9] but how did banning the cult of Mary affect attitudes toward women and sexual identity?

Let us ask some of these large questions about an important category of women in France—not the great noblewomen already examined by Nancy Roelker, but the women of the cities. Hopefully, some of the conclusions drawn about France may, with appropriate adjustments, be relevant to other parts of Europe.

[1]

The growing cities of sixteenth-century France, ranging from ten thousand inhabitants in smaller places to sixty thousand in Lyon and a hundred thousand in Paris, were the centers of organization and dissemination of Protestantism. The decades in question here are especially those up to the Saint Bartholomew's Day Massacre of 1572—the years when it still seemed hopeful, in the words of a female refugee in Geneva, that the new Christians might deliver their cities from the tyranny and cruelty of the papist Pharaohs.[10] For a while they were successful, with the growth of a large Protestant movement and the establishment in 1559 of an official Reformed Church in France. After 1572, the Huguenot party continued to battle for survival, but it was now doomed to remain a zealous but small minority.

Apart from the religious, almost all adult urban women in the first half of the sixteenth century were married or had once been so. The daughter of a rich merchant, lawyer, or financial officer might find herself betrothed in her late teens. Most women waited until their early twenties, when a dowry could be pieced together from the family or one's wages or extracted from a generous master or mistress.

And then the babies began and kept appearing every two or three years. The wealthy woman, with her full pantry and her country refuge in times of plague, might well raise six or seven children to adulthood. The artisan's wife might bury nearly as many as she bore, while the poor woman was lucky to have even one live through the perils of a sixteenth-century childhood. Then, if she herself had managed to survive the first rounds of child-bearing and live into her thirties, she might well find that her husband had not. Remarriage was common, of course, and until certain restrictive edicts of the French king in the 1560's a widow could contract it quite freely. If she then survived her husband into her forties, chances are she would remain a widow. At this stage of life, women outnumbered and outlived men,[11] and even the widow sought after for her wealth might prefer independence to the relative tutelage of marriage.

With the death rate so high, the cities of sixteenth-century France depended heavily on immigration for their increasing populations. Here, however, we find an interesting difference between the sexes: men made up a much larger percentage of the young immigrants to the cities. The male immigrants contributed to every level of the vocational hierarchy—from notaries, judges, and merchants to craftsmen and unskilled day laborers. And although most of the men came from nearby provinces, some were also drawn from faraway cities and from regions outside the kingdom of France. The female immigrants, on the other hand, clustered near the bottom of the social ladder and came mostly from villages and hamlets in surrounding provinces to seek domestic service in the city.[12]

Almost all the women took part in one way or another in the

economic life of the city. The picture drawn in Renaissance courtesy books and suggested by the quotation from Robert Mandrou —that of women remaining privily in their homes—is rather far from the facts revealed by judicial records and private contracts. The wife of the wealthy lawyer, royal officer, or prosperous merchant supervised the productive activities of a large household but might also rent out and sell rural and urban properties in her own name, in her husband's name, or as a widow. The wives of tradesmen and master craftsmen had some part in running the shops, not just when they were widowed but also while their husbands were alive: a wife might discipline apprentices (who sometimes resented being beaten by a woman's hand), might help the journeymen at the large looms, might retail meats while her husband and his workers slaughtered cattle, might borrow money with her husband for printing ventures, and so on.[13]

In addition, a significant proportion of women in artisanal families and among the *menu peuple* had employ on their own. They worked especially in the textile, clothing, leather, and provisioning trades, although we can also find girls apprenticed to pinmakers and gilders. They sold fish and tripe; they ran inns and taverns. They were painters and, of course, midwives. In Paris they made linen; in Lyon they prepared silk. They made shoes and gloves, belts and collars. In Paris, one Perette Aubertin sold fruit at a stall near the Eglise des Mathurins while her husband worked as a printer. In Lyon, one Pernette Morilier made and sold wimples while her husband worked as a goldsmith. And in an extraordinary document from Lyon, a successful merchant-shoemaker confesses that his prosperity was due not so much to his own profits as to those made by his wife over the preceding 25 years in her separate trade as a linen merchant.[14]

Finally, there were the various semiskilled or unskilled jobs done by women. Domestic service involved a surprisingly high number of girls and women. Even a modest artisanal family was likely to have a wretchedly paid serving girl, perhaps acquired from within the walls of one of the orphan-hospitals recently set up in many urban centers. There was service in the bath-houses, which sometimes slid into prostitution. Every city had its *filles de joie*, whom the town council tried to restrict to certain streets and to stop from brazenly soliciting clients right in front of the parish church. And there was heavy work, such as ferrying people across the Saône and other rivers, the boatwomen trying to argue up their fares as they rowed. If all else failed, a woman could dig ditches and carry things at the municipal construction sites. For this last, she worked shoulder to shoulder with unskilled male day workers, being paid about one-half or two-thirds as much as they for her pains.[15]

This economic activity of women among the *menu peuple* may explain in part the funny nicknames that some of them had. Most French women in the sixteenth century kept their maiden names all their lives: when necessary, the phrase "wife of" or "widow of" so-and-so was tacked on. Certain women, however, had sobriquets: *la Capitaine des vaches* (the Captain of the cows) and *la reine d'Hongrie* (the queen of Hungary) were nicknames given to two women who headed households in Lyon; *la Catelle* was a schoolmistress in Paris; *la Varenne*, a midwife in Le Mans; and *la Grosse Marguerite*, a peddler of Orléans.[16] Such names were also attached to very old women. But in all cases, we can assume not only that these women were a little eccentric but also that these names were bestowed on them in the course of public life— in the street, in the marketplace, or in the tavern.

The public life of urban women did not, however, extend to the civic assembly or council chamber. Women who were heads of households do appear on tax lists and even on militia rolls and were expected to supply money or men as the city government required. But that was the extent of political participation for the *citoyenne*. Male artisans and traders also had little say in these oligarchical city governments, but at least the more prosperous among them might have hoped to influence town councillors through their positions as guild representatives. The guild life of women, however, was limited and already weaker than it had been in the later Middle Ages. In short, the political activity of women on all levels of urban society was indirect or informal only. The wives of royal officers or town councillors might have hoped to influence powerful men at their dining tables. The wives of poor and powerless journeymen and day laborers, when their tables were bare because the city fathers had failed to provide the town with grain, might have tried to change things by joining with their husbands and children in a well-timed grain riot.[17]

What of the literacy of urban women in the century after the introduction of printing to Europe? In the families of the urban elite the women had at least a vernacular education—usually at the hands of private tutors—in French, perhaps in Italian, in music, and in arithmetic. A Latin education among nonnoble city women was rare enough that it was remarked—"learned beyond her sex," the saying went—and a girl like Louise Sarrasin of Lyon, whose physician-father had started her in Hebrew, Greek, and Latin by the time she was eight, was considered a wondrous prodigy. It was women from these wealthy families of bankers and jurists who organized the important literary salons in Paris, Lyon, Poitiers, and elsewhere.[18]

Once outside these restricted social circles, however, there was a dramatic drop in the level of education and of mere literacy among city women. An examination of contracts involving some 1,200 people in Lyon in the 1560's and 1570's to see whether those people could simply sign their names[19] reveals that, of the women, only 28 percent could sign their names. These were almost all from the elite families of well-off merchants and publishers, plus a few wives of surgeons and goldsmiths. All the other women in the group—the wives of mercers, of artisans in skilled trades, and even of a few notaries—could not sign. This is in contrast to their husbands and to male artisans generally, whose ability to sign ranged from high among groups like printers, surgeons, and goldsmiths, to moderate among men in the leather and textile trades, to low—although still well above zero—among men in the food and construction trades. Thus, in the populous middle rank of urban society, although both male and female literacy may have risen from the mid-fifteenth century under the impact of economic growth and the invention of printing, the literacy of the men increased much more than that of the women. Tradesmen might have done business with written accounts; tradeswomen more often had to use finger reckoning, the abacus, or counting stones. Only at the bottom of the social hierarchy, among the unskilled workers and urban gardeners, were men and women alike. As with peasants, there were few of either sex who were literate.[20]

And where would women of artisanal families learn to read and write if their fathers and husbands did not teach them? Nunnery schools received only a small number of lay girls, and these only from fine families. The municipal colleges set up in the first half of the sixteenth century in Toulouse, Nîmes, and Lyon were for boys only; so were most of the little vernacular schools that mushroomed in even quite modest city neighborhoods during these years. To be sure, a few schoolmistresses were licensed in Paris, and there were always some Parisian schoolmasters being chided for illegally receiving girls along with their boy pupils. But in Lyon, where I have found only five female teachers from the 1490's to the 1560's, I have come upon 87 schoolmasters for the same decades.[21]

Thus, in the first half of the sixteenth century, the wealthy and well-born woman was being encouraged to read and study by the availability to her of printed books; by the strengthening of the image of the learned lady, as the writings of Christine de Pisan and Marguerite de Navarre appeared in print; and by the attitude of some fathers, who took seriously the modest educational programs for women being urged by Christian humanists like Erasmus and Juan Luis Vives. Reading and writing for women of the *menu peuple* was more likely to be ridiculous, a subject for farce.[22]

All this shows how extraordinary was the achievement of Louise Labé, the one lowborn female poet of sixteenth-century France. From a family of Lyon ropemakers, barber-surgeons, and butchers, in which some of the women were literate and some (including her own stepmother) were not, Louise was beckoned to poetry and publication by her talent and by profane love. Her message to women in 1555 was "to lift their minds a little above their distaffs and spindles . . . to apply themselves to science and learning . . . and to let the world know that if we are not made to command, we must not for that be disdained as companions, both in domestic and public affairs, of those who govern and are obeyed."[23]

[11]

The message of Calvinist reformers to women also concerned reading and patterns of companionship. But before we turn to it, let us see what can be said about the Catholic religious activity of city women on the eve of the French Reformation.

In regard to the sacramental life of the church, the women behaved very much like their husbands. The prominent families, in which the husband was on the parish building committee, attended mass and confession with some regularity. The wealthiest of them also had private chapels in their country homes. Among the rest of the population attendance was infrequent, and it was by no means certain that all the parishioners would even get out once a year to do their Easter duty of confession and communion. (The clergy itself was partly to blame for this. Those big city parishes were doubling and even tripling in size in these decades, and yet the French Church took virtually no steps to increase accordingly its personnel in charge of pastoral functions or even to guarantee confessors who could understand the language and dialect of the parishioners.) Baptism was taken more seriously, however, as were marriage and extreme unction. Every two or three years the husband appeared before the *curé* with the new baby, bringing with him one or two godfathers and up to five godmothers. The wife was most likely at home, waiting till she was ready to get up for her "churching," or purification after childbirth (the *relevailles*).[24] Moreover, the wills of both men and women show an anxious preoccupation with the ceremonial processions at their funerals and masses to be said for the future repose of their souls. A chambermaid or male weaver might invest many months' salary in such arrangements.[25]

In regard to the organizational and social aspects of Catholic piety on the eve of the Reformation, however, the woman's position was somewhat different from the man's. On the one hand, female religious life was less well organized than male religious life; on the other, the occasions in which urban women participated jointly with men in organized lay piety were not as frequent as they might have been.

To be sure, parish processions led by the priests on Corpus Christi and at other times included men, women, and children, and so did the general processions of the town to seek God's help in warding off famine or other disasters. But the heart of lay religious activity in France in the early sixteenth century was in the lay confraternities organized around crafts or around some devotional interests. Here laymen could support common masses, have their own banquets (whose excesses the clergy deplored), and mount processions on their own saints' days—with "blessed bread," music, costumes, and plays. City women were members of confraternities in much smaller numbers than men at this period. For instance, out of 37 confraternities at Rouen in the first half of the sixteenth century, only six mention female members, and these in small proportion. Women were formally excluded from the important Confraternity of the Passion at Paris, and some confraternities in other cities had similar provisions. Young unmarried men were often organized into confraternities under the patronage of Saint Nicholas; young unmarried women prayed to Saint Catherine, but religious organizations of female youth are hard to find.[26]

Even the convents lacked vitality as centers of organization at this time. Fewer in number than the male religious houses in France and drawing exclusively on noble or wealthy urban families for their membership, the convents were being further isolated by the "reform" movements of the early sixteenth century. Pushed back into arid enclosure, the nuns were cut off not only from illicit love affairs but also from rich contact with the women in the neighborhoods in which they lived.[27] Nor in France during the first part of the sixteenth century do we hear of any new female experiments with communal living, work, and spiritual perfection like the late medieval Beguinages or the imaginative Ursuline community just then being created in an Italian city.

Thus, before the Reformation the relation of Catholic lay women to their saints was ordinarily private or informally organized. The most important occasions for invoking the saints were during pregnancy and especially during childbirth. Then, before her female neighbors and her midwife, the parturient woman called upon the Virgin—or, more likely, upon Saint Margaret, patron of pregnant women—that God might comfort her peril and pain and that her child might issue forth alive.[28]

Into this picture of city women separated from their parish clergy and from male religious organizations, one new element was to enter, even before the Reformation. Women who could read or who were part of circles where reading was done aloud were being prompted by vernacular devotional literature and the Bible to speculate on theology. "Why, they're half theologians," said the Franciscan preachers contemptuously. They own Bibles the way they own love stories and romances. They get carried away by questions on transubstantiation, and they go "running around from . . . one [male] religious house to another, seeking advice and making much ado about nothing." What the good brothers expected from city women was not silly reasoning but the tears and repentance that would properly follow a Lenten sermon replete with all the rhetorical devices and dramatic gestures of which the Franciscans were masters.[29]

Even a man who was more sympathetic than the Franciscans to lettered females had his reservations about how far their learning should take them. A male poet praised the noble dame Gabrielle de Bourbon in the 1520's for reading vernacular books on moral and doctrinal questions and for composing little treatises to the honor of God and the Virgin Mary. But she knew her limits, for "women must not apply their minds to curious questions of theology and the secret matters of divinity, the knowledge of which belongs to prelates, rectors and doctors."[30]

The Christian humanist Erasmus was one of the few men of his time who sensed the depths of resentment accumulating in women whose efforts to think about doctrine were not taken seriously by the clergy. In one of his *Colloquies*,[31] a lady learned in Latin and Greek is being twitted by an asinine abbot (the phrase is Erasmus'). She finally bursts out, "If you keep on as you've begun, geese may do the preaching sooner than put up with you tongue-tied pastors. The world's a stage that's topsy-turvy now, as you see. Every man must play his part—or exit."[*]

[III]

The world was indeed topsy-turvy. The Catholic Church, which Erasmus had tried to reform from within, was being split by Protestants who believed that man was saved by faith in Christ alone and that human work had nothing to do with it, who were changing the sacramental system all around and overthrowing the order of the priesthood. Among this welter of new ideas, let us focus here on the new image of the Christian woman as presented in Calvinist popular literature.

We can find her in a little play dated around 1550. The heroine is not a learned lady but a pure and simple woman who knows her Bible. The villain is not a teasing, harmless abbot but a lecherous and stupid village priest. He begins by likening her achievements to those of craftsmen who were meddling with Scripture, and then goes on: "Why, you'll even see a woman /

---

[*] Erasmus' colloquy makes an interesting contrast with a well-known fifteenth-century dialogue between a woman and her confessor, *Schwester Katrei*. Part of the corpus of mystical literature attributed to Meister Eckhart, the tract portrays a woman who ultimately knows more than her confessor—not through religious study or reading, but through experience and illumination. See Robert E. Lerner, *The Heresy of the Free Spirit in the Later Middle Ages* (Berkeley and Los Angeles, 1972), pp. 215-18, and Franz Pfeiffer, *Meister Eckhart*, trans. C. de B. Evans (London, 1923), 1: 312-34.

Knock over your arguments / With her responses on the Gospel."
And in the play she does, quoting Scripture to oppose the adora-
tion of Mary and the saints and to oppose the power of the popes.
The priest can only quote from glosses, call her names, and
threaten to burn her.[32]

Wherever one looks in the Protestant propaganda of the 1540's
to the 1560's, the Christian woman is identified by her relation to
Scripture. Her sexual purity and control are demonstrated by her
interest in the Bible, and her right to read the New Testament in
the vernacular is defended against those who would forbid it to
her, as to such other unlearned persons as merchants and artisans.
The author of the pamphlet *The Way to Arrrive at the Knowledge
of God* put the matter sharply enough: "You say that women who
want to read the Bible are just libertines? I say you call them lewd
merely because they won't consent to your seduction. You say it's
permitted to women to read Boccaccio's *Flamette* or Ovid's *Art of
Love* . . . which teach them to be adulterers, and yet you'll send a
woman who's reading a Bible to the flames. You say it's enough
for a woman's salvation for her to do her housework, sew and
spin? . . . Of what use then are Christ's promises to her? You'll
put spiders in Paradise, for they know how to spin very well."[33]

The message was even put to music during the First Religious
War in the 1560's. The Huguenot queen of Navarre sings:

> Those who say it's not for women
> To look at Holy Writ
> Are evil men and infamous
> Seducers and antichrist.
> Alas, my ladies.
> Your poor souls
> Let them not be governed
> By such great devils.[34]

And in reality as well as in popular literature Protestant women
were freeing their souls from the rule of priests and doctors of
theology. Noble churchmen were horrified at the intemperance
with which Protestant females abused them as godless men. The

pages of Jean Crespin's widely read *Book of the Martyrs*, based on the real adventures of Protestant heretics, record the story of one Marie Becaudelle, a servant of La Rochelle who learns of the Gospel from her master and argues publicly with a Franciscan, showing him from Scripture that he does not preach according to the Word of God. A bookseller's wife disputes doctrine in a prison cell with the bishop of Paris and with doctors of theology. An honest widow of Tours talks to priests and monks with the witness of Scripture: "I'm a sinner, but I don't need candles to ask God to pardon my faults. You're the ones who walk in darkness." The learned theologians did not know what to make of such monstrous women, who went against nature.[35]

To this challenge to the exclusion of women, the Catholic theologians in mid-century responded not by accommodating but by digging in their heels. It wasn't safe, said an important Jesuit preacher, to leave the Bible to the discretion of "what's turning around in a woman's brain." "To learn essential doctrine," echoed another cleric, "there is no need for women or artisans to take time out from their work and read the Old and New Testament in the vernacular. Then they'll want to dispute about it and give their opinion . . . and they can't help falling into error. Women must be silent in Church, as Saint Paul says." Interestingly enough, when a Catholic vernacular Bible was finally allowed to circulate in France at the end of the sixteenth century, it did not play an important role in the conversion or devotional life of Catholic leaders like Barbe Acarie and Saint Jeanne Frances de Chantal.[36]

Thus, into a pre-Reformation situation in which urban women were estranged from priests or in tension with them over the matter of their theological curiosity, the Protestant movement offered a new option: relations with the priestly order could be broken, and women, like their husbands (indeed *with* their husbands), could be engaged in the pure and serious enterprise of reading and talking about Scripture. The message being broadcast to male artisans and lesser merchants was similar but less momentous. In the first place, the men were more likely already to be literate; and anyway, the only natural order the men were being asked to violate was the separation between the learned and unlearned. The women were *also* being called to a new relation with men. It is worth noting how different is this appeal to women from that which Max Weber considered most likely to win females over to a new religion. Rather than inciting to orgy and emotion, it was summoning to intellectual activity and self-control.

How was the appeal received? France never became a Protestant kingdom, of course, and even in cities where the movement was strong only one-third to one-half of the population might be ardent Calvinists. City men who became caught up in Protestantism ranged from wealthy bankers and professionals to poor journeymen, but they were generally from the more skilled and complex, the more literate, or the more novel trades and occupations. A printer, a goldsmith, or a barber-surgeon was more likely to disobey priests and doctors of theology than was a boatmaster, a butcher, or a baker.

What of the Calvinist women? As with the men, they did not come from the mass of poor unskilled people at the bottom of urban society, although a certain percentage of domestic servants did follow their masters and mistresses into the Reformed Church. The Protestant women belonged mostly to the families of craftsmen, merchants, and professional men, but they were by no means exclusively the literate women in these circles. For all the female martyrs who answered the Inquisitors by citing Scripture they had read, there were as many who could answer only by citing doctrines they had heard. It is also clear that in Lyon in the 1570's, more than a decade after the Reformed Church had been set up, a significant percentage of Reformed women still could not write their names.[37] For this last group, then, the Protestant path was not a way to express their new literacy but a way finally to associate themselves with that surge of male literacy already described.

But there is more that we can say about city women who turned

Protestant. A preliminary examination of women arrested for heresy or killed in Catholic uprisings in many parts of France, of women among the Protestant suspects in Toulouse in 1568-69, and of a very large sample of Protestant women in Lyon (about 750 women) yields three main observations. First, there is no clear evidence either that the wives mainly followed their husbands into the movement or that it worked the other way around.* We can find women converted by their husbands who became more committed than their men; we can find wives who converted while their husbands remained "polluted in idolatry" and husbands who converted while their wives lagged behind.[38] Second, the Protestant women seemed to include more than a random number of widows, of women with employ of their own—such as dressmakers, merchants, midwives, hotel-keepers, and the like—and of women with the curious nicknames associated with public and eccentric personalities.[39] But finally, the Protestant movement in the sixteenth century did not pull in the small but significant group of genuinely learned women in the city—neither the patronesses of the literary salons nor the profane female poets. Louise Labé, who pleaded with women to lift their heads above their distaffs, always remained in the church that invoked the Virgin, although one of her aunts, a female barber, joined the Calvinists.[40]

What do these observations suggest about the state of life of city women before their conversion to the new religion? They do not indicate a prior experience of mere futility and waste or restrictive little family worlds. Rather, Protestant religious commitment seems to have complemented in a new sphere the scope and independence that the women's lives had already had. Women already independent in the street and market now ventured into the male preserve of theology. And yet the literary woman, al-

---

* Nancy Roelker found a different pattern among Huguenot noblewomen, who more often than their husbands took the first step toward conversion ("The Appeal of Calvinism to French Noblewomen in the Sixteenth Century," *The Journal of Interdisciplinary History* 2 [1972]: 402). Class differences help explain this contrast, such as the more significant roles in public life enjoyed by noblewomen than those allowed to city women.

ready admitted to the castle of learning, does not seem to have needed the Religion of the Book. A look at developments within the Reformed Church will indicate why this should have been so.

[IV]

After 1562 the Reformed Church of France started to settle into its new institutional structures and the promise of Protestantism began to be realized for city women. Special catechism classes in French were set up for women, and in towns under Huguenot control efforts were made to encourage literacy, even among all the poor girls in the orphanages, not just the gifted few. In certain Reformed families the literate husbands finally began teaching their wives to read.[41]

Some Protestant females, however, had more ambitious goals. The image of the new Christian woman with her Bible had beckoned them to more than catechism classes or reading the Scriptures with their husbands. Consider Marie Dentière. One-time abbess in Tournai, but expelled from her convent in the 1520's because of heresy, Dentière married a pastor and found her way to Geneva during its years of religious revolution. There, according to the report of a nun of the Poor Clare order, Marie got "mixed up with preaching," coming, for instance, to the convent to persuade the poor creatures to leave their miserable life. She also published two religious works, one of them an epistle on religious matters addressed to Princess Marguerite de Navarre. Here Dentière inserted a "Defense for Women" against calumnies, not only by Catholic adversaries but also by some of the Protestant faithful. The latter were saying that it was rash for women to publish works to each other on Scriptural matters. Dentière disagreed: "If God has done the grace to some poor women to reveal to them by His Holy Scriptures some good and holy thing, dare they not write about it, speak about it, and declare it, one to the other? . . . Is it not foolishly done to hide the talent that God has given us?"[42]

Dentière maintained the modest fiction that she was addressing herself only to other females. Later women did not. Some of the women prisoners in the French jails preached to "the great consolation" of both male and female listeners. Our ex-Calvinist jurist Florimond de Raemond gave several examples, both from the Protestant conventicles and from the regular Reformed services as late as 1572, of women who while waiting for a preacher to arrive had gone up to pulpits and read from the Bible. One *théologienne* even took public issue with her pastor. Finally, in some of the Reformed Churches southwest of Paris—in areas where weavers and women had been early converts—a movement started to permit lay persons to prophesy. This would have allowed both women and unlearned men to get up in church and speak on holy things.[43]

Jean Calvin, Théodore de Bèze, and other members of the Venerable Company of Pastors did not welcome these developments. The social thrust of the Reformation, as they saw it, was to overthrow the hierarchical priestly class and administer the church instead by well-trained pastors and sound male members of the Consistories. That was enough topsy-turvy for them. And like Catholic critics who had quoted Paul's dictum from I Corinthians that "women keep silence in the churches" against Protestants who were reading and talking about the Bible, now the Reformed pastors quoted it against Protestant women who wanted to preach publicly or have some special vocation in the church.[44] Pierre Viret explained in 1560 that the elect were equal in that they were called to be Christian and faithful—man and woman, master and servant, free and serf. But the Gospel had not abolished within the church the rank and order of nature and of human society. God created and Christ confirmed that order. Even if a woman had greater spiritual gifts than had her husband, she could not speak in Christian assembly. Her task, said Pastor Viret, was merely to instruct her children in the faith when they were young; she might also be a schoolteacher to girls if she wished.*

* At Nîmes in the early 1560's four women were charged by the Consistory to seek alms for the poor (Samuel Mours, *Le protestantisme en France au*

And when a female—even a member of the royal family, like Renée de France—tried to go beyond this and meddle in the affairs of the Consistory, the ministers could be very blunt. As a pastor wrote to Calvin about Renée, "She is turning everything upside-down in our ecclesiastical assembly. . . . Our Consistory will be the laughing-stock of papists and Anabaptists. They'll say we're being ruled by women."[45]

Women had been incited to disobey their priests: were they now going to be allowed to disobey their pastors? The pastors quelled them rather easily, and the noisy women subsided into silence or, in a few cases, returned to the Catholic Church. Interestingly enough, during the 1560's, when so many urban churches needed pastors, even a few men of artisanal background were scooped in as ministers of the Word. Consistories were dominated by wealthy merchants and professional men but usually included one or two prosperous master craftsmen.[46] But the women, no matter how rich or well read, were just wives: together with men in a new relation to the Word—but unequal nevertheless.

It cannot be said that the French Calvinist women expressed much bitterness about this role. Radical sects of the Anabaptist type did not form in France, as they did in the Netherlands or in Germany, where—in a less professional, less bookish, less hierarchical order—women were allowed to prophesy or speak in tongues along with men. Nor, apart from later witchcraft trials, did the French Reformation ever turn against troublemaking women with the fury of the Jacobins during the French Revolution, who guillotined the feminist leaders and denied women any political rights whatsoever, including the right even to wit-

seizième siècle [Paris, 1959], p. 218), but women were not made deaconesses. A proposal that women serve as deaconesses in the Reformed Church was actually made by Jean Morély, former tutor in the court of Jeanne d'Albret. Appearing in his *Traicté de la discipline et police chrestienne* (1562) along with other imaginative ideas for a more decentralized and democratic church polity, the proposal was never realized. Rather, Morély's work was roundly condemned by pastors in Geneva and national synods in France (Robert Kingdon, *Geneva and the Consolidation of the French Protestant Movement* [Madison, Wis., 1967], pp. 46-84, esp. p. 59).

ness political debate. What is notable about Calvinist women is not that they were subsequently discontented but that the Reformed solution gave a certain style to their activities on behalf of the Gospel. However enterprising the city women were in the cause of the New Jerusalem—and their activities ranged from marching to martyrdom—there were two things they did not do. No Calvinist woman showed (or was allowed to show) the organizational creativity of the great Catholic females of the Counter-Reformation—of an Angela Merici, for instance, who conceived and set up an extraordinary new order for nonenclosed women in Brescia in the 1530's. Nor did Reformed women outside the circles of the nobility publish as much as did Catholic women of the same social milieu. After Marie Dentière's *Letter to the Queen of Navarre* with its "Defense of Women" in 1538 (which, incidentally, caused a scandal in Geneva because of its sharp criticism of pastors), no book by a woman was printed in Geneva for the rest of the century. In France there was no Protestant counterpart in the sixteenth century for such an urban poet as Louise Labé.[47]

Now we can understand better why Louise Labé would not have flourished under the discipline of a Calvinist Consistory or have been readily attracted to the Huguenot movement. To be sure, many male poets of sixteenth-century France were discomfited by Calvinism, too. But at least one of them, no less than Pastor Théodore de Bèze, was able to hold on to some of the threads of his literary identity, even after his conversion to the new religion.[48] But the public and independent identity of Louise Labé was based on behavior that was unacceptable in a modest and brave Reformed woman. The books Louise read and wrote were lascivious; her salons an impure gathering of the sexes; and her literary feminism impudent. She was talked of in Geneva as a lewd female who had corrupted the wife of a Lyon surgeon, persuading her to abandon her Christian husband for the sake of pleasure. In a Protestant poem against the scandalous new fashion of hoop skirts, Louise seems to have been the model of the libertine—a woman who talks loud and often, affecting to know divine things but really living a life of debauchery. A Catholic deacon in Lyon, Guillaume Paradin, himself a humanist and literary man, thought Louise virtuous, angelic of face, and with an understanding superior to her sex. Calvin said she was a strumpet. There was some truth in both evaluations.[49]

[v]

An examination of a few other areas of Protestant reform reveals the same pattern as in reading Scripture and preaching: city women revolted against priests and entered new religious relations that brought them together with men or likened them to men but left them unequal.

The new Calvinist liturgy, with its stress on the concerted fellowship of the congregation, used the vernacular—the language of women and the unlearned—and included Psalms sung jointly by men and women. Nothing shocked Catholic observers more than this. When they heard the music of male and female voices filtering from a house where a conventicle was assembled, all they could imagine were lewd activities with the candles extinguished. It was no better when the Protestant movement came into the open. After the rich ceremony of the mass, performed by the clergy with due sanctity and grandeur, the Reformed service seemed, in the words of a Catholic in Paris in the 1560's, "without law, without order, without harmony." "The minister begins. Everybody follows—men, women, children, servants, chambermaids. . . . No one is on the same verse. . . . The fine-voiced maidens let loose their hums and trills . . . so the young men will be sure to listen. How wrong of Calvin to let women sing in Church."[50]

To Protestant ears, it was very different. For laymen and laywomen in the service the common voice in praise of the Lord expressed the lack of distance between pastor and congregation. The Catholic priests had stolen the Psalms; now they had been returned. As for the participants in the conventicles, the songs gave them courage and affirmed their sense of purity over the hypocritical papists, who no sooner left the mass than they were singing love songs. The Protestant faithful were firmly in control of their sexual impulses, they believed, their dark and sober clothes a testimonial to their sincerity. And when the women and men sang together in the great armed street marches of the 1560's, the songs were a militant challenge to the hardened Catholics and an invitation to the wavering listeners to join the elect.[51]

For the city women, there was even more novelty. They had had a role smaller than men's in the organized lay ceremonial life of the church, and the confraternities had involved them rather little. Previously, nuns had been the only women to sing the office. Now the confraternities and the convents would be abolished. The ceremonial was simplified and there was only one kind of group for worship, one in which men and women sang together. For Protestant tradesmen, many of whom were immigrants to the city, the new liturgical fellowship provided religious roots they had been unable to find in the inhospitable parishes. For Protestant women, who were not as likely to have been immigrants, the new liturgy provided roots in religious organizations with men.

But this leveling, this gathering together of men and women, had its limits. Singing in church did not lead women on to preaching or to participating in the Consistory any more than Bible-reading had. Furthermore, there was some effort by the pastors to order the congregations so as to reflect the social order. In Geneva, special seats were assigned to minimize the mingling of the sexes. And in some Reformed churches the sexes were separated when communion was taken: the men went up first to partake of the Holy Supper.[52]

Psalms were added to the religious life of the Protestants and saints were taken away—from prayer, image, and invocation. Here the matter of sex was indifferent: Saint Damian departed as did Saint Margaret; Saint Nicholas departed as did Saint Catherine. Protestant men and women affirmed before the Inquisition that one must not call upon the Virgin, for, blessed though she was, she had no merit. And when the magistrates were slow to purify the churches of their idolatrous statues, zealous members of the *menu peuple* smashed the saints. Females were always included in these crowds.[53] Indeed, like the armed march of the psalm-singers, the iconoclastic riot was a transfer of the joint political action of the grain riot into the religious sphere.

But the loss of the saints affected men and women unequally. Reformed prayer could no longer be addressed to a woman, whereas the masculine identity of the Father and Son was left intact. It may seem anachronistic to raise the matter of sexual identity in religious images during the Reformation, but it is not. Soon afterward, the Catholic poet Marie le Jars de Gournay, friend and editor of Montaigne, was to argue in her *Equality of the Sexes* that Jesus' incarnation as a male was no special honor to the male sex but a mere historical convenience; given the patriarchal malice of the Jews, a female savior would never have been accepted. But if one were going to emphasize the sex of Jesus, then it was all the more important to stress the perfection of Mary and her role in the conception of our Lord.[54] So, if the removal from Holy Mother Church cut off certain forms of religious affect for men, for women the consequences for their identities went even deeper. Now during their hours of childbirth—a "combat," Calvin described it, "a horrible torment"—they called no more on the Virgin and said no prayers to Saint Margaret. Rather, as Calvin advised, they groaned and sighed to the Lord and He received those groans as a sign of their obedience.[55]

Obedience to the Lord was, of course, a matter for both men and women. But women had the additional charge of being obedient to their husbands. The Reformed position on marriage provides a final illustration of the pattern "together but unequal."

The Protestant critique of clerical celibacy involved first and foremost a downgrading of the concept that the male had a greater capacity than the female to discipline his sexual impulses. Since the time of the Greeks, physicians had been telling people that physiology made the female the more lustful, the more uncontrollable sex. As Doctor François Rabelais put it, there are many things a man can do, from work to wine, to control "the pricks of venery"; but a woman, with her hysteric animal (the womb) within, could rarely restrain herself from cuckolding her husband. Given these assumptions, clerical celibacy for the superior sex had been thought a real possibility whereas for the female it had appeared an exceptional achievement.[56]

The Reformers' observation that continence was a rare gift of God and their admonition "Better to marry than to burn" were, then, primarily addressed to the numerous male clergy and less to the small fraction of female religious. Indeed, sermons on clerical marriage stressed how the groom would now be saved from fornication and hellfire but said little of the soul of the bride. It is surely significant, too, that male religious joined the Reformation movements in proportionately larger numbers than did female. The nuns were always the strong holdouts, even when they were promised dowries and pensions. Though some of them may have been afraid to try their chances on the marriage market, many simply preferred the separate celibate state and organization. When Marie Dentière tried to persuade the nuns of the Poor Clare order at Geneva to end their hypocritical lives and marry, as she had, the sisters spat at her.[57]

The argument for clerical marriage, then, equalized men and women somewhat in regard to their appetites. It also raised the woman's status by affirming that she could be a worthy companion to a minister of God. The priest's concubine, chased from his house in ignominy by Catholic reformers and ridiculed as a harlot by Protestants, could now become the pastor's wife! A respectable girl from a good city family—likely, in the first generation, to be the daughter of a merchant or prosperous craftsman—would be a helpful companion to her husband, keeping his busy household in order and his colleagues entertained. And she would raise her son to be a pastor and her daughter to be a pastor's wife.[58]

Since marriage was now the only encouraged state, the Reformers did what they could to make it more tolerable according to their lights. Friendship and companionship within marriage were stressed, as many historians have pointed out, although it is a mistake to think that this was unique to Protestant thought. Catholic humanist writers valued these relations within marriage as well.[59] In other ways, the Reformed position was more original.* A single sexual standard would now be enforced rather than talked about; and the victorious Huguenot Consistories during the Wars of Religion chased out the prostitutes almost as quickly as they silenced the mass. The husband would be compelled insofar as possible to exercise his authority, in Calvin's words, "with moderation and not insult over the woman who has been given him [by God] as his partner." Thus, in a real innovation in Christian Europe, men who beat their wives were haled before Consistories and threatened with denial of communion. The men grumbled and complained—"I beat my wife before and I'll beat

---

* It does not seem justified to argue, as does Roelker, that Calvin's position on divorce "advanced women to a position of equality with their husbands." "By permitting wives as well as husbands to instigate divorce proceedings," she maintains, "Calvin elevated their dignity and increased their legal rights. Enacted into Genevan law, this could not help but raise the position of women to a higher level" ("The Appeal of Calvinism," p. 406). The institution of divorce with permission to remarry in cases of adultery or very prolonged absence was, of course, an important innovation by Calvin and other Protestant reformers. But this change did not remedy an *inequality* in the existing marriage law. The canon law had long allowed either male or female the right to initiate proceedings in an ecclesiastical court for separation in case of the partner's adultery, as well as for annulment and dissolution in certain circumstances. What determined whether men and women in fact had equal access to separation or divorce before or after the Reformation was, first, the informal operation of the double standard, which tolerated the husband's adultery more readily than the wife's, and, second, the relatively greater economic difficulty faced by the single woman supporting herself and her children in the interval before she was able to remarry. For all but the very wealthy man or woman, divorce or legal separation was an unlikely possibility. In any case, the exhaustive research of René Stauffenegger has shown that divorces were very rarely granted in Geneva in the late sixteenth and early seventeenth centuries—pastors and Consistory always pressing for couples to solve their disputes. See Keith Thomas, "The Double Standard," *Journal of the History of Ideas* 20 (1959): 200-202; John T. Noonan, Jr., *Power to Dissolve* (Cambridge, Mass., 1972), chaps. 1-3, 7; R. Stauffenegger, "Le mariage à Genève vers 1600," *Mémoires de la société pour l'histoire du droit* 27 (1966): 327-28.

her again if she be bad," said a Lyon typecaster—but the situation had improved enough in Geneva by the end of the century that some called it "the women's Paradise."[60]

But despite all this, the Reformed model of the marriage relation subjected the wife to her husband as surely as did the Catholic one. Women had been created subject to men, said Calvin, although before the fall "this was a liberal and gentle subjection." Through sin, it had become worse: "Let the woman be satisfied with her state of subjection, and not take it amiss that she is made inferior to the more distinguished sex." Nor was this view restricted to pastors. There are many examples from sixteenth-century France of Protestant husbands instructing their wives, "their dear sisters and loyal spouses," telling them of their religious duties, telling them of their responsibilities toward their children, warning them that they must never do anything without seeking advice first. And if Protestant wives then told their husbands to go to the devil or otherwise insulted them so loudly that the neighbors heard, the women might soon find themselves brought before the Consistories and even punished (as the criminal records of Geneva reveal) by three days in prison on bread and water.[61]

Undoubtedly there were many Reformed marriages in commercial and artisanal circles where the husbands and wives lived together in peace and friendship. And why not? Women had joined the Reformation to rebel against priests and pope, not to rebel against their husbands. Although they wanted certain "masculine" religious activities opened to them, Calvinist wives—even the most unruly of them—never went so far as to deny the theory of the subjection of women within marriage.[62] The practice of subjection in individual marriages during those heroic decades of the Reformation may have been tempered by two things: first, the personality of the wife herself, which sustained her revolt against priestly power and her search for new relations with books and men; and second, the common cause of reform, which for a while demanded courageous action from both husbands and wives.

And what could a city woman accomplish for the cause if she were not rich and powerful like a noblewoman? On a Catholic feast day, she could defy her Catholic neighbors by sitting ostentatiously spinning in her window. She could puzzle over the Bible alone or with her husband or with Protestant friends. If she were a printer's wife or widow, she could help get out a Protestant edition to spread the word about tyrannical priests. She could use her house for an illegal Protestant conventicle or assembly. She could put aside her dissolute hoop skirts and full gowns and start to wear black. She could harangue priests in the streets. She could march singing songs in defiance of royal edicts. She could smash statues, break baptismal fonts, and destroy holy images. She could, if persecution became very serious, flee to London or Geneva, perhaps the longest trip she had ever taken. She could stay in France and dig the foundations for a Reformed temple. She could even fight—as in Toulouse, where a Huguenot woman bore arms in the First Religious War. And she could die in flames, shouting to her husband, as did one young wife of Langres, "My friend, if we have been joined in marriage in body, think that this is only like a promise of marriage, for our Lord . . . will marry us the day of our martyrdom."[63]

Many of these actions, such as Bible-reading, clearly were special to Protestant city women. A few were not. The Catholic city women in Elizabethan England, for instance, hid priests in their quarters and, if captured, went to the "marriage" of martyrdom as bravely as did any Huguenot. It was the same among the radical Anabaptists. One kind of action, however, seems to have been special to Catholic city women (as also to the radical Quaker women of the seventeenth century): organized group action among women. On the highest level, this was expressed in such attempts to create new forms of common life and work among females as the Ursulines and the Sisters of Charity and the Christian Institutes of Mary Ward. On the lowest level, this was reflected in the violent activity of all-female Catholic crowds— throwing stones at Protestant women, throwing mire at pastors, and, in the case of a group of female butchers in Aix-en-Provence, beating and hanging the wife of a Protestant bookseller.[64]

These contrasts can point the way to some general conclusions about the long-range significance of the Reformed solution for relations between the sexes. In an interesting essay, Alice Rossi suggests three models for talking about equality. One is assimilationist: the subordinate group is somewhat raised by making it like the superior group. A second is pluralistic: each group is allowed to keep its distinctive characteristics but within a context of society at large that is still hierarchical. The third is hybrid (or, better, transformational), involving changes within and among all groups involved.[65] Whatever transformations in social relations were accomplished by either the Reformation or the Counter-Reformation, it seems that as far as relations between the sexes go the Reformed solution was assimilationist; the Catholic solution, with its female saints and convents, was pluralistic. Neither, of course, eliminated the subject status of women.*

Is one position clearly better than the other? That is, within the context of the society of the sixteenth and seventeenth centuries did one solution seem to offer greater freedom to men and women to make decisions about their lives and to adopt new roles? One important school of sociologists always answers such questions in favor of Protestantism. It is the superior sect: its transcendent and activist Father, less hierarchical religious symbolism, and this-worldly asceticism all make for a more evolved religion, facilitating the desacralization of society. More different choices are also facilitated, so this argument goes, and more rapid social change.[66]

Certainly it is true that the Reformed solution did promote a certain desexualization of society, a certain neutralizing of forms

* The same point can be made in regard to class relations within the two Reformations, the Reformed Church assimilating artisans and even peasants upward in styles of religious behavior and the Catholic allowing greater scope to "peasant religion." Although Calvinism reduced the levels of angelic and ecclesiastical hierarchy, neither church challenged the *concept* of social hierarchy.

of communication and of certain religious places so that they became acceptable for women. These were important gains, bringing new tools to women and new experience to both sexes. But the assimilationist solution brought losses, too. This-worldly asceticism denied laymen and laywomen much of the shared recreational and festive life allowed them by Catholicism. It closed off an institutionalized and respectable alternative to private family life: the communal living of the monastery. By destroying the female saints as exemplars for both sexes, it cut off a wide range of affect and activity. And by eliminating a separate identity and separate organization for women in religious life, it may have made them a little more vulnerable to subjection in all spheres.

As it turned out, women suffered for their powerlessness in both Catholic and Protestant lands in the late sixteenth to eighteenth centuries as changes in marriage laws restricted the freedoms of wives even further, as female guilds dwindled, as the female role in middle-level commerce and farm direction contracted, and as the differential between male and female wages increased.[67] In both Catholic France and Protestant England, the learned lady struggled to establish a role for herself: the female schoolteacher became a familiar figure, whether as a spinster or as an Ursuline; the female dramatist scrambled to make a living, from the scandalous Aphra Behn in the seventeenth century to the scandalous Olympe de Gouges in the eighteenth.

Thus it is hard to establish from a historical point of view that the Reformed assimilationist structure always facilitated more rapid and creative changes in sex roles than did the relatively pluralistic structure found in the Catholicism of the sixteenth and seventeenth centuries. Both forms of religious life have contributed to the transformation of sex roles and to the transformation of society. In the proper circumstances, each can serve as a corrective to the other.[68] Whatever long-range changes may be achieved, the varied voices heard in this essay will have played their part: the immodest Louise Labé telling women to lift their minds a little above their distaffs, the servant Marie Becaudelle disputing with her priest, the ex-nun Marie Dentière urging women to speak and write about Scripture, and yes, the Catholic Marie le Jars de Gournay reminding us that, after all, it was only a historical accident that our Lord Jesus Christ was born a male.

FOUR

The Reasons of Misrule

[1]

"It is sometimes expedient to allow the people to play the fool and make merry," said the French lawyer Claude de Rubys at the end of the sixteenth century, "lest by holding them in with too great a rigor, we put them in despair. . . . These gay sports abolished, the people go instead to taverns, drink up and begin to cackle, their feet dancing under the table, to decipher King, princes, . . . the State and Justice and draft scandalous defamatory leaflets."[1] De Rubys' view is a traditional one, but it tells us more about the thought of urban magistrates than about the real uses of popular recreation. I hope to show that rather than being a mere "safety valve," deflecting attention from social reality, festive life can on the one hand perpetuate certain values of the community (even guarantee its survival), and on the other hand criticize political order. Misrule can have its own rigor and can also decipher king and state.

The festivities that de Rubys favored for his native Lyon were found in all the cities of France, and indeed of Europe, in the later Middle Ages and the sixteenth century: masking, costuming, hiding; charivaris (a noisy, masked demonstration to humiliate some wrongdoer in the community), farces, parades, and floats; collecting and distributing money and sweets; dancing, music-making, the lighting of fires; reciting of poetry, gaming, and athletic contests—the list in all its forms and variations would be longer than the 81 games in Bruegel's famous painting or the 217 games that Rabelais gave to Gargantua. They took place at regular intervals, and whenever the occasion warranted it; they were timed to the calendar of religion and season (the twelve days of Christmas, the days before Lent, early May, Pentecost, the feast of Saint Jean Baptiste in June, the Feast of the Assumption in mid-August, and All Saints) and timed also to domestic events, marriages, and other family affairs.

One of these urban festivals was sponsored by clerics—namely the Feast of Fools at Christmastime, when a choirboy or chaplain would be elected bishop and preside while the minor clergy burlesqued the mass and even confession, and led an ass around the church. By the late fifteenth century this topsy-turvy saturnalia was being slowly banished from the cathedrals,[2] and apart from it virtually all the popular recreations were initiated by laymen. They were not, however, "official" affairs in the sixteenth-century French city; that is, city governments ordinarily did not plan, program, and finance them as they did the great Entry parades for royalty or other important personages or the parades in celebration of peace treaties. Rather, the festivities were put on by informal circles of friends and family,[3] sometimes by craft or professional guilds and confraternities, and very often by organizations that literary historians have called "*sociétés joyeuses*" (or "fool-societies" or "play-acting societies")[4] but that I will call Abbeys, since that name comes closest to what they usually called themselves—the Abbeys of Misrule.

To their officers the Abbeys gave diverse titles, but certain common themes are played upon: power, jurisdiction, youth, misrule, pleasure, folly, even madness. Thus around 1500 there were Abbots of Misrule (Abbés de Maugouvert) in Lyon, Mâcon, Poitiers, Rodez, Briançon, and Abbeville; an Abbot of Gaiety (Liesse) and his Good Children at Arras; a Prince of Pleasure at Valenciennes; a Prince of Youth at Soissons; a Prince of Fools (Prince des Sots) at Amiens; an Abbot of Conards or Cornards* at Rouen; and a Mère d'Enfance and her Children at Bordeaux and a Mère Folle and her Infanterie at Dijon (both of them men dressed up as women).⁵ In some cities there were a host of other dignitaries: for instance, Rouen's Abbot of Conards had serving him in 1541 the Prince of Improvidence, the Cardinal of Bad Measure, Bishop Flat-Purse, Duke Kickass, and the Grand Patriarch of Syphilitics, to mention only a few.⁶

These Abbeys acted like courts and used their jurisdictions. Mock coins were issued and distributed to spectators during parades (see Plate 5).⁷ Lyon had both a Judge of Misrule and a Bench of Bad Advice.⁸ In Dijon and Rouen, cases were heard— foolish cases and also those concerning the honor of the Abbeys or the behavior of their dignitaries.⁹ Proclamatory letters were issued such as those of 1536 from the Abbot of Conards and his court permitting all men for 101 years to take two wives. What

---

* Both Conard and Cornard were used as names for the members of the Misrule Abbey at Rouen, though Conard was more frequent. To sixteenth-century observers, the words suggested the various uses of folly, sexuality, power, and noise. A *conard* was defined as a *sot*, or fool. The word also had associations with *con*, as in sixteenth-century pictures purporting that the female genitalia made fools out of men and were the source of male energy. A *cornard* was a cuckolded husband, the husband wearing the phallic horns on his head. The two words were related, according to a seventeenth-century commentator, because of their similar sound, because both fools and deceived husbands wore horns, and because a husband was a fool to let himself be cuckolded. The wearing of horns could also evoke the diabolic, the pagan, and the Jewish, as well as the ancient meanings of honor and victory and the medieval horned mitre of the bishop, sometimes worn by an abbot as well. Finally, a woodcut of the Abbot of Conards from the 1530's shows him blowing a horn, which has a flag with a horn on it and the words "O Conardz" upside down. The mocking noise made by a Misrule Abbey may be what is intended here. See E. Picot and P. Lacombe, eds., *Querelle de Marot et Sagon* (Rouen, 1920), pièce 1; Pierre Borel, *Trésor de Recherches et Antiquitez Gauloises et Françoises* (Paris, 1655), pp. 101, 110; *Grand Larousse de la langue française* (Paris, 1972), II, 1847; Eduard Fuchs, *Die Frau in der Karikatur* (Munich, 1907), p. 183; J. A. Pitt-Rivers, *The People of the Sierra* (London, 1954), p. 116; William Willeford, *The Fool and His Scepter* (Evanston, Ill., 1969), p. 184; Ruth Mellinkoff, *The Horned Moses in Medieval Art and Thought* (Berkeley, Calif., 1970), chaps. 8, 10.

reason was given? The Turks have put out to sea to destroy Christendom and we must appease them by becoming polygamous.[10]

With the Turkish fleet, which in fact had been threatening the Mediterranean under the Admiral Khairad-Din Barbarossa, a note of reality was sounded in the midst of the May revels of the Abbey of Conards. This was no exceptional occurrence. Real life was always deeply embedded in these carnivals, and not only because Misrule always implies the Rule that it parodies. Real people were mocked by the Abbeys in clamorous charivaris and parades for their real everyday behavior: husbands beaten by their wives were led by a noisy, masked, and costumed throng through the town facing backwards on an ass (see Plate 7), or if not the husband himself then a neighbor who shouted "it is not for my deed, it is for my neighbor's."[11] Often the form in which this monstrous reversal of nature had occurred was acted out: thus a 1566 festival in Lyon included seven floats in which husbands identified by street and occupation were being beaten variously with tripe, wooden sticks, knives, forks, spoons, frying pans, trenchers, and water pots; were having stones thrown at them; were having their beards pulled; and were being kicked in the genitalia—each, as the printed description said, representing the actual "martyr" of the quarter.[12]

Nor were these the only victims of charivaris: widows or widowers remarrying were vulnerable, as were husbands deceived by their wives and husbands who beat their wives during the month of May (a special month for women).[13]

There were many other occasions for mockery by the Abbeys of Misrule, but readers are surely wondering (as I did when I had this preliminary data in front of me, most of it from sixteenth-century printed scenarios and other *urban* sources) what kind of organizations these really were, what they were really up to, where they came from and where they were going, and what linked together their seemingly disparate recreations. Most books on "everyday life" in the late Middle Ages and early modern period do not help us very much, for they merely describe the curious charivaris and carnivals and stop short of analysis. Thus to search for the meaning of Misrule, I went first to men who had lived during the Renaissance, then to modern historians of literature who had treated festive organizations and customs as sources for the Renaissance theatre, and then to the theoreticians of play and recreation.

Both in the Renaissance and in our own day, two modes of explanation have been used to account for the form and content of popular festivities and games—one historical, the other functional. A 1556 treatise by Guillaume Paradin, dean of Beaujeu, traced mumming back to Greek and Roman festivals in which it was permissible to mask oneself, imitate magistrates, and publicly proclaim the vices and faults of others. Indeed, said the good cleric, all dances, games, and kingdoms on saints' days were but *"ethnicisme et paganisme."*[14] Some fifty years later Claude Noirot, a judge of Langres, gave a similar account in his *Origin of Masks, Mumming and . . . Charivari*, but added information on the use of public humiliation and the parade backward on an ass as legal penalties in the classical world, as well as on Roman law regarding second marriages (which, as we have seen, were occasions for charivari).[15]

Modern scholarship, working not only with ancient sources but with studies of primitive and peasant religion, has enriched this picture of historical transmission. As E. K. Chambers said in his great study of the medieval stage, "the traditional beliefs and customs of the medieval or modern peasant are in nine cases out of ten but the *detritus* of heathen mythology and heathen worship. . . . Village festivals . . . are but fragments of the naïve cults addressed by a primitive folk to the beneficent deities of field and wood and river." The Feast of Fools then not merely went back to the Roman Kalends of January, but also had primitive features that had passed through peasant communities to the city cathedrals: the holiday bishop of the Christmas revels, like all other holiday lords, was a survival of that temporary king, described in Fraser's *Golden Bough*, once elected by his fellows for human sacrifice.[16]

How then do we account for the specific features of Abbeys and Kingdoms of Misrule and their charivaris and carnivals? According to Chambers and the literary school, they were simply a secularization during the fifteenth century of the declining Feast of Fools.[17] According to others, they represented commoners imitating their betters, that is, imitating the judicial role of the seigneur[18] or certain allegedly aristocratic customs of late chivalry.[19] These theories are wrong. The imagery of the lay organizations was usually monastic rather than episcopal as in the Feast of Fools. The lay societies had mock jurisdiction over marriages and domestic affairs, for which there is no precedent in the Feast of Fools and no clear precedent in feudal law. And the Misrule Abbeys existed in some form in French cities from the thirteenth century on, contemporaneous with the cathedral fête and prior to the flowering of late medieval chivalry.[20]

Finally, these last theories do not clarify for us the uses of Misrule, for they rest on a picture of city-dwellers either acting out ancient and magical customs whose meaning had long since been forgotten or copying their social superiors just for the sake of copying. Thus we must turn to a second, functional, approach to find the sense in popular recreations. "Foolishness . . . is our second nature," said a fifteenth-century defender of the Feast of Fools, "and must freely spend itself at least once a year. Wine barrels burst if from time to time we do not open them and let in some air."[21]

For us, *homo ludens* is a more complex person than this (as he was for Shakespeare and Rabelais), and modern theoreticians have tried to sort out his games as they appear and are used in different cultures. In these typologies, the carnival, masks, and misrule are usually seen as functional characteristics of primitive, or at least traditionalist, preindustrial societies. Roger Caillois argues in *Les jeux et les hommes* that such festivities bring coherence to primitive societies; their apparent disorder is actually a source of order in societies lacking in contractual relationships.[22] In a less paradoxical view ably developed by Keith Thomas, the carnival is seen as a prepolitical safety valve for the members of a structured, hierarchical society, and because of its spontaneity and irregular rhythm, the expression and reinforcement of "a pre-industrial sense of time."[23]

In contrast, the anthropologist Victor Turner and the Soviet structuralist Mikhail Bakhtin see topsy-turvy play or rite as present in *all* societies. For Turner, the ritual of status reversal—whether of an Ashanti ceremony, a Christian sect, or a teenage street gang—serves to loosen the rigors of a structured society and to "infuse" through the system at least temporarily the values of an egalitarian community. For Bakhtin, in his beautiful study of Rabelais, the carnival is always a primary source of liberation, destruction, and renewal, but the scope it is allowed changes in different periods. Before the existence of classes and the state, the comic realm was equal to the serious; with slave and feudal societies, including that of the sixteenth century, the carnival becomes a second life, a second reality for the people, separated from power and the state but still public and perennial; in bourgeois society (and alas, one feels, in Bakhtin's socialist society as well) it is reduced to the home and the holiday. The carnival does not, however, reinforce the serious institutions and rhythms of society as in the other functional theories just mentioned; it helps to change them. In Rabelais' day, says Bakhtin, it provided the people with an actual experience of life without hierarchy as against the fixed categories of "official" medieval culture.[24]

These historical and functional formulations provide us with a framework and some alternatives for interpreting the Abbeys of Misrule. They are, however, very general; we need accurate historical precedents closer to the sixteenth century than the Roman Empire or the sacrificial king, and we need more information about the Abbeys themselves in order to ascertain their uses and to decide where the balance lies in their recreations between tradition and innovation and between the prepolitical and the political.

[11]

To track down the source of Misrule, I left the streets of Rouen
and Dijon and Lyon and other cities and went to the villages. I
left the works of historians, with their literary or political bias,
and went to those of the anthropologists, especially the many systematic studies of France by Arnold Van Gennep. Everything I
shall say about the villages, however, I have confirmed in hundreds of royal pardons from the later Middle Ages, from which a
French archivist, Roger Vaultier, has extracted and published all
material bearing on folk customs.[25]

We discover from the twelfth century (and undoubtedly before), throughout France, organizations of the unmarried men in
peasant communities who have reached the age of puberty. When
precisely they joined or whether there were initiation rites has not
been discovered. These young men were called *varlets* and *varlets à
marier* or *compagnons* and *compagnons à marier*; their organizations were known as *bachelleries* (in the Poitou, Berry, the Angoumois, the Vendée, and elsewhere), Kingdoms of Youth, and in
wide areas—Burgundy, the Dauphiné, Savoie, and the Midi—
Abbeys of Youth (Abbayes de la Jeunesse).[26] Since village boys
usually did not marry until their early or middle twenties in the
fifteenth through seventeenth centuries,[27] their period of *jeunesse*
lasted a long time and the number of bachelors relative to the total
number of men in the village was quite high. Each year before
Lent, after Christmas, or at some other time, they elected a King
or Abbot from among their midst.[28] The Abbey of Misrule was
in its inception a youth group!

Now these youth-abbeys had a surprising range of jurisdiction
and festive responsibility. They met the youth of other parishes at
Mardi Gras for *soules*, a violent football game, and at other times
pitted their strength against the married men in their own village.[29]
In the Fête des Brandons at the beginning of Lent it was they who
bore the brands of blazing straw and jumped and danced to ensure
the village's agricultural and sexual fertility for the coming year;

and at All Souls' Day it was they who rang the bells for the dead ancestors of the village.[30]

The Abbeys had jurisdiction over villagers their own age, including marriageable girls,* in front of whose houses they planted May bushes (or a smelly bush, if they wished to suggest a girl's morals were dubious),[31] and over young strangers coming to court their girls, whom they would fight or hold up for a fine.[32] They had prescribed roles in the wedding ceremony, such as putting up chains across the path of the procession or bursting into the wedding chamber on some pretence—obstacles, like our western shivaree, to the consummation of the marriage that could be removed only by the payment of flowers, money, or a drink.[33]

More important, the rural youth-abbeys had jurisdiction over the behavior of married people—over newlyweds when the wife had failed to become pregnant during the year, over husbands dominated by their wives, sometimes over adulterers. The penalties were in some villages ducking in water, in others a humiliating parade backwards on the ass or a charivari.[34] The earliest known French use of the term charivari† and the most frequent occasion for it in villages, however, was in connection with second marriages, especially when there was a gross disparity in age between the bride and groom.[35] Then the masked youth with their pots,

* The unmarried adolescent girls also had prescribed roles in rural festive life: they danced with the young men; they participated in May festivities; they sometimes went out with the young males on the New Year's *"quête de l'Aquilanneuf"* or *"l'aguileneuf"* (corruption of *"au guy l'an neuf"* and deriving from the Druid collecting of the mistletoe; M. du Tilliot, *Mémoires pour servir à l'histoire de la Fête des Foux* [2d ed.; Lausanne and Geneva, 1751], pp. 67-71). Temporary Queens were also elected among the young unmarried women of the village at certain times of year, especially in May. But were the village girls organized into youth groups of their own? Van Gennep reports various *reinages* and confraternities of unmarried girls in honor of Saint Catherine (Arnold Van Gennep, *Manuel de folklore français* [Paris, 1943-49], 1: 207-12), but gives no evidence that they existed in the countryside in the Middle Ages or sixteenth century.

† Van Gennep provides many variants for the word charivari in different parts of France: chalivali, calvali, chanavari, coribari, kériboeéri—even hourvari and others (*Manuel*, 1: 622 and 622, n. 2).

tambourines, bells, rattles, and horns might make their clamor for a week outside the house of their victims, unless they settled and paid a fine. Others in the village might join them, but it was the young men who took the initiative (see Plate 8).

Nor were these activities, as E. K. Chambers and others have claimed, a mere playing with primitive and magical customs of forgotten meaning. Rather they were a carnival treatment of reality, with an important function in the village. Let us take the question of second marriages. Canon law had long since overcome the scruples of the early Church Fathers about remarriage, and though no benediction was given the pair and the ceremony was held modestly at night, second and third marriages were completely licit. The church had dropped the old Roman prescription of a waiting period before remarriage—a loosening enthusiastically supported by feudal law—and there were no rules regarding disparity in age either, as long as the partners were sexually mature.[36]

Why then the charivaris? First there was the dead spouse to be placated. He was sometimes present at the charivari as an effigy.[37] Then there were the children from the first marriage to be thought about, psychologically and economically. Folktales about the wicked stepmother or stepfather express the former worry; the latter one is reflected in the *coutumier* of Paris of 1510, which introduced legal restrictions on the woman who remarried in order to protect the revenues due to existing children.[38] And last and most fundamental, there was resentment when someone had been inappropriately removed by an older widow or widower from the pool of young eligibles.* In principle this jeopardized the chances of the village young to find a mate of a seemly age and also meant a marriage that was unlikely to produce many chil-

---

* Charivaris were especially violent when the remarriage involved a marked difference in age. Sometimes they did not occur if *both* of the spouses had been married before. Fines collected from lads from another village who came to court local girls and the fights that sometimes broke out on these occasions also reflect, in my view, a recognition of the threat to the pool of young eligibles.

dren.[39] In fact, with life expectancy as short as it was, remarriages were necessary and common. Thus the air could be cleared and the community reminded of the imbalance by a noisy mocking laugh at the *"Vieille Carcasse, folle d'amour"* ("old carcass, crazy with love"), or at the old man surely incapable of satisfying his young wife. The couple then acquitted themselves toward the village (and toward the young people who had not received the food and money of a traditional daytime ceremony) *"au triple de tes noces"*—at three times the wedding costs, as one charivari chant demanded.[40]

What then can we conclude about the character of Misrule in the French countryside in the late Middle Ages and sixteenth century? The use of the imagery of "Kingdoms" and especially of "Abbeys" not only provided a carnival reversal of status in regard to a faraway king or a nearby monastery, to whom peasants might owe services and dues, but—more important—provided a *rule* that the youth had over others and perhaps too a brotherhood existing among themselves; and it gave enormous scope to mockery and derision. But license was not rebellious. It was very much in the service of the village community, dramatizing the differences between different stages of life,[41] clarifying the responsibilities that the youth would have when they were married men and fathers, helping to maintain proper order within marriage and to sustain the biological continuity of the village. Total violence or disorder in the course of Misrule was a mistake, an accident (so we learn from the brawls and murder cases that ultimately found their way to the royal courts); and when a rural carnival became political, it was turned, as we will see, not against the *laboureurs*, the rich peasants in the village, or the village elders, but against oppressors from without.

Thus the activities of the youth-abbeys functioned rather like *rites de passage*, here spaced over a number of years, in communities where the older generation's expectations for the young and the younger generation's expectations for themselves did not differ very much. They refute, incidentally, the assertion of Philippe

Ariès that Europeans made no distinction between childhood and adolescence before the end of the eighteenth century, that "people had no idea of what we call adolescence," that "there [was] no room for adolescence" in the earlier centuries.[42] Though villagers obviously had no theory of the psychodynamics of male adolescent development, and though rural society did not stimulate the possibility of exploring alternate identities (except for the lad who decided to move to the city), nevertheless these youth groups played *certain* of the functions that we attribute to adolescence. They gave the youth rituals to help control their sexual instincts and also to allow themselves some limited sphere of jurisdiction or "autonomy" in the interval before they were married. They socialized them to the conscience of the community by making them the raucous voice of that conscience.* And it

---

* I follow here the definition of adolesence of Elizabeth Douvan and Joseph Adelson, *The Adolescent Experience* (New York, 1966), pp. 4-21, 346-47. The work of Philippe Ariès, Kenneth Keniston, and John and Virginia Demos has helped us understand the development of modern concepts of adolescence (see n. 42). But we should not reserve the term "adolescence" only for the forms and definitions which that stage of life enjoys in Western countries in the nineteenth and twentieth centuries. This seems especially important since the study of Douvan and Adelson on a very large American sample shows that some of the allegedly typical traits of adolescence—disaffection, *Sturm und Drang*—are characteristic of only a small percentage of adolescents even today (pp. 350-51). Thus one might better assume that adolescence, the period from the onset of puberty to the full assumption of adult roles, is given some recognition, however slight, in every society; and one might then examine systematically the different ways in which it is defined, valued, and organized. David Hunt has made a similar suggestion in regard to Ariès' treatment of infancy and early childhood (*Parents and Children in History. The Psychology of Family Life in Early Modern France* [New York, 1970], ch. 2).

In the preface to his new edition of *L'enfant et la vie familiale*, M. Ariès has considered some of the evidence presented in my essay (Paris, 1973, pp. vii-ix). He asks about the age of members of the youth-abbeys, and points out that they were organizations of bachelors ("*célibataires*") at a period in history when men often married late. "The opposition was, then, between the married and the unmarried." As I have already suggested, the period of male *jeunesse* in the sixteenth-century countryside might well last from fourteen to the early twenties, but that does not mean that it was lacking in distinctive and youthful characteristics. Contemporaries thought of the word "*bachelier*"

should be noted that youth-abbeys and youth-kingdoms with the same constellation of characteristics just described are found throughout rural Europe in Switzerland,[43] Germany,[44] Italy,[45] Hungary, Rumania,[46] and perhaps England and Scotland[47] and Spain.[48]

Finally, these groups make us attend the message of the anthropologist André Varagnac and the sociologist S. N. Eisenstadt about the importance of age categories or age groups in the traditional rural community. As Eisenstadt says, "In primitive and traditional societies, youth groups are usually part of a wider organization of age groups that covers a very long period of life, from childhood to late adulthood and even old age."[49] They exist despite the economic differentiation among the peasants from rich *laboureur* to landless hired hand, and despite changes in the demographic pyramid.[50] Like parish institutions, they help explain how the peasant community defended its identity against the outside world.

[III]

The youth-abbeys and youth-kingdoms had, of course, developed in French cities from the thirteenth century on. Whereas in the French countryside their basic organization and customs had changed very little even as late as the eighteenth century (they sometimes took on military functions without, however, dropping their other roles),[51] in the cities, with the relative literacy and complexity of urban life, this festive form evolved and proliferated in important ways. Most obvious was the enrichment of the dramatic and literary content of Misrule, of the whole vocabulary of

---

as having an initial sense of "youth" ("a young adolescent, beginning to enter the age of manhood," Borel, *Dictionnaire*, p. 31); and the rites and festivities described above depended for their meaning both on the youthful and on the unmarried state of the actors. Finally, the number of older bachelors in a village was small relative to the number of youthful ones. There is some evidence suggesting that after a certain age, bachelors were not merely the butt of the village youth-abbey, but may have been assimilated in certain ways into the status of the married or widowed (A. Varagnac, *Civilisation traditionelle et genres de vie* [Paris, 1948], pp. 99-100, 117-18, 253).

Folly. Whereas only a limited number of rural Abbeys called themselves Abbayes de Maugouvert, this and other merry and paradoxical titles multiplied in the cities, perhaps especially in the
fifteenth century, when urban literacy rates began to rise somewhat. Whereas the rural drama accompanying charivaris is quite
modest, when it occurs at all (usually a mere carrying around of
effigies of the guilty parties or of the widow, her new husband, and
dead spouse), now the dramatic productions are more elaborate
(as we saw earlier in the floats mocking the martyred husbands
of Lyon), and have verses to go with them. The village literary
production consists of a simple charivari song; the urban verses
are more complex and contributed to the development of the
sottie style and the *coq à l'asne* (poetic dialogue that jumps from
one thing to another). Whereas the rural player might deck himself out on the spur of the moment (we have a wonderful picture
from the royal pardons of a fifteenth-century miller's son, an
homme joyeux, improvising a messenger's outfit so that he could
quickly deliver a message to a harvest queen), the urban players
fabricate complicated and sometimes sumptuous costumes.[52] And
finally, the rural Abbeys left their Misrule to memory alone; the
city Abbeys of the sixteenth century often put theirs down in
print.[53]

There were changes in the organization of the Abbeys as well,
changes in their social and age composition. Even a city of 6,000
is too big for a single Abbey. By the sixteenth century, Lyon, with
its population growing up to 60,000, had about twenty of them,
with a full range of Abbots, Barons, Captains, Admirals, Princes,
Counts, Princesses, Judges, and Patriarchs of Misrule at their
head. Though organized separately, they called each other out
and paraded together at feast time. Most of them were organized
around the quarter or neighborhood, and the same seems to have
been partly true of Rouen.[54]

In some cases the distinctive functions of the Abbey—of carnival misrule, of charivari and jurisdiction over domestic affairs
and community morals—were taken up and transformed by occu-

pational groupings. Thus the Basoche, the organization of the law clerks (originally the young members of the profession) in Paris, Lyon, Bordeaux, and other French cities, developed with officers called Abbots, Kings, and Princes, planted May bushes, pleaded mock cases, and put on public comedies and farces at Mardi Gras in which real persons, in their jurisdiction and out of it, were represented and their faults derided.[55] Thus in sixteenth-century Lyon, the printers' journeymen acted as an Abbey of Misrule, with the Lord of Misprint (Seigneur de la Coquille) as its leader; the painters elected a Judge of Fools and the silk-dyers' journeymen a Captain of Misrule.[56]

Furthermore, and very significant, the urban Abbeys, especially in the large cities, were no longer necessarily organizations of unmarried youth as they had been in the villages. In Rouen there were enough married men in the Abbey of Conards in 1541 for the Abbot to issue a mock proclamation that any Conard with a wife confined in childbirth could provide for himself with a serving-girl or neighbor-woman. In Dijon at the end of the century, a well-known lawyer was elected as Mère Folle regularly until his death, when he was succeeded by his son-in-law.[57] (For Mère Folle's costume and chariot, see Plate 6). Only in smaller towns like Chalon-sur-Saône does the complete identity between Abbey and youth regularly remain.[58] Elsewhere the idea of youth lingers on in names like the Infanterie Dijonnoise or the Enfants-sans-souci (a former youth-abbey that had evolved especially in Paris into a semiprofessional players' group[59]), or the youth groups are confined (1) to a limited social category, as in Lyon or Rouen, where the Enfants de la Ville are the sons of municipal magistrates,[60] or (2) to limited functions, as in Geneva, where the Abbaye des Enfants, once in charge of dances, mummeries, and masking, formed the basis of the urban militia established at the end of the fifteenth century.[61]

Why does this happen? Why do traditional festive organizations often lose their age-specificity in the big sixteenth-century cities, outside the college[62] and the urban patriciate? It was not because city people stopped recognizing that there was a period of adolescence—here again I am taking issue with Philippe Ariès[63] —for medical literature, religious manuals, and popular prints distinguish it and recognize it as a period of sexual maturation.* As Eisenstadt points out, "However great the differences among various societies, there is one focal point within the life span of an individual which in most known societies is to some extent emphasized: the period of youth, of transition from childhood to full adult status, or full membership in the society." What differs from society to society and from sector to sector within a society, he goes on, is "the extent to which age in general and youth in

* Sixteenth-century medical literature said that on the average puberty begins for males at 14, and that "l'age d'adolescence" usually lasts from 14 to 20 or 21, being a period of "natural robustness" in which exercise is important (Laurent Joubert, *Erreurs populaires au fait de la medecine et regime de santé . . . la premiere partie* [Bordeaux, 1578], Book II, chap. 2; Hierosme de Monteux, *Commentaire de la conservation de santé* [Lyon, 1559], pp. 202-3). Prints representing the stages of life, as M. Ariès points out himself, show the older adolescent in the process of courting. Though the long debate over the precise age at which children should begin to confess and receive the sacrament of penance was still unresolved at the Council of Trent, theologians always stated that sexual sins could start occurring only around the age of fourteen. Confessors' manuals attended to the voluptuous thoughts of the teenager and his desire to touch others, and college rulings separated the 16-year-olds from the boys aged 8 or 9 for similar reasons. See H. C. Lea, *A History of Auricular Confession and Indulgences in the Latin Church* (Philadelphia, 1896), 1: 400-404; Jean Gerson, "Brève manière de confession pour les jeunes," *Opera omnia,* ed. Mr. Glorieux (Paris, 1966), 7: 408-9; Astrik Gabriel, *Student Life in Ave Maria College, Mediaeval Paris* (Notre Dame, Indiana, 1955), p. 105. Another kind of distinction between childhood, adolescence, and adulthood is made by the liberal Protestant Sébastien Castellion in his description of the stages of God's education of the human race. During the Age of Law, or of the Father, God commands mankind as a father does the young child, expecting only outward obedience; during the Age of the Gospel, or of the Son, Christ brings adolescent humanity instruction through the Gospel; during the Age of the Holy Ghost, the adult man is directed by the perfect inspiration of the Spirit (F. Buisson, *Sébastien Castellion* [Paris, 1892], 2: 193-97). See also the discussion of the distinctive perils and joys of the years from puberty to marriage in Charles V. Langlois, *La vie en France au moyen âge* (Paris, 1925), 2: 217-25. The characterization of adolescent development in these works is not exactly the same as would be made today, but it is a characterization!

particular form a criterion for the allocation of roles ... [and] the extent to which [there] develop specific age groups, specific corporate organizations, composed of members of the same 'age.' "[64] Now sixteenth-century cities continued to see informal groupings such as street gangs of males in their teens who played games and threw stones at neighborhood enemies. But the character of economic and social life made it likely that male adolescents would be organized into groups either with adults or more directly dominated by adults than were the village Abbeys.

Let us consider the craft world. The median age for apprenticeship in sixteenth-century French cities was twelve (later than in the fourteenth century, it would get later still in the seventeenth).[65] Sometime in his middle or late teens the apprentice became a journeyman. Then he might become part of his master's guild, in a wholly dependent status of course, or he might be initiated into a secret journeymen's organization in which there would be journeymen of all ages. Here the *rite de passage* led to an economic status, not a new stage of life.

The *compagnon à marier* in the countryside might well grow up and marry; the *compagnon imprimeur* in the city might well remain a dependent worker for years and years.[66]

As for the poor and the unskilled, we have little information about their social life, though we know that their children had to go to work early and that the beggars' kingdom encompassed young and old alike. The militia in most places at this period was also made up of men of different ages.[67]

Where the traditional youth group persists in the large sixteenth-century city—among the sons of rich lawyers, merchants, and magistrates—much of the Misrule is missing. In Lyon, the Enfants de la Ville might get into a brawl to avenge the honor of one of their number, but they dropped their titular Abbot and their charivaris shortly after 1500. The city fathers could hardly allow their own sons to bruit their *mauvais ménage* throughout the town. And anyway the *sottie* verse forms of the charivari, the rhymes in the Lyonnais dialect, the crude parade on the ass seemed hopelessly old-fashioned to young men who were being taught by rich Italian bankers resident in Lyon to play ancient Roman games and to mask in classical fashion. So the Enfants took their place in the official ceremonies that their fathers organized for visiting dignitaries, played their appointed role in society weddings, supported a confraternity, and organized banquets for the best ladies in town. This youth group served less to prepare them for the way of life of a married man, and more to confirm their participation in an exclusive social circle.[68]

Thus the characteristic Abbeys of Misrule in the large sixteenth-century city were professional or more likely neighborhood groupings, which encompassed men* both young and old. They also differed from the rural Abbeys in the range of their social composition. Whereas in the village, the youth-abbeys could include the sons of well-off peasants and landless ones, in the sixteenth-century French city, not even within the individual neighborhood could men from all estates be drawn together in a festive organization. The urban elite would be missing from the Abbey and had their own entertainments, as would the unskilled *gagnedenier* (day workers); certain classes of newcomers and foreign residents might be excluded too. In Nice, four Abbots were elected separately by "nobles," merchants, artisans, and a group of urban gardeners and fishermen.[69] In Lyon, the Abbeys were made up

---

* As in the countryside, membership in the Abbeys was confined to males. All of the officers with female names were men who dressed as women (see Chapter 5). Women participated in and watched the festivities, of course. In the 1541 parade in Rouen, the Conards visited women, danced with them, and gave them sweets and flowers. In the 1566 *chevauchée de l'âne* at Lyon, some real women paraded in female costumes along with the Abbeys, that is, twelve women dressed as "Egyptiennes." The closest we come to festive organizations for females are temporary Queens, as in Abbeville from the fourteenth century on, where Queens were elected in every quarter on Easter Tuesday (R. Vaultier, *Le folklore pendant la Guerre de Cent Ans d'après les lettres de rémission du Trésor des Chartes* [Paris, 1965], pp. 61-62). In the fifteenth and sixteenth centuries, French brothels were sometimes called "Abbayes," with an Abbess at their head, but these were pleasure organizations of quite another kind.

of artisans and small and medium merchants. The Judge of Fools in 1534 was a painter, who ended up on the city poor-relief rolls.[70] The literary output of Rouen's Abbey of Conards suggests that a higher percentage of educated men participated there than in Lyon, but the Conards were still not drawn from the "best families." Of two known important Conards, one was a process-server for the Parlement of Rouen, the other a miller.[71] Dijon's Infanterie had members of high status at the end of the sixteenth century, including lawyers in the Parlement of Dijon; but earlier a simple tailor was able to start Mère Folle on one of her promenades, and there is some evidence that even wine-growers living in the city took part.[72]

The fragmenting of festive organizations in the cities, the limiting of the Kingdom of Misrule, was a consequence of urban growth, of vocational differentiation, and of changes in economic and social structure. But just because there was so much innovation and disorder, the Abbeys had a new role to play in the city. A neighborhood grouping can be more coherent and informative than an age grouping on a busy street, with families jammed into every story of the house, *haute, moyenne, et basse*. A notarized account of a May 1517 meeting of 42 members of the Abbey of Misrule of the rue Mercière in Lyon (I came on it in the archives;[73] it may be the only such document yet found) shows them electing an Abbot and other officers, and setting up councillors to "govern" the street and "keep peace and amity" among the members. Fines were collected when the Abbey's rules were broken in regard to swearing and blasphemy (good signs that a fight was brewing); and in severe cases, members could be banned from the Abbey. This peace-keeping function is not unique to Lyon. The fifteenth-century statutes of the Abbey of Fools of Turin say members are to keep themselves in peace and love, eliminating all dissension that might develop among them.[74] The intervention of Rouen's Abbot of Conards in a literary quarrel between two poets was intended not to support one side, but to bring peace between the two:

Parquoy enfants . . . [says the Abbot]
Pour eviter querelles et debatz
Ie vous defendz toute iniure intedicte . . .
Vous mettre en paix. . . .[75]

The Abbeys also carried on charivaris, as we have seen, in familiar circumstances and also in circumstances the village passed over in silence. We catch the Abbey of the rue Mercière in Lyon planning a parade on the ass against a well-off tanner in the neighborhood about whose recent beating by his wife "we have made good and sufficient inquiry." This *chevauchée* was needed "in order to repress the temerity and audacity of women who beat their husbands and of those who would like to do so; for according to the provision of divine and civil law, the wife is subject to the husband; and if husbands suffer themselves to be governed by their wives, they might as well be led out to pasture." Anyway it is the month of May now, the 1517 report goes on, and this season requires frolics and diversion.[76]

Here again we have the loud and mocking laugh of Misrule intended to keep a traditional order. Interestingly enough, while charivaris against second marriages were central in country misrule, in the cities charivaris against domineering wives were the most frequent.* Grotesque disparities in age between bride and groom could still scandalize the city-dwellers. (Claude de Rubys recalled not only the hubbub of pots and pans but also the wooden cannon with which the newly married widow or widower was "besieged" in his house in Lyon.)[77] But remarriage in the city represented less of a threat to the pool of young eligibles than in the countryside, for population size and patterns of mortality and migration assured a better supply of mates of appropriate social background in the city. Further, widows may have found it easier

---

* Rabelais passes over second marriages with an anticlerical joke, but dwells on the husband-beater. "At the creation of the world, or a little after, the women conspired together to flay the men alive for trying to lord it over them everywhere." Panurge worries about marrying such a woman and plans to beat her instead (*Le Tiers Livre*, chaps. 6, 9, 12, 14, 18).

in the French city to maintain households on their own, as has been recently shown to be the case in fifteenth-century Tuscan towns. In addition, there were important and little-understood changes going on in the relations between men and women in the fifteenth and sixteenth centuries, reflected in the charivaris against henpecked husbands, in the worsening position of women in French law,[78] and in the independent interest of some city women in Protestantism.

The city charivari was used to mark other affronts to the sense of order or justice of the neighborhood. To quote a later writer on the Mère Folle of Dijon: "If anything singular occurred in town, like thefts, murders, bizarre marriages, seductions, then the Chariot and the Infantry got on foot; people in the troupe were dressed the same as those to whom the thing had happened and represented them realistically." In Amiens grocers who sold false wax were likely victims. Indeed any "vicious deed" might prompt the horns of the Conards of Rouen.[79]

Not surprisingly, the charivari and carnival license to deride could also be turned against the political authorities, and with the changed social and age composition of the urban Abbeys it sometimes was. Those Judges of Misrule, that company of Princes, Patriarchs, and Bishops, were more likely to direct their barbs at the powerful than was the young village Abbot. It was not the domestic disorder of the governing families that was criticized, but rather their political misrule. And this was an important channel for criticism in those oligarchical cities, where even rather substantial artisans and merchants had little, if any, chance to make political decisions.

The relations of the Abbeys to city councils, Parlements, and kings were more complex and ambivalent than that of the court fool to his king. If the Parlements of Rouen and Grenoble sometimes tolerated charivaris, there are decrees of the Parlements of Toulouse and Dijon against them. The Consulate of Lyon and royal officials there instituted proceedings against the Abbey of the rue Mercière because it had established a jurisdiction infringing on their prerogatives; whereas in Orange the town council allowed the Abbey its charivaris so long as it turned over part of the fines collected to the city. There are numerous royal and local edicts against masking and mumming, all intended to protect the cities and the king himself against brawling and fighting, conspiracy, and seditious activity.[80] In short, the Abbeys survived under a kind of legal sufferance—at their easiest moments, as in Rouen, receiving yearly license from the Parlement for their Misrule and even being invited to join the Entry Parade honoring Henri II; at their most difficult, again in Rouen, having their Abbot arrested by the sergeants right off his festive float in 1541 because it attacked the city fathers too sharply.[81]

The Mardi Gras revels at Rouen illustrate well the possibilities of political criticism and commentary. One year they dramatized the venality of specific local magistrates who had demanded a large sum from a pleader instead of the modest hare he offered them; the judges claimed their wives did not like to eat game.[82] The Mardi Gras parade of 1540 was less personal, the political observation more general or veiled. We hold up "a Socratic mirror" to the world, said the Abbot. Business was so bad that the procession began with an elaborate funeral for Merchandise, followed by a float bearing Hope in a laughing and joyous mask. Another float bore a king, the pope, the emperor, and a fool playing catch with the globe of the world: *"Tiens-cy; baille-ça, Rist'en, Moque-t'en."* There was also a procession of Old Testament prophets uttering prophetic riddles with reference to current political responsibility for pauperization and religious troubles.[83]

In Paris the king might be attacked under his very nose, as in 1516, when the Basoche put on a farce demonstrating that Mère Sotte reigned at court and that she was taxing, pillaging, and stealing everything. At Dijon, the 1576 *Anerie* of Mère Folle and her children ridiculed the king's Grand Master of Streams and Forests in Burgundy not only for beating his wife in May, but also for devastating for his own profit the forests he was supposed to protect.[84] In Lyon the Lord of Misprint and his band used their carnival license in the 1580's to protest the folly of religious war, the high cost of bread, and the empty stalls of the merchants. Like the verses of the Abbey of Conards, these were printed at the time of the festival and brought this carnival criticism to the attention of those who had not heard it.[85]

These elements of political and social criticism in the midst of carnival were intended to destroy-and-renew political life in Mikhail Bakhtin's sense, but not to lead directly to further political action. There are fascinating examples, however, in both city and countryside, of carnivals where the tension between the festive and everyday official realms was broken and uprising and rebellion ensued. Sometimes this was partially planned ahead of time, sometimes it was spontaneous. Thus in 1513, three hundred young peasants from villages near Berne, Switzerland, marched on the city after some June revels to punish the *"mangeurs de couronnes"* and sacked it.[86] During the revolt of the Netherlands, in Cambrai (where the Abbé de L'Escache-Profit and other dignitaries held court) the rebels were costumed and carried fools' scepters with the head of the hated governor Cardinal Granvelle.[87] In sixteenth-century France in the Côtes du Rhône region, E. Le Roy Ladurie reports that "the societies of youth in the parishes . . . [were] the cells for insurrection." Indeed, an entire uprising and its terrible suppression occurred in the course of the Mardi Gras carnival of 1580 at Romans, "a long series of symbolic actions" ending in blood.[88]

Finally, a 1630 uprising in Dijon against royal tax officers took the form of a masquerade; Mère Folle and her Infanterie were implicated and the Abbey was abolished by an angry and obscene royal edict.[89]

The relationship between popular festivals and politics clearly warrants further study, and so does their relation to religious institutions and movements. Here I will outline only a few of the major questions. The Abbeys' relations with the Catholic Church were as complex and ambivalent as with the secular authorities. Charivaris against second marriages were regularly forbidden by French provincial synods from the thirteenth century on.[90] But there was no systematic attempt before the mid-seventeenth cen-

tury to do away with Abbeys of Misrule, as there had been with
the campaign of the Paris Theology Faculty against the clerical
Feast of Fools. Catholic reformers with humanist tastes (like Guillaume Paradin, dean of Beaujeu) might fume about the pagan and
superstitious elements in the popular recreations and cite the
writings of the early Fathers against masking and mumming as
vicious and unnatural activities.[91] But the church simply prohibited masked indecency within church buildings or cemeteries,
letting it go on elsewhere. The canons of the cathedral of Rouen
reacted punitively only when Conards carried around scandalous
effigies of two of *them* during Mardi Gras.[92]

The Protestant response was different. Interestingly enough, the
youth-abbeys in the Savoie and in Switzerland, the Fools in Geneva, and the Enfants-sans-souci in some towns in the Guyenne
were early supporters of the new religion and integrated Protestant
themes into their festivities.[93] Once the Reformation was established, however, the new church was fair game: thus the youth-
abbey of Lausanne mocked the Consistory for imprisoning two
prostitutes in the 1540's.[94] Pastors and Consistories then tried
hard to stamp out the Abbeys and all their customs in Reformed
Switzerland and in any French towns that fell under their control
during the Religious Wars. For instance, the author of the Calvinist *Histoire ecclésiastique* recounts with pride that at Mardi Gras,
1562, just before the Protestant Revolution in Rouen, the Conards
tried to put on their usual "insolent masquerades," but the evangelical *menu peuple* stopped them by throwing stones at them.[95]

The Calvinist antipathy to the Abbeys was not owing, of course,
just to their insolence and mockery. It was part of a deeper hostility to the whole psychology of two worlds, of two levels upon
which life could be lived.[96] "This-worldly asceticism," in Max
Weber's phrase, offered many choices to Protestants, but all of
them were to be made within the same serious time scheme. Only
within the solemn halls of the Consistory could criticism be given
of morals and marriages, of men who beat their wives (yes, it was
the other way around in Geneva—and not just during the month
of May[97]). Laughter and charivari could be used only to over-

turn the Catholic enemy; even revolutions should be carried on with decorum. Popular iconoclasm was wrong, said Calvin, as were rollicking parades bearing the relics seized from the Roman churches. Stones and bones must be removed and registered by the authorities.[98] As one might expect, the Consistories had a hard time doing away with this festive life: in the mid-seventeenth century, Misrule Abbeys and charivaris against beaten husbands were still being punished in Geneva, and there were signs of the Abbeys in Protestant rural areas as late as the nineteenth century.[99]

Meanwhile, in the last part of the sixteenth century, despite the puritan streak in Counter-Reformation sensibility, some Catholic authorities in France began to perceive the value of Misrule to their cause. Here I refer not to the harnessing of carnival color and festive spirit to the religious processions of the Holy Catholic League in Paris, but rather to the utilization of the Abbeys themselves. After all, some of them actually had chapels and organized confraternities,[100] many of their revels were timed to the feast days the Protestants had abolished, and the existence of festive Abbots could be taken to suggest that there were serious abbots as well. The charivaris against domineering women in Lyon in the 1560's seemed to mock not only monstrous wives, but those monstrous women who had so recently been badgering and insulting priests in the streets of the city.[101] The lawyer Claude de Rubys, the ardent League supporter with whose quotation I began this essay, encouraged the Abbey festivals and all efforts to inject Catholic propaganda into them. In fact the Abbeys were harder to capture than he realized (both in Lyon and Rouen they were ultimately opposed to the League), but then Folly always is.[102]

[IV]

In my own attempt to seize Misrule, I have tried to relate it to several things: to the history of youth groups; to the history of social forms among the lower orders; and to the problem of play and its functions. First, I have taken a group of disparate festive customs and organizations in sixteenth-century cities and have shown that they derive not merely from Roman or primitive sources, but from a cluster of festive roles assigned primarily to the organization of young unmarried men in the village. Although the traditional youth group lasted for a very long time in the countryside and to some extent in smaller towns, the conditions of big-city life were dissolving it by the sixteenth century, except in the colleges and the urban upper class, in favor of formal groupings based on profession or occupation or neighborhood or class. As far as I know, it was not until the end of the eighteenth or the beginning of the nineteenth century that there appeared fully articulated the variety of youth movements and youth groups of a "modern" kind, which respond to feelings of discontinuity between childhood and the adult world.[103] To be sure, the Reformation in its *early* decades, with its attack on the paternal authority of the clergy and its imagery of the young Christian combating the old doctor of theology, sometimes seems to have the character of a youth movement; but it gave birth to no genuine youth organizations.

Meanwhile, the festive Abbeys did not atrophy, but were maintained and transformed by craftsmen, merchants, and lawyers. The Abbeys' rule was extended to cope with new situations—to keep peace and just order among neighbors in a growing city. Their Misrule was enriched dramatically, and to their old function of maintaining order in the family was added a new one of political criticism. I am struck here, as I was earlier in studying the formation of *compagnonnages*,[104] by the social creativity of the so-called inarticulate, by the way in which they seize upon older social forms and change them to fit their needs.

As for theories of play, I have stressed the rule and rationale in popular festivals and the extent to which they remain in close touch with the realities of community and marriage. These are natural consequences of the carnival license to deride and the historical nature of festive organizations. It is an exaggeration to view the carnival and Misrule as merely a "safety valve," as merely a primitive, prepolitical form of recreation. Victor Turner and Mikhail Bakhtin are closer to the truth in seeing it as present in all cultures. I would say not only that it is present, but that the structure of the carnival form can evolve so that it can act both to reinforce order and to suggest alternatives to the existing order. (Eric Hobsbawm in his *Primitive Rebels* has evaluated the transformational capacities of millenarian movements in a similar way.)[105] The urban Abbeys of Misrule lost much of their vitality by the eighteenth century, but along the way they had called on members of the lower orders to noise their political complaints. Indeed charivaris of a political nature are found in city and countryside into the nineteenth century. It is no accident that the celebrated satirical newspaper in which Daumier published his cartoons—founded in 1832 and prosecuted twenty times by Louis Philippe's government—was entitled *Charivari*.[106]

Finally, to literary specialists I may have offered a new source for comedy, and perhaps for tragedy, too. C. L. Barber has talked of some of Shakespeare's plays as saturnalia; is Hamlet perhaps a charivari of the young against a grotesque and unseemly remarriage, a charivari where the effigy of the dead spouse returns, the vicious action is replayed? And perhaps we have in the Abbeys of Misrule another source for Rabelais' Abbaye de Thélème.[107]

But enough reasons for Misrule. Readers will have to decide whether all I have said is folly. If so, I will try to answer. Or then again I might not, and claim as did Erasmus' Queen of Misrule that I have forgotten "all that I have spoken, after such a rabblement of words poured forth." No matter. I say now with Erasmus' Stultitia, "Fare ye well. Clap your hands in token of gladness, live careless and drink all out, ye the trusty servants and solemn ministers of folly."

FIVE

Women on Top

[I]

The female sex was thought the disorderly one par excellence in early modern Europe. *"Une beste imparfaicte,"* went one adage, *"sans foy, sans loy, sans craincte, sans constance."* Female disorderliness was already seen in the Garden of Eden, when Eve had been the first to yield to the serpent's temptation and incite Adam to disobey the Lord. To be sure, the men of the lower orders were also believed to be especially prone to riot and seditious unrest. But the defects of the males were thought to stem not so much from nature as from nurture: the ignorance in which they were reared, the brutish quality of life and conversation in the peasant's hut or the artisan's shop, and their poverty, which led to envy.[1]

With the women the disorderliness was founded in physiology. As every physician knew in the sixteenth century, the female was composed of cold and wet humors (the male was hot and dry), and coldness and wetness meant a changeable, deceptive, and tricky temperament. Her womb was like a hungry animal; when not amply fed by sexual intercourse or reproduction, it was likely to wander about her body, overpowering her speech and senses. If the Virgin Mary was free of such a weakness, it was because she was the blessed vessel of the Lord. But no other woman had been immaculately conceived, and even the well-born lady could fall victim to a fit of the "mother," as the uterus was called. The male might suffer from retained sexual juices, too, but (as Doctor François Rabelais pointed out) he had the wit and will to control his fiery urges by work, wine, or study. The female just became hysterical.* In the late seventeenth century, when vanguard physicians were abandoning humoral theories of personality in favor of more mechanistic notions of "animal spirits" and were beginning to remark that men suffered from emotional ills curiously like hysteria, they still maintained that the female's mind was more prone to be disordered by her fragile and unsteady temperament. Long before Europeans were asserting flatly that the "inferiority" of black Africans was innate, rather than the result, say, of climate, they were attributing female "inferiority" to nature.[2]

The lower ruled the higher within the woman, then, and if she were given her way, she would want to rule over those above her outside. Her disorderliness led her into the evil arts of witchcraft, so ecclesiastical authorities claimed; and when she was embarked on some behavior for which her allegedly weak intellect disqualified her, such as theological speculation or preaching, that was blamed on her disorderliness, too. The rule of a queen was impossible in France by the Salic law, and mocked by the common proverb *"tomber en quenouille."* For Pastor John Knox it was a "monstrous regimen," "the subversion of good order . . . all equitie and justice," whereas the more moderate Calvin "reckoned it among the visitations of God's anger," but one that should be borne, like any tyranny, with patience. Even a contemporary defender of queenship, John Aylmer, still had to admit that when he thought of the willfulness of women, he favored a strong role for Parliament. As late as 1742, in the face of entomological evi-

---

* Female medical practitioners also accepted the theory of the "wandering womb" and provided remedies for female hysteria. See *A Choice Manual of . . . Select Secrets in Physick . . . Collected and Practised by . . . the Countesse of Kent* (London, 1653), pp. 114, 145; *Recueil des Remedes . . . Recueillis par les Ordres Charitables de . . . Madame Fouquet* (4th ed.; Dijon, 1690), pp. 168-89; Jean de Rostagny, *Traité de Primerose sur les erreurs vulgaires de la medecine* (Lyon, 1689), p. 774; Angélique Du Coudray, *Abrégé de l'art des Accouchemens* (Paris, 1759), p. 173.

dence to the contrary, some apiologists pretended that nature required the rule of a King Bee.[3]

What were the proposed remedies for female unruliness? Religious training that fashioned the reins of modesty and humility; selective education that showed a woman her moral duty without enflaming her undisciplined imagination or loosing her tongue for public talk; honest work that busied her hands; and laws and constraints that made her subject to her husband.[4]

In some ways, that subjection was gradually deepening from the sixteenth to the eighteenth centuries as the patriarchal family streamlined itself for more efficient property acquisition, social mobility, and preservation of the line, and as progress in state-building and the extension of commercial capitalism were achieved at a cost in human autonomy. By the eighteenth century, married women in France and England had largely lost what independent legal personality they had formerly had, and they had less legal right to make decisions on their own about their dowries and possessions than at an earlier period. Propertied women were involved less and less in local and regional political assemblies. Working women in prosperous families were beginning to withdraw from productive labor; those in poor families were increasingly filling the most ill-paid positions of wage labor. This is not to say that females had no informal access to power or continuing vital role in the economy in these centuries; but the character of those relations was in conflict.[5]

Which side of the conflict was helped by the disorderly woman? Since this image was so often used as an excuse for the subjection of women, it is not surprising to find it opposed by one strain in early feminist thought, which argued that women were *not* by nature more unruly, disobedient, and fickle than men. If anything it was the other way around. "By nature, women be sober," said the poet Christine de Pisan, "and those that be not, they go out of kind."* Women are by nature more modest and

* Some female writers from the sixteenth to the early eighteenth centuries, such as Marguerite de Navarre, Madame de Lafayette, Aphra Behn, and Mary de la Rivière Manley, did not accept this view. Although they did not portray

shamefaced than men, claimed a male feminist, which is demonstrated by the fact that women's privy parts are totally covered with pubic hair and are not handled by women the way men's are when they urinate. Why, then, did some men maintain that women were disorderly by nature? Because they were misogynists—vindictive, envious, or themselves dissolute.[6]

These claims and counterclaims about sexual temperament raise questions not merely about the actual character of male and female behavior in preindustrial Europe, but also about the varied uses of sexual symbolism. Sexual symbolism, of course, is always available to make statements about social experience and to reflect (or conceal) contradictions within it. At the end of the Middle Ages and in early modern Europe, the relation of the wife—of the potentially disorderly woman—to her husband was especially useful for expressing the relation of all subordinates to their superiors, and this for two reasons. First, economic relations were still often perceived in the medieval way as a matter of service. Second, the nature of political rule and the newer problem of sovereignty were very much at issue. In the little world of the family, with its conspicuous tension between intimacy and power, the larger matters of political and social order could find ready symbolization.*

women as necessarily more lustful than men, they did give females a range of sexual appetites at least equal to that of males.

* The English characterization of a wife's killing of her husband as petty treason rather than as homicide may be an early example of the kind of symbolism being described here. Petty treason appeared as a crime distinct from high treason in the fourteenth century, and lasted as such till the early nineteenth century. It included the killing of a master by his servant, a husband by his wife, and a prelate by a secular cleric or religious. As Blackstone presents the law, it seems to differ from earlier Germanic practice, which treated the murder of *either* spouse by the other as an equally grave crime. The development of the concept and law of treason was closely connected with the development of the idea of sovereignty. J. G. Bellamy, *The Law of Treason in England in the Later Middle Ages* (Cambridge, Eng., 1970), pp. 1-14, 225-31; William Blackstone, *Commentaries on the Laws of England* (Oxford, 1770), Book IV, chap. 14, including note t.

The use of male/female as an expression of social relationships (master/servant, sovereign/subject, and the like) is not the only kind of sexual sym-

Thus, Jean Calvin, himself a collapser of ecclesiastical hierarchies, saw the subjection of the wife to the husband as a guarantee of the subjection of both of them to the authority of the Lord. Kings and political theorists saw the increasing legal subjection of wives to their husbands (and of children to their parents) as a guarantee of the obedience of both men and women to the slowly centralizing state—a training for the loyal subject of seventeenth-century France or for the dutiful citizen of seventeenth-century England. "Marriages are the seminaries of States," began the preamble to the French ordinance strengthening paternal power within the family. For John Locke, opponent of despotic rule in commonwealth and in marriage, the wife's relinquishing her right of decision to her husband as "naturally . . . the abler and stronger" was analogous to the individual's relinquishing his natural liberties of decision and action to the legislative branch of government.[7]

Indeed, how could one separate the idea of subordination from the existence of the sexes? Gabriel de Foigny's remarkable fictitious land of Australie (1673), a utopia of hermaphrodites, shows how close the link between the two was perceived to be. The Australian, in whom the sexes were one, could not understand how a conflict of wills could be avoided within the "mutual possession" of European marriage. The French traveler answered that it was simple, for mother and child were both subject to the father. The hermaphrodite, horrified at such a violation of the total autonomy that was the sign of complete true "men," dismissed the European pattern as bestial.[8]

The female's position was used to symbolize not only hierar-

bolism in early modern Europe, though it is the basis for discussion in this essay. Eric Wolf considers male/female as an expression of the relationships public/domestic and instrumental-ordering/expressive-ordering in "Society and Symbols in Latin Europe and in the Islamic Near East," *Anthropological Quarterly* 42 (July 1968): 287-301. For an attempt at a very broad theory of sexual symbolism, see Sherry B. Ortner, "Is Female to Male as Nature Is to Culture?" in Michelle Zimbalist Rosaldo and Louise Lamphere, eds., *Woman, Culture, and Society* (Stanford, Calif., 1974), pp. 67-87.

chical subordination but also violence and chaos. Bruegel's terrifying *Dulle Griet*, painted during the occupation of the Netherlands by Spanish soldiers, makes a huge, armed, unseeing woman, Mad Meg, the emblem of fiery destruction, of brutal oppression and disorder. Bruegel's painting cuts in more than one way, however, and shows how female disorderliness—the female out of her place—could be assigned another value. Next to Mad Meg is a small woman in white on top of a male monster; it is Saint Margaret of Antioch tying up the devil. Nearby other armed women are beating grotesque animals from Hell.[9]

Bruegel's Margarets are by no means alone in preindustrial Europe. In hierarchical and conflictful societies that loved to reflect on the world-turned-upside-down, the *topos* of the woman-on-top was one of the most enjoyed. Indeed, sexual inversion—that is, switches in sex roles—was a widespread form of cultural play in literature, in art, and in festivity. Sometimes the reversal involved dressing and masking as a member of the opposite sex—the prohibitions of Deuteronomy 22, Saint Paul, Saint Jerome, canon law, and Jean Calvin notwithstanding.[10] Sometimes the reversal involved simply taking on certain roles or forms of behavior characteristic of the opposite sex. Women played men; men played women; men played women who were playing men.

It is the uses of sexual inversion, and more particularly of play with the image of the unruly woman in literature, in popular festivity, and in ordinary life, that will be the subject of the rest of this essay. Evidently, the primary impulse behind such inversion in early modern Europe was not homosexuality or disturbed gender identity. Although Henri III expressed special wishes of his own when he and his male "mignons" masked as Amazons in the 1570's, and although the seventeenth-century Abbé de Choisy, whose mother had dressed him as a girl through adolescence, had special reasons for using a woman's name and wearing female clothes until he was thirty-three,[11] still most literary and festive transvestism at this time had a wider psychosexual and cultural significance than this.

Anthropologists offer several suggestions about the functions of magical transvestism and ritual inversion of sex roles. First, sexual disguise can ward off danger from demons, malignant fairies, or other powers that threaten castration or defloration. Second, transvestism and sexual reversal can be part of adolescent rites of passage, either to suggest the marginality of the transitional state (as when a male initiate is likened to a menstruating woman) or to allow each sex to obtain something of the other's power (as in certain initiation and marriage customs in early Greece). Third, exchange of sex can be part of what Victor Turner has called "rituals of status reversal," as when women in certain parts of Africa usurp the clothing, weapons, or tasks of the superior males and behave in lewd ways to increase the chance for a good harvest or to turn aside an impending natural catastrophe. Finally, as James Peacock has pointed out, the transvestite actor, priest, or shaman can symbolize categories of cosmological or social organization. For instance, in Java the transvestite actor reinforces by his irregularity the importance of the categories high/low, male/female.

However diverse these uses of sexual inversion, anthropologists generally agree that they, like other rites and ceremonies of reversal, are ultimately sources of order and stability in a hierarchical society. They can clarify the structure by the process of reversing it. They can provide an expression of, and a safety valve for, conflicts within the system. They can correct and relieve the system when it has become authoritarian. But, so it is argued, they do not question the basic order of the society itself. They can renew the system, but they cannot change it.[12]

Historians of early modern Europe are likely to find inversions and reversals less in prescribed rites than in carnivals and festivities. Their fools are likely to escape the bounds of ceremony,[13] and their store of literary sources for inversion will include not only the traditional tales of magical transformation in sex, but also a variety of stories in which men and women *choose* to change their sexual status. In addition, there are comic conventions and genres, such as the picaresque, that allow much play with sexual roles. These new forms offered increased occasions and ways in which topsy-turvy could be used for explicit criticism of the social order. Nevertheless, students of these festive and literary forms have ordinarily come to the same conclusion as anthropologists regarding the limits of symbolic inversion: a world-turned-upside-down can only be righted, not changed. To quote Ian Donaldson's recent study *Comedy from Jonson to Fielding*: "The lunatic governor . . . , the incompetent judge, the mock doctor, the equivocating priest, the hen-pecked husband: such are the familiar and recurrent figures in the comedy of a society which gives a general assent to the necessity of entrusting power to its governors, judges, doctors, priests, and husbands."[14]

I would like to argue, on the contrary, that comic and festive inversion could *undermine* as well as reinforce that assent through its connections with everyday circumstances outside the privileged time of carnival and stage-play. Somewhat in contradistinction to Christine de Pisan and the gallant school of feminists, I want to argue that the image of the disorderly woman did not always function to keep women in their place. On the contrary, it was a multivalent image that could operate, first, to widen behavioral options for women within and even outside marriage, and, second, to sanction riot and political disobedience for both men and women in a society that allowed the lower orders few formal means of protest. Play with the unruly woman is partly a chance for temporary release from the traditional and stable hierarchy; but it is also part of the conflict over efforts to change the basic distribution of power within society. The woman-on-top might even facilitate innovation in historical theory and political behavior.

[II]

Let us begin with a review of the major types of sexual inversion we find in literary sources—sources sober and comic, learned and popular. Then we will consider the disorderly woman in more detail. What kinds of license were allowed through this turnabout? First of all, we have stories of men who dress as women to save themselves from an enemy or from execution, to sneak into the opponent's military camp, or to get into a nunnery or women's quarters for purposes of seduction. In all of these cases, the disguise is not merely practical but exploits the expected physical frailty of women to prevent harm to the male or to disarm his victim. A more honorable trickery is ventured by Pyrocles in Sidney's *Arcadia*, by Marston's Antonio, and by d'Urfé's Céladon, for they dress as brave Amazons or as a Druid priestess in order to have access to the women they wish to woo. Here no more than in the first case does the inversion lead to criticism of social hierarchy. Rather Pyrocles is rebuked by his friend for "his effeminate love of a woman," for letting his "sensual weakness" rebel against his manly reason.

Only with the male fool or clown do we find literary examples of male transvestism serving to challenge order. In the seventeenth-century *commedia dell'arte*, a black-faced Harlequin dolls himself up as a ridiculous Diana, goddess of the chase, replete with crescent-moon ruff, fancy clothes, and a little bow. The result is so absurd that not only are boundaries between high and low effaced, but, as William Willeford has suggested, reality itself seems to dissolve.[15]

The stories, theater, and pictorial illustration of preindustrial Europe offer many more examples of women trying to act like men than vice versa, and more of the time the sexual inversion yields criticism of the established order. One set of reversals portrays women going beyond what can ordinarily be expected of a mere female; that is, it shows women ruling the lower in themselves and thus deserving to be like men. We have, for instance, tales of female saints of the early Church who lived chastely as male monks to the end of their lives, braving false charges of fathering children and withstanding other tests along the way. Five of these transvestite ladies appear in Voragine's *Golden Leg-*

end, which had wide circulation in manuscript and printed editions in both Latin and the vernacular.[16]

Other uncommon women changed their roles in order to defend established rule or values associated with it. Disguised as men, they prove fidelity to lovers whom they wish to marry or, as in the case of Madame Ginevra in Boccaccio's tale, prove their chastity to doubting husbands. Disguised as men, they leave Jewish fathers for Christian husbands and plead for Christian mercy over base Jewish legalism. Disguised as men, they rescue spouses from prison and the family honor from stain. For example, in *The French Amazon*, one of Mademoiselle l'Héritier's reworkings of an old French tale, the heroine maintains her father's connections with the court by fighting in the place of her slain and rather incompetent twin brother. She, of course, ultimately marries the prince. Along with Spenser's Britomart, Tasso's Clorinda, and others, the French Amazon is one of a line of noble women warriors, virtuous viragos all, magnanimous, brave, and chaste.[17]

To what extent could such embodiments of order serve to censure accepted hierarchy? They might reprove by their example the cowardice and wantonness of ordinary men and women. But they used their power to support a legitimate cause, not to unmask the truth about social relationships. By showing the good that could be done by the woman out of her place, they had the potential to inspire a few females to exceptional action and feminists to reflection about the capacities of women (we will see later whether that potential was realized), but they are unlikely symbols for moving masses of people to resistance.

It is otherwise with comic play with the disorderly woman, that is, inversion that can be expected of the female, who gives rein to the lower in herself and seeks rule over her superiors. Some portraits of her are so ferocious (such as Spenser's cruel Radagunde and other vicious viragos) that they preclude the possibility of fanciful release from, or criticism of, hierarchy. It is the same with those tales, considered humorous at the time, that depict a savage taming of the shrew, as in the fabliau of *La Dame escoillée*, where the domineering lady is given a counterfeit but painful "castration" by her son-in-law, and in the sixteenth-century German cartoon strip *The Ninefold Skins of a Shrewish Woman*, which are stripped off one by one by various punishments. The legend of the medieval Pope Joan also has limited potential for mocking established order. As told by Boccaccio, it is a hybrid of the transvestite saint and the cruelly tamed shrew: Joan wins the papacy by her wits and good behavior, but her illicit power goes to her head, or rather to her womb. She becomes pregnant, gives birth during a procession, and dies wretchedly in the cardinals' dungeon.[18]

There are a host of situations, however, in which the unruly woman is assigned more ambiguous meanings. For our purposes we can sort out three ways in which the multivalent image is used. First, there is a rich treatment of women who are happily given over to the sway of their bodily senses or who are using every ruse they can to prevail over men. There is the wife of Bath, of course, who celebrates her sexual instrument and outlives her five husbands. And Rabelais' Gargamelle—a giant of a woman, joyously and frequently coupling, eating bushels of tripe, quaffing wine, joking obscenely, giving birth in a grotesque fecal explosion from which her son Gargantua somersaults shouting "Drink, drink." Then the clever and powerful wife of the *Quinze joies de mariage*—cuckolding her husband and foiling his every effort to find her out, wheedling fancy clothes out of him, beating him up, and finally locking him in his room. Also Grimmelshausen's Libuschka, alias Courage, one of a series of picaresque heroines— fighting in the army in soldier's clothes; ruling her many husbands and lovers; paying them back a hundredfold when they take revenge or betray her; whoring, tricking, and trading to survive or get rich. Husband-dominators are everywhere in popular literature (see Plate 9), nicknamed among the Germans St. Cudgelman (Sankt Kolbmann) or Doktor Siemann (she-man). The point about such portraits is that they are funny and amoral: the women are full of life and energy, and they win much of the time; they stay on top of their fortune with as much success as Machiavelli might have expected for the Prince of his political tract.[19]

A second comic treatment of the woman out of her place allows her a temporary period of dominion, which is ended only after she has said or done something to undermine authority or denounce its abuse. When the Silent Wife begins to talk and order her husband about in Ben Jonson's *Epicoene*, she points out that women cannot be mere statues or puppets and that what her husband calls "Amazonian" impudence in her is simply reasonable decorum.* When the Woman-Captain of Shadwell's comedy puts aside her masculine garb and the sword with which she has hectored her jealous and stingy old husband, she does so only after having won separate maintenance and £400 a year. The moral of the play is that husbands must not move beyond the law to tyranny. In *As You Like It*, the love-struck Rosalind, her tongue loosed by her male apparel and her "holiday humor," warns Orlando that there is a limit to the possession he will have over a wife, a limit set by her desires, her wit, and her tongue. Though she later gives herself to Orlando in marriage, her saucy counsel cannot be erased from the real history of the courtship.

The most popular comic example of the female's temporary rule, however, is Phyllis riding Aristotle, a motif recurring in stories, paintings, and household objects from the thirteenth through the seventeenth centuries (see Plate 11). Here Aristotle admonishes his pupil Alexander for his excessive attention to a certain Phyllis, one of his new subjects in India. The beautiful Phyllis gets revenge before Alexander's eyes by coquettishly persuading the old philosopher to get down on all fours and, saddled

---

* The ambiguities in *Epicoene* were compounded by the fact that the Silent Wife in the play was a male playing a female, that is, a male actor playing a male playing a female. Professional troupes, of course, always used males for female parts in England until the Restoration and in France until the reign of Henri IV. See J. H. Wilson, *All the King's Ladies. Actresses of the Restoration* (Chicago, 1958) and Léopold Lacour, *Les premières actrices françaises* (Paris, 1921).

and bridled, carry her through the garden. Here youth overthrows age, and sexual passion, dry sterile philosophy; nature surmounts reason, and the female, the male.[20]

Phyllis' ambiguous ride brings us to a third way of presenting the woman-on-top, that is, where the license to be a social critic is conferred on her directly (see Plate 10). Erhard Schoen's woodcuts (early sixteenth century) portray huge women distributing fools' caps to men. This is what happens when women are given the upper hand; and yet in some sense the men deserve it. Erasmus' female Folly is the supreme example of this *topos*. Stultitia tells the truth about the foibles of all classes and defends the higher folly of the Cross, even though paradoxically she's just a foolish gabbling woman herself.[21]

These varied images of sexual topsy-turvy—from the transvestite male escaping responsibility and harm to the transvestite fool and the unruly woman unmasking the truth—were available to city people who went to the theater and to people who could read and afford books. They were also familiar to the lower orders more generally in both town and country through books that were read aloud and through stories, poems, proverbs, and broadsheets.[22]

In addition, popular festivals and customs, hard though they are to document, show much play with switches in sex roles and much attention to women-on-top. In examining these data, we will notice that sexual inversion in popular festivity differs from that in literature in two ways. Whereas the purely ritual and/or magical element in sexual inversion was present in literature to only a small degree, it assumed more importance in the popular festivities, along with the carnivalesque functions of mocking and unmasking the truth. Whereas sexual inversion in literary and pictorial play more often involved the female taking on the male role or dressing as a man, the festive inversion more often involved the male taking on the role or garb of the woman, that is, the unruly woman—though this asymmetry may not have existed several centuries earlier.

The ritual and/or magical functions of sexual inversion were filled in almost all cases by males disguised as grotesque cavorting females. In sections of Germany and Austria, at carnival time male runners, half of them masked as female, half as male, jumped and leaped through the streets. In France it was on St. Stephen's Day or New Year's Day that men dressed as wild beasts or as women and jumped and danced in public (or at least such was the case in the Middle Ages). The saturnalian Feast of Fools, which decorous doctors of theology and prelates were trying to ban from the French cathedrals in the fifteenth and sixteenth centuries, involved both young clerics and laymen, some of them disguised as females, who made wanton and loose gestures. In parts of the Pyrénées at Candlemas (February 2), a Bear Chase took place* involving a lustful bear, costumed hunters, and young men dressed as women and often called Rosetta. After an amorous interlude with Rosetta, the bear was killed, revived, shaved, and killed again.[23]

In England, too, in Henry VIII's time, during the reign of the Boy Bishop after Christmas some of the male children taken from house to house were dressed as females rather than as priests or bishops. The most important English examples of the male as grotesque female, however, were the Bessy and Maid Marian. In the northern counties, a Fool-Plough was dragged about the countryside, often on the first Monday after Epiphany, by men

* Though evidence for the Candlemas Bear Chase is fullest and clearest from the French and Spanish Pyrénées, there are suggestions that it was more widespread in the Middle Ages. In the ninth century, Hincmar of Reims inveighed against "shameful plays" with bears and women dancers. Richard Bernheimer has argued for the connection between the bear hunt and the wild-man hunt, performed in several parts of Europe, and this has been confirmed by Claude Gaignebet, who relates it further to the popular play of Valentin and Ourson. Bruegel represented this game in an engraving and in his painting of the Battle of Carnival and Lent: a male, masked and dressed as a female, holds out a ring to the wild man. See R. Bernheimer, *Wild Men in the Middle Ages* (Cambridge, Mass., 1952), pp. 52-56; C. Gaignebet, "Le combat de Carnaval et de Carême de P. Bruegel (1559)," *Annales. Economies, Sociétés, Civilisations* 27 (1972): 329-31.

dressed in white shirts. Sword dances were done by some of them, while old Bessy and her fur-clad Fool capered around and tried to collect from the spectators. Maid Marian presided with Robin Hood over the May games. If in this capacity she was sometimes a real female and sometimes a disguised male, when it came to the Morris Dance with Robin, the Hobby Horse, the dragon, and the rest, the Marian was a man. Here again the Maid's gestures or costume might be licentious.[24]

All interpreters of this transvestism see it, like the African example mentioned earlier, as a fertility rite—biological or agricultural[25]—embedded into festivities that may have had other meanings as well. In the European context the use of the female garb was especially appropriate, for it drew not merely on the inevitable association of the female with reproduction, but on the contemporary definition of the female as the lustier sex. Did it also draw on other features of sexual symbolism in early modern Europe, e.g. the relation of the subordinate to the superior? Did it (as with our transvestite Harlequin of the *commedia dell'-arte*) suggest to peasants or city folk the blurring or reversing of social boundaries? Perhaps. When we see the roles that the woman-on-top was later to play, it is hard to believe that some such effect was not stimulated by these rites. In the urban Feast of Fools, in any case, the fertility function of the transvestism was already overshadowed by its carnivalesque derision of the celibate priestly hierarchy.

Along with these instances of festive male transvestism, we have some scanty evidence of a more symmetrical switch. During the Twelve Days of Christmas or on Epiphany, mummers and guisers in northern England, the Scottish Lowlands, and northern France might include men *and* women wearing the clothes of the opposite sex. At Fastnacht in fifteenth-century Nuremberg men dressed as women and women as men, and the same was the case at Shrovetide in sixteenth-century England and perhaps at Mardi Gras in early modern France. Possibly here too there is some old relation to fertility rites, but the exchange may well be connected with the more flexible license of carnivalesque inversion. At least in the case of "goose-dancing" at Eastertime on the Scilly Islands in the mid-eighteenth century, we know the license was used to tell the truth: "the maidens are dressed up for young men and the young men for maidens: thus disguised they visit their neighbours in companies, where they dance, and make jokes upon what has happened on the island; when everyone is humorously told their own without offense being taken."[26]

The truth-telling of Europe's male festive societies was much less gentle than that of the Scilly geese. These organizations were the Kingdoms and Abbeys of Misrule[27] discussed in the previous essay. (In England and Scotland we have Lords of Misrule and Abbots of Unreason, though the exact character of their bands remains to be studied.) Among other roles in town and countryside, the Abbeys expressed the community's interest in marriages and their outcome much more overtly than the cavorting Bessy or Rosetta. In noisy masked demonstrations—charivaris, scampanete, katzenmusik, cencerrada, rough music, and the like—they mocked newlyweds who had not produced a baby soon enough and people marrying for the second time, especially when there was a gross disparity in age between bride and groom. Indeed, any local scandal might be made the target for their pots, tambourines, bells, and horns.

The unruly woman appeared in the Abbeys' plays in two forms. First as officers of Misrule. In rural areas, these were usually called Lords and Abbots; in the French cities, however, they took all kinds of pompous titles. Among these dignitaries were Princesses and Dames and especially Mothers: we find Mère Folle in Dijon, Langres, and Chalon-sur-Saône; Mère Sotte in Paris and Compiègne; and Mère d'Enfance in Bordeaux. In Wales, though I know of no female festive titles, the men who conducted the *ceffyl pren*, as the local rough music was called, blackened their faces and wore women's garb.[28] In all of this there was a double irony: the young villager who became an Abbot, the artisan who became a Prince directly adopted for their Misrule a symbol of licit power; the power invoked by the man who became Mère Folle, however, was already in defiance of natural order—a dangerous and vital power, which his disguise made safe for him to assume.

The unruly woman not only directed some of the male festive organizations; she was sometimes their butt. The village scold or the domineering wife might be ducked in the pond or pulled through the streets muzzled or branked or in a creel.[29] City people from the fifteenth to the eighteenth centuries were even more concerned about husband-beating, and the beaten *man* (or a neighbor playing his part) was paraded through the streets backward on an ass by noisy revelers. In the English Midlands the ride was known as a Skimmington or a Skimmety, perhaps from the big skimming ladle sometimes used by women in beating their husbands (see Plate 13). In northern England and Scotland, the victim or his stand-in "rode the stang" (a long hobbyhorse), and a like steed was used in the *ceffyl pren* in Wales. In some towns, effigies of the offending couple were promenaded. In others, the festive organization mounted floats to display the actual circumstances of the monstrous beating: the wives were shown hitting their husbands with distaffs, tripe, sticks, trenchers, water pots; throwing stones at them; pulling their beards; or kicking them in the genitalia.[30]

With these last dramatizations, the Misrule Abbeys introduced ambiguities into the treatment of the woman-on-top, just as we have seen in the comic literature. The unruly woman on the float was shameful, outrageous; she was also vigorous and in command. The mockery turned against her martyred husband. And the message of the urban carnival was mixed: it both exhorted the henpecked husband to take command and invited the unruly woman to keep up the fight.

Real women in early modern Europe had less chance than men

to initiate or take part in their *own* festivals of inversion. To be sure, a female fool named Mathurine flourished at the courts of Henri IV and Louis XIII and, dressed as an Amazon, commented on political and religious matters; but there is no sign of festive organizations for young women. Confraternities for young unmarried women, where they existed at all, stayed close to religious devotion. Queens were elected for special occasions, such as Twelfth Night or Harvest, but their rule was gentle and tame. The young May queens in their flowers and white ribbons begged for money for dowries or for the Virgin's altar, promising a mere kiss in return. Some May customs that were still current in early modern Europe, however, point back to a rowdier role for women. In rural Franche-Comté during May, wives could take revenge on their husbands for beating them by ducking the men or making them ride an ass; wives could dance, jump, and banquet freely without permission from their husbands; and women's courts issued mock decrees. (In nearby Dijon by the sixteenth century, interestingly enough, Mère Folle and her Infanterie had usurped this revenge from the women; May was the one month of the year when the Misrule Abbey would charivari a man who had beaten his wife.) Generally, May—Flora's month in Roman times—was thought to be a period in which women were powerful, their desires at their most immoderate. As the old saying went, a May bride would keep her husband in yoke all year round. And in fact marriages were not frequent in May.[31]

In Nuremberg it was at carnival time that women may have assumed some kind of special license in the sixteenth and seventeenth centuries. Illustrated proclamations in joking pompous language granted every female with "a wretched dissolute husband" the right to deny him his freedom and to beat him till "his asshole [was] roaring." Another decree, issued by Foeminarius, the Hereditary Steward of Quarrel and Dispute Valley, gave three years of Privileges to the suffering Company of Wives so that they might rule their husbands: they could bear arms, elect their own mayor, and go out and entertain as they wished while their spouses could buy nothing or drink no wine or beer without the wives' permission. And, of course, the men did all the housework and welcomed any bastards that the wives might bear.[32]

[III]

The relationship between real marriages and May license, between real pregnancy and Fastnacht games returns us to the question posed earlier in this paper. What were the overall functions of these festive and literary inversions in sex roles? Clearly they filled in part the role attributed to them by anthropologists and historians of literature: they afforded an expression of, and an outlet for, conflicts about authority within the system; and they also provided occasions by which the authoritarian current in family, workshop, and political life could be moderated by the laughter of disorder and paradoxical play. Accordingly, they served to reinforce hierarchical structure.

Indeed, in the early modern period, up to the late eighteenth century, the patriarchal family is not challenged as such even by the most searching critics of relations between the sexes. The late seventeenth-century feminists François Poullain de La Barre and Mary Astell believed the submission of the wife to her husband not to be justified by any natural inferiority of females, but to be necessary nonetheless. As Astell said, "There can be [no] Society great or little, from Empires down to private Families, without a last Resort, to determine the Affairs of that Society by an irresistible sentence. . . . This Supremacy must be fixed somewhere." The best they could imagine was an impossible hermaphroditic utopia or a primitive state of equality between the sexes, now irrevocably lost (perhaps the experience of festive role-reversals at least helped keep this egalitarian dream alive, as Victor Turner has suggested in another connection). The best they could hope for and recommend, like Shadwell's Woman-Captain, were ways to prevent husbandly tyranny: better education for women or a better choice of marriage partners. The only countermodel for the family they had come to recognize by the mid-eighteenth century was the equally hierarchical one of matriarchy.[33]

Thus, this study does not overturn the traditional theory about rites and festivities of inversion; but it does hope to add other dimensions to it. Rather than expending itself primarily during the privileged duration of the joke, the story, the comedy, or the carnival, topsy-turvy play had much spillover into everyday "serious" life, and the effects there were sometimes disturbing and even novel. As literary and festive inversion in preindustrial Europe was a product not just of stable hierarchy but also of changes in the location of power and property, so this inversion could prompt new ways of thinking about the system and reacting to it.

Let us begin with a historical reflection about the family. Europeans of the fifteenth to eighteenth centuries found it remarkably difficult to conceive of the institution of the family as having a "history," of changing through time. Its patriarchal form went back either to the Garden of Eden, where the woman's subjection to the man was at least a gentle one, or to the first moment in human history, when monogamous marriage set mankind off from the promiscuous horde. Political forms might follow each other in a predictable cyclical fashion; economic, religious, and cultural systems might change along with them (as Vico thought). But the family stayed the same. To be sure, curious sexual customs were noted in the New World, but they were used merely to satirize European abuses or dismissed as products of savagery or degeneration. Play with the various images of woman-on-top, then, kept open an alternate way of conceiving family structure.* Ultimately, when the Jesuit Lafitau found an order in the strange

---

* The Amazons play a role, for instance, in Thomas Hobbes' remarkable theoretical discussion of dominion within the family. As is usual in his period, he insists that it must be vested in one person only; but "whereas some have attributed the dominion to the man only, as being of the more excellent sex; they misreckon in it. For there is not always that difference of strength, or prudence between the man and the woman, as that the right can be determined without war." In commonwealths, the conflict is settled by law, which for the most part decides for the father. But in the state of nature, the deci-

family patterns (matrilineal and matrilocal) that he had observed among the Iroquois and heard about in the Caribbean, he was able to refer back to legends of the Amazons and to the Lycians, whom he had read about in Herodotus. Lafitau's new theory of "gynae-cocracy," as he called the matriarchal stage, was published in 1724 in his *Moeurs des sauvages ameriquains, comparées aux moeurs des premiers temps*. It owed something to the unruly woman.[34]

Play with the exceptional woman-on-top, the virtuous virago, was also a resource for feminist reflection on women's capacities. Although she did not argue that men and women should change the separate offices to which God had ordained them, nevertheless Christine de Pisan was glad to use examples of ancient female conquerors, stock figures in the legends about Amazons and in the stories and proverbs about women's rule, to show that "in many women there is . . . great courage, strength, and hardiness to undertake all manner of strong things and to achieve them as did . . . great men and solemn conquerors." Subsequent writers on "Women Worthies" almost always included some viragos, readily incorporating Joan of Arc into the company. By the early eighteenth century, speculation about virtuous Amazons could be used not only to praise the wise rule of contemporary lawful queens (as it had been already in Elizabeth I's day), but also to hint at the possibility of a wider role of citizenship for women.[35]

Furthermore, the exceptional woman-out-of-her-place enriched the fantasy of a few real women and might have emboldened them to exceptional action. Marie Delcourt has argued convincingly that Joan of Arc's male garb, to which she clung obdurately to the end, was not the product of mere practical military considera-

---

sion is made by those who generate the children. It may be made by contract. "We find in history that the Amazons contracted with the men of the neighboring countries, to whom they had recourse for issue, that the issue male should be sent back, but the female remain with themselves: so that the dominion of the females was in the mother." Where there is no contract, the dominion lies with the mother—that is, in the absence of matrimonial laws, with the only person who knows who the true parents are and who has the power to nourish the child. *The Leviathan*, Second Part, chap. 20.

tions, but was inspired by the example of the transvestite saints of the *Golden Legend*. The unusual seventeenth-century mystic Antoinette Bourignon started her career by fleeing from an impending marriage in the clothes of a male hermit. Among her later visions was that of humankind created originally as androgynous, a state of whole perfection to which it would return at the resurrection of the dead. The Recusant Mary Ward, founder of an innovating unenclosed teaching order for women with no male superior but the pope, was taking the Jesuits as her model but may also have received encouragement from traditions of sexual inversion. Galloping over the countryside in the vain effort to reconvert the English to Holy Mother Church, she and the members of her Company struck observers as "apostolic Amazons."[36]

Two of these women ultimately went to prison; the third narrowly escaped arrest. The virtuous virago could be a threat to order after all. But what about the majority of unexceptional women living within their families? What could the woman-on-top mean to them?

Girls were brought up to believe that they ought to obey their husbands; and boys were brought up to believe that they had the power of correction over their wives. In actual marriage, subjection might be moderated by the common causes of economic support, to which they both contributed, of sexual need, of childrearing, or of shared religious interest. It might be reversed temporarily during the lying-in period, when the new mother could boss her husband around with impunity. And subjection might be aggravated by the husband's repeated beatings of his wife. Some women accepted these arrangements. Some women got around them by sneaky manipulations that made their husbands fancy themselves the sole decision-makers. Still other wives rebelled, told their husbands to go to the devil, badgered them, thrashed them. Many circumstances might produce a wife of the third type. Here I wish only to speculate that the ambiguous woman-on-top of the world of play made the unruly option a more conceivable one within the family.[37]

Ordinary women might also be disorderly in public. In principle, women could pronounce on law and doctrine only if they were queens, had unusual learning, or fell into an ecstatic trance. Virtually never were they to take the law into their own hands. In fact, women turn up telling off priests and pastors, being central actors in grain and bread riots in town and country, and participating in tax revolts and other rural disturbances. In England in the early seventeenth century (so Thomas Barnes has discovered), a significant percentage of the rioters against enclosures and for common rights were female. In Calvinist Edinburgh in 1637, the resistance to Charles I's imposition of the Book of Common Prayer was opened by a crowd of "rascally serving women" at Saint Giles' Church, who drowned out the Dean's reading, threw stools at the Bishop of Edinburgh, and when evicted, stoned the doors and windows. The tax revolt at Montpellier in 1645 was started by women, led down the streets by a virago named la Branlaïre, who shouted for death for the tax-collectors who were taking the bread from their children's mouths.[38]

There are several reasons for this female involvement that we cannot consider here, but part of its background is the complex license accorded the unruly woman. On the one hand, she was not accountable for what she did. Given over to the sway of her lower passions, she was not responsible for her actions; her husband was responsible, for she was subject to him. Indeed, this "incapacity" was embodied in varying degrees in English law and in some French customary law. In England, in most felonious acts by a married woman to which her husband could be shown to be privy or at which he was present, the wife could not be held entirely culpable. If indicted, she might be acquitted or receive a lesser sentence than he for the same crime. In Normandy and Brittany, the husband might have to answer for her crimes in court, and everywhere the *sexus imbecillus* might be punished less severely. The full weight of the law fell only on the ruling male. Small wonder that the husbands sometimes thought it safer to send their wives out to do the rioting alone. And small wonder that the Star Chamber grumbled in 1605 that some women who had torn down enclosure fences were "hiding behind their sex."[39]

On the other hand, sexual inversion also gave a more positive license to the unruly woman: her right as subject and as mother to rise up and tell the truth. When a great pregnant woman at the front of a crowd curses grain-hoarders or cheating authorities, the irreverent Gargamelle is part of her tradition. When Katherine Zell of Strasbourg dares to write an attack on clerical celibacy in the 1520's and claims "I do not pretend to be John the Baptist rebuking the Pharisees. I do not claim to be Nathan upbraiding David. I aspire only to be Balaam's ass, castigating his master," then Dame Folly is part of her tradition.[40]

It turns out, however, that Dame Folly could serve to validate disobedient and riotous behavior by men, too. They also could hide behind that sex. Much has been written by historians on the ideals, traditions, symbols, and solidarities that legitimated the numerous rural and urban uprisings of early modern Europe. Among these traditions was the carnival right of criticism and mockery, which sometimes tipped over into real rebellion. In 1630 in Dijon, for instance, Mère Folle and her Infanterie were part of an uprising in masquerade against royal tax officers. In fact, the donning of female clothes by men and the adopting of female titles for riots were surprisingly frequent, beginning (so our still scanty data suggest) in the seventeenth century. In many of these disturbances, the men were trying to protect traditional rights against change; in others, it was the rioters who were pressing for innovation. But in all cases, they were putting ritual and festive inversion to new uses.

So in the Beaujolais in the 1770's, male peasants blackened their faces and dressed as women and then attacked surveyors measuring their lands for a new landlord. In the morning, when the police agents came, the peasants' wives knew nothing, and said the attackers were "fairies" who came from the mountains from time to time.* Among the market women who marched to Versailles in

---

* The association of these costumed figures with "fairies," which was also made in a few other riots, adds another dimension to political transvestism. Fairy beliefs were still strong in rural Europe in the eighteenth century, having originated from diverse traditions, including one that associated them with

October 1789, it is very likely there were men in female garb. And in 1829-30, the "War of the Demoiselles" took place in the Department of Ariège in the Pyrénées. The peasants dressed themselves in long white shirts, suggesting women's clothes, and wore women's hats, and defended their desperately needed rights to wood and pasturage in the forests, then being threatened by a new Forest Code.[41]

In England we find the same thing. In 1629, "Captain" Alice Clark, a real female, headed a crowd of women and male weavers dressed as women in a grain riot near Maldon in Essex. They sacked a ship thought to be exporting grain to the Netherlands. In 1631, in the dairy and grazing sections of Wiltshire, bands of men rioted and leveled fences against the king's enclosure of their forests. They were led by men dressed as women, who called themselves "Lady Skimmington." In May 1718, Cambridge students followed "a virago, or man in woman's habit, crowned with laurel" to assault a Dissenting meeting house. Two years later, laborers in Surrey rioted in women's clothes, and at mid-century country men disguised as women tore down the hated tollbooths and turnpike gates at the Gloucestershire border to the sound of drumming and loud shouts. In April 1812, "General Ludd's Wives," two weavers dressed as women, led a crowd of hundreds to smash steam looms and burn a factory at Stockport.[42]

In Wales and Scotland, too, there were uprisings in female disguise. The *ceffyl pren*, with its blackfaced transvestite males, gave way in the 1830's and 1840's in west Wales to the Rebecca riots against the detested turnpike tolls and other sources of agrarian complaint. They were led by one "Rebecca" and noisy men in women's clothes. And in 1736 in Edinburgh, the Porteous Riots,

---

the spirits of the dead. Fairies might assume male or female form, might have various sizes and shapes, and might dress in different ways; but they all had a spiritual power that could be used on human beings either malevolently or benevolently. Female and fairy combine their power in these riots to help the peasants. See K. M. Briggs, *The Fairies in Tradition and Literature* (London, 1967), and Keith Thomas, *Religion and the Decline of Magic* (London, 1971), pp. 606-14.

which were sparked by a hated English officer, oppressive customs laws, and resistance to the union of Scotland with England, were carried out by men disguised as women and with a leader known as Madge Wildfire.[43]

Finally, in Ireland, where old stories told of the ritual killing of the king at Samhain by men dressed as animals and as women, and where the funeral wakes involved fertility rites with women dressed as men, we have the most extensive example of disturbances led by men disguised as women. For about a decade, from 1760 to 1770, the Whiteboys, dressed in long white frocks and with blackened faces, set themselves up as an armed popular force to provide justice for the poor, "to restore the ancient commons and redress other grievances." They tore down enclosures, punished landowners who raised the rents, forced masters to release unwilling apprentices, and fought the gouging tithe-farmers mercilessly. Those who opposed their rule they chastised and ridiculed. They sometimes said they acted under "sanction of being fairies," and a favorite signature on their proclamations was Sieve Outlagh (or Sadhbh Amhaltach)—"Ghostly Sally." Ultimately they were suppressed by the armed might of the gentlemen and magistrates, but not before they had left a legacy for the Molly Maguires and the Ribbon Societies of the nineteenth century.[44]

The female persona was only one of several folk disguises assumed by males for riots in the seventeenth and eighteenth centuries, but it was quite popular and widespread. Our analysis of sexual symbolism and of the varieties of sexual inversion should help us understand why this was so. In part, the black face and female dress were a practical concealment, and readily at hand in households rarely filled with fancy wardrobes. More important, however, were the mixed ways in which the female persona authorized resistance. On the one hand, the disguise freed men from full responsibility for their deeds and perhaps, too, from fear of outrageous revenge upon their manhood. After all, it was mere women who were acting in this disorderly way. On the other hand, the males drew upon the sexual power and energy of the unruly

woman and on her license (which they had long assumed at carnival and games)—to promote fertility, to defend the community's
interests and standards, and to tell the truth about unjust rule.

The woman-on-top was a resource for private and public life
in the fashions we have described only so long as two things were
the case: first, so long as sexual symbolism had a close connection
with questions of order and subordination, with the lower female
sex conceived as the disorderly lustful one; second, so long as the
stimulus to inversion play was a double one—traditional hierarchical structures *and* disputed changes in the distribution of power
in family and political life. As we move into the industrial period
with its modern states, classes, and systems of private property,
and its exploitation of racial and national groups, both symbolism and stimuli were transformed. One small sign of the new order
is the changing butt of domestic charivaris: by the nineteenth
century, rough music in England was more likely to be directed
against the wife-beater than against the henpecked husband, and
there are signs of such a shift in America and even in France.[45]

The woman-on-top flourished, then, in preindustrial Europe
and during the period of transition to industrial society. Despite
all our detail in this essay, we have been able to give only the
outlines of her reign. Variations in sexual inversion from country
to country or between Protestants and Catholics have been ignored for the sake of describing a large pattern over time. Cultural
play with sex roles intended to explore the character of sexuality
itself (Where did one sex stop and the other begin?) has been ignored to concentrate on hierarchy and disorder. The timing of the
transvestite riots needs to be examined. (Why do they apparently
start only in the seventeenth century?) Also, the nature of play
with sex roles before the fourteenth century must be investigated.
(Is it not likely that there were female transvestite rituals in areas
where hoeing was of great consequence? Can the unruly woman
have been so much an issue when sovereignty was less at stake?)
The asymmetry between male and female roles in festive life from

the fifteenth through the eighteenth centuries remains to be explored, as do some of the contrasts between literary and carnivalesque inversion. What has been established are the types of symbolic reversal in sex roles in early modern Europe and their multiple connections with orderliness in thought and behavior. The holiday rule of the woman-on-top confirmed subjection throughout society, but it also promoted resistance to it. The Maid Marian danced for a plentiful village; the Rosetta disported with the doomed old bear of winter; the serving women of Saint Giles threw stools for the Reformed Kirk; Ghostly Sally led her Whiteboys in a new kind of popular justice. The woman-on-top renewed old systems, but also helped change them into something different.

The Rites of Violence

These are the statutes and judgments, which ye shall observe to do in the land, which the Lord God of thy fathers giveth thee. . . . Ye shall utterly destroy all the places wherein the nations which ye shall possess served their gods, upon the high mountains, and upon the hills, and under every green tree:

And ye shall overthrow their altars, and break their pillars and burn their groves with fire; and ye shall hew down the graven images of their gods, and destroy the names of them out of that place [Deuteronomy 12: 1-3].

Thus spoke a Calvinist pastor to his flock in 1562.[1]

If thy brother, the son of thy mother, or thy son, or thy daughter, or the wife of thy bosom, or thy friend, which is as thine own soul, entice thee secretly, saying Let us go serve other gods, which thou hast not known, thou, nor thy fathers. . . . Thou shalt not consent unto him, nor hearken unto him. . . . But thou shalt surely kill him; thine hand shall be first upon him to put him to death, and afterwards the hand of all the people. . . .

If thou shalt hear say in one of thy cities, which the Lord thy God hath given thee to dwell there, saying, Certain men, the children of Belial are gone out from among you, and have withdrawn the inhabitants of their city, saying Let us go and serve other gods, which ye have not known. . . . Thou shalt surely smite the inhabitants of that city with the edge of the sword, destroying it utterly and all that is therein [Deuteronomy 13: 6, 8-9, 12-13, 15].

And [Jehu] lifted up his face to the window and said, Who is on my side? Who? And there looked out to him two or three eunuchs. And he said, Throw her down. So they threw [Jezebel] down: and some of her blood was sprinkled on the wall, and on the horses: and he trode her under foot. . . . And they went to bury her: but they found no more of her than the skull and the feet and the palms of her hands. . . . And [Jehu] said, This is the word of the Lord, which he spake by his servant Elijah . . . saying, In the portion of Jezreel shall dogs eat the flesh of Jezebel: And the carcase of Jezebel shall be as dung upon the face of the field [2 Kings 9: 32-33, 35-37].

Thus in 1568 Parisian preachers held up to their Catholic parishioners the end of a wicked idolater.[2] Whatever the intentions of pastors and priests, such words were among the many spurs to religious riot in sixteenth-century France. By religious riot I mean, as a preliminary definition, any violent action, with words or weapons, undertaken against religious targets by people who were not acting *officially and formally* as agents of political and ecclesiastical authority. As food rioters bring their moral indignation to bear upon the state of the grain market, so religious rioters bring their zeal to bear upon the state of men's relations to the sacred. The violence of the religious riot is distinguished, at least in principle, from the action of political authorities, who can legally silence, humiliate, demolish, punish, torture, and execute, and also from the action of soldiers, who at certain times and places can legally kill and destroy. In mid-sixteenth-century France, all these sources of violence were busily producing, and it is sometimes hard to tell a militia officer from a murderer and a soldier from a statue-smasher. Nevertheless, there are occasions when we can separate out for examination a violent crowd set on religious goals.

The sixteenth century itself had its own generalizations about crowd violence. Once in a while it was seen as having a kind of system or sense. In Corpus Christi Day drama, the violence against Christ is represented as a series of formal competitive "games," which hide from His tormentors the full knowledge of what they do.[3] In Dürer's *Martyrdom of the Ten Thousand*, the Persian torturers of the Christians are spaced apart, doing their terrible business in an orderly, methodical way.[4] Most of the time, however, as in Bruegel's *The Triumph of Death*, the image of the crowd was one of chaos. Learned writers talk of grain-rioters in Lyon as "the dregs of the populace, with no order, no rein, no leader . . . a beast of many heads . . . an insane rabble," and of the Paris mob as "an ignorant multitude, collected from all nations . . . governed by the appetite of those who stir them up [to] extreme rage, just looking for the chance to carry out any kind of cruelty."[5]

Nowadays this hydra-headed monster has taken on a more orderly shape, as a result of the work of George Rudé, Eric Hobsbawm, E. P. Thompson, Charles Tilly, Emmanuel Le Roy Ladurie, and others.[6] We may see these crowds as prompted by political and moral traditions that legitimize and even prescribe their violence. We may see urban rioters not as miserable, uprooted, unstable masses, but as men and women who often have some stake in their community; who may be craftsmen or better; and who, even when poor and unskilled, may appear respectable to their everyday neighbors. Finally, we may see their violence, however cruel, not as random and limitless but as aimed at defined targets and selected from a repertory of traditional punishments and forms of destruction.

This picture of preindustrial crowd violence has been drawn primarily from the study of grain and bread riots, tax riots, craft violence, and certain kinds of peasant revolts. The broad spectrum of religious riot, however, has not received analytical attention except in the case of the anti-Semitic pogrom and the millenarian movement,[7] both of which have evident contemporary significance and nonreligious features. To present-day church historians, especially in an age of ecumenicalism, the popular violence of their Calvinist and Catholic ancestors may be an embarrassment (as is that of Belfast). To social historians it is the seeming "irrationality" of most sixteenth-century religious riot that has been puzzling. To bear the sword in the name of a millenarian dream might make some sense, but why get so excited about the Eucharist or saints' relics? It is hard to decipher the social meaning of such an event.

Not surprisingly, the pioneering remarks of C. Verlinden and his colleagues on popular iconoclasm, and of Janine Estèbe on popular Catholic violence, insist upon a strong linkage between religious conflict and economic issues. It has been argued that a rise in grain prices triggers these disturbances, and that the Saint Bartholomew's massacres are also a "class-crime," "rich Huguenots being attacked and pillaged by preference." Beyond this, Estèbe accounts for the crowd action in the massacres as an expression of the primitive soul of the people, pushed by events into pathological hatred. Similarly, in Philippe Wolff's study of anti-Semitic pogroms in Valencia and Barcelona in 1391 and in George Rudé's analysis of anti-Catholic riots in eighteenth-century London, there is a tendency to identify the "real" elements in the disturbance as the social ones, social being defined only in terms of a conflict of poor against rich, artisans against wealthy burghers or craftsmen, and wage earners against manufacturers and merchants.[8] There is no doubt that some religious violence has this character—Wolff's evidence for Barcelona is very good indeed—but is this the only kind of social meaning inherent in a religious riot? What does one make of popular religious violence where class conflict of this type is not present?

I will try to answer these questions in regard to sixteenth-century France in the course of this essay. My first purpose is to describe the shape and structure of the religious riot in French cities and towns, especially in the 1560's and early 1570's. We will look at the goals, legitimation, and occasions for riots; at the kinds of action undertaken by the crowds and the targets for their violence; and briefly at the participants in the riots and their organization. We will consider differences between Protestant and Catholic styles of crowd behavior, but will also indicate the many ways in which they are alike. Our sources will be contemporary Catholic and Protestant accounts of religious disturbance, from which we will do our best to sort out utter fabrication from likely fact.* I

---

* Where possible, I have tried to use both Catholic and Protestant accounts of the same episode. For instance, for events in Toulouse in 1562, I have used

hope this inquiry will put the massacres of Saint Bartholomew's Day in a new perspective, and also deepen our understanding of the religious riot as a type of collective disturbance.

[1]

What then can we learn of the goals of popular religious violence? What were the crowds intending to do and why did they think they must do it? Their behavior suggests, first of all, a goal akin to preaching: the defense of true doctrine and the refutation of false doctrine through dramatic challenges and tests. "You blaspheme," shouts a woman to a Catholic preacher in Montpellier in 1558; and, having broken the decorum of the service, she leads part of the congregation out of the church. "You lie," shouts a sheathmaker in the midst of the Franciscan's Easter sermon in Lyon, and his words are underscored by the gunshots of Huguenots waiting in the square.[9] "Look," cries a weaver in Tournai, as he seizes the elevated host from the priest, "deceived people, do you believe this is the King, Jesus Christ, the true God and Savior? Look!" And he crumbles the wafer and escapes. "Look,"

---

among others the account of the Catholic G. Bosquet (*Histoire de M. G. Bosquet, sur les troubles Advenus en la ville de Tolose l'an 1562* [Toulouse, 1595]) and that of the Reformed *Histoire ecclésiastique*. I have taken especially seriously descriptions of Catholic violence coming from Catholic writers (as in the *Mémoires* of the priest Claude Haton) and descriptions of Protestant violence coming from the *Histoire ecclésiastique*. These sources are not necessarily telling the *whole* truth about their party's violence, but at least we can assume that what they positively describe did occur. I have also taken especially seriously the *omission* of certain kinds of violence in accusations made by one party about the opposing party, since these writers show so little willingness to put their opponents in a favorable light. If certain kinds of violence are regularly *not* attributed to the enemy, then I think we can assume that they did not in fact occur very often.

In regard to accepting evidence about acts of desecration of corpses, torture, and acts of filth, where there is no way of getting "impartial" eyewitness accounts, I have used my judgment, based on a general understanding of the range of possibilities in sixteenth-century behavior. My guides here have been French legal practice and penalty, Rabelais, descriptions by Pierre de L'Estoile of behavior in Paris in the late sixteenth century, and the comments of Montaigne on tortures in his time ("On Cruelty," "Of Cannibals").

says a crowd of image-breakers to the people of Albiac in 1561, showing them the relics they have seized from the Carmelite monastery, "look, they are only animal bones."[10] And the slogan of the Reformed crowds as they rush through the streets of Paris, of Toulouse, of La Rochelle, of Angoulême is "The Gospel! The Gospel! Long live the Gospel!"[11]

Catholic crowds answer this kind of claim to truth in Angers by taking a French Bible—well-bound and gilded, seized in the home of a rich merchant—and parading it through the streets on the end of a halberd. "There's the truth hung. There's the truth of the Huguenots, the truth of all the devils." Then, throwing it into the river, "There's the truth of all the devils drowned."[12] And if the Huguenot doctrine was true, why didn't the Lord come and save them from their killers? So a crowd of Orléans Catholics taunted its victims in 1572: "Where is your God? Where are your prayers and Psalms? Let him save you if he can." Even the dead were made to speak in Normandy and Provence, where leaves of the Protestant Bible were stuffed into the mouths and wounds of corpses. "They preached the truth of their God. Let them call him to their aid."[13]

The same refutation was, of course, open to Protestants. A Protestant crowd corners a baker guarding the holy-wafer box in Saint Médard's Church in Paris in 1561. "Messieurs," he pleads, "do not touch it for the honor of Him who dwells here." "Does your God of paste protect you now from the pains of death?" was the Protestant answer before they killed him.[14] True doctrine can be defended in sermon or speech, backed up by the magistrate's sword against the heretic. Here it is defended by dramatic demonstration, backed up by the violence of the crowd.

A more frequent goal of these riots, however, is that of ridding the community of dreaded pollution. The word "pollution" is often on the lips of the violent, and the concept serves well to sum up the dangers that rioters saw in the dirty and diabolic enemy. A priest brings ornaments and objects for singing the Mass into a Bordeaux jail. The Protestant prisoner smashes them all. "Do you want to blaspheme the Lord's name everywhere? Isn't it enough that the temples are defiled? Must you also profane prisons so nothing is unpolluted?"[15] "The Calvinists have polluted their hands with every kind of sacrilege men can think of," writes a doctor of theology in 1562. Not long after, at the Sainte Chapelle, a man seizes the elevated host with his "polluted hands" and crushes it under foot. The worshipers beat him up and deliver him to the agents of Parlement.[16] The extent to which Protestants could be viewed as vessels of pollution is suggested by a popular belief about the origin of the nickname "Huguenots." In the city of Tours, *le roi Huguet* was the generic name for ghosts who, instead of spending their time in Purgatory, came back to rattle doors and haunt and harm people at night. Protestants went out at night to their lascivious conventicles, and so the priests and the people began to call them Huguenots in Tours and then elsewhere. Protestants were thus as sinister as the spirits of the dead, whom one hoped to settle in their tombs on All Souls' Day.[17]

One does not have to listen very long to sixteenth-century voices to hear the evidence for the uncleanliness and profanation of either side. As for the Protestants, Catholics knew that, in the style of earlier heretics, they snuffed out the candles and had sexual intercourse after the voluptuous psalm-singing of their nocturnal conventicles. When their services became public, it was no better, for their Holy Supper was perceived (in the words of a merchant-draper of Lyon) as disordered and drunken, "a bacchanalia."[18] But it was not just the fleshly license with which they lived that was unclean, but the things they said in their "pestilential" books and the things they did in hatred of the mass, the sacraments, and the whole Catholic religion. As the representative of the clergy said at the Estates of Orléans, the heretics intended to leave "no place in the Kingdom which was dedicated, holy, and sacred to the Lord, but would only profane churches, demolish altars, and break images."[19]

The Protestants' sense of Catholic pollution also stemmed to some extent from their sexual uncleanness, here specifically of the clergy. Protestant polemic never tired of pointing to the lewdness of the clergy with their "concubines." It was rumored that the Church of Lyon had an organization of hundreds of women—sort of temple prostitutes—at the disposition of priests and canons; and an observer pointed out with disgust how after the First Religious War the mass and the brothel reentered Rouen together. One minister even claimed that the clergy were for the most part sodomites.[20] But more serious than the sexual abominations of the clergy was the defilement of the sacred by Catholic ritual life, from the diabolic magic of the mass to the idolatrous worship of images. The mass is "vile filth"; "no people pollute the House of the Lord in every way more than the clergy." Protestant converts talked of their own past lives as a time of befoulment and dreaded present "contamination" from Catholic churches and rites.[21]

Pollution was a dangerous thing to suffer in a community, from either a Protestant or a Catholic point of view, for it would surely provoke the wrath of God. Terrible windstorms and floods were sometimes taken as signs of His impatience on this count.[22] Catholics, moreover, had also to worry about offending Mary and the saints; and though the anxious, expiatory processions organized in the wake of Protestant sacrilege might temporarily appease them, the heretics were sure to strike again.[23] It is not surprising, then, that so many of the acts of violence performed by Catholic and Protestant crowds have (as we shall see more fully later on) the character either of rites of purification or of a paradoxical desecration, intended to cut down on uncleanness by placing profane things, like chrism, back in the profane world where they belonged.

This concern of Catholic and Protestant crowds to destroy polluting elements is reminiscent of the insistence of revolutionary millenarian movements that the wicked be exterminated that the godly may rule. The resemblance is real, but is limited. Our Catholic and Protestant rioters have a conviction not so much of their immanent godliness as of the rightness of their judgment, envisage not so much a society of saints as a holier society of sinners.

For Catholic zealots, the extermination of the heretical "vermin" promised the restoration of unity to the body social* and the reinforcement of some of its traditional boundaries:

> And let us all say in unison:
> Long live the Catholic religion
> Long live the King and good parishioners,
> Long live faithful Parisians,
> And may it always come to pass
> That every person goes to Mass,
> One God, one Faith, one King.[24]

For Protestant zealots, the purging of the priestly "vermin" promised the creation of a new kind of unity within the body social, all the tighter because false gods and monkish sects would no longer divide it. Relations within the social order would be purer, too, for lewdness and love of gain would be limited. As was said of Lyon after its "deliverance" in 1562:

> Lyon has changed indeed. . . .
> The profit of Mercury, the dance of Venus
> And presumption, too, each man has left aside.

And again:

> When this town so vain
> Was filled
> With idolatry and dealings
> Of usury and lewdness,
> It had clerics and merchants aplenty.

---

*I have tried in this section to generalize Janine Estèbe's important insight in regard to the popular aspect of the Saint Bartholomew's Day massacres: that the Protestants appeared as "profaners" (*Tocsin pour un massacre. La saison des Saint-Barthélemy* [Paris, 1968], pp. 194-95). There seems to me very little evidence, however, that the Catholic killers wished to exterminate "a foreign race" (p. 197). This exaggerates and misreads the evidence in regard to the killing of pregnant women and the castration of males (see below, pp. 175 and 179). Heretics were hated for their polluting, divisive, and disorderly actions, not as a "race"; and the crowds sometimes forced them back to the mass rather than kill them.

For a helpful discussion of the relation between pollution fears and concern for social boundaries, see Mary Douglas, *Purity and Danger. An Analysis of Concepts of Pollution and Taboo* (London, 1966), chap. 7.

But once it was purged
And changed
By the Word of God,
That brood of vipers
Could hope no more
To live in so holy a place.[25]

Crowds might defend truth, and crowds might purify, but there was also a third aspect to the religious riot—a political one. E. P. Thompson has shown how in the eighteenth-century English food riot, the crowd's behavior was legitimated by a widely held belief that it was acting in place of the government. If the justices of the peace failed to do their legal duty in guaranteeing the food supply, then the crowd would carry out the provisions of the Assize for them.[26] I have found the same thing to be true, at least as far as the *menu peuple* are concerned, in the great grain riot, or *rebeine*, of Lyon in 1529. Under the slogan "the commune is rising against the hoarders of grain," the crowd met on the grounds where municipal assemblies were ordinarily held and then went about opening the municipal granary and seizing grain from wealthy people with ample supplies—actions which the city council had undertaken in the past but had failed to do promptly during the current crisis. In the grain riot of Provins in 1573, the artisans seized grain that had been sold at a high price to nonresidents of the city because the civic authorities had failed to provision the town at an honest price.[27]

Now we can deduce some of the same assumptions from the actions of the religious crowds of the mid-sixteenth century. When the magistrate had not used his sword to defend the faith and the true church and to punish the idolaters, then the crowd would do it for him. Thus, many religious disturbances begin with the ringing of the tocsin, as in a time of civic assembly or emergency. Some riots end with the marching of the religious "wrongdoers" on the other side to jail. In 1561, for instance, Parisian Calvinists, fearing that the priests and worshipers in Saint Médard's Church were organizing an assault on their services in the Patriarche garden next door, first rioted in Saint Médard and then seized some fifteen Catholics as "mutinous" and led them off, "bound like galley slaves," to the Châtelet prison.[28]

If the Catholic killing of Huguenots has in some ways the form of a rite of purification, it also sometimes has the form of an imitation of the magistrate. The mass executions of Protestants at Merindol and Cabrières in Provence and at Meaux in the 1540's, duly ordered by the Parlements of Aix and of Paris as punishment for heresy and high treason, anticipate crowd massacres of later decades. The Protestants themselves sensed this: the devil, unable to extinguish the light of the Gospel through the sentences of judges, now tried to obscure it through furious war and a murderous populace. Whereas before they were made martyrs by one executioner, now it is at the hands of "infinite numbers of them, and the swords of private persons have become the litigants, witnesses, judges, decrees, and executors of the strangest cruelties."[29]

Similarly, *official* acts of torture and *official* acts of desecration of the corpses of certain criminals anticipate some of the acts performed by riotous crowds. The public execution was, of course, a dramatic and well-attended event in the sixteenth century, and the woodcut and engraving documented the scene far and wide. There the crowd might see the offending tongue of the blasphemer pierced or slit, the offending hands of the desecrater cut off. There the crowd could watch the traitor decapitated and disemboweled, his corpse quartered, and the parts borne off for public display in different sections of the town. The body of an especially heinous criminal was dragged through the streets, attached to a horse's tail. The image of exemplary royal punishment lived on for weeks, even years, as the corpses of murderers were exposed on gallows or wheels, and the heads of rebels on posts.[30] We are not surprised to learn, then, that the body of Admiral Coligny had already been thrown out of the window by the king's men and stoned by the Duc de Guise hours before the popular attacks on it began in 1572. Furthermore, crowds often took their victims to places of official execution, as in Paris in 1562, when the Protestant printer

Roc Le Frere was dragged for burning to the Marché aux Pourceaux, and in Toulouse the same year, when a merchant slain in
front of a church was dragged for burning to the town hall. "The
king salutes you," said a Catholic crowd in Orléans to a Protestant trader, then put a cord around his neck as official agents
might do, and led him off to be killed.[31]

Riots also occurred in connection with judicial cases, either to
hurry the judgment along or when verdicts in religious cases were
considered too severe or too lenient by "the voice of the people."[32]
Thus in 1569 in Montpellier, a Catholic crowd forced the judge
to condemn an important Huguenot prisoner to death in a hasty
"trial," then seized him and hanged him in front of his house. In
1551 a masked Protestant group kidnapped and released a goldsmith's journeyman who had been condemned in Lyon for heresy
and was being removed to Paris. And in 1561 in Marsillargues,
when prisoners for heresy were released by royal decree, a Catholic crowd "rearrested" them and executed and burned them in
the streets.[33] The most fascinating example of the assumption of
the magistrate's role by a crowd, however, is the mock trial held
by the boys of Provins in October 1572. A Huguenot had been
hanged for thefts and killings committed during the religious troubles. Groups of boys put ropes around his neck and his feet, but
a tug-of-war could not resolve which way the corpse was to be
dragged. The boys then elected lawyers and judges from among
their midst for a trial. Before the eyes of a hundred spectators,
they argued the penalty, appealing from the decision of the real
judge that the Huguenot be only hanged and not burned alive as
befitted a heretic. After the boys' decision, the corpse was dragged
through the streets by the feet and burned.[34]

The Calvinist crowds that seized religious buildings and destroyed images also believed they were taking on the role of the
authorities. When Protestants in Montpellier occupied a church
in 1561, they argued that the building belonged to them already,
since its clergy had been wholly supported by merchants and
burghers in the past and the property belonged to the town. In

Agen the same year, with Reformed ministers preaching that it was the office of the magistrate alone to eradicate the marks of idolatry, Protestant artisans decided one night that "if one tarried for the Consistory, it would never be done" and proceeded to break into the town's churches and destroy all the altars and the images.[35]

To be sure, the relation of a French Calvinist crowd to the magisterial model is different from that of a French Catholic crowd. The king had not yet chastised the clergy and "put all ydolatry to ruyne and confusyon," as Protestants had been urging him since the early 1530's.[36] Calvinist crowds were using his sword as the king *ought* to have been using it and as some princes and city councils outside of France had already used it. Within the kingdom before 1560 city councils had only *indicated* the right path, as they set up municipal schools and lay-controlled welfare systems, or otherwise limited the sphere of action of the clergy.[37] During the next years, as revolution and conversion created Reformed city councils, governors, and rulers (such as the queen of Navarre) within France, Calvinist crowds finally had local magistrates whose actions they could prompt or imitate.

In general, then, the crowds in religious riots in sixteenth-century France can be seen as sometimes acting out clerical roles—defending true doctrine or ridding the community of defilement in a violent version of priest or prophet—and sometimes acting out magisterial roles. Clearly some riotous behavior, such as the extensive pillaging done by both Protestants and Catholics, cannot be subsumed under these heads; but just as the prevalence of pillaging in a war does not prevent us from typing it as a holy war, so the prevalence of pillaging in a riot should not prevent us from seeing it as essentially religious.

[11]

What ever made the people think they could rightfully assume the roles of priest, pastor, and magistrate? Like other Catholic writers, the Jesuit Emond Auger, when he composed his *Peda-*

gogue d'Armes in 1568 to urge a holy war to exterminate the heretics, addressed his instruction only to Charles IX.[38] Like other Reformed preachers, Pastor Pierre Viret told his flock that private individuals should never take it upon themselves to stop public scandals under cover of having some "extraordinary vocation." There was no way that one could get certain evidence from a Scripture to show that a particular private individual had such a calling, and everything was best left to those who held political power.[39] When Protestant resistance theory was fully developed it too never conceded a clear right of violent disobedience to private persons.[40] Nor were secular authorities in sixteenth-century cities in the habit of telling the *menu peuple* that they had a right to riot when they felt like it.

Yet the crowds did riot, and there are remarkably few instances reported of remorse on the part of participants in religious disturbances. Of the many Catholic murderers mentioned in Crespin's *Book of Martyrs*, only three were said to have fallen ill in the wake of their deeds, to have become mad and died invoking devils or denying God. Leading killers in the Lyon Vespers of 1572 exhibited their bloody pourpoints in the streets and bragged of the numbers they had slain; their subsequent absolution by a papal legate appears a formal, political affair. In cases where Protestants returned to Mother Church, there may well have been some regret for smashing statues or assaulting priests, but here only as part of a whole pattern of "heretical" behavior. So long as rioters maintained a given religious commitment, they rarely displayed guilt or shame for their violence. By every sign, the crowds believed their actions legitimate.[41]

One reason for this conviction is that in some, though by no means all, religious riots, clerics and political officers were active members of the crowd, though not precisely in their official capacity. In Lyon in 1562, Pastor Jean Ruffy took part in the sack of the Cathedral of Saint Jean with a sword in his hand.[42] Catholic priests seem to have been in quite a few disturbances, as in Rouen in 1560, when priests and parishioners in a Corpus Christi parade broke into the houses of Protestants who had refused to do the procession honor.[43] (In other cases, the clergy was said to have been busy behind the scenes organizing the crowds.[44]) At Aix a band of Catholic rioters was headed by the First Consul of that city, and at Lyon in 1562 the merchant-publisher and Consul Jean de La Porte led a Protestant group to an assault on the cloister of Saint Just.[45] The fighting crowd of Protestants that "arrested" Catholics at Saint Médard's Church in 1561 had in its midst the chief officer of the "royal watch" in Paris. And among the image-smashers of Agen the same year was the town executioner. "It is my office to set fire," he said as he put the statues to the flames.[46] Finally, there is the well-known participation of some of the militia officers in the Saint Bartholomew's Day massacres in Paris and in the Lyon Vespers. Their murdering and sacking, as Janine Estèbe has pointed out for Paris, went beyond any informal encouragement that they had from the king and clearly beyond the official orders given them by the Bureau de la Ville.[47]

On the other hand, not all religious riots could boast of officers or clergy in the crowd, and other sources of legitimation must be sought. Here we must recognize what mixed cues were given out by priests and pastors in their sermons on heresy or idolatry. If we do not know whether to believe the Catholic priest Claude Haton in his claim that a Huguenot preacher at Sens told his congregation that "to exterminate papal vermin would be a great sacrifice to God," it is surely significant that iconoclastic riots in Gien and Rouen both occurred on May 3, 1562, after sermons on the text from Deuteronomy 12 with which I opened this essay.[48] However much Calvin and other pastors opposed such disturbances (preferring that all images and altars be removed soberly by the authorities), they nevertheless were always more ready to understand and excuse this violence than, say, that of a peasant revolt or of a journeymen's march. Perhaps, after all, the popular idol-smashing was the result of "an extraordinary power (*vertu*) from God." How else was it possible, says Jean Crespin about iconoclasm in the Netherlands in 1566, for a small number of men, women, and children, badly equipped and of modest condition, to demolish in four days what it would have taken many masons twice as long to do? How else to explain the fact that artisans, women, and children had been able to clean out fifty churches in Rouen in only twenty-four hours?[49] Pastor Pierre Viret may have similarly wondered about God's role in a crowd seizure of the cathedral at Nîmes in December 1561. Though he had opposed such actions, he was nevertheless willing to preach to the Calvinists in the church three days later.[50]

The role of Catholic preachers in legitimating popular violence was even more direct. If we do not know whether to believe the Protestant claim that Catholic preachers at Paris were telling their congregations in 1557 that Protestants ate babies, it is surely significant that, in the year of the attack on the rue St. Jacques conventicle, Catholic preachers did blame the loss of the battle of Saint Quentin on God's wrath at the presence of heretics in France.[51] In the next years, they held up Ahab and his wife Jezebel, and Belshazzar and others, as examples of the terrible end that would come to those who tolerated idolatry. Before a Catholic riot at the Cimetière des Innocents, Brother Jean de Han told his listeners in the church that they could not count on royal judges to punish Lutherans and would have to take matters into their own hands.[52] On St. Michael's Day 1572 at Bordeaux, a few days before the massacres there, the Jesuit Emond Auger preached on how the Angel of the Lord had already executed God's judgment in Paris, Orléans, and elsewhere, and would also do so in Bordeaux.[53] And if Protestant pastors could timidly wonder if divine power were not behind the extraordinary force of the iconoclasts,*

---

* Protestant writers also stressed divine intervention to show God's disapproval of Catholic rioters and violence. For instance, in Draguignan two Protestants killed by a crowd were found three months later, so it was claimed, with no sign of corruption in their bodies and with their wounds still fresh in appearance. A Catholic who had been guarding the corpses was killed by Protestant soldiers and his body instantly became rotten, and was eaten by crows and dogs. In Marennes (Charente-Maritime), a rich burgher who tried to prevent the holding of Protestant services and beat up one of

priests had no doubts that certain miraculous occurrences in the wake of Catholic riots were a sign of divine approval—such as a copper cross in Troyes that began to change color and cure people in 1561, the year of a riot in which Catholics bested Protestants, and the long-barren hawthorn tree at the Cimetière des Innocents that began to bloom from the beginning of the Saint Bartholomew's Day massacres.[54]

In all likelihood, however, there are sources for the legitimation of popular religious riot that come directly out of the experience of the local groups that often formed the nucleus of a crowd—the men and women who had worshiped together in the dangerous days of the night conventicles; the men in confraternities, in festive groups, in youth gangs, and in militia units. It should be remembered how often conditions in sixteenth-century cities required groups of the *menu peuple* to take the law into their own hands. Royal edicts themselves enjoined any person who saw a murder, theft, or other misdeed to ring the tocsin and chase after the criminal.[55] Canon law allowed certain priestly roles to laymen in times of emergency; an example of one was the midwife's responsibility to baptize a baby in danger of dying.[56] Also, the role of preaching the Gospel was often assumed by Protestant laymen in decades before the Reformed Church was set up. Talking about the Bible among themselves, some Calvinist city folk decided that private persons might be obliged to act independently of the magistrate in defense of religion, and even published a tract—*The Civil and Military Defense of the Innocents and of the Church of Christ*—in support of this view with Old Testament precedents.[57]

Finally, the very experience of singing the Psalms together in French in a large armed group intent on challenging the religious practices of the world around it, the very experience of being part of a Corpus Christi Day procession at a time when danger threat-

---

the Protestants died shortly afterward from apoplexy. This was viewed as the "hand of God" and led to the conversion of his children to the new religion. *Histoire ecclésiastique des Eglises Réformées au Royaume de France,* ed. G. Baum and E. Cunitz (Paris, 1883-89), 1: 428, 357.

ened the sanctity of the host—these processional experiences in themselves would feed a popular certitude that the group did indeed have the right on occasion to move into the realm of violence for the sake of religion.

[III]

What then of the occasions for religious riot? By "occasions" I do not mean here the specific things, such as the Saint Bartholomew's rumor of conspiracy to kill the king, that have triggered particular instances of religious riot. Nor do I mean anything as grand as theories of structural strain, relative deprivation among the people, or crises among the elite that might account for the timing of all riots. In fact, I am considering the chronological question of timing very little in this paper—that is, I am not asking why there are a cluster of religious disturbances in Lyon, say, in the early 1550's,[58] a cluster of religious disturbances throughout France in the early 1560's, and so on. I do not have the extensive data upon which to base such an analysis. Working from the crowd behavior itself, I have merely stressed the fact that religious riot is likely to occur when it is believed that religious and/or political authorities are failing in their duties or need help in fulfilling them.

All I would add in regard to the timing and triggers of religious riot is that a rise in grain prices does not seem to be a significant variable. For instance, the religious disturbances in Toulouse in the first five months of 1562 correspond to a period of grain prices that were the same as, or lower than, those of the preceding two years. The supply was surely more abundant there than during the hard times in the spring and early summer of 1557, when there was no religious disturbance.[59] The Catholic attack on the conventicle on the rue Saint Jacques in September 1557 occurred at a time when grain had dropped to a good low price in Paris and was plentiful. The Saint Médard riot at the end of 1561 took place when prices were rising but were far from what contemporaries would have thought a famine level.[60] As for the 1572 massacres, they occurred at a time of slowly rising grain prices, but not yet of serious dearth, with August-September prices in Paris being a little lower than those of October 1571, and in Toulouse lower than those of the immediately preceding summer months.[61] In short, grain prices are relevant to religious riot in France only in the general and indirect sense that the inflation of the last 40 years of the sixteenth century had an effect on many aspects of life, as did the Religious Wars themselves.* Perhaps it is only in this broad sense that they are part of the background to the Flemish icono-clastic movement of 1566 (I am here raising a query about the interpretation of Verlinden and his colleagues), the specific trigger for the riots being more likely, as Crespin claimed, the sudden upsurge in public Protestant preaching.[62] What are *specific* rises in grain prices correlated with in France? Why, with grain riots and penitential white processions to beg for rain.[63]

Questions of chronological timing apart, then, the occasion for most religious violence was during the time of religious worship or ritual and in the space which one or both groups were using for sacred purposes. There were exceptions, of course. Profana-tion of religious statues and paintings might occur at night, espe-cially in the early years when it was a question of a small number of Protestants sneaking into a church.[64] Widespread murder, as in the 1572 massacres, might occur anywhere—in the streets, in bedrooms. But much of the religious riot is timed to ritual, and the violence seems often a curious continuation of the rite.

Almost every type of public religious event has a disturbance associated with it. The sight of a statue of the Virgin at a cross-road or in a wall-niche provokes a Protestant group to mockery of those who reverence her. A fight ensues. Catholics hide in a house to entrap Huguenots who refuse to doff their hats to a

---

* A recent study of fifteenth-century Spain has shown how complex the relation was between a rise in food prices and anti-Semitic pogroms. Its author suggests that a rise in food prices is part of the *general* background for a variety of popular risings. The sharper the price rise, the more likely the dis-turbance was *not* to be "exclusively anti-Semitic in character." Angus Mac-Kay, "Popular Movements and Pogroms in Fifteenth-Century Castile," *Past and Present* 55 (May 1972): 58-59.

Virgin nearby, and then rush out and beat up the heretics.[65] Baptism: in Nemours, a Protestant family has its baby baptized on All Souls' Day according to the new Reformed rite. With the help of an aunt, a group of Catholics steals it away for rebaptism. A drunkard sees the father and the godfather and other Protestants discussing the event in the streets, claps his sabots and shouts, "Here are the Huguenots who have come to massacre us." A crowd assembles, the tocsin is rung, and a three-hour battle takes place.[66] Funeral: in Toulouse, at Easter time, a Protestant carpenter tries to bury his Catholic wife by the new Reformed rite. A Catholic crowd seizes the corpse and buries it. The Protestants dig it up and try to rebury her. The bells are rung, and with a great noise a Catholic crowd assembles with stones and sticks. Fighting and sacking ensue.[67]

Religious services: a Catholic mass is the occasion for an attack on the host or the interruption of a sermon, which then leads to a riot.[68] Protestant preaching in a home attracts large Catholic crowds at the door, who stone the house or otherwise threaten the worshipers.[69] In the years when the Reformed services are public, the rivalry of the rites becomes graphic. At Saint Médard's Church, the Vesper bells are rung to drown out the pastor's sermon nearby; at Provins, the Huguenots sing their Psalms to drown out the mass.[70]

But these encounters are as nothing compared to the disturbances that cluster around processional life. Corpus Christi Day, with its crowds, colored banners, and great crosses, was the chance for Protestants *not* to put rugs in front of their doors; for Protestant women to sit ostentatiously in their windows spinning; for heroic individuals, like the painter Denis de Vallois in Lyon, to throw themselves on the "God of paste" so as "to destroy him in every parish in the world." Corpus Christi Day was the chance for a procession to turn into an assault on, and slaughter of, those who had so offended the Catholic faith, its participants shouting, as in Lyon in 1561, "For the flesh of God, we must kill all the Huguenots."[71] A Protestant procession was a parade of armed men and women in their dark clothes going off to services at their temple or outside the city gates, singing Psalms and spiritual songs that to Catholic ears sounded like insults against the church and her sacraments. It was an occasion for children to throw stones, for an exchange of scandalous words—"idolaters," "devils from the Pope's purgatory," "Huguenot heretics, living like dogs"— and then finally for fighting.[72] Sometimes the two processions encountered each other, as in Sens in 1562. The Calvinists would not give way and insisted upon passing through the center of the Catholic procession. The groups confronted each other again after services, and the Catholics, aided by processions from peasant villages, prevailed in a bloody battle.[73]

The occasions that express most concisely the contrast between the two religious groups, however, are those in which a popular festive Catholicism took over the streets with dancing, masks, banners, costumes, and music—"lascivious abomination," according to the Protestants. In Lyon, when Catholics did their traditional summer dancing on St. Peter's Day 1565, the Huguenots attacked them in a riot that led eventually to the exile of Pierre Viret and another pastor from the city. In Montpellier in the summer of 1561, the confraternities organized Sunday processions of hundreds of men, women, and children with *pains bénits* ("blessed loaves of bread")—dancing, jumping, and crying "in spite of the Huguenots we dance."[74]

But festivities led to more than spite and intimidation. For Mardi Gras at Issoudun in 1562, a Catholic group organized a dramatic costumed dance for thirteen pilgrims, thirteen reapers, thirteen wine-harvesters and thirteen tithe-collectors, all armed with large macabre tools. The Protestants got hold of the scenario for this grisly carnival and were able to get the players arrested.[75] In Pamiers in 1566, however, the festive youth society, with its popes, emperors, bishops, and abbots, was able to dance its Pentecostal dance to the end. The Calvinists, who had stoned earlier dances, tried to prevent the affair, but the Catholic group insisted. "If [the heretics] can preach secretly, then we can dance—or it will cost five hundred heads." After a procession with relics and a silver statue of St. Anthony, the dancing began, three by three, with tambourines and minstrels. When they got to the quarter where Pastor Du Moulin was preaching, the song turned into "kill, kill," and serious fighting began that was to divide the town for three days. "It's a long time since I was up to my elbows in Huguenot blood," one of the dancers said. He was to be disappointed, for this time it was the Huguenots who won.[76]

These occasions for religious riot show us how characteristic was the scenario for the Paris St. Bartholomew's Day Massacre. A marriage—one of the great rites of passage, but here, as with the baptism of Nemours and the burial at Toulouse, conflict over whether its form should be Catholic or Protestant—and then wedding masques of all kinds. In one, later seen as an allegory of coming events, the king and his brothers prevent wandering knights from entering Paradise and are pulled down to Hell by demons.[77] Soon after, as in Pamiers, the festivity turned into a rite of violence.

[IV]

As with liturgical rites, there were some differences between the rites of violence of Catholic and Protestant crowds. The good Calvinist authors of the *Histoire ecclésiastique* went so far as to claim that outside of the murder of a certain Seigneur de Fumel, killed in the Agenois "not for religion but for his tyrannies," "those of the Reformed Religion made war only on images and altars, which do not bleed, while those of the Roman religion spilled blood with every kind of cruelty."[78] Though there is some truth in this distinction, Protestant rioters did in fact kill and injure people, and not merely in self-defense; and Catholic rioters did destroy religious property. At the Patriarche garden in Paris, at Vassy, at Senlis, Catholics smashed the pulpits and benches used in Reformed worship; at Amiens they went on to burn them.[79] As houses that had been used for Protestant worship in Meaux and Paris were ordered to be razed by Parlementary decree, so in Lyon in 1568 a Catholic crowd razed the Protestant Temple de Paradis, which hundreds of psalm-singing men, women, and children had erected only a few years before (see Plate 14).[80] *Both* Protestant and Catholic crowds destroyed books. The Catholic target was especially the French Bibles that they had so often seen burned publicly by the authorities in the 1540's and 1550's.[81] The Calvinist targets were especially the priests' manuals, the missals, and the breviaries, which Protestant writers like Viret had already desecrated in gross and comic satire.[82]

Nevertheless, when all this is said, the iconoclastic Calvinist crowds still come out as the champions in the destruction of religious property ("with more than Turkish cruelty," said a priest). This was not only because the Catholics had more physical accessories to their rite, but also because the Protestants sensed much more danger and defilement in the *wrongful use of material objects*. In Pamiers, the Catholic vicar might drop his Black Virgin of Foix when she failed to bring good weather; but then he tenderly repaired her broken neck with an iron pin. When the Protestants found her, they promptly burned the head in Pamiers and the body in Foix.[83]

In bloodshed, the Catholics are the champions (remember we are talking of the actions of Catholic and Protestant crowds, not of their armies). I think this is owing not only to their being in the long run the stronger party numerically in most cities, but also to their having a greater sense of *the persons of heretics* as sources of danger and defilement. Thus, injury and murder were a preferred mode of purifying the body social.

Furthermore, the preferred targets for physical attack differ in the Protestant and Catholic cases. As befitting a movement intending to overthrow a thousand years of clerical "tyranny" and "pollution," the Protestants' targets were primarily priests, monks, and friars. That their ecclesiastical victims were usually unarmed (as Catholic critics hastened to point out) did not make them any less harmful in Protestant eyes, or any more immune from the wrath of God.[84] Lay people were sometimes attacked by Protestant crowds, too, examples being the festive dancers who were stoned at Pamiers and Lyon and the worshipers who were killed at Saint Médard's Church.[85] But there is nothing that quite resembles the style and extent of the slaughter of the 1572 massacres. The Catholic crowds were, of course, happy to catch a pastor when they could,[86] but the death of any heretic would help in the cause of cleansing France of these perfidious sowers of disorder and disunion. Indeed, although the number of women killed by Protestant crowds seems to have been very small, observers' reports[87] show that about one out of ten people killed by Catholic crowds in the provinces in 1572 was a woman (one of those "presumptuous" females we have considered in Chapter 3), and the ratio was higher in Paris.*

Clearly, crowds that attacked unarmed priests and unarmed women were not trying to destroy only the physically powerful. But is Janine Estèbe right in suggesting that the 1572 massacres were also an expression of class hatred, by which she means a

---

* Estimates in Jean Crespin's *Histoire des Martyrs* of persons killed in the 1572 massacres give for Rouen about 550 men and about 50 women; for Orléans, 1,800 adult men and 150 adult women. No female deaths were reported from the Lyon Vespers. So many women were victims at Paris that word went out on August 28 or 29 that no more women were to be killed, especially pregnant women. Even here, the listings show many fewer female deaths than male. The same is true for earlier crowd actions by Catholics, as in Provence in 1562 (see n. 87). It is clear from these estimates that pregnant women could not have been the *preferred* targets, though they obviously were not spared. Whether they were the "choice victims" (*victimes de choix*) of Catholic crowds, as Estèbe claims (*Tocsin*, p. 197), I do not know. She associates this, as well as the castration of male corpses, with an attempt to extinguish "a foreign race, a hated and cursed race." As suggested above, I find no evidence of the perception of the Huguenots as a "race." By their heresy, they appeared outsiders and finally nonhuman to their killers, but this is not a *racial* distinction. See further below on the castration of corpses. As for Protestant killing of women, Catholic sources (see n. 87) report women killed by the Huguenots in the Saint Médard massacre at Paris, in the May events at Toulouse in 1562, and in the diocese of Angoulême. Nuns were reported raped at Montauban in 1562. On the whole, accounts of Protestant crowd action say little about assaults on females. With *statues* of the Virgin and female saints, it is another matter.

rising of the people against the rich Huguenots?[88] We can even broaden her question and ask whether it is true of other Catholic disturbances and of Protestant riots as well. As Charles Tilly and James Rule have asked in *Measuring Political Upheaval*, is the "isomorphy" of these disturbances high or low, by which they mean is there a high or low "degree of correspondence between the divisions separating the antagonists in a . . . disturbance and those prevailing in the social system within which the disturbance occurs"?[89]

Though only extensive quantitative research could establish the point, it seems to me that Estèbe's view does not hold for these *urban* disturbances. To be sure, pillaging played its role in all riots. To be sure, the Catholic crowds who threw slime and shouted *"putains"* at the Protestant noblewomen being led from the rue Saint Jacques conventicle to prison in 1557 were savoring social resentment as well as religious hatred. So probably were the embroiderer's journeyman who slew a prominent jewel merchant in 1572 at Paris and the cutler who slew a lawyer in Orléans.[90] For Protestants at Valence in 1562 who killed the Sire de La Motte Gondrin, lieutenant governor of the Dauphiné, there were political grievances to reinforce religious and social complaint.[91]

Nevertheless, despite such individual cases of "high isomorphy," the overall picture in these urban religious riots is not one of the "people" slaying the rich.[92] Protestant crowds expressed no preference for killing or assaulting powerful prelates over simple priests. As for Catholic crowds, contemporary listings of their victims in the 1572 massacres show that artisans, the *menu peuple*, are represented in significant numbers. In Lyon, for instance, in a list of 141 males killed in the Vespers, 88 were artisans, 34 were merchants, and six were lawyers.[93] Reports from other cities give a similar spread, as can be seen in Table 1. Only in Orléans were more merchants reported to have been killed than artisans, whereas in Rouen and Meaux the *menu peuple* outnumbered the wealthier merchants among the victims many times over. The distributions are all the more significant because the prominent and

TABLE I

Social-Occupational Distribution of Male Victims
in Contemporary Listings of the 1572 Massacres

City	Nobles	Lawyers, officers	Mer- chants	Teach- ers, pastors	Arti- sans	Un- skilled, ser- vants	Occu- pation un- known	Total
Bourges	—	7	6	—	8	—	2	23
Meaux	—	5	13	—	10[a]	1	—	29
Troyes	—	1	11	—	22	2	—	36
Orléans	2	15	50	2	47	11	15	142
Rouen	3	9	18	3	119	3	31	186
Lyon	—	6	34	3	88	5	5	141
Paris	36	14	13	5	40	2	11	121

SOURCES: For Lyon, see note 93; for other cities, Jean Crespin, *Histoire des Martyrs*, ed. D. Benoît (Toulouse, 1885–89), III.

NOTE: Nobles are here defined as persons listed with the title "Sieur de" in Crespin. Some of the lawyers and high officers killed may also have been ennobled.

[a] The names of ten artisans are listed for Meaux, after which the author says "[and] other artisans to the number of 200 or more." This figure is of doubtful accuracy, but it does reflect the impression contemporaries had of the level of the population hit by the massacres.

rich who were slain were especially likely to be remarked. If we had fuller evidence about the massacres, it would doubtless multiply the names of victims of modest background. As I show in detail in another place, Catholic and Protestant movements in French cities up to 1572 cut vertically through the social structure, but had each a distinctive occupational distribution.* On the basis of limited evidence, that distribution seems to be fairly well reflected in the victims of crowd action, and (as we will see more fully in a moment) in the makeup of the crowds. Only the most vulnerable of the urban poor—the *gagnedenier*, that is; the unskilled, the day laborers, and the jobless—are not among the killers or the killed. Neither committed to the Calvinist cause nor well integrated into the Catholic city parish, these "*bélîtres*" (rascals) appear only after the violence is over, stolidly robbing clothing from the corpses.[94]

* In my forthcoming book on Lyon in the Reformation, an analysis of the social and vocational distribution of several thousand male Protestants there in the period up to 1572 shows them to be drawn from the Consular elite, the notables, and the *menu peuple* in numbers roughly proportional to their distribution in the population at large; but the analysis shows them to

Is popular religious violence in sixteenth-century France never then correlated in a *systematic* way with socioeconomic conflict? Not when it is among the city folk, who account for most of the disturbances; but when peasants raise their arms for the faith, the relationship is more likely to exist. How else to explain the dispatch with which peasant pilgrims fell upon the Huguenot burghers of Sens, surprising even the urban Catholics by their initiative? And when Protestant peasants in the Agenois pursued their persecuting lord, the Seigneur of Fumel, they were shouting, "Murderer! Tyrant!" Even Catholic peasants joined in the siege of his chateau.[95]

Before turning to the composition of the urban crowds, let us look a little further at what I have called their rites of violence. Is there any way we can order the terrible, concrete details of filth, shame, and torture that are reported from both Protestant and Catholic riots? I would suggest that they can be reduced to a repertory of actions, derived from the Bible, from the liturgy, from the action of political authority, or from the traditions of popular folk justice, intended to purify the religious community and humiliate the enemy and thus make him less harmful.

The religious significance of destruction by water or fire is clear

have come especially from the newer or more skilled occupations, occupations where the literacy rate was higher, or occupations (such as tavern-keeping) that had been transformed by the urban developments of the early sixteenth century. At the top of urban society, it is the new elite rather than the more established elite that tends to produce Protestants (in Lyon, therefore, among the Consular families it is the wealthy merchants rather than the lawyers who tend to become Protestant). This vocational distribution is, of course, not perfectly expressed in the victims of the massacres, since so many factors operated in the choice of any one person as a victim. For instance, very few persons from the publishing trade were killed in the Vespers at Lyon (the *libraires* Jean Honoré, Mathieu Penin, and Jean Vassin, the bookbinder Mathurin Le Cler, and the proofreader Jean de Saint Clément), though a very large percentage of the industry had been Protestant in the 1560's and many masters and publishers still were so in 1572. It is my impression that in other cities, members of the publishing trade, though certainly found among the victims, were underrepresented relative to their presence in the Reformed Church. This can probably be explained by the special relations among the men in the trade or by their absence from France.

enough. The rivers that receive so many Protestant corpses are not merely convenient mass graves, they are temporarily a kind of holy water, an essential feature of Catholic rites of exorcism. The fire that razes the house of a Protestant apothecary in Montpellier leaves behind it not the smell of death, of the heretic whom the crowd had hanged, but of spices, lingering in the air for days, like incense. If Protestants have rejected holy water and incense, they still follow Deuteronomy in accepting fire as a sacred means of purification.[96]

Let us take a more difficult case, the troubling case of the desecration of corpses. This is primarily an action of Catholic crowds in the sixteenth century. Protestant crowds could be very cruel indeed in torturing living priests, but paid little attention to them when they were dead.[97] (Perhaps this is related to the Protestant rejection of Purgatory and prayers for the dead: the souls of the dead experience immediately Christ's presence or the torments of the damned, and thus the dead body is no longer so dangerous or important an object to the living. Popular Protestant poetry represented priests as ghouls who fed off the dead roasted in Purgatory.[98]) What interested Protestants was digging up bones that were being treated as sacred objects by Catholics and perhaps burning them, after the fashion of Josiah in 1 Kings.[99] The Catholics, however, were not content with burning or drowning heretical corpses. That was not cleansing enough. The bodies had to be weakened and humiliated further. To an eerie chorus of "strange whistles and hoots," they were thrown to the dogs like Jezebel, they were dragged through the streets, they had their genitalia and internal organs cut away, which were then hawked through the city in a ghoulish commerce.[100]

Let us also take the embarrassing case of the desecration of religious objects by filthy and disgusting means. It is the Protestants, as we have seen, who are concerned about objects, who are trying to show that Catholic objects of worship have no magical power. It is not enough to cleanse by swift and energetic demolition, not enough to purify by a great public burning of the images, as in

Albiac, with the children of the town ceremonially reciting the
Ten Commandments around the fire.[101] The line between the sacred and the profane was also redrawn by throwing the sacred
host to the dogs, by roasting the crucifix upon a spit, by using holy
oil to grease one's boots, and by leaving human excrement* on
holy-water basins and other religious objects.[102]

And what of the living victims? Catholics and Protestants humiliated them by techniques borrowed from the repertory of folk
justice. Catholic crowds lead Protestant women through the streets
with muzzles on—a popular punishment for the scold in some
parts of Europe—or with a crown of thorns.[103] A form of charivari
is used, where the noisy throng humiliates its victim by making
him ride backward on an ass. In Blois in 1562, the Catholics did
this to a Protestant saddler, poking him with a pike and shouting,
"Oh, don't touch him, he belongs to the Queen Mother." In Montauban, a priest was ridden backward on an ass, his chalice in one
hand, his host in the other, and his missal at an end of a halberd.
At the end of his ride, he must crush his host and burn his own
vestments. And, just as in the festive parade on an ass of henpecked husbands it was sometimes necessary to get a neighbor to
replace the husband, so sometimes a Protestant had to replace the
priest. Dressed in holy vestments, he would be led through the
streets pretending to say mass, while the crowd with him sang in
derision *Te Deum Laudamus* or a requiem.[104]

With such actions, the crowds seem to be moving back and forth
between the rites of violence and the realm of comedy. Are we at
a Mardi Gras game, with its parodies and topsy-turvy mockery?
At Lyon, a Protestant, in the midst of sacking the Church of Saint
Irénée, dresses up as the Saint with his episcopal ring around his
neck. At Rouen, the host is paraded at the end of a Rogation Day's

---

* Excrement is also thrown by Catholic crowds at Protestants in several
places (Crespin, *Martyrs*, 2: 545; 3: 203-4, 672). In an extraordinary episode
in Toulouse, Protestants hiding in the sewers along the river were flushed out,
covered with excrement, by great streams of water poured into the *cloacas* by
Catholics, and were then drowned (*Hist. eccl.*, 3: 19).

lance with a dragon on it: "The dragon has eaten the host!"[105] At Mâcon in 1562, the familiar blessing from Numbers 6: 24-26 is parodied as Protestants are slain: "The lord God of Huguenots keep you, the great Devil bless you, the Lord make his face to shine upon you who play the dead." Murder finally began to be called a "farce" in Mâcon,* the "farce of Saint Point," named after the lieutenant governor. The game was to go with some women after a party and get one or two Protestant prisoners from jail, have the ladies chat pleasantly with them as they walked to the Saône bridge, and then drown them.[106]

These episodes disclose to us the underlying function of the rites of violence. As with the "games" of Christ's tormentors, which hide from them the full knowledge of what they do, so these charades and ceremonies hide from sixteenth-century rioters a full knowledge of what they are doing. Like the legitimation for religious riot examined earlier in this essay, they are part of the "conditions for guilt-free massacre," to use a phrase from a recent study of violence in our own day.[107] The crucial fact that the killers must forget is that their victims are human beings. These harmful people in the community—the evil priest or hateful heretic—have already been transformed for the crowd into "vermin" or "devils." The rites of religious violence complete the process of dehumanization. So in Meaux, where Protestants were being slaughtered with butchers' cleavers, a living victim was trundled to his death in a wheelbarrow while the crowd cried, "vinegar, mustard." And the vicar of the parish of Fouquebrune in the Angoumois was attached with the oxen to a plow and died from Protestant blows as he pulled.[108]

---

* There are other examples of renaming objects or actions of violence. Protestants in Béziers and Montpellier called the clubs with which they hit priests and religious and other Catholic enemies *épousettes* or "feather-dusters." Catholics in Mont-de-Marsan and its region used the same term for the clubs with which they hit Protestants. At Agen, the gibbet on which Protestants were hanged was called the "Consistory." At Rouen, Catholic crowds referred to killing Huguenots as "accommodating" them. See n. 106.

[v]

What kinds of people made up the crowds that performed the range of acts we have examined in this essay? First, they were not by and large the alienated rootless poor that people the pages of Norman Cohn's *Pursuit of the Millennium*.[109] A large percentage of men in Protestant iconoclastic riots and in the crowds of Catholic killers in 1572 were characterized as artisans. Sometimes the crowds included other men from the lower orders, as in 1562 in Gaillac, where Catholic boatmen from Montauban participated in the May massacres, and in Dieppe, where Protestant sailors entered the churches at night to smash statues. More often, the social composition of the crowds extended upward to encompass merchants, notaries, and lawyers, as well as the clerics whose role has already been mentioned.[110] Depending on the size,* extent, and occasion of the disturbance, the leaders of the crowd were sometimes artisans themselves, but frequently a mixed group. Iconoclastic disturbances, unless carried out by Protestant nobles and their soldiers, were ordinarily led by the *menu peuple*, but notables led the Protestant rioters into Saint Médard's Church in 1561. Of twenty leaders of the 1572 massacres at Orléans, three were lawyers, eight were merchants, and others were various kinds of craftsmen—tanners, butchers, and candlemakers.[111]

In addition, there was significant participation by two other groups of people who, though not rootless and alienated, had a more marginal relationship to political power than did lawyers, merchants, or even male artisans—namely, city women and teen-age boys. As the wives of craftsmen marched with their husbands

* The crowds ranged in size from a handful of people to several hundred (Crespin, *Martyrs*, 3: 726). A large urban disturbance of some duration might involve a total of a few thousand persons on both sides, but never an entire city population. Many people merely watched; still others stayed at home. In a forthcoming study of "Reformed Preaching and Iconoclasm in the Netherlands in 1566," Phyllis Mack Crew makes an interesting analysis of the political and religious situation there that produced such small iconoclastic crowds.

in the great psalm-singing parades, so they were always busy in the iconoclastic riots of the Protestants. Sometimes they were active in other ways, as in Pamiers, where a bookseller's wife set fire to the house of the leading enemy of the Huguenots there, and in Toulouse, where La Broquière, a solicitor's wife, fought Catholics with firearms.[112] As the wives of Catholic tradesmen marched with their husbands in Corpus Christi Day processions, so they participated in Catholic religious disturbances. They shouted insults at a Protestant funeral in Montauban and threw mire at a minister in Vassy, screaming, "Kill him, kill the evil-doer who has caused so many deaths"; but their most extreme violence seems directed against other women. At Aix-en-Provence in 1572, a group of butcher women tormented a Protestant woman, the wife of a bookseller, finally hanging her from a pine tree that had marked a meeting place for Protestant worship.[113]

Adolescent males and even boys aged ten to twelve played a strikingly important role in both Catholic and Protestant crowds. In Lyon and Castelnaudary in 1562, *enfants* stoned Protestant worshipers on their way to services. In several towns in Provence —Marseille, Toulon, and elsewhere—Catholic youths stoned Protestants to death and burned them. The reputation of the adolescents in Sens and Provins was so frightening that a member of a well-known Huguenot family was afraid to walk through the streets lest the *enfants de Provins* massacre him.[114] In Toulouse, Catholic students took part in the massacres of 1572, and a decade earlier Protestant students had had the university in an uproar, whistling and banging in lectures when the canon law or the "old religion" was mentioned. In Poitiers in 1559, and again in 1562, Protestant youngsters from ten to twelve and students took the initiative in smashing statues and overturning altars. Indeed, youths are mentioned as part of almost all the great iconoclastic disturbances—in the Netherlands, in Rouen, and elsewhere.[115]

I am struck here by the similarity between the license allowed youth to do violence in religious riot and the festive license allowed adolescents in the youth-abbeys in villages and small towns to act as the conscience of the community in matters of domestic discord. As young teenagers and children participated in the processional life of, say, Rouen ("their prayers are of great merit before God, especially because they are pure and clean in their conscience and without malice," noted a Rouennais priest) and led some of the great League penitential processions in Paris in 1589, so Catholic adolescents moved into religious violence without much criticism from their elders.[116] In the Protestant case, where sons might sometimes disagree about religion with their fathers and where the revolt is in part against the paternal authority of the clergy, youthful violence seems to have more of the character of generational conflict. But ultimately Calvinism, too, was a movement cutting across generational lines, within which adolescents or artisans sometimes took the early initiative in open militant action. Thus in Lyon in 1551, the first public psalm-singing marches were organized by printers' journeymen, and in Montpellier in 1560-61 it was the "young people" who first invited a minister to the city and began public psalm-singing in French in front of the city hall.[117]

Finally, as this essay has already suggested, the crowds of Catholics and Protestants, including those bent on deadly tasks, were not an inchoate mass, but showed many signs of organization. Even with riots that had little or no planning behind them, the event was given some structure by the situation of worship or the procession that was the occasion for many disturbances. In other cases, planning in advance led to lists of targets and ways of identifying friends or fellow rioters (white crosses on Catholic doors in Mâcon in 1562; red bonnets worn by the killers in the Bande Cardinale in Bordeaux in 1572; passwords and slogans— "Long live the Cross," "The Wolf," "Long live the Gospel").[118] Existing organizations could provide the basis for subsequent religious disturbance; these might be confraternities and festive youth societies for Catholics; and for both Protestants and Catholics, units of the militia and craft groupings.[119]

Zeal for violent purification also led to new organizations. Sometimes the model was a military one, as in the companies of Catholic artisans in Autun, Auxerre, and Le Mans raised by the lifting of an ensign; the "marching bands" organized in Béziers by both Protestants and Catholics; and the *dizaines* set up by the Reformed Church of Montauban in 1561.[120] Sometimes the model was a youth group,* as in the case of a band of young unmarried lesser nobles in Champagne, who went around terrorizing Catholics.[121] The creation which best expresses the spirit of religious riot, however, is the band of the Sieur de Flassans in Aix-en-Provence. This nobleman, First Consul of Aix, in 1562 organized a troop of *menu peuple*, butchers among them, and monks, to seek out Protestants in the area and stone their houses, shout at them, and kill or imprison them. They wore rosaries and special feathered hats with white crosses on them; they sang special songs against the Huguenots; they carried an ensign with the Pope's keys upon it; and they went everywhere led by a Franciscan with a great wooden cross.[122]

That such splendor and order should be put to violent uses is a disturbing fact. Disturbing, too, is the whole subject of religious violence. How does a historian talk about a massacre of the magnitude of St. Bartholomew's Day? One approach is to view extreme religious violence as an extraordinary event, the product of frenzy, of the frustrated and paranoiac primitive mind of the people. As Estèbe has said, "The procedures used by the killers of Saint Bartholomew's Day came back from the dawn of

---

* The most interesting new youth group formed in this period was the Whistlers (*Sifflars*) of Poitiers—so called from a whistle the members wore around their necks. Founded among students around 1561, it initially mocked both religions. Initiates had to swear by flesh, belly, death, and "the worthy double head, stuffed with Relics" and by all the Divinity in this pint of wine, that they would be devoted Whistlers, and that instead of going to Protestant service, mass, or Vespers, they would go twice a day to a brothel, etc. The group grew to include some 64 youths and became especially hostile to the Reformed Church and its services, perhaps because of Reformed hostility to it. Its members began to go around armed. *Hist. eccl.*, 1: 844-45.

time; the collective unconscious had buried them within itself, they sprang up again in the month of August 1572."[123] Though there are clearly resemblances between the purification rites of primitive tribes and those used in sixteenth-century religious riots, this essay has suggested that one does not need to look so far as the "collective unconscious" to explain this fact, nor does one need to regard the 1572 massacres as an isolated phenomenon.

A second approach sees such violence as a more usual part of social behavior, but explains it as a somewhat pathological product of certain kinds of child-rearing, economic deprivation, or status loss. This essay has assumed that conflict is perennial in social life, though the forms and strength of the accompanying violence vary, and that religious violence is intense because it connects intimately with the fundamental values and self-definition of a community. The violence is explained not in terms of how crazy, hungry, or sexually frustrated the violent people are (though they may sometimes have such characteristics), but in terms of the goals of their actions and in terms of the roles and patterns of behavior allowed by their culture. Religious violence is related here less to the pathological than to the normal.

Thus, in sixteenth-century France, we have seen crowds taking on the role of priest, pastor, or magistrate to defend doctrine or purify the religious community—either to maintain its Catholic boundaries and structure, or to re-form relations within it. We have seen that popular religious violence could receive legitimation from different features of political and religious life, as well as from the group identity of the people in the crowds. The targets and character of crowd violence differed somewhat between Catholics and Protestants, depending on their perception of the source of danger and on their religious sensibility. But in both cases, religious violence had a connection in time, place, and form with the life of worship, and the violent actions themselves were drawn from a store of punitive or purificatory traditions current in sixteenth-century France.

In this context, the cruelty of crowd action in the 1572 massacres was not an exceptional occurrence. St. Bartholomew was certainly a bigger affair than, say, the Saint Médard's riot; it had more explicit sanction from political authority, it had elaborate networks of communication at the top level throughout France, and it took a more terrible toll in deaths. Perhaps its most unusual feature was that, in contrast to earlier attacks, this one did not see the Protestants fight back.[124] But on the whole, it still fits into a pattern of sixteenth-century religious disturbance.

This inquiry also points to a more general conclusion. Even in the extreme case of religious violence, crowds do not act in a mindless way. They will to some degree have a sense that what they are doing is legitimate, the occasions will relate somehow to the defense of their cause, and their violent behavior will have some structure to it—here dramatic and ritual. But the rites of violence are not the rights of violence in any *absolute* sense. They simply remind us that if we try to increase safety and trust within a community, try to guarantee that the violence it generates will take less destructive and cruel forms, then we must think less about pacifying "deviants" and more about changing the central values.

1. Goddess of the printers' journeymen of Lyon, 1594

2. Emblem of the Aumône-Générale of Lyon, 1539

3. Float of the Abbé des Conards of Rouen, 1539

4. Distribution of bread and money by the Aumône-Générale of Lyon, 1539

5. Mock coin of the Baron of the rue Neuve, Lyon, 1596, with device *"Nostre iustice regnera en tous temps"*

6. Chariot of Mère Folle of Dijon, about 1610

7. Parade on an ass of a
husband beaten by his wife,
Langres, ca. 1609

8. Charivari from a manu-
script of the *Roman de
Fauvel*, early 14th c.

9. Husband-dominators. (*a*) German playing card by Peter Floetner, ca. 1520. (*b*) Engraving by Martin Treu, ca. 1540-43. (*c*) French broadsheet, Orléans, 1650. (*d*) French engraving, 1690

10. Woman makes fools of men, by the Petrarch-Master of Augsburg, ca. 1526

Phyllis riding Aristotle, by Hans Baldung, alias Grien, 1513.

12. Dialogue of Solomon and Marcolf, late 15th c., probably French

13. Skimmington Ride, by William Hogarth, ca. 1726

14. Protestants at worship, Lyon, mid-1560's

. Author portrait of the midwife
ouise Bourgeois, 1608

16. Author portrait of the reckonmaster Milles de Norry, 1574

. Catholic view of Protestant crowd violence in France, late 16th c.

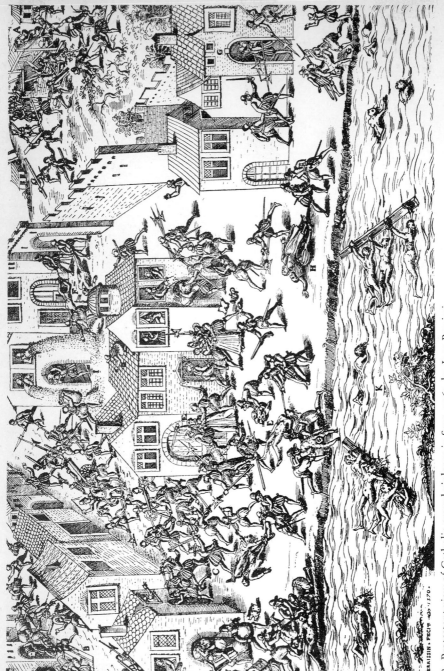

18. Protestant view of Catholic crowd violence in Sens, 1562, by Jean Perrissin

Printing and the People

Here are some voices from the sixteenth century. "The time has come . . . for women to apply themselves to the sciences and disciplines." Thus the ropemaker's daughter Louise Labé addresses her sex when her collected poems are printed in Lyon in 1556. "And if one of us gets to the point where she can put her ideas in writing, then take pains with it and don't be reluctant to accept the glory." Ten years later in Cambrai, a Protestant linen-weaver explains to his judges about the book in his life: "I was led to knowledge of the Gospel by . . . my neighbor, who had a Bible printed at Lyon and who taught me the Psalms by heart. . . . The two of us used to go walking in the fields Sundays and feast days, conversing about the Scriptures and the abuses of priests." And listen to the printers' journeymen of Paris and Lyon in 1572, in a brief they printed to convince Parlement and public that they needed better treatment from their employers: "Printing [is] an invention so admirable, . . . so honorable in its dignity, and profitable above all others to the French. Paris and Lyon furnish the whole of Christendom with books in every language." And yet "the Publishers and master Printers . . . use every stratagem to oppress . . . the Journeymen, who do the biggest and best part of the work of Printing." And finally, Pierre Tolet, doctor of medicine, justifying in 1540 his translation of some Greek texts into French, printed for the use of surgeons' journeymen: "If you want

a servant to follow your orders, you can't give them in an unknown tongue."[1]

These quotations suggest the several and complex ways in
which printing entered into popular life in the sixteenth century,
setting up new networks of communication, facilitating new
options for the people, and also providing new means of controlling the people. Can this be true? Could printing have mattered
that much to *the people* in a period when literacy was still so low?
How can one detect its influence? And what do I mean anyway by
"popular" and "the people"?

Indeed, these words were ambiguous in sixteenth-century literate usage, as in our own. On the one hand, "the people" could
refer to all the natives in the kingdom (*le peuple françoys*) or the
body of citizenry and inhabitants to which a law was promul-
gated. On the other hand, the word could refer to a more limited
but still large population: those who were commoners, not noble;
of modest means or poor, not wealthy; unschooled, not learned.
For Claude de Seyssel in his *Grand' Monarchie* of 1519, the "little
people" lived in both the town and the countryside, and were
those who worked the land and those who carried on the crafts
and lesser mysteries.[2] Recent studies of popular culture in the
seventeenth and eighteenth centuries have used "people" in de
Seyssel's sense, but have stressed peasants more than city-dwellers.
Geneviève Bollème has talked of the *"petites gens"*; Robert Mandrou has been concerned with "popular milieus," especially in the
countryside.[3]

The connection between these milieus and the printed book has
been considered in several ways. First, there are those studies that
take "popular literature" as their source material and make a
thematic analysis of its contents. Lewis B. Wright's *Middle-Class
Culture in Elizabethan England* (1935) is the classic example of
such an undertaking for a literate urban grouping comprising
merchants, tradesmen, and skilled artisans. Robert Mandrou's
subject has been the blue-covered books that were peddled out
of Troyes in the seventeenth and eighteenth centuries to villages

over a wide geographical area, whereas Geneviève Bollème has examined a large sample of French almanacs. Their goal has been to discover not so much new or continuing patterns of communication, but rather "the outlook of the average citizen" (Wright), or a popular "vision of the world" (Mandrou). Why this confidence in inferring from the book its readers' outlook? Because, so it is argued, the Elizabethan literature was written "for or by the plain citizen"; because the publishers of the *Bibliothèque bleue* stayed in close touch through their peddlers with village needs and tastes.[4]

In establishing the characteristics of a body of printed literature, these studies have been invaluable and even surprising. For disclosing the outlook of a given social group, though, they have some methodological drawbacks. Popular books are not necessarily written by *petites gens*. Master André Le Fournier, author of a 1530 compilation of household recipes and cosmetics for women, was a regent of the Faculty of Medicine at Paris,[5] and he was by no means the only university graduate to engage in such an enterprise. Nor are popular books bought and read only by *petites gens*. The *Grand Calendrier et compost des bergers*, for instance, the archetype of the French almanac, was read perhaps by countryman but surely by king. François Ier had a copy in the royal collection, and a mid-sixteenth-century edition, now at the Houghton Library, belonged to the king's advocate at Sens.[6] The *Tresor des povres*, a traditional collection of medical remedies, was owned in sixteenth-century Paris by a councillor's wife and a bookbinder.[7]

Finally, it is especially important to realize that people do not necessarily agree with the values and ideas in the books they read. For instance, M. Mandrou concludes from the fairy stories and saints' lives in the *Bibliothèque bleue* that it functioned as escape literature for the peasants, an obstacle to the understanding of social and political realities. Perhaps. But without independent evidence, can we be sure of how a rural audience took its tales of marvels, especially at a period when people might dress up as ghosts to teach children a lesson or might protect peasant rebels by saying they were "fairies" who came from time to time?[8] When a peasant read or was read to, it was not the stamping of a literal message on a blank sheet; it was the varied motion of "a strange top" (to use Jean-Paul Sartre's metaphor for the literary object), set to turning only by the combined effort of author and reader.[9]

Thus we can best understand the connections between printing and the people if we do two things: first, if we supplement thematic analysis of texts with evidence about audiences that can provide context for the meaning and uses of books; second, if we consider a printed book not merely as a source for ideas and images, but as a carrier of relationships. The data to support such an approach are scattered in the pages of the original editions themselves; in studies of literacy and dialects, book ownership and book prices, authorship and publication policy; and in sources on the customs and associational life of peasants and artisans. The theory to assist such an approach can be found in part in the work of Jack Goody and his collaborators on the implications of literacy for traditional societies—especially in their discussion of the relations between those who live on the margins of literacy and those who live at its center. Additional theoretical support exists in the fertile essays of Elizabeth L. Eisenstein on the impact of printing on literate elites and on urban populations in early modern Europe—especially when she talks of "cross-cultural interchange" between previously "compartmentalized systems." Both Goody and Eisenstein have insisted to critics that they do not intend technological determinism, and I am even more ready than they to emphasize the way that social structure and values channel the uses of literacy and printing.[10]

This essay, then, will consider the context for using printed books in defined popular milieus in sixteenth-century France and the new relations that printing helped to establish among people and among hitherto isolated cultural traditions. Were there new groups who joined the ranks of known authors? What was the composition of "audiences"—those who actually read the books

—and of "publics"—those to whom authors and publishers addressed their works?*

These relations are especially interesting to trace in the sixteenth century. In the cities, at any rate, the basic innovations occurred quite rapidly. By mid-century all the major centers of publication had been established in France: Paris, Lyon, Rouen, Toulouse, Poitiers, Bordeaux, Troyes. Some forty towns had presses by 1550; about sixty had them by 1600. Moreover, economic control in the industry was not yet firmly in the hands of merchant-publishers and commercial booksellers, as it would be after the Religious Wars. Decisions about what was profitable and/or beneficial to print were made also by "industrial capitalists" and artisans, that is, by publisher-printers like Jean I de Tournes in Lyon and the Marnef brothers in Poitiers; such decisions were even sometimes made by simple master printers publishing their own editions. This diversity may help explain the wide range in the *types* of books that appeared before mid-century. In these decades there proliferated most of the forms to be published in France up to 1700. The same is true of patterns in book ownership. For example, virtually no Parisian artisans other than printers in the generation that died around 1500 owned printed books; by 1560, the percentage of Parisian artisans and tradesmen possessing books in inventories after death had reached the level (not very high, to be sure) that Henri-Jean Martin has documented for mid-seventeenth-century Paris.[11]

This brings me to a last point about method. Rather than thinking diffusely about "the people," I am trying wherever possible to ask how printing affected more carefully defined milieus—namely, cohesive social groups some of whose members were literate. In the countryside this means the entire settled population of a village where anyone was literate. In the cities this means the small merchants and the craftsmen (masters and journeymen),

* This distinction is a necessary one, but is not made in everyday speech. I follow the terminology of T. J. Clark, *Image of the People. Gustave Courbet and the Second French Republic, 1848-1851* (New York, 1973), p. 12.

and even semiskilled workers (such as urban gardeners and fishermen) having some connection with urban organizations such as confraternities or guilds. It means their wives, themselves ordinarily at work in the trades, and even women in the families of the wealthier merchants. It means domestic servants, male or female, who might be living in their households. It does not include the unskilled dayworkers, the *gagnedenier* and *manouvriers*, the *portefaix* and *crocheteurs*, the vagabonds and permanent beggars. This floating mass was just illiterate; and however resourceful their subculture, the only reader to whom they listened with any regularity was the town crier ordering them to show up for work cleaning sewage or else leave town under penalty of the whip.

Nor am I including the lower clergy or the backwoods noblemen and their wives, even though they might in the sixteenth century sometimes cluster on the borderline between literacy and illiteracy and as individuals play a role in village social life. They are distinguished from the peasants and the urban *menu peuple* not by the criterion of literacy but by their estate and their relations to spiritual and emotional power, to jurisdiction and to property.

[1]

Let us look first to the peasants. The penetration of printing into their lives was a function not just of their literacy but of several things: the cost and availability of books in a language that they knew; the existence of social occasions when books could be read aloud; the need or desire for information that they thought could be found in printed books more easily than elsewhere; and in some cases the desire to use the press to say something to someone else.

In the countryside we meet a world that sees letters infrequently, whether written or printed. Suggestive of their relevance in the days before printing is a rural festival in Torcy around 1450, where a mock herald—a miller's son—with a mock seal pretends to read to the harvest queen from a blank parchment, whereas in fact he is improvising farcical jokes. Parchment or paper might come into the peasants' life when transactions were being recorded by courts, seigneurs, or rent-collectors, but peasants might equally expect to see these materials used, say, in a humiliating headdress for local offenders. (In the Ile-de-France in the fifteenth century a dishonest chicken-grower is led to punishment wearing a miter with chicks and other fowl painted on it and "an abundance of writing," and in 1511 a lax forest ranger is paraded around in a paper miter decorated with standing and fallen trees.)[12]

Rural literacy remained low throughout the sixteenth century. Of the women, virtually none knew their ABC's, not even the mid-wives. As for the men, a systematic study by Emmanuel Le Roy Ladurie of certain parts of the Languedoc from the 1570's through the 1590's found that three percent of the agricultural workers and only ten percent of the better-off peasants—the *laboureurs* and *fermiers*—could sign their full names.* In the regions north and southwest of Paris, where the speech was French, the rates may have been slightly higher, and rural schools have been noted in several places. But the pupils who spent a couple of years at such places learning to read and write and sing were drawn from special families (such as that of a barber-surgeon in the Forez, who sent his boys to a school and rewarded its rector with a chapel in 1557) or were intended for nonagricultural occupations (such as the serf's son in the Sologne who went to school "to learn science" because he was "weak of body and could not work the soil").[13]

Surely a lad ambitious to be a *fermier* in the mid-sixteenth cen-tury would need to keep accounts, yet not all economic pressures

---

*Estimates of ability to read based on studies of ability to sign one's name are, of course, approximate. One can learn to read without learning to write and vice versa. Nevertheless, the two skills were most often taught together in the sixteenth century. Statistics on ability to sign, then, give us the order of magnitude of the number of readers. For a discussion of techniques of measuring literacy in the early modern period, see R. S. Schofield, "The Mea-surement of Literacy in Pre-Industrial England," in J. R. Goody, ed., *Literacy in Traditional Societies* (Cambridge, Eng., 1968), pp. 311-25, and F. Furet and W. Sachs, "La croissance de l'alphabétisation en France, XVIIIe-XIXe siècle," *Annales. Economies, Sociétés, Civilisations* 29 (1974): 714-37.

pushed the prosperous peasant to literacy. Charles Estienne's agricultural manual advised the landed proprietor that his tenant farmer need not have reading and writing (one can lie on paper, too) so long as he was experienced and wise in agricultural ways. A peasant in the Haut-Poitou in 1601, designated tax assessor of his village, tried to get out of it by pleading illiteracy. As for sales of land, marriage contracts, and wills, there were itinerant scribes and notaries aplenty who were happy to add to their income by performing these services for the peasants.[14]

The country boys who really learned their letters, then, were most likely those who left for the city to apprentice to crafts or to become priests, or the few lucky sons of *laboureurs* who, at a time when fellowships for the poor were being taken over by the rich, still made it to the University of Paris. One such, the son of a village smith from Brie, became a proofreader in Lyon after his university years, and at his death in 1560 was in possession of a precious manuscript of the Theodosian Code.[15]

But when they came back to visit, such men did not leave books in their villages. "Our little Thomas talks so profoundly, almost no one can understand him" was the observation of Thomas Platter's relatives when he passed through his Swiss mountain home during his student years in the early sixteenth century. One can imagine similar remarks exchanged by peasants in France about a son who had studied books in a strange language or learned his craft in a different dialect. As the peasants' inventories after death* were virtually without manuscripts in the fifteenth

---

* No study has yet been made of the book holdings of rural *curés* in sixteenth-century France. Albert Labarre examined inventories after death of 23 *curés* of rural parishes in the Amiénois from 1522 to 1561 (fifteen had books, eight had none), but, as he points out, these men were all living in Amiens. Except when the resident *curé* kept a school, we would expect that he would possess little more than a breviary and a missal, and perhaps a book of saints' lives. In his *Propos rustiques* of 1547, Noel du Fail pictured a rural *curé* of earlier decades at a feast-day banquet, not reading aloud, but chatting with parishioners about the text for the day and with the old midwife about medicinal herbs. The education of the rural clergy was, of course, very uneven well into the seventeenth century. Only then do we find French bishops re-

century, so they were almost without printed books in the sixteenth.[16] Why should this be so? Surely a *laboureur* who could afford many livres worth of linens and coffers in the 1520's could afford three sous for a *Calendrier des bergers,* two sous for the medical manual *Le Tresor des povres,* or even two and a half livres for a bound and illustrated Book of Hours, which might be a credit to his family for generations.[17]

Yet just because one can afford books does not mean that one can have ready access to them or need them or want them. A literate *laboureur* in some parts of France during the sixteenth century might never meet a bookseller: his nearest market town might have no presses if it were a small place, and peddlers' itineraries still reached relatively few parts of the countryside.[18] If he did come upon a bookseller, his wares might be in a language the peasant had difficulty reading, since so little printing was done in vernaculars other than French. Only five books printed in Breton during the sixteenth century could be found by an eighteenth-century student of that language, and the first work in Basque came out in 1545 and had very few imitators.[19] Provençal was favored by several editions, mostly of poetry, but the various regional dialects, from Picard to Poitevin, rarely appeared in print at all.[20]

In any case, how much were printed books really needed in the sixteenth-century village? A *Shepherds' Calendar* was a useful, though not always essential, supplement to oral tradition. (Indeed, sometimes as I read the different sixteenth-century editions of the *Calendrier des bergers,* I wonder to what extent contemporary compilers and publishers envisaged a peasant public for them. They appear a cross between a folklorist's recording and a pastoral, a shaped vision of the peasant world for country gentlemen

quiring *curés* to own specified books. A. Labarre, *Le livre dans la vie amiénoise du seizième siècle* (Paris, 1971), pp. 107-11. Noel du Fail, *Les propos rustiques,* ed. A. de la Borderie (Paris, 1878), p. 21. T.-J. Schmitt, *L'organisation ecclésiastique et la pratique religieuse dans l'archidiaconé d'Autun de 1650 à 1750* (Autun, 1957), pp. 132-33. J. Ferté, *La vie religieuse dans les campagnes parisiennes, 1622-1695* (Paris, 1962), pp. 186-94.

and city people and a way for such readers to identify themselves with the simple wisdom of "the great shepherd of the mountain." The appearance in Paris in 1499 of a *Shepherdesses' Calendar*, a literary contrivance modeled after the earlier *Calendrier* and printed by the same atelier, tends to support this view.[21]) The *Shepherds' Calendar* told which sign the moon was in and its phases, the dates of fixed and movable feast days, and the timing of solar and lunar eclipses. For the most important findings about the year in which the calendar was printed, pictorial devices were given to aid the barely literate. For full use of the various tables, genuine ability to read was required.*

Now except for the eclipses, peasants had their own equivalent devices to calculate these results, which they then recorded "in figures on little tablets of wood." These "hieroglyphic Almanacs" were still being made by peasants in the Languedoc in 1655: "On a morsel of wood no bigger than a playing card," said an observer in the Albigeois region, "they mark by a singular artifice all the months and days of the year, with the feast days and other notable things."[22] Why should they then feel the lack of a *Shepherds' Calendar*?

Other parts of the *Calendrier* might have been enjoyable for peasants, such as the recommendations on regimen or the physiognomic signs that warned one who was crafty and who was kind. Yet here, too, rural communities were well supplied with proverbs and old sayings that covered many of these contingencies, sometimes even more aptly than the uniform teaching of the *Calendar*. (Can both Provençaux and Picards have agreed that black curly hair meant a melancholy, lewd, evil-thinking person? Can both

---

* The *Shepherds' Calendar* was not published annually. The dates for the new moon could be read off for 38 years; the eclipses were predicted for a century or more. For any year after the year of its printing, the dates of the days of the week, the exact time of the new moon, and the position of the moon in the zodiac had to be worked out from the tables.

In Noel du Fail's *Propos rustiques*, the village copy of the *Calendrier des bergers* is owned by old Maistre Huguet, former village schoolteacher, who reads aloud from it from time to time (p. 15).

Bretons and Gascons have agreed that redheads were foolish, senseless, and disloyal?[23]) The gynecological sections of some *Calendars* (such as Troyes, 1541, and Lyon, 1551) were trifling compared to the wide lore of the village midwife. And let us hope that traveling barbers did not base their bleeding only on the crude illustration of the veins that recurred in these editions.[24]

Similarly, the agricultural advice in the *Shepherds' Calendar* was only of occasional usefulness. Peasants did not really need its woodcuts—a delight though they were to the eyes—to teach them, for instance, that in March it was time to prune the vines. As the old saying went:

> Le vigneron me taille
> Le vigneron me lie
> Le vigneron me baille
> En Mars toute ma vie.[25]

Finally, though I have come upon no example before 1630 of a rural *curé* in possession of a *Shepherds' Calendar*, we can imagine such a priest in the earlier period reading aloud from the extensive religious passages of the book, or even better, showing the villagers the articulated trees of virtue and vice and the pictures of punishments in Hell.[26] This might happen, but could these woodcuts compete with the Last Judgments, the dance of death, the saints' lives, and the Biblical scenes already coloring the walls and filling the windows of so many rural churches at the end of the Middle Ages? And would the seven ways of knowing God and self and the six ways of fulfilling baptism, wise though they might be, do much to lessen the peasants' dependence on ritual, to move peasant religion toward reading? In short, *Le Grand Calendrier des bergers*, if any of its editions found their way to the village in the sixteenth century, may have jogged the peasants' memory and enriched and perhaps helped standardize its visual store. But it can hardly have brought them much new information or changed significantly their reliance on oral transmission and their relationships with nonpeasant groups.

The festive and musical life of the peasants was also nourished primarily by local tradition and experience and by what the peasants learned from traveling players and saw and heard themselves at fairtime in a nearby center. For example, the unmarried youth of the village, organized into Abbayes de Jeunesse, composed chants and playlets to mock the domestic and sexual foibles of older villagers. Thus a mid-sixteenth-century charivari song might be made up on the spur of the moment because a newly wed husband had failed three nights running to consummate his marriage. In the version that has come down to us:

> Quand ils ont sceu au village
> Que ce mary
> N'avoit non plus de courage
> Q'une soury
> Ils ont faict charyvary
> Pour la riser. . . .
> En tres grande diligence
> Un bon garcon
> Du village par plaisance
> Fit la chanson.[27]

In parts of the Auvergne, *reinages* were organized annually in which the right to costume oneself as king, queen, dauphin, constable, and the like was auctioned off to the villager who gave the most wax to the parish church or a local convent.[28] Religious drama also emerged from this nonliterate milieu: in the late fifteenth century, four inhabitants of Triel (Ile-de-France) put on the Life of Saint Victor and got into trouble for taking a statue from the church and using it irreverently as a prop; in 1547, three *laboureurs*, unable to sign their names, contracted with a village painter to make "portraits" for the Life of the child martyr Saint Cyr that they were playing on Sundays in their hamlet of Villejuive.[29]

Farces, moralities, and mysteries were pouring from the presses of Paris and Lyon in the first part of the sixteenth century, but these rural performances used no printed book and probably did not even have a text behind them. So too, it became the fashion in the mid-century to publish so-called *"chansons rustiques"* as part of general collections of songs without music, but there is no evidence that these were aimed at or bought in the villages.[30]

And yet there were a few ways that printing did enter rural life in the sixteenth century to offer some new options to the peasants. The important social institution for this was the *veillée*, an evening gathering within the village community held especially during the winter months from All Saints' Day to Ash Wednesday.[31] Here tools were mended by candlelight, thread was spun, the unmarried flirted, people sang, and some man or woman told stories—of Mélusine, that wondrous woman-serpent with her violent husband and sons; of the girl who escaped from incest to the king's palace in a she-donkey's hide; of Renard and other adventuresome animals.[32] Then, if one of the men were literate and owned books, he might read aloud.

In principle, printing increased significantly the range of books available for the *veillée*. In fact, given the limited channels of distribution in the sixteenth century and the virtuosity of the traditional storyteller, even a rural schoolteacher might have very few books. According to Noel du Fail, a young lawyer from a seigneurial family in upper Brittany who wrote in 1547 a story of a peasant village, the village books were "old": *Aesop's Fables* and *Le Roman de la Rose*. Now both of these had printed editions and urban readers in the late fifteenth and early sixteenth centuries. By the 1540's, however, the learned were enjoying Aesop in fresh Latin and Greek editions or in new French rhyme; and, though still appreciative of the thirteenth-century *Roman*, they were feeling ever more distant from its sense and style, even in the updated version given them by Clément Marot. In contrast, peasants would have had no reason to supplant the early editions that Marot and his publisher disdained as full of printing errors and *"trop ancien langaige."*[33]

Did such reading aloud change things much in the village? *Reading* aloud? We might better say "translating," since the reader was inevitably turning the French of his printed text into a dialect

his listeners could understand. And we might well add "editing"—
if not for *Aesop's Fables*, whose form and plots were already familiar to peasants, then for the 22,000 lines and philosophical
discourses of the *Roman*. In a community hearing parts of the
Roman for the first time, new relationships were perhaps set up
with old chivalric and scholastic ways of ordering experience;
some new metaphors were acquired and varied images of women
and love added to the listeners' existing stock.[34] Who do you yearn
to be, or to love? Mélusine or the Rose? A good question, but it
hardly constitutes a connection with the distinctive features of
"print culture."*

As early as the 1530's, however, some *veillées* were being treated
to a book that was in the vanguard and more disruptive of traditional rural patterns than Aesop, the *Roman de la Rose*, or the
Calendrier: the vernacular Bible. In Picardy a cobbler reads it to
the villagers at the *veillées* until he is discovered by a nearby abbey.
Here the literalness of the text was important. The Bible could
not be "edited" or reduced to some formulaic magic. It had to be
understood, and there were probably no pictures to help. In the
Saintonge and elsewhere during the 1550's, Philibert Hamelin, his

---

* Noel du Fail was quite particular about the books that he placed in the
village. When a pirated edition of his *Propos* came out in Paris in 1548 with
other books added to his list, he suppressed them in his new edition at Lyon
in 1549. In 1573, however, the Parisian publisher Jean II Ruelle added five
titles that may have had some hearing in the countryside: a late-fifteenth-
century poetic history of the reign of Charles VII; two medieval romances (including *Valentin et Orson*, which has thematic material relating to the old
rural custom of the chase of the wildman or of the bear); an account by
Symphorien Champier of the chivalric deeds of the good knight Bayard; and
the Miracles of Our Lady. Some of these were part of the *Bibliothèque bleue*
of the seventeenth century (du Fail, *Propos*, pp. iv-xii, 138, 187).

On a rainy evening in February 1554, the Norman gentleman Gilles de
Gouberville read to his household, including the male and female servants,
from *Amadis de Gaule* (A. Tollemer, *Un Sire de Gouberville, gentilhomme
campagnard au cotentin de 1553 à 1562*, with introduction by E. Le Roy
Ladurie [reprint of the 1873 ed., Paris, 1972], p. 285). This chivalric tale had
only recently been translated from the Spanish and printed in France.

I think these books would have been received by peasants in the same way
as the *Roman de la Rose* and *Aesop's Fables*.

pack filled with Bibles and prayer books that he had printed at Geneva, comes to sit with peasants in the fields during their noonday break and talks of the Gospel and of a new kind of prayer. Some are delighted and learn; others are outraged and curse and beat him. He is sure that one day they will know better.[35]

In the Orléanais a forest ranger buys a vernacular New Testament, a French Psalter, and the Geneva catechism from a bookseller at a fair and goes alone into the forest of Marchenoir to read them. Over in the mountains of the Dauphiné a peasant somehow teaches himself to read and write French and divides his time between plowing and the New Testament. The story goes that when reproached by the priests because he did not know the Scripture in Latin, he laboriously spelled it out until he could contradict them with Latin citations.[36]

Finally, evangelical peddlers begin to work the countryside systematically. A carter, a native of Poitiers, loads up in Geneva with Bibles, Psalters, and Calvinist literature published by Laurent de Normandie and looks for buyers in the Piedmont and the rural Dauphiné. Five craftsmen from scattered parts of France are arrested in 1559 in a village in the Lyonnais with literature from Geneva in their baskets. Even the Inquisitor wonders why they should want to sell such books to *"gens rustiques."*[37]

As it turned out, of course, the Calvinist message never won the massive support of the French peasants. Rural Protestantism was to be chiefly the affair either of seigneurs and great noble houses, whose tenants or subjects would then attend Reformed services perforce, or of special regions like the Cévenol, where (as Le Roy Ladurie has shown) initial commitment came from the relatively high concentration of rural artisans, especially in the leather trades.[38] For most peasants, the religion of the Book, the Psalm, and the Consistory gave too little leeway to the traditional oral and ritual culture of the countryside, to its existing forms of social life and social control.

This Calvinist inflexibility is illustrated by the character of a new *Calendrier* that originated in Geneva in the late 1550's and was published in great numbers in the 1560's there, in Lyon, and elsewhere. The engravings for each month still depicted rural scenes, sometimes with great charm. But information on the moon's location in the zodiac either was given not in tables but in *words*, or more often was suppressed altogether (perhaps because it was feared that it would be put to astrological use); and the many saints whose names and pictures marked the traditional *Calendrier* were banished as "superstitious and idolatrous." Instead, the Reformed *Calendar* listed "historical" dates that would show God's ways to man. Thus Noah's progress in the ark and events in the life of Christ were recorded in their place. On January 26 or 27, 815, Charlemagne died. On February 18, "the feast of fools was celebrated at Rome, to which corresponds Mardi Gras of the Papists . . . successors of the Pagans." March was the month of Martin Bucer's death, July that of Edward VI. Constantinople was taken by Mahomet II May 29, 1453. On August 27, the "reformation according to the truth" took place in Geneva. Under October was remembered Martin Luther's attack on indulgences.[39]

It was an interesting innovation, this slender *Calendrier historial*, which was often slipped in with the Reformed Psalter or New Testament (and even appeared, as they did, in Basque).[40] But how would peasants have responded to it? First, it was harder for the semiliterate to decipher than the Catholic calendar, and it had less astronomical fact. But most of all, no matter how curious the new historical items were, the peasants' year was here stripped beyond recognition, empty even of the saints by which they named their days. Protestant publishers wanted *gens rustiques* to buy these books, but they had not tailored them to a peasant public.*

* The *Calendriers historials* were all anonymous and were given their form and content by those that published them. The *Calendrier*'s first creator was Conrad Badius, son of a printer in Paris. Of sixteen other *libraires* and *imprimeurs* associated with the editions in Geneva and Lyon in the 1560's, nine of them—and these the most important—were of urban origin. The pictures show some attention to agricultural detail: the ox-drawn light plows (*araires*) of the Languedoc figure in some, whereas the horse-drawn heavier plows

Still, even if the Bible did not become a permanent fixture in most rural households, merely to think of selling to them on a large scale was something new. Who first opened up the rural markets for the peddlers' books of the seventeenth century? Not a simple printer of rural background; he would remember the illiteracy of his village. Not an ordinary publisher of popular literature; he would worry about meager profits. But zealous Protestants could overlook all that, could face the possibilities of destroyed merchandise and even death for the sake of "consoling poor Christians and instructing them in the law of God."[41]

If printing and Protestantism opened new routes for selling books in the countryside, the press also facilitated the *writing* of a few new books for a peasant public. What happened, I think, was that the printing of "peasant lore," as in the *Shepherds' Calendar* and in books of common proverbs, brought it to the attention of learned men in a new way. These men were discovering the thoughts not of their local tenants or of the men and women from whom they bought grain at market, but of The Peasants. And, dedicated to the "illustration" of the national tongue and to the humanist ideal of practical service, they decided that they must correct rural lore and instruct The Peasants. Thus, Antoine Mizaud, doctor of medicine, mathematician, and professor at Paris, writes an *Astrologie des Rustiques* to tell countryfolk without the time to acquire perfect knowledge of the heavens how to predict the weather by sure terrestrial signs. (Mariners, military commanders, and physicians should find it useful, too.)[42] Thus, somewhat later, the royal surgeon Jacques Guillemeau writes a book on pregnancy and childbirth "not for the learned . . . but for young Surgeons, little versed in the art, dispersed here and there, far away from the cities."[43]

Some new kinds of almanacs appear on an annual basis now,

(*charrues*) of the north appear in others. But some calendars put animal and instrument together in less likely combinations; and a 1566 Lyon edition has placed mowing in the month before reaping—and none provides advice on crops.

authored by doctors of medicine and "mathematicians," containing bits of possibly novel *agricultural* information, such as when to plant fruits and market vegetables. ("Tested by M. Peron and Jean Lirondes, old gardeners at Nîmes," says one edition, which then tells about the *choux cabus*, artichokes, melons, and other plants that distinguished the seventeenth-century Languedoc garden from its modest fifteenth-century forebear.)[44] Though these almanacs were conceived for a diverse public, they probably were expected to reach some peasant readers—certainly more than were the justly celebrated agricultural manuals of Charles Estienne, Jean Liebault, and others. These latter treatises were intended for landowners, gentlemen farmers, and seigneurs, who would then teach their lessees, tenants, and hired servants what to do.*

The most interesting of these new almanacs, however, was written by Jean Vostet in 1588 and occasioned by the Gregorian calendar reform of six years before. As his patron, the prior of

* As Corinne Beutler points out in an excellent review of sixteenth-century agricultural literature, these manuals were addressed to the nobility and landed proprietors, who were then expected to teach their unlettered peasants ("Un chapitre de la sensibilité collective: la littérature agricole en Europe continentale au XVIe siècle," *Annales. Economies, Sociétés, Civilisations* 28 [1973]: 1282, 1292-94). This is clear not only from the introductions to the manuals, but from the assumed public for some of their chapters. Charles Estienne devotes a long section to the kind of *fermier* and *fermière* that the proprietor should hire after he has constructed his farmhouse. Literacy is not a requirement for the tenant, as we have seen, and thus Estienne is not thinking of him as the *reader* of his text (*L'agriculture et la maison rustique de M. Charles Estienne Docteur en Medecine* [Paris: Jacques Du Puys, 1564], chaps. 7-8).

Olivier de Serres, after a preface discussing the limitations of the agricultural understanding of unlettered peasants (an understanding based on experience alone), goes on to a chapter on the different kinds of arrangements by which the Father of the Family may rent out or administer his land. We are long past the time, he writes with ironic wistfulness, when the Father of the Family dirtied his hands working the soil himself. He thinks some of his readers may have to be absent from their property because of service to the king, judicial or financial office, or commercial enterprise. (*Theatre d'Agriculture et Mesnage des Champs d'Olivier de Serres, Seigneur de Pradel* [Paris: Jamet Mettayer, 1600], Preface and Book I, chap. 8. Signature at the end of Table in copy at the Bancroft Library: "de Menisson." Marginalia in French, German, and Latin, by different hands, in the chapter on medicinal plants.)

Flammerécourt in Champagne, had said, the ten cut days "had rendered useless the ancient observations of the peasants . . . had ruined their verses and local memory [*leurs vers et mémoire locale*]." So Vostet went through the year's poems and proverbs— culled from sayings and from old manuscript and printed *Calendars* and *Prognostications*—occasionally correcting them when he thought the advice bad or "superstitious" and rewriting them to make up for the lost days. For example, the Bear decides about winter's length no more at Candlemas but on February 12; the hog's acorns are put in doubt not by a rainy Saint James' day but by a rainy Saint Gengoul's. Instead of it being a good idea to bleed your right arm on March 17, Saint Gertrude's Day, you now should do it two days after the Annunciation. This will keep your eyes clear for the whole year. All this is rather different from the Calvinist *Calendrier historiale*, and not merely because the Protestants refused to accept the pope's reformed calendar until the eighteenth century. (Did Vostet's new sayings catch on? At least in the printed literature they did. We find them in the seventeenth- and eighteenth-century almanacs, but coupled, alas, with the verses they were supposed to supersede.[45])

Jean Vostet was a man of minor learning, but another book imagined for a peasant public (though actually printed only in Latin during the sixteenth century) was by the eminent jurist René Choppin. It was called *On the Privileges of Rustic Persons*, and Choppin wrote it in 1574 at his estate at Cachan, where he, "half-peasant," was on vacation from the Parlement of Paris.[46] Surveying his fields and flocks, he thought how little jurists had done to recompense the men by whose labor they lived. Why had no one told the peasants of their legal privileges and rights, so they need not be diverted from the plow to wasteful cases in the courts? He would relieve their ignorance in a treatise which, drawing on Roman law, customary law, royal ordinances, and decisions of the Parlements, would answer a host of questions concerning peasants—from the status of persons to disputes over pasture.

Was Choppin really trying to make the law accessible to the

peasants? Despite the claims of this "semi-paganus" that he wished the "Diligent Husbandman" to read his own law, the promised French translation did not appear till several years after his death. He spoke of the countryfolk with a pastoral nostalgia for their sincerity and an employer's suspicion of their laziness. But especially he visualized peasants as clients or opposing parties, and the book was directed to lawyers who would plead for or against them in various courts. It was a genuine contribution to the slow process of unification of French law—though one about which Choppin felt defensive. Writing about rustic things after writing about the royal domain might be thought, as the proverb said, to be going from horses to asses.⁴⁷ As for the "asses," it seems unlikely that they read about their privileges. Indeed, we have no *sure* evidence that any of these books addressed to a rural public ever actually reached a peasant audience. Probably some of the almanacs did circulate in the countryside, for they appear in the peddlers' packs in the seventeenth century.

What can we conclude, then, about the consequences of printing for the sixteenth-century peasant community? Certainly they were limited. A few lines of communication were opened between professor and peasant—or rather between bodies of cultural materials, as in the case of some traditional lore that was standardized and disseminated by the press, perhaps with a little correction from above. Expectations were higher by 1600 that a printed book might come into the village and be read aloud at the *veillée*, even where the little spark of Protestantism had burned out in the countryside. But oral culture was still so dominant that it transformed everything it touched; and it still changed according to the rules of forgetting and remembering, watching and discussing. Some printed medieval romances may have come to the peasants from the cities, but they cannot have played the escapist role that Mandrou has claimed for them in the seventeenth century. Peasants in the Lyonnais, in the Ile-de-France, and in the Languedoc put on tithe strikes just the same; villages in Burgundy forced their lords to enfranchise about half of their servile population; peasants in Brittany, the Guyenne, Burgundy, and the Dauphiné organized themselves into emergency communes, communicated with each other, and rebelled under traditional slogans, ensigns, and captains with festive titles—all neither deflected nor aided by what was being said in print.[48] Indeed, those who wished to control the countryside and bring it to order by means other than sheer force—whether bishop, seigneur, or king—would have to send not books but messengers, whose seals would not be mock and who would disclose verbally the power behind the papers that they read.

[11]

In the cities, the changes wrought or facilitated by printing in the life of the *menu peuple* had greater moment. The literacy rate had long been higher among urban artisans and tradesmen than among peasants, but the gap widened—at least for males—in the early sixteenth century. The old choirboy schools still performed their service for the sons of some artisans and petty traders, and more important, the numbers of vernacular schoolteachers and reckonmasters multiplied. For instance, in Lyon in the 1550's and 1560's, some 38 male teachers of reading, writing, and arithmetic can be identified (very roughly one for every 400 males under the age of twenty in the city), quite apart from the masters at the Latin Collège de la Trinité. They marry the daughters of taverners and the widows of millers; they live in houses with pouchmakers and dressmakers; they have goldsmiths, printers, barber-surgeons, coopers, and gold-thread-drawers among their friends.[49] In addition to these teachers, newly established municipal orphanages in some cities provided simple instruction for poor boys, and at times even orphan girls were taught their ABC's.[50]

This press for literacy was associated with technological, economic, and social developments. Printing itself created a populous cluster of crafts (including bookbinding and typecasting) where literacy rates were high. Of 115 printers' journeymen assembled in Lyon in 1580 to give power of attorney, two-thirds could sign

their names fully; and the journeymen were already demanding
that all apprentices know how to read and write, even those who
would be but simple pressmen. In other crafts, such as painting
and surgery, literacy was spurred by the desire for a higher, more
"professional" status and the availability of vernacular books for
training. Even the royal sergeants, a group among the *menu peuple*
previously noted only for their skill with the rod, began to live
up to a 1499 decree requiring them to read and write.[51]

Literacy was not, of course, distributed evenly among the *menu
peuple*. An examination of the ability to sign of 885 males involved
in notarial acts in Lyon in the 1560's and 1570's spreads the trades
out as follows (masters and journeymen combined):

Very high: apothecaries, surgeons, printers.
High: painters, musicians, taverners, metalworkers (including
   gold trades).
Medium (about 50 percent): furriers and leatherworkers, artisans in textile and clothing trades.
Low to very low: artisans in construction trades, in provisioning, transport; urban gardeners; unskilled dayworkers.

In Narbonne, for about the same time, Le Roy Ladurie found that
one-third of the artisans could sign their names; another third
could write initials; and only one-third were totally foreign to
letters. At Montpellier the percentage of craftsmen who could
make only marks was down to 25 percent. This range among the
artisans contrasts both with the almost complete literacy of well-
off merchants of all kinds and with the low rate of literacy among
urban women outside the families of lawyers, merchant-bankers,
and publishers.[52]

City-dwellers were also more likely than countryfolk to be able
to understand French. Towns were, of course, constantly replen-
ished by people from rural areas with their local patois and even
by people from foreign lands, and the urban speech itself was not
independent of the big patterns of regional dialect. Nevertheless,
French was increasingly the language of royal government (after
1539 all judicial acts were to be in French) and of other kinds of

exchange; in an important southern center like Montpellier it could be heard in the streets already by 1490.[53] Thus the urban artisan had potentially a more direct access to the contents of the printed book—whose vernacular was French, as we have seen— than a peasant who could read handwritten accounts in Provençal but would have had to struggle over a printed *Calendrier*.

From simple literacy to actual reading is something of a step. Studies based only on inventories after death in sixteenth-century Paris and Amiens suggest that the step was not always taken. In the early years of the century, if an artisan or small shopkeeper in Paris owns a book at all, it is likely to be a manuscript Book of Hours. By 1520 printed books appear, displacing the manuscripts but existing along with the religious paintings, sculpture, and wall hangings that even quite modest families possess. Most artisans, however, had no books at their death. They represent only about ten percent of book owners in Paris and twelve percent of book owners in Amiens (or seventeen percent, if we include barbers and surgeons), that is, well below the proportion of the *gens mécaniques* in the urban population at large. And when they do have books, outside of printers' stock, there are not very many of them. Out of all the editions in the Amiens inventories, only 3.7 percent were in artisanal hands (six percent, if we include barbers and surgeons); and apart from the latter group, the median size of the library was one book![54]

In Amiens that one book was most likely to be a Book of Hours, or perhaps a French *Golden Legend* (the medieval book of saints' lives popular throughout the sixteenth century), or a vernacular Bible. Or else it might be a technical work, such as a pattern book for cabinetmaking or painting. In Paris in 1549, a tanner dies owning a *Golden Legend* and the *Mer des Histoires*, a thirteenth-century historical work still being printed in the 1530's and 1540's; a barber-surgeon leaves behind six French volumes on the art of surgery.[55] Clearly the literate were often without private libraries and, at least on their deathbed, do not appear to have taken much advantage of the varied fruits of the "admirable invention."

There were some economic reasons for this, even though printed books were cheaper by far than manuscripts had been. A twenty-four page sermon on poor relief cost as much as a loaf of coarse bread in the 1530's; an easy little arithmetic, half a loaf. A few years later, a full news account of the seizure of Rhodes could be almost as expensive as a pair of children's shoes; a book of Christmas carols, as much as a pound of candlewax. In the 1540's a French history could cost more than half a day's wages for a painter's journeyman or a printer's journeyman, and almost a whole day's wages for a journeyman in the building trades.[56] In the 1560's the cheapest "hand-size" New Testament in French was not much less. Understandably, some artisans complained that they could not afford to buy it, thus prompting a Protestant polemicist to ask them whether "they didn't have all the Instruments of their craft, however much poverty made it difficult to buy them" and how could they pass up a Book of such utility as the Bible?[57]

In fact, artisans found ways to have access to printed materials without collecting them privately. They bought a book, read it until they were finished, or until they were broke or needed cash, and then pawned it with an innkeeper or more likely sold it to a friend or to a *libraire*. Thus one Jean de Cazes, a native of Libourne, purchased a Lyon Bible in Bordeaux for two écus (an expensive edition), read it, and sold it to someone from the Saintonge before he was arrested for heresy in 1566 at the age of 27.[58] Books were relatively liquid assets and were less subject to depreciation than many other personal items. One kept to the end, if one could afford it, only those editions that were needed for constant reference or were wanted as permanent family property —thus the Hours, the Bibles, and the workbooks that show up in the inventories after death. Possibly, too, in the absence of public libraries, literate artisans and shopkeepers lent each other books from their small stores as did more substantial collectors (the poet François Béroald had three leaves of his account book devoted to loaned books[59]); and they may even have passed on books as gifts more often than we know. Theirs was a world in which "secrets"—the secrets of craft, the secrets of women—had never been private possessions but corporate ones, shared, told, passed on so they would not be forgotten. What happens when scarce printed books enter such a world? They flow through the literate segments of the *menu peuple* rather than remain hoarded on an artisan's shelf.

Books were also shared in reading groups which, as in the countryside, brought the literate and illiterate together. The traditional winter *veillée* was not the regular setting, however; for outside the building trades many craftsmen worked winter and summer, by candlelight if necessary, till eight or even ten o'clock at night.[60] Gatherings of family and friends for singing, games, cards, storytelling, and perhaps reading were more likely special occasions, like feast days. Certain books were designed to be read aloud or consulted in the shop, such as pattern books for textile design and the French translation of Birunguccio's *Pirotechnia*, an excellent manual on metallurgical processes.[61] So, too, the oft-printed little arithmetics that taught petty business operations "by the pen" in Arabic numerals and by counting stones (*jetons*) "for those who don't know how to read and write" were resources for apprentices and adults in an atelier even more than for an instructor in a little school. One *Brief Arithmetic* promised to teach a tradesman all he needed to know in fifteen days' time and added mnemonic verses to help him catch on.[62]

Reading aloud in one connection or another must have been especially common in the printing shop. I am thinking not merely of the discussion of copy among scholar-printers, authors, and editors, but of reading in snatches that could reach out to the journeymen and to the spouses and daughters helping to hang up the freshly printed sheets. Thus one Michel Blanc, a simple pressman in Lyon in the late 1530's, knew enough of Marot's poems, which were printed in his shop, for his son to remember later how he had been "brought up in his youth on Marot."[63] Possibly men may sometimes have taken books into the tavern for reading. As for the women, they surely did some of their reading aloud among their own sex; an example might be the Life of Saint Margaret, with prayers for the pregnant and the parturient.[64]

But the most innovative reading groups were the secret Protestant assemblies on feast days or late at night in private homes—innovative among other reasons because they brought together men and women who were not necessarily in the same family or craft or even neighborhood. Thus a 1559 assembly in Paris included a goldsmith's journeyman from the Gâtinais, a university student from Lyon, a shoemaker's journeyman, and several others, all from different parts of the city. An early conventicle in the town of Saintes, organized by two poor artisans in 1557, had access to one printed Bible, from which passages were written down for discussion. Encouraged by Deuteronomy 6: 7 to speak of God's law however small their learning, the artisans scheduled written exhortations every Sunday by the six members who could read and write. Like the heretical linen-weavers of Cambrai, with their printed Bible in the fields, these Protestants read, talked, sang, and prayed.[65]

In short, reading from printed books does not silence oral culture. It can give people something fresh to talk about. Learning from printed books does not suddenly replace learning by doing. It can provide people with new ways to relate their doings to authority, new and old.

Nor should printing be viewed merely as purveying to the *menu peuple* the science of university graduates, the doctrine of the religious, the literary production of the educated, and the orders of the powerful. Artisans, tradesmen, and women composed themselves a few of the books they read.* To be sure, some such persons had in the fourteenth and fifteenth centuries quietly authored

---

* Anonymous city lore and song, like peasant sayings, found their way into print, as did innumerable stories and poems in which artisans and servants were the actors (such as *Le caquet de bonnes Chambrieres, declarant aucunes finesses dont elles usent vers leurs maistres et maistresses*, printed at Lyon about 1549). The authorship of such material and its relation to actual popular life and sources are such complex problems that we cannot consider them here.

manuscripts—of craft secrets, of mechanical inventions, of poems. But the authors had failed to become widely known and, with the exception of outstanding figures like the literary Christine de Pisan, their works were not reproduced later by the presses.

But now many individuals without the ordinary attributes expected of an author in the later Middle Ages get their books printed—and they have an audience. Their tone might range from the confident ("I've tested sundials for a long time") to the apologetic ("Excuse my unadorned language . . . I am not Latin"), but they are sure that their skills, observations, or sentiments give them something distinctive to say.[66] Like the learned writer, they imagine varied publics for their work: their own kind and those on a higher level. Like the learned writer, they present themselves to the unknown buyers of their books in proud author portraits quite different from the humble donor picture characteristic of the medieval manuscript. Thus Milles de Norry, previously a modest reckonmaster in Lyon, gazes from his 1574 commercial arithmetic, fitted out with a ruff and a Greek device (see Plate 16).[67]

This widening of the circle of authors had diverse causes besides printing, but it was given some permanence by the new form of publication. Now practicing apothecaries get into print, like Pierre Braillier of Lyon, who dared to attack *The Abuses of Ignorance of Physicians*, and Nicolas Houel of Paris, who encroached on the physicians' field by writing on the plague and who published a treatise on poor relief as well.[68] Now surgeons write on their art and even on medicine (and we must remember that they are still considered *gens mécaniques* in the sixteenth century, despite the gains of some of them in learning, status, and wealth). Ambrose Paré's first book appears in 1545, when he is a mere army surgeon and master at the Hôtel-Dieu in Paris; and at least nineteen other surgeons have vernacular texts printed from the 1540's through the 1580's.[69] Sailors publish accounts of their travels to the New World. Poems come out from a cartwright in the Guyenne, a wine merchant in Toulouse, and a trader in Béthune, the last including a "Hymn to Commerce."[70]

The most self-conscious artisan-author, however, was the potter Bernard Palissy. To the readers of his important dialogues on chemistry and agriculture he says that some will think it impossible that "a poor artisan ... destitute of Latin" could be right and ancient learned theorists wrong. But experience is worth more than theory. If you don't believe what my books say, get my address from the printer and I will give you a demonstration in my own study.[71] What we see here is not merely fresh communication between craftsman and scholar (much discussed by historians of science), and between practice and theory (the participants in Palissy's dialogues); we see also a new kind of relation between an author and his anonymous public.*

Another entrant into the ranks of authors was, of course, the self-educated scholar-printer. Elizabeth Eisenstein has rightly stressed the novelty of this figure, who combined intellectual, physical, and administrative forms of labor.[72] Indeed, it was not only men like Badius, the Estiennes, Gryphius, and the de Tournes who had such a creative role; lesser masters and even journeymen could shape the content of the books they printed. Sometimes their

---

* This formal invitation from the author for direct response from readers is found in other printed books as well. It is the product of a situation in which the author expects that a large number of unknown readers will be seeing his work in the near future and will be able to locate him easily. (It goes well beyond the practice of the medieval author who, as John Benton has informed me, either urged his readers to write improvements on the manuscript or—more likely—anathemized readers and scribes who tampered with his text, but who did not invite correspondence.) Robert I Estienne asked readers of his *Dictionaire Francoislatin* to send him any words he might have omitted that they found in Latin authors and "good French authors," as well as to correct any faults they found in his definitions of hunting terms (Paris: Robert I Estienne, 1549, "*Au lecteur*" and p. 664). Both the physician Laurent Joubert and the bibliophile François de La Croix du Maine asked for information from their readers, as we will see below. Authors may also have received unsolicited letters: Ambrose Paré asked young surgeons using his *Oeuvres* (1575) to let him know graciously of any faults they might find rather than slander him. The reckonmaster Valentin Mennher did not especially want to hear from readers about the mistakes in his arithmetic texts: "Please just make corrections on the page rather than by useless words." The errors in a 1555 Lyon edition of his work were the printer's fault, not his (*Arithmetique Seconde par M. Valentin Mennher de Kempten* [Antwerp, Jean Loc, 1556], f. Z viii^r).

names are appended to prefaces; sometimes, as with the proof-reader Nicolas Dumont, it is only by luck that we catch a glimpse of their work as authors. A native of Saumur, Dumont was so busy preparing and correcting copy in Paris in the years 1569 to 1584 "that he scarcely had time to breathe." Yet he sometimes got hold of a press and printed pamphlets; he translated various works from Latin to French; and, in particular, he composed little news stories about Henri III's doings in France and Poland, the seizure of Tunis from the Turks, and other current happenings. Whether he presented his stories as "letters" from unnamed gentlemen observers or as anonymous eyewitness accounts, Dumont in many ways anticipated the reporter of the periodical press.[73]

Female writers also appeared in print in noticeable numbers—more than twenty had some reputation. Mostly they came from families of gentlemen or lawyers, were involved in humanist circles, and published poems or translations.[74] Their works still show signs of womanly modesty: they are dedicated to other women ("because women must not willingly appear in public alone, I choose you for my guide"); they address themselves to "female readers"; they defend themselves against the reproach that silence is the ornament of women.[75] A few of them transformed the image of the author even more: Louise Labé, the rope-maker's daughter, whose appeal to women to publish we heard at the opening of this essay (and contemporary evidence indicates that many well-born women did shyly keep their poems in manuscript);[76] Nicole Estienne, printer's daughter and physician's wife, whose verses on "The Miseries of the Married Woman" had two editions; and the midwife Louise Bourgeois. Once midwife to the poor of her Paris neighborhood, later midwife to the family of Henri IV, Bourgeois wrote on her art, believing herself the first woman to do so. Her wide practice, she claimed, would show up the mistakes of Physicians and Surgeons, even of Master Galen himself. She looks out with poise from her engraving at the reader, this skilled woman who corrected men, publicly and in print (see Plate 15).[77]

Finally, groups among the *menu peuple* sometimes spoke to

the public collectively through the press. The *compagnonnages* of the journeymen of Lyon and Paris, as we have seen, printed the brief that they presented to the Parlement of Paris in 1572. This document raised a dozen objections to a royal edict on printing and attacked the journeymen's employers as tyrannical and avaricious oppressors, who worked them to poverty and illness. Their employers answered, also in print, that the journeymen were debauched conspiratorial "monopolists," trying to reduce their masters to servitude and destroy the industry. A printed protest was used again in Lyon in 1588, when master printers and journeymen were on the same side against the merchant-publishers, who were ignoring them in favor of the cheaper labor of Geneva.[78] Here are precocious examples of artisans trying to influence literate public opinion in a labor dispute.

Groups also tried on occasion to influence public opinion in regard to political matters. Here I am thinking of the urban Abbeys of Misrule, festive societies of neighborhood or craft, which directed their charivaris and mockery not only against domestic scandals but against misgovernment by their betters. For a long time, the Abbeys had left their recreations unrecorded; but in the sixteenth century they began to print them. Thus readers outside Rouen could learn about the 1540 Mardi Gras parade at that city —with its float bearing a king, the pope, the emperor, and a fool playing catch with the globe—and could ponder its mocking verses about hypocrisy in the church, about how faith was turning to contempt (*foy* to *fy*) and nobility to injury (*noblesse* to *on blesse*). In the Lyon festivals of the 1570's through the 1590's, the Lord of Misprint tossed printed verses to the spectators and subsequently published the scenarios, with their complaints about the high cost of bread and paper, about the fluctuations in the value of currency, and especially about the folly of war in France.[79]

This body of pamphlet literature, small and ephemeral though it is, suggests two interesting things about the relation of printing to the development of political consciousness. First, though most early polemical literature disseminated outward and downward the political and religious views of persons at the center (whether at the center of royal government or at the center of strong resistance movements like the Huguenots and the Holy Catholic League), it occurred to some city people on the margins of power to use the press to respond. Second, the addition of printed pamphlets to traditional methods for spreading news (rumor, street song, private letters, town criers, fireworks displays, bell-ringing, and penitential processions) increased the *menu peuple*'s stock of detailed information about national events. In the 1540's, the Rouen festive society could count on spectators and readers knowing the facts of local political life, but references to national or European events were usually general and even allegorical. By the end of the century in Lyon, however, the Lord of Misprint could expect that his audience would also recognize joking references to recent sumptuary legislation and to controversial decisions of the Parlement of Paris.[80]

Readers may be thinking that these varied works authored by the *menu peuple* were such a tiny fraction of the total printed corpus of sixteenth-century France that no educated contemporary would have paid attention to them. In fact they were noticed, favorably and unfavorably. The visionary bibliographer François de La Croix du Maine, who built up a library of thousands of volumes and who sent out printed requests all over Europe for information about authors, was happy to include most of the people and books we have been considering here in his *Bibliotheque* of 1584.* He made no critical exclusions: Nicole Estienne

---

* Thus among sixteenth-century authors either writing in French or translating into French, La Croix listed 110 physicians, but also 25 surgeons (22 of whom had works in print) and nine apothecaries (eight with works in print). He included 40 female writers from the end of the fifteenth century to 1584 (at least sixteen had works in print, as far as he knew); Christine de Pisan, composing her *City of Ladies* around 1405, seems to have been aware of no other contemporary female authors.

In 1579 at Le Mans, La Croix had 350 copies printed of the initial statement of his project, including his request for information about or from authors. He received six answers. He repeated the request in the 1584 edition of the *Bibliotheque*, this time remembering to suggest ways in which mail might reach him

and Nicolas Dumont are set in their alphabetical places just as are Pierre de Ronsard and Joachim du Bellay in his "general catalogue" of all authors, "women as well as men, who had written in our maternal French."[81]

We also have a reaction from a humanist and poet deeply concerned about the character of French culture. As a member of the Pléiade, Jacques Peletier had devoted himself to the vernacular tongue and had also celebrated the printing press:

> Ah . . . one can print in one day
> What it would take thirty days to say
> And a hundred times longer to write by hand.

High quality in vernacular publication would be guaranteed, so he had argued hopefully, by right and clear Method—right method for ordering poetry, mathematics, medicine, music, even spelling. But what would happen now that all kinds of people were publishing books? In an ironic anonymous essay, he urged every village, every curate, every trader, every captain to write his piece; every parish, every vineyard must have its historian. *"Ecrivons tous, sçavans et non sçavans!"* And if we do badly? Well, never mind. Our books can be used by the ladies who sell toilet paper at the Paris bridges.[82]

How indeed could the learned control not only aesthetic quality but also true doctrine and science if just anyone could get books printed, and if these books were being made available by the press in the vernacular to large numbers of ill-educated city people? The central book in the religious debate was, of course, the vernacular Bible, and for several decades the doctors of theology (strongly backed by secular law) tried to defend their monopoly on its interpretation by denying the right of the uneducated to read it. The debate was sometimes face to face, between doctor of theology and craftsman: "Do you think it's up to you to read the Bible," asked the Inquisitor in a Lyon prison in 1552, "since you're just

---

at Paris (*Premier volume de la Bibliotheque du sieur de la Croix-du-Maine* [Paris: Abel l'Angelier, 1584], *"Preface aux lecteurs"* and pp. 523, 529, 538-39).

an artisan and without knowledge?" "God taught me by His Holy Spirit," said the craftsman. "It belongs to all Christians to know it in order to learn the way to salvation."[83]

The debate also took place in print. "God does not want to declare his secrets to a bunch of *menu peuple*," said the great Jesuit Emond Auger. "Intoxicated by I know not what phrases from the Apostles, badly quoted and even worse understood, they start to abuse the Mass and make up questions." Understanding comes not from "a bare and vulgar knowledge of the words," but from the special vocation of those who have studied.[84] A young Protestant pastor answered: the pope and his doctors of theology forbid the Bible to everyone but themselves, because they know that once their lives and doctrine are examined by the Word of God, they will have to give their goods to the poor and start working with their hands. They permit a poor craftsman to read a book on love or folly, to dance or play cards, but they see him with a New Testament in his hands and he is a heretic. But our Lord has commanded us "Search the Scriptures." And the early Fathers exhorted the people—craftsmen, women, and everybody in general—to read it in their houses and often, and especially before going to sermons so they could understand them.[85] The pastor ends up reminding his readers that reading *alone* was not the path to true doctrine. The Protestant method for guaranteeing orthodoxy was in the last instance censorship and punishment; but in the first instance it was *the combination of reading with listening to a trained teacher.*

Ultimately, despite the triumphs of the Counter-Reformation in France, the doctors of theology had to abandon their position, in fact if not always in public. Force simply would not work. What had guaranteed the clerical monopoly two hundred years before had really been a limited technology and the Latin language. Already at the end of the fourteenth century, vernacular Bibles, Biblical digests, and picture books were being used by lay families here and there. Once the first presses were installed in France, the stream of French Bibles and Bible versions began without waiting for the Reformation. No legislation, no inquisition, no procedures of censorship could stop the new relations between reading, listening, and talking that had grown up among city people—relations which Catholic humanists as well as Protestants had been ready to encourage. After the 1570's, it became legal for a French Bible— a Catholic revision of the Genevan Scripture approved by the Theology Faculty of Louvain—to circulate in France. In cheap, small format, the New Testament had some success among Catholic laymen in the cities.[86]

What was needed to maintain Catholic orthodoxy was a mode of control more suited to printing than an archaic form of sacerdotal monopoly and more effective than censorship. In 1524, a Franciscan religious who was translating and commenting a Book of Hours for a circle of noblewomen pointed the way. Everyone is admitted to preaching, no matter how unlearned, said Brother Gilles; need seeing words be more dangerous than hearing them? The answer was to make the bare text safe by clothing it with orthodox exposition. The Jesuits were to go on and fix the meaning of a devotional text by an accompanying standardized religious picture or emblem. By 1561 in Lyon, the Jesuit Possevino paid for the printing of orthodox little booklets and distributed them free in the streets. By the late sixteenth century, the Catholic laity had a growing body of spiritual literature *in which the eye was guided by exposition and illustration.*[87]

A similar though less intense debate occurred over the dissemination of medical information to laymen. Vernacular *Regimens against the Plague* and collections of remedies for ill health and women's disorders were old genres; printing did no more than increase their numbers. In the 1530's, however, doctors of medicine began to publish translations of Greek medical texts and of Doctor Guy de Chauliac's fourteenth-century Latin treatise on surgery, as well as systematic examinations of medicine and surgery in French for the specific use of surgeons' journeymen, "who have begged us to do it," "whose ignorance must be dispelled," and "who are today more studious than many physicians." These books were used by the young surgeons who attended occasional lectures and dissections given by physicians at the Hôtel-Dieu at Lyon, special courses at the Faculty of Medicine at Montpellier, and the classes supported by the surgeons' confraternity of Saint-Côme at Paris; they were used also by older surgeons in the cities who wanted to improve their skill.[88] The next step was the publication by doctors of medicine of new regimens of health and medical advice on child-rearing in the vernacular, very often dedicated to women.[89]

The arguments used in defense of these editions, offered by Catholic humanists and Protestants alike, resemble those used in defense of vernacular Bibles and doctrinal literature. As printers pointed out that Saint Jerome had translated the Bible into a vernacular, so the physician Vallembert pointed out in his 1565 pediatric manual that Galen and Avicenna had written in their vernacular. An English medical popularizer spoke against his critics in the very terms that the early Protestant Antoine de Marcourt had used against the engrossing "merchants" of the Faculty of Theology: "Why grutch [grudge] they phisike to come forth in Englysche? Wolde they have no man to know but onley they? Or what make they themselves? Marchauntes of our lyves and deathes, that we shulde bye our healthe onely of them, and at theyr pryces?" A French work by the Protestant Laurent Joubert makes the comparison explicit: those doctors of medicine who say that it is wrong to teach people how to maintain their health are no better than doctors of theology who deprive them of spiritual food. To those who objected to instructing surgeons in French, Joubert's son answered that good operations could be performed in any language and that misunderstanding of a Latin text was as possible as misunderstanding of a French one ("should we burn all Latin books because of the danger that some clerk will misinterpret the law therein?"). And anyway, if we are willing to read books aloud to surgeons' journeymen, why not put them in French? "Must we put a lower value on the living voice than on the written paper?"[90]

Laurent Joubert's volumes are especially useful for a study of the new relations between groups of people and between cultural traditions facilitated by printing. For twenty-five years he had been trying to stamp out false opinions in medicine, and in 1578 he decided to compile a new kind of book—*Erreurs Populaires* about health and medicine from conception to grave that he would collect and correct. "Popular errors" came from several sources, he explained: from weaknesses in the soul and human reasoning; from ignorant oral traditions, especially those of midwives; and from people's having heard too much from physicians and having a crude understanding of it. It seems to me, however, that as the sense of the errors in peasant lore was sharpened for the learned by the printing of that lore (as we have seen above), so the printing of all kinds of vulgar regimens, traditional books of secrets, and remedies created for Joubert the concept of general errors and made them accessible to correction.*

In any case, in Volume One he got through conception and infancy, demonstrating, for instance, that it was *not* true that male children were born at full moon and female children at new moon and that it *was* true that at certain times of night or monthly period one could be sure of conceiving a male. He then told his readers that he would wait to publish Volume Two until they had had a chance to send him more popular errors. They could just address him at the University of Montpellier, where he was Chancellor of the Faculty of Medicine. Dr. Joubert received 456 sayings and queries from readers within a year, which he duly published and, where possible, corrected or explained in Volume Two.[91]

Joubert's *Popular Errors* illustrates the central paradox in the impact of printing on the people. On the one hand, it can destroy traditional monopolies on knowledge and authorship and can sell and disseminate widely both information and works of imagination. It can even set up a new two-way relationship between author and anonymous audience. But printing can also make

---

* The origin and history of books on popular errors in medicine are discussed further in Chapter 8.

possible the establishment of new kinds of control on popular thought. To quote once more the physician and translator Pierre Tolet, "If you want a servant to follow your orders, you can't give them in an unknown tongue."[92] Joubert's goal and that of the other popularizers was not to eliminate the distinction between expert and inexpert or to weaken the profession of medicine. It was to raise the surgeons from their "routine illiterate practice" while defining their field to keep even the most skillful of them under the authority of the physicians. It was to raise the people to a better understanding of how to take care of themselves while convincing them more effectively to obey the doctor's orders.

On the whole, it seems to me that the first 125 years of printing in France, which brought little change in the countryside, strengthened rather than sapped the vitality of the culture of the *menu peuple* in the cities—that is, added both to their realism and to the richness of their dreams, both to their self-respect and to their ability to criticize themselves and others. This is because they were not passive recipients (neither passive beneficiaries nor passive victims) of a new type of communication. Rather they were active users and interpreters of the printed books they heard and read, and even helped give these books form. Richard Hoggart, in his remarkable study of working-class culture in present-day England (*The Uses of Literacy*) has found a salty, particularistic, resourceful layer of culture existing along with a "candy-floss," slack, uniform one. If this is possible in the twentieth century, with its powerful and highly competitive mass media and centralized political institutions, all the more readily could the sixteenth-century populace impose its uses on the books that came to it. Oral culture and popular social organization were strong enough to resist mere correction and standardization from above. Protestantism and certain features of humanism converged with printing to challenge traditional hierarchical values and to delay the establishment of rigid new ones. Economic control of publishing was not concentrated in the houses of great merchant-publishers, but was shared by a variety of producers. Monopolies in knowledge had broken down but had not been replaced by effective political and religious censorship and by the theory and laws of private property in ideas.

If in a different context printing may lead the people to flaccidity, escape, and the ephemeral, in the sixteenth century the printers' journeymen could claim with some reason that printing was "the eternal brush which gave a living portrait to the spirit."[93]

EIGHT

Proverbial Wisdom and Popular Errors

In the late fifteenth century, when Europe's new presses were has-
tening into print the most appreciated works of the medieval
manuscript corpus, there appeared in Paris and in several other
cities a little book called *The Sayings of Solomon with the Answers
of Marcolf*. On the title page of one of them was a woodcut of a
bookish, decorous king talking with a disheveled, barefoot rustic
(see Plate 12). In the text Solomon gave forth rhymed proverbs of
high moral tone; Marcolf then answered back in earthy verse,
either redoing Solomon's sayings in shrewd practical language or
going him one better in a joke. Thus Solomon observes:

> A load upon a mare
> May be silver or be brass
> Which one the beast won't care.

To which Marcolf responds:

> The whore doesn't care
> Which man jumps on her ass,
> To her it's all one fare.

The manuscript tradition of this dialogue, which existed in various
versions and in several vernaculars, went back to the tenth century. In the twelfth century it was widely narrated, and in the
sixteenth century Rabelais had his characters play it as a game,
like "the dozens."[1]

Three centuries later, on the 30th of Floréal in the year XIII (1805), the newly formed Académie Celtique in Paris envisaged a rather different exchange between the learned man and the peasant. The now lustrous nation of France must uncover the glories of its earliest days. To this end, the Academicians drew up a questionnaire on the proverbs, customs, "superstitious" medicine, and ritual of the peasants in order to gain information that would assist in reconstructing the language, myths, and history of the Celts. The questionnaire would be distributed, so they hoped, to prefects and scholars in the *départements*. There was some cause for speed, for with the Code Civile and other new institutions in France, it was to be expected that the old sayings and ways would soon disappear. When the answers came back over the next few years, no Marcolf was among the respondents.[2]

It is the change from the living dialogue of Solomon and Marcolf to the roundabout studious questionnaire of the Celtic Academy that poses the central problem of this essay. Each shows the learned engaged in collecting materials about or from the peasant; each suggests a different attitude toward the peasant and different uses for his words. Each then becomes a valuable source for the student of social boundaries, of the early history of anthropology and folklore, and of the actual customs and behavior of the lower orders.

Collecting popular customs was certainly not a major interest of the educated and wellborn in early modern Europe. They wrote pastorals, eclogues, and domestic comedies more often than observations on peasants or servants. They described the customs of the Turks, the Africans, the Iroquois, and the Aztecs more frequently than those of local folk. The Druids and old Celtic ways were the subject of more dissertations from the 1580's to the 1650's than, say, the current practices of peasants in Brittany or Burgundy.[3] Cultural and social boundaries might be as readily explored in reflections on the relation of humans to ape or beast, of civilized man to wild man, and of male to female as in reflections on the relation of noble to commoner and of master to servant.*

Despite these preferences, there nevertheless exists a body of literature from the fifteenth to eighteenth centuries in which learned persons present information about the behavior and sayings of the "people." Such were the theologians' compilations of "superstitions," where the authors went to some trouble to record the practices and beliefs they wished to modify or extirpate: examples include the fifteenth-century *Tractatus de superstitiosis* by Henricus de Gorinchem; the late-seventeenth-century *Traité des superstitions* by Jean-Baptiste Thiers, *curé* of rural parishes in the Maine; and *The Antiquities of the Common People* (1725) by the Newcastle clergyman Henry Bourne.[4] Such were collections of and commentaries on song and dance in the sixteenth and seventeenth centuries, which claimed to have "rustic" and/or popular creations among their pages. Such were the books of fairy tales and folktales, which—assigned no distinctive popular origin in the fifteenth- and sixteenth-century editions—were attributed to the people, to Mother Goose, or to old nurses in the versions prepared by Charles Perrault, Mademoiselle Lhéritier, and others in the late seventeenth and early eighteenth centuries.[5]

Such, finally, were the two genres that will be our point of concentration here: collections of common proverbs, and collections of popular beliefs and practices in regard to health and medical cures. In reviewing them, I will ask several questions that may have a bearing on other kinds of collecting as well. Why were the learned writing about common sayings and doings, and for whom? Can we tell how they acquired their information and whether they altered it for publication? What sense did they have of how proverbs and remedies functioned in the lives of the people? That is, to what extent did men who never used the word "culture" in its anthropological definition still conceive (as did

---

* See the discussion of the meanings of sexual symbolism in Chapter 5, "Women on Top."

Thomas More when he wrote of Utopians and Montaigne when he wrote of Cannibals) that there was some meaningful order in the language and usage of peasants and city folk, even when such language and usage might differ from their own? An analysis of these questions—already so fruitful in Marc Soriano's study of the *Contes de Perrault*—may here tell us something new about the changing relations between learned and popular culture in preindustrial France.[6] It may also guide us in the venture that first attracted me to these collections—to use them to hear the voice of the people therein.

[I]

The *Sayings* of Solomon and Marcolf were only a small part of the recorded proverbial stock that sixteenth-century scholars acquired from the past. Adages and proverbs were assembled and transcribed repeatedly in the Middle Ages. The manuscript collections fell into two categories: those proverbs and maxims attributed to ancient sages and philosophers (Aristotle, Seneca, Cato the Elder, and others), and those vernacular proverbs attributed to peasants or common people (*Li proverbes au vilain*, *Proverbes communs*, and *Proverbes ruraux et vulgaux*). The compilers of the common proverbs seem to have been obscure clerics, though one collection was commissioned by a Count of Flanders and another by a Count of Burgundy. The lists might include as many as five or six hundred sayings, some of them still in use in France today.[7]

Whether rhymed or unrhymed, the proverbs were presented either in a way that dramatized their usage in speech, or else in a way that assumed that readers knew their meaning. Solomon and Marcolf exchange their sayings, as we have seen; the proverbs of the *"vilain"* follow upon a verse to which each one applies. The *proverbes ruraux et vulgaux* simply stand alone in no special order. Not until the late fifteenth century did a Latin prose exposition appear in collections of the popular proverbs.[8]

Are the proverbs, then, really from the peasants' lips? The authority of the collections clearly depended on readers thinking so, but the compilers do not say where precisely they heard or saw their sayings. In all likelihood, some of the proverbs did have a genuinely rural or "common" origin, but they have been modified for use by nonpeasants. On the one hand, their metaphors drew upon subjects familiar to countryfolk—oxen, horses, dogs, grains, fallow fields—and were sometimes coarse or ribald.[9] On the other hand, they were in Old French rather than in the regional dialects peasants spoke in the late Middle Ages. All their particularistic edges (of which we shall hear more in a moment) have been rubbed away.

Common proverbs thus were made generally available for the speech of knights and clerks, who wanted to supplement their own store, memorized in childhood or perhaps learned from the *Distichs of Cato*. They were used by writers: not only did Chaucer put them in the mouth of the lusty wife of Bath, but Chrétien de Troyes gave some of the *vilain*'s proverbs to diverse characters in his courtly romances.[10] They were used in preaching, too, both in the vernacular and in Latin: "Love me, love my dog" was being said in a Latin sermon by Bernard of Clairvaux at about the same time that it was being recorded in *Li proverbes au vilain*.[11] They may well have been used by landowning laymen at vassalic and manorial courts: the medieval common proverbs *"Qui veut le roi, si va la loi"* and *"Oignez vilain, il vous poindra: poignez vilain, il vous oindra"* had acquired the status of legal aphorisms by the late sixteenth century when Antoine Loisel was drawing up his manual of French customary law.[12] Learned men bound collections of vulgar proverbs in together with lofty rhetorical manuscripts on letter-writing and oratory. Noblemen had them transcribed along with "philosophic" sentences and little vernacular treatises on morality and history.[13]

In short, clerical and literary languages were seen as separate from common rural speech; but, as in the dialogue between Solomon and Marcolf, under certain conditions they were equivalent. They shared the same speech form—the proverb—and none had an absolute monopoly on wisdom. Though the proverb *"Vox populi, vox Dei"* already had some currency in Europe, it was not widely accepted or used. The vulgar proverbs were collected not as the voice of God but because they had a claim to tell some of the truth. To quote *Li proverbes au vilain*, "The wise man takes mutton in place of venison."[14]

This view of the common proverb and its use in clerical and knightly circles are related to several features of medieval society and culture. First of all, the level of literacy among the laity in northern Europe was low until the fifteenth century (those were the days when only the clergy were learned, said Etienne Pasquier, looking back from the sixteenth century, thus the old saying about "speaking Latin before clerks").[15] The mnemonic proverb was appreciated not simply because ancient writers had praised it as a rhetorical device, but because it was necessary to so much of the business of society.

Second, as Jacques Le Goff has argued, from the twelfth through the fourteenth centuries in France, knights and noble landowners were trying to set themselves off from the clergy and forge an independent cultural identity. This involved in part certain "folk" tastes taken over from their peasants, such as a love for Mélusine and other fairy tales. Interest in their peasants' proverbs is of a piece with this. Nor would they have been put off by the frank references to bodily orifices and processes found in the common sayings. We know, since Nykrog's work, that bawdy and scatological tales were told to aristocratic audiences along with the expected chivalric romance. Indeed, some sayings that emerged from the knightly milieu (such as *"la verge anoblit et le ventre affranchit"*) would have been thought indelicate by a later age.[16]

Third, a part of the clergy, however Latin and scholastic its training, still had to preach to the people in their own language. From the twelfth century on, sermons can be found addressed to distinct social or vocational groups—peasants among them.[17] Common proverbs were a way of setting up a familiar universe of discourse and of helping people to remember the sermon's message. Furthermore, until the mid-fifteenth century, most clerics shared the willingness of their hierarchical society (with its rural rituals and its Pauline tradition of the wondrous "foolishness of preaching" [1 Cor. 1: 18-20]) to play at turning the world upside down.[18] We have looked at their games and rites of reversal in earlier chapters. So, too, the words of the peasant fool Marcolf could on occasion topple Solomon's wisdom.

[11]

In the sixteenth century, this whole picture changed. Learned interest in proverbs intensified in a way that would not be seen again in Europe until the romantic national movements of the late eighteenth and nineteenth centuries; and the collectors were not just modest clerics but often important humanists. New compilations of classical and common proverbs were made and printed; proverbs were compared from one language to another; the stylistic and linguistic features of the proverb were discussed afresh. To the older practical, moral, and rhetorical reasons for collecting proverbs was added a new concern with the enrichment of the national tongue. The old inattention to historical and/or geographical origins was no longer general, as some collectors began to consider where precisely a common proverb came from and what it meant to its users. Interestingly enough, these last two developments—though simultaneous and sometimes initiated by the same people—were ultimately in conflict with each other, reflecting (as we shall see) contradictory goals in the collection of the people's speech.

The first step was taken with regard to the "learned" proverbs, and involved verifying, correcting, and expanding the welter of sayings attributed to real or legendary classical sages. Even before the work of Erasmus, the Italian humanist Beroaldo had published an oration on ancient views of the proverb, and Polydore Vergil had brought out in Paris his new collection of proverbs from Greece and Rome.[19] Then in 1500, the *Adagia* of Erasmus began to appear (some eight hundred in the first edition;

more than four thousand when he had done with them in the 1530's). Though he presented there only aphorisms culled from ancient writers in Latin, Greek, and Hebrew, his method and material had important implications for the study of popular sayings in the vernacular.

To begin with, Erasmus set up a definition of the proverb— or, at least, of the proverb worth collecting—that made it neither the exclusive possession of esoteric circles nor the natural property of the people. Aristotle's definition could be taken to support either view: proverbs were "brief and pregnant" sayings, whose authority came from their being an "ancient witness" and universally known; they were also "the truest remains of the ancient philosophy," and thus full of "hidden meaning."[20] To his contemporaries who wanted to make the proverb into a kind of hieroglyph that only an elite could fully decipher, Erasmus pointed out that many proverbs were not dark enigmas. Some of them were clear, and they were all widely known and commonly said. To those collectors who thought a proverb could be just any trite saw mouthed by the people, Erasmus insisted that a proverb had to have style. It had to be pithy and witty, with an unusual turn or figure; short and neat; "clear-cut as a gem." Both peasant and scholar could share such language: in the Gospel itself there were "many things . . . from the common people," Christ taking on our "familiar language" as he took on our body. Nevertheless, there was a limit to the vulgarity of speech in which wisdom could be expressed. When Erasmus "made a show of kitchen pots" (one of his Greek proverbs), that is, when he used Dame Folly to tell the truth about the great, she spoke in pleasant jokes, not in a "vile offensive" fashion. Marcolf's tongue would have to be bridled a bit.[21]

Erasmus went on to demonstrate a method for studying proverbs. The adage was for him not only an occasion for moral, literary, or satirical comment on his own day, but "a window on the ancient world." For each saying he wanted to find its meaning, its origin, and how it should be used; and since ancient customs were often so different from modern ones, he had to read carefully in many classical authors. Some of their proverbs no longer made sense (tightrope walking was an easy matter now); some were still being said by the common people ("he carries water in one hand and fire in another" to indicate a double-dealer); but the proverb was first and foremost embedded in its own culture. Context could be so important that Erasmus admitted "Some proverbs have this peculiarity, that they need to be quoted in their native tongue, otherwise they lose much of their charm; just as some wines refuse to be exported."[22]

For those learned persons interested in proverbs in their native tongue, the celebrated classicist and humanist had a double message. Collect and use your common proverbs, for there are gems among them; but follow your judgment and taste about what to include. Study proverbs carefully, even if they reflect customs different from your own; notice what they mean to the common people who have been using them.

What was in fact the treatment of the vernacular proverb? In the early years of the century, between about 1510 and 1519, the collating of vernacular proverbs was begun by two clerics teaching in the University of Paris—Nicolas Du Puy (alias Bonaspes), who had corrected Polydore Vergil's classical proverbs, and his friend Master Jean Gilles de Noyers. Combining French proverbs from several medieval manuscripts,* they published them together with their own Latin translations but without any commentary. Entitled variously *Proverbia communia, Proverbia gallicana, Proverbia popularia,* and *Proverbes communs,* the editions were advertised not as a way to study the people but as a source for eloquence, for learning French and Latin, and for moral instruction of boys and even of unmarried girls. They were not precisely what

---

* In the 1490's, at Lyon and Paris, printed editions appeared of a late-fifteenth-century manuscript collection of French proverbs by Jean de la Veprie, prior of Clairvaux, entitled *Les proverbes communs.* Gilles de Noyers drew heavily, though by no means exclusively, on this collection and may have used it in printed form rather than in manuscript. See note 23.

Erasmus would have recommended, but they still aroused the interest of humanist printers (such as Josse Bade) and of lawyers and poets. As one of them remarked in a 1549 dedication, the ancients prized their proverbs, so why should the French look down on theirs? Finally, after many printings, at the opening of the seventeenth century the common proverbs (in the version of Gilles de Noyers) were all incorporated into the important *Treasure of the French Tongue, Ancient and Modern.* The store of proverbs came to more than a thousand; they covered a multitude of subjects; and they ranged in imagery from the fecal to the celestial.[23]

Understandably, the *Proverbia communia* did not satisfy some humanists. The traditional popular corpus was founded on older compilations alone. Origin, meaning, and use were not there explored, and some of the proverbs were objectionable. The innovator was the canon Charles de Bouelles of Noyon in Picardy, onetime member of the circle of Lefèvre d'Etaples, mathematician and philosopher. Bouelles had developed a deep though ambivalent curiosity about vernacular language long before the members of the Pléiade had begun their defense and illustration of the French tongue. Unlike them, he saw no possibility for creating a regulated, correct vernacular that would equal Latin in splendor. Regional variations in customs and temperament (the influence of the stars was important here; yet somehow it did not affect the savants' international Latin), geographical mobility, and the ignorance of the people would always keep pronunciation, grammar, and idioms faulty and in flux. "Today in France there are as many customs and languages as there are peoples, regions, and towns," he observed in his 1533 Latin treatise on vernacular languages.[24]

However regrettable these differences, Bouelles found them worth writing about. In addition to his work on vernacular pronunciation and etymology, he published two books of popular proverbs—*Proverbiorum Vulgarium Libri tres* in 1531, and *Proverbes et dicts sententieux* in 1557. His vulgar subject embarrassed him a little, it is true. His dedications were in Latin; he indexed the vernacular proverbs in the 1531 edition by their first letter in Latin translation; he had done them only because his young nephews asked him to. Compared with the *Adages* of Erasmus, his were ludicrous and light—what else could you expect from plebeians? And yet he thought there was some truth spoken here, even if common proverbs were hard on soft ears.[25]

So he listened, and was the first French compiler to state that he had gone out into the streets, roads, and doorways and taken down the sayings directly from the mouth of the people. Moreover, he was the first French commentator to provide some social context for his explications. "*A longue voye, paille poise* [from the 1557 collection of Bouelles, this saying was also recorded in the mid-fifteenth century by a canon in nearby Lille]. This proverb is frequent and very common among the people, and refers to those who, even if sober and of little expense, live off others and are hard on their friends. Thus, straw is light, but on a long journey, it weighs a lot." "*A toute heure, femme pleure.* The common people, speaking of the lightness of women, say while laughing, 'a woman laughs when she can and cries when she wants to.'" "*De tout grain on faict pain.* These words are said very often by the poor against the high cost of grain." "*Qui pert le sien Il pert le sens.* This proverb is more common among the *menu peuple* than among the rich and opulent."[26]

A modest achievement perhaps, especially when one remembers that Bouelles, who had elsewhere noted eight different pronunciations for "yes" and six for "no" in various regions of France,[27] here put all his proverbs into a standard French, with no word about variations. Moreover, of the nine hundred sayings that he collected—wide-ranging though they were—none was what Erasmus would have thought "offensive." Some of what Bouelles heard he did not record.

Bouelles' initial quest for the context of common proverbs was carried on in the next decades by a few literary men who had no lingering doubts about the value of French. For instance, Jean Nicot, editor of the 1606 *Treasure of the French Tongue*, included an anonymous work of *Moral Explications*, with one hundred and twenty current sayings, that made frequent reference to rural, commercial, and craft practice. Admittedly, the author's close observation of the people is put in doubt when the explanation for "*Escorcher l'anguille par la queue*" begins "Those who have seen an eel skinned know that it is absolutely necessary to begin from the tail." But elsewhere his untangling of metaphors leads to descriptions of how muleteers give oats to their mules, how winegrowers prop their vines, how peasants cheat in paying their tithes ("to give God a sheaf of straw," a proverb going back to Scripture), how cardplayers conceal their emotions (wearing a scarf over part of the face helps), how millers overcharge, and how bakers put their dough in the oven. One proverb he quotes as a shout between two haggling tradesmen; for another he gives the hand gestures that always go with it. Especially noteworthy are a few sayings that, instead of floating geographically as "common," are characterized as "peculiar" to Troyes or to the Champagne. Thus a distinctive proverb about losing the substance of one's work by continual fussing with it ("*De l'arbre d'un pressoir le manche d'un cernoir*"—a very rough English equivalent might be "You've sanded your mast to a matchstick") calls forth data on winepresses, nutcrackers, and carpentry in the rural Champenois.[28]

Still, if proverbs and regional sentiment sometimes pushed the author of the *Explications morales* to detailed observation of popular customs, it was the French language rather than the culture of the people that concerned him. As the scholar-publisher Henri Estienne was to say in 1579 in his *Précellence du langage françois*, the range in subject of the vernacular proverbs and the grace possessed by some of them proved once again that French could compete in power and beauty of expression with Italian, Greek, and Latin. This was also the view of the lawyer Etienne Pasquier, who devoted many pages of his *Recherches de la France* to discussing selected common proverbs. Like his other antiquities, these were nuggets from which he could mine the national past. Some proverbs fell out of use as customs changed* (Erasmus had remarked this in his *Adagia*), some changed their wording, some stayed the same; but they could all be studied as expressions of the national character.[29]

Finally, the several new editions of common proverbs without commentaries that appeared in the last half of the sixteenth century and during the reign of Henri IV were not prompted by a yearning for Marcolf's wisdom or for a window on the popular world. None bothered with translations of the vulgar proverbs into Latin; one "enriched" the French collection with translations of Italian or classical proverbs; three placed French proverbs next to their equivalents in vernaculars outside the kingdom (French/ Italian, 1547; Flemish/French, 1568; Spanish/French, 1609). But no one recorded proverbs "peculiar" to a place, or in regional dialects or languages like Provençal or Breton†—not even the physician Jean Le Bon of Lorraine, who declared he was collecting his proverbs from all provinces in order to embellish French without going abroad. If Gabriel Meurier remarked in his 1568 preface that "it's commonly said and believed that the common people do not lie," it was not really that firmly believed. More characteristic was the position of Le Bon in the 1570's that the proverb was a remarkable form of speech—ancient, graceful, elegant, a

---

* For instance, Pasquier discussed *"Je veux qu'on me tonde"* (that is, "I want to be shaved" if such and such a thing I say isn't true or if I don't do such and such a thing) as a saying of "our fathers and ancestors" that he had heard in his childhood, but that was no longer used. This was because long hair was once respected, and the common people, seeing kings with long wigs, thought a shaved head ignominious. Nowadays, when everyone wore his hair short, the saying could no longer suggest a punishment. *Les recherches de la France* (Paris, 1633), Book VIII, chap. 9, pp. 699-700.

† The earliest example known to me of a collection of proverbs in one of the regional dialects is Voltoire's list of Gascon proverbs (*"montets gasconns"*) incidental to his 1607 treatise on commerce, *Le Marchand traictant des proprietez et particularitez de commerce et négoce* (Toulouse, 1607). See G. Brunet, *Anciens proverbes basques et gascons, recueillis par Voltoire* (Paris, 1845). The earliest example of a dictionary of special slang is Pechon de Ruby, *La vie généreuse des mercelots, gueuz et boesmiens, contenans leur façon de vivre, subtilitez et gergon* (Lyon, 1596).

"voix de ville" that in any conversation might serve as the final arbiter and judge—but that the people used proverbs without appreciating all this. In a sense, the proverbs existed above *"le parler peuplacier"* and were best understood by the learned.[30]

We come then to the basic paradox in the learned collecting of popular speech and customs during the sixteenth century. The more collectors wished to share the speech forms and language of the people, the less able they were to grasp the concrete particularity and order in popular culture. The more collectors wished to study popular proverbs in their context, the less able they were to value them as something that could be used to enrich current national culture.

At work here were changes that loosened social and cultural boundaries only to redraw some of them more securely than before. On the one hand, French had been established as a learned and literary language in its own right, as against the Latin of the clergy and the universities, and this had involved in part the assimilation of popular speech forms into it. Furthermore, common proverbs were really used by the learned. The collections went through numerous printed editions and were bought by lawyers and schoolteachers among others. *Proverbes vulgaires* were quoted in a wide range of genres (*"plusieurs yeux voyent mieux que peu,"* said lawyer Claude de Rubys in the midst of a defense of Lyon's political institutions), and were kept in handwritten lists by scholarly jurists such as Pierre Pithou and Antoine Loisel.[31] So well-known were they that Rabelais could count on his readers getting the joke without commentary when the officers of Queen Whim in the Kingdom of Entelechy "ploughed a sandy shore with three couples of foxes in one yoke and did not lose their seed," "sheared asses and got long fleece wool anyway," "gathered grapes off of thorns and figs off of thistles," and "skinned an eel from the tail"; in the same way, Bruegel could count on viewers understanding much of his painted rendition of Flemish proverbs.[32]

On the other hand, the popular proverbs in the collections had been adjusted to the requirements of learned taste and use—more consciously, in my view, than in the medieval manuscript compilations. Much was at stake when one was trying to develop the national tongue rather than just setting down sayings in an everyday vernacular alongside a serious Latin. In addition, educated persons in the sixteenth century, in their relatively literate urban milieu, stood at a greater cultural distance from the oral world of the peasants than had knights and aristocrats of two or three hundred years before. However fluid social boundaries were for a while among the wealthy classes, however loose the criteria for the use of "familiar" and common speech, no learned collector wanted to erase the language boundaries that distinguished the prosperous and powerful from the lower orders.

To be sure, the learned had provincial roots, too, that shaped their speech and cultural interests. We have seen how regional loyalties prompted some of the best proverb-recording by Charles de Bouelles and the author of the *Explications morales*. But these loyalties were to some extent in conflict with their work as French collectors: they had to take what came from the mouth of the common people and adapt it for common use in the national tongue. The printed editions then spread the standardized proverb far and wide. A similar tension existed for the poets and other major writers. "I speak my Vandomois," said Pierre de Ronsard; and Jean-Antoine de Baïf mingled his Angevin with words from other provinces. In fact, it was "our French" that Ronsard was trying to perfect, and regional dialects would only assist with a word from time to time. One had to be careful not to use them too much, as Pasquier thought Montaigne had done with his Gasconisms. The "naiveté"—a kind of naturalness—that was sought for French style was not going to be found literally in peasant speech or verse.[33]

What happened to popular proverbs and words in dialect happened in other areas as well. Already in the fifteenth century, court dance and folk dance had parted ways in France, so Curt Sachs has told us. "They . . . continue to influence each other, but they have fundamentally different aims and different styles." Such influences were felt in the mid-sixteenth century, when the solemn ceremonial dances of the court were transformed by contact with lively animated peasant dance. At a banquet at Bayonne in 1565, for example, Catherine de Médicis had peasant girls and musicians brought in from provinces all over the kingdom, each group to dance as it did in the village (an affirmation of national character, incidentally, that can hardly have pleased the Huguenot party at court). The *branles* and *gaillards* performed by courtiers, however, were no literal imitation of these rural dances: movements were tamed, motifs were amalgamated, gestures and rhythm were altered.[34]

So, too, with the collection of French customary law. The humanist lawyer Antoine Loisel worked for forty years on the diverse *coutumiers* and local legal traditions of France in an effort (to quote his friend Pasquier) to find "the true and *naif* [native or natural] law of France" as opposed to the foreign judgments of Roman law. His materials concerned the peasants in part and were sometimes couched, as we have seen, in proverbial form. What he did in his *Institutes coutumières* of 1607 was to give one rule or sentence where before there had been several, and to arrange them in the topical order that lawyers like instead of leaving them in the jumble he had seen before. (How peasants and local seigneurs managed with this confusion he did not ask.) This would make it easier to teach to law students and would be a step toward "the conformity, reason and equity of a SINGLE LAW . . . under the authority of His Majesty."[35]

These examples bring us to a last consideration about the learned collectors of popular proverbs in the sixteenth century. Not only had they put their sayings into a "common" French, not only had they excised those with unseemly metaphors,* but

* Apart from the *Proverbes communs* of Gilles de Noyers, which eventually found their way into the *Treasure of the French Tongue*, most of the compilations presented no coarse sayings at all. The *Explications morales* included "*On auroit aussitost un pet d'un asne mort*" (to refer to a person who will not say anything no matter how often he is asked) with the comment "among these adages which are a little dirty, this is one" (p. 20, see n. 28). On the

also they envisaged different uses for proverbs from those that they had among the peasants (and even perhaps from those they had among the *menu peuple* in the cities, though I cannot here speculate on this difficult question).

Let us make this comparison by piecing together what we know from varied historical and critical sources and from present-day anthropological studies of proverb use.[36] In the first place, lawyer, writer, artisan, and peasant in the sixteenth century all delighted in the *form* of the proverb—its generally balanced structure and its brevity. Its very compactness, they thought, helped to convince and persuade. For the peasants, however, in their primarily unlettered and still quite local world, proverbs were an essential resource; whereas for the literary and the learned they were simply a helpful tool, an additional device. The peasants' stock was memorized, learned by ear in concrete situations in childhood and adolescence. It was all the more weighty because of its assumed connection with local or regional tradition, and it probably increased very little during a generation in the village. That of learned men was also in part acquired in situations during childhood, but it was enlarged by reading at school and afterward and enriched by translations of foreign sayings. It was partly memorized (and then more likely by "rehearsal" than by living usage) and partly left in books.

To the villager, his common proverbs—wide-ranging in metaphor and tone, inconsistent with each other and flexible—were available for many different circumstances and for recommending different courses of action. Indeed, the meaning of any individual proverb might vary with the situation to which it was applied and the status of the speaker and listener. Thus, Peter Seitel has shown from his careful observation of the Haya in Tanzania how the same proverb can be used to unite speaker and listener in agreement or to divide them in anger and hostility, depending

---

whole matter of "billingsgate" and "obscene" language in Renaissance writing, see Mihail Bakhtin, *Rabelais and His World*, trans. Helene Iswolsky (Cambridge, Mass., 1968).

on the context and the participants.[37] Erasmus' discussion of the
saying "to have Dutch ears" gives us an inkling of this process,
as he turns the insult of the "rustic, untutored, boorish" ear into
a praise for sincerity and virtue.[38] Similarly, we can imagine how
"the goslings lead the geese to grass" could be given opposite
meanings, though the author of the *Explications morales* perceived it only as a criticism of that situation, "against nature,"
in which inexperienced young people try to rule their elders.*

The gifted proverb-speakers in the village, then, were not those
with new sayings, but those who knew how to apply the old ones
most tellingly. Proverbs could be used to remind peasants of what
they might do for good health or a good harvest. They could provide formulas for summing up the meaning of an event. They
could be used to give orders in a courteous fashion, to call someone back to duty without a humiliating confrontation, to rebuke,
to argue, or to insult. Further, we have evidence that villagers
both expected an exchange of proverbs to have some role in legal
argumentation and probably used them themselves before manorial courts and in village disputes. "Wherever you can attach a
proverb, do so," was the advice to a lawyer in a late medieval
manuscript, "for the peasants like to judge according to proverbs."[39]

Now, this advice at least was familiar to some lawyers in the
sixteenth century, for peasants were involved in litigation. Moreover, lawyers had their own legal proverbs, *regulae*, and maxims,
which they memorized to help them learn the law and plead.[40]

---

* So, too, "*Homme de porc et de boeuf*" is certainly a multivalent saying,
though the author of the *Explications morales* interprets it only one way.
"By these words one indicates a gross, uncivil, dishonest, ill-taught man, such
as those who are ordinarily among the lowest degree of the people. For the
familiar food of such persons is lard, pork, beef, and other heavy meats. They
differ from men who are more honest, delicate, and of good life and manners,
who are also nourished by more delicate foods, like mutton, capons, partridge,
and other dainty meats." (*Explications morales*, p. 18; compare the different
evaluation of mutton in *Li proverbes au vilain*, p. 232 above. Mutton was
more expensive than beef in the sixteenth century.)

Yet none of the compilations of common proverbs discussed this similarity between lawyers' ways and peasants' ways, nor, indeed, any of the social functions of proverbial speech in the village. Rather they were geared to the uses of the educated and the literary. Instead of offering diverse meanings for a single proverb, they gave several examples of a single meaning. Whether listed in alphabetical order, as they usually were (an arrangement already found in a manuscript of the 1450's), or placed at random,[41] the proverbs were disposed for a literate person who had time to look things up or wished to read out of curiosity. They helped one learn and ornament one's language (and perhaps a foreign one as well); they inspired to moral reflection; they could make one more persuasive, witty, or severe. These were the ways one circulated one's proverbs when there were so many other written and printed words in the treasury.

What character, then, did the sixteenth-century proverb collectors seem to be giving to the culture of "the people"? It was old, though not unchanging. It was capable of sustaining a valued form of speech, but was lacking in consciousness about itself and was undiscriminating. Montaigne might still assert that the popular *villanelles* of Gascony were as beautiful as the poets' perfect art,[42] but there was growing doubt among the learned that Marcolf—the real Marcolf, not some fanciful shepherd—had an equivalent wisdom. At the end of the sixteenth century, Olivier de Serres was writing in his *Theater of Agriculture* that the experience of unlettered peasants by itself was no sure rule for cultivating the fields,[43] and (as we shall see below) a French physician was publishing the first book to brand as erroneous the traditional peasant proverbs on health. Increasingly, Solomon was to be the sole judge.

[III]

In the seventeenth century, of course, learned attitudes toward "the people" became more critical, and interest in the stylistic potential of the proverb form began to wane. The authority of old and vulgar sayings could hardly be compelling to enlightened Libertines with their contempt for foolish tales, to Cartesian rationalists, or to any other opponents of "superstition" and credulity. As the sense of social distance and social boundaries sharpened after the relative fluidity of the sixteenth century, so now there was less laxity in regard to the character of speech in the upper circles of the city, the world of officers, and the court. Already Ronsard had wondered whether familiar proverbs were a suitable ornament for courtly poetry, and now the arbiters of French taste insisted they were not. If François de Malherbe was supposed to have tested his poems on serving girls and joked that good usage could be found among the porters of Paris, his elegant language was quite free of popular expressions. The stylist Vaugelas stated flatly in 1647 that "the people is master only of bad usage"; the language of the court and the best authors would not be corrupted by provincialisms, words in dialect, and vulgar sayings. Even the literary genres must know their place; there was to be no mixing of tragedy and comedy. Within the comic theatre, common proverbs might be used by Molière's valets and by Harlequin and Columbine, but they were not to be heard in the mouth of a *grand seigneur*.[44]

To be sure, common proverbs need not be totally cut from learned and "honest" conversation, but they were reserved for special occasions. As the Jesuit Dominique Bouhours remarked, proverbs were like old clothes in the wardrobes of great houses— suitable to be taken out only for masquerades. And in fact, courtiers played at proverbs—not the quick repartee of Solomon and Marcolf, but slower guessing games. In 1654, young Louis XIV and his friends put on costumes and danced in ballet "For little peddlers, little baskets" and "Don't tease the dogs till you're outside the village."[45] Later, Madame de Maintenon and others wrote entire plays based on proverbs that the audience was to try and guess. Those knowing proverbs well seem to have been fewer than in the sixteenth century: around 1660, when Jacques Lagniet published his remarkable engravings illustrating popular proverbs, he had to add captions everywhere so they could be understood.[46]

New compilations of proverbs continued to be printed in seventeenth-century France, albeit in smaller numbers than before. On the whole, they reflect learned disdain for the culture of the people. For instance, Antoine Oudin's *Curiositez françoises* of 1657 was an effort "to purge the language of Errors," a dictionary of vulgar and low phrases, most of which he thought should not be used. (Interestingly enough, he censured not only phrases like "*Bas de cul, bas de fesses*," but also proverbs that Bouelles had thought seemly enough a century earlier, such as "*Ung barbier rase l'autre*," "One barber shaves another gratis.") Two collections of the 1650's—the anonymous *Illustres proverbes*, and Fleury de Bellingen's *L'Etymologie ou Explication des Proverbes françois*—revived the medieval dialogue form. But here Marcolf has dwindled to the peasant Manant or to the city-dweller Simplician, and Solomon has become the Philosopher or Cosimo; and now it is the latter who has the last word. Manant and Simplician start off naively using proverbs whose origins and meanings they do not understand. The Philosopher and Cosimo then explain the sayings at considerable length. The peasant "bundles" his phrases together in disorder, said one of the compilers; the philosopher composes them into a delightful discourse. "Profit from their talk . . . and after having jeered . . . at the ignorance of our Peasant, admire the incomparable science of our Doctor."[47]

Two works contrasted with the above in tone. In 1657, the Navarrais lawyer Arnauld Oihenart published his *Basque Proverbs*—over seven hundred of them—in Basque and in French, followed by his own Basque poems. His praise of proverbs was unstinting. Used by common people and learned alike, they were, in Aristotle's words, "the remains of the Ancient Philosophy" (other French compilers were not citing his phrase anymore). After listing collections in several languages from Erasmus on,

Oihenart said, "I thought I would render a service to *'ma patrie'* if, after the pains I have taken since my youth to collect her proverbs from the mouth of the People, I made them more familiar and permanent by printing them."* He suspected that there must be many more among the Basques on the other side of the Pyrénées, whose unjust domination by Spain he had denounced in another work some years before. Of his local proverbs he had omitted only those that were "vulgar" or lacking in character. He concluded with a discourse on Basque orthography and ancient Basque handwriting.[48]

The other work, *Les origines de quelques coutumes anciennes, et de plusieurs façons de parler triviales* (1672), was written by the Norman Jacques Moisant de Brieux, a former lawyer in the Parlement of Rouen, a Latin poet, a Protestant, a voyager to England, and the founder of the Académie de Caen, one of France's earliest provincial academies. His feelings for his *patrie* and its common proverbs were more restrained than those of Oihenart, but nevertheless he was deeply curious about Norman folkways. "Our People" is what he called the Norman peasants, and he rose to defend them against the malicious proverb "He's a Norman; he gives his word and retracts it."† He described himself as following the tradition of Pasquier's *Recherches de la France*, "seeking rusty pins and little Antiquities," but it was really Normandy that was his bailiwick. It was there that he could verify the pronunciations of a Rouen New Year's chant, could

---

* In fact there had been some Basque proverbs included in a work by Voltoire earlier in the century: *Interprect ou traduction du François, Espagnol et Basque* (Lyon, n.d.), described by Brunet, *Anciens proverbes basques*. Oihenart's enthusiasm for the language is also found in the first work printed in Basque. The *Linguae Vasconum Primitiae* of Bernard Dechepare (Bordeaux, 1545) opens with a dedication in which Dechepare says he writes "to show the world that Basque . . . lends itself marvelously well to the rules of writing." He hopes that others will imitate his example and increase the number of *"publications euskariennes"* (G. Brunet, *Poésies basques de Bernard Dechepare* [Bordeaux, 1847]. See also above, Chap. 7, p. 197.).

† " *'Il est Normant, il a son dit et don dédit.'* It is very unjust that a liberty given by our old Custom, to annul or ratify a contract within twenty-four hours, has been turned into a reproach of faithlessness" (p. 56, see n. 49).

correspond with other observant antiquarians, and could then compare what he had seen and heard with the customary law. *"C'est un ris de Boucher, il ne passe point le noeu de la gorge"*— "It's a butcher's laugh," that is, an insincere laugh—"a Proverb common among the People of upper Normandy and comes from that fact . . . that butchers hold their knife between their teeth." *"Faire mérienne, fair rincie"* (to interrupt one's work at noon, eat, and take a nap). "Agricultural dayworkers do this depending on the season. After All Saints', the days are too short."[49]

Moisant de Brieux's "rusty pins" and Oihenart's native proverbs can illustrate some of the ways in which seventeenth-century collectors related to popular material. In the first place, collecting for direct use—collecting from a community whose words one used in poetry or whose sayings one fought in sermons—continued to put a strain on the accuracy or fullness of reporting. Thus Oihenart left out the Basque proverbs he thought too broad. Thus, several decades later (as we shall see again), Charles Perrault and Mademoiselle Lhéritier readily altered motifs and details in the folk tales they had collected to please and instruct the young and old in their aristocratic audience. And, thus, the doctor of theology Jean-Baptiste Thiers in his remarkable *Traité des superstitions* suppressed certain signs and words in the rituals he was condemning (he put in dots to indicate deletions) so that his readers would not try them out.[50] In contrast, collectors with antiquarian detachment from their popular material, whatever other bases for selection they used, did not worry about quoting Paris street slang or describing "silly customs."[51]

In the second place, Moisant de Brieux and Oihenart show us that for a few savants a new impetus to the study of what the people were saying and doing could come from love of "country"; but the country was one's own region rather than "our France."*

* Regional sentiment did not automatically promote an interest in popular behavior. Histories of Provence and of Béarn mention the peasants and townsfolk only incidentally to their political narrative (Caesar de Nostradame, *L'histoire et chronique de Provence* [Lyon, 1624]; Antoine de Ruffi, *Histoire des Comtes de Provence* [Aix-en-Provence, 1655]; Pierre de Marca, *Histoire*

Contemporary etymological dictionaries were also displaying a more conscious concern with regional dialect and local words— and thus with words used by peasants and the *menu peuple*—than had been the case in the sixteenth century. For his *Origins of the French Language*, Gilles Ménage regretted that he did not know Breton and "the diverse idioms of our Provinces and the parlance of the Peasants, among whom Languages are conserved the longest." But he still managed to discuss, say, regional variations on the word "toil" (*ahan*), old words for "midwives," and the changing meanings of "*putain*" and "*garce.*" Pierre Borel's *Treasure . . . of Gallic and French Antiquities* (1655) began with a description of certain peasant customs "in our Languedoc" (such as giving no surnames in the villages around Castres, but identifying men only as "son of . . . , son of . . ."). The remains of the old French tongue could best be found, he thought, in Brittany, Provence, and parts of the Languedoc.[52]

The context for this connection between the regional and the popular was a centralizing, absolutist government. Not that these collectors were opposed to king and France—Oihenart wanted not an independent Basque country, but one free of any Spanish domination—but their interests were rooted in their regional world. In different circumstances in the seventeenth century, the national and the popular might similarly be associated. Let us look first at the English grammarian and man of letters James Howell, simply to sharpen the significance of the French examples. His *Proverbs* were printed in London in 1659, and began with a poem:

> The Peeples voice, the Voice of God we call,
> And what are Proverbs but the peeples voice?
> Coin'd first, and current made by common choice,
> Then sure they must have Weight and Truth withal.
>   They are a publick Heritage entayled
>   On every Nation, or like Hireloomes nayld,

---

de Bearn [Paris, 1640]). On the other hand, the *curé* Gabriel du Moulin opened his *Histoire generale de Normandie* (Rouen, 1631) with a portrait of contemporary customs and regional character that included material on peasant families as well.

Which pass from Sire to Son and from Son
Down to the Grandchild till the world be done;
They are Free-Denisons by long Descent,
Without the grace of Prince or Parlement,
The truest Commoners and Inmate guests,
We fetch them from the Nurse and Mothers breasts;
They can Prescription plead gainst King and Crown,
And need no Affidavit but their own.

Vox populi, vox Dei, he exclaimed elsewhere; *"voz de Pleu, voz de Deu"* says the Gascon proverb, "for it must needs be true what every one sayes." Nor was he bothered by the coarseness of some proverbs. "Now let the squeamish Reder take this Rule along with him, that Proverbs being Proleticall, and free familiar Countrey sayings do assume the Libertie to be sometimes in plain, down-right and homely termes, with wanton natural Expressions . . . yet they can not be tax'd of beastliness or bawdry." Howell listed proverbs in Spanish, Italian, French, and English, most of them taken from previous collections, and also sayings in "Cambrian," (that is, Welsh)—the island's first language and the language of the place where he had been born.[53]

Howell, too, had some regional roots that held him and favored his collecting, but mostly he was involved in national issues. With attitudes such as those in the *Proverbs,* where did he stand in regard to the great Civil War that had disturbed his country? For the king. He had worked for Charles I, spent several years in Fleet prison for his loyalty, dedicated his proverbs to Royalist peers, and became historiographer to Charles II. If his celebration of the balanced constitution of Venice had won him release from republican prisons in 1651, even in that work he had especially praised Venice for her constancy "to her first fundamentalls and principles," for her enmity to change. Howell must have believed that, like the people's Royalist maypoles of 1660, the people's ancestral proverbs would support the king, too.[54]

That a learned Royalist would sentimentalize popular tradition is understandable in the wake of Charles I's martyrdom and Puritan rule. That the person or rule of Louis XIV could inspire a

French scholar to celebrate the people's voice in Howell's fashion is hard to imagine. The Gascon *"Voz de Pleu, voz de Deu"* was not the basis of the Sun King's reign, and it was surely not one of the proverbs that he danced at court in the 1650's.* Only in the case of the Basque country, with its particular culture and suppressed administrative unity could a poet identify romantically with the peasant.

What of Charles Perrault then? His *Tales of Mother Goose*, first published in 1697, was really based on folktales that he had heard from old countrywomen in the Ile de France and Champagne as well as on stories in the printed peddlers' books. And yet he had been Colbert's aide for twenty years, suggesting and supervising cultural policies to glorify the king; and the poem with which he opened a new round in the Quarrel between the Ancients and the Moderns was entitled "Le siècle de Louis le Grand." He was both "a man of the court" and "one of the rare men of his time who listened to the voice of the people," to quote Marc Soriano's study, which I follow here. Nevertheless, the relations between the royal, the national, and the popular in his work were different from those of James Howell. Rather than calling upon traditional popular wisdom to support traditional kingship, Perrault was trying to remake an old folk tradition to serve "modern" causes.† An Aca-

---

* In fact, the style of dance at the court had many fewer popular elements in it than in the mid-sixteenth century. Using aristocratic ballet for popular proverbs was an amusing conceit. According to Curt Sachs, "the *branle, courante,...gavotte*, [and] *minuet*...had forgotten their rustic origin and adapted themselves to the ceremonial formality of the *bal paré*." Madame de Sévigné thought the *bourrées* that she saw in Auvergne charming, but contrasted them with what was known at court (Curt Sachs, *World History of the Dance* [New York, 1963], pp. 391-97, 407-10).

† So, too, Colbert had an interest in regional traditions for the sake of "modern causes." On the one hand, he wanted the French language to spread into all the corners of France and tried to get French-speaking priests to stay in lower Brittany (F. Brunot et al., *Histoire de la langue française* [Paris, 1905-53], 3: 719, n. 1). On the other hand, as Orest Ranum has pointed out to me, he did what he could in the 1660's to encourage the writing of regional history, partly out of curiosity and partly because such information could serve as a basis for policy. Mr. Ranum talks about the question of provincial

demician wholly opposed to "popular superstitions," he saw the tales as the French equivalent of Homeric poetry and ancient fables. They treated themes fundamental in all human societies, but were more suitable to his times because they had grown out of a Christian and national culture. The marvelous in the stories could be made safe through Perrault's ironic voice: these were tales of the past and directed especially to children. The immoralities of the stories could be changed to suit the needs of Christian education.[55]

By such means, says Soriano, folk literature entered into "great" literature by the front door. But it was at the cost of putting the multiple voices of the people into a single clear French, as was the case with proverb collectors of the sixteenth century. And if Soriano is right that willy-nilly the *Contes de Perrault* have a "pure" and "profoundly popular" character,[56] it is also true that they have been pulled up from the context in which they were told, heard, and interpreted. Neither Perrault's Mother Goose nor Moisant de Brieux's "little Antiquities" pretends to tell us what the culture of the people really meant.

In the next century, learned interest in common proverbs in France was at its lowest ebb. Playlets around proverbial sentences continued to amuse salons in Paris and elsewhere, but the proverb was not an appreciated literary device. New maxims, perhaps; old saws, no. Between 1710 and 1750, four compilations of proverbs appeared, all called "dictionaries," all organized primarily by publishers, and all copied from earlier compilations or from each other.[57] As for the *Encyclopédie*, it dismissed the proverb in a few inches. To *philosophes* eager to correct defective ideas by eliminating false associations and inadequate proof, the common proverb could recommend itself neither by its conciseness, nor by its familiarity, and certainly not by its claim to truth by long existence.[58]

---

and national identities in his "Introduction" to *National Consciousness, History, and Political Culture in Early Modern Europe* (Baltimore, Md., 1974) and in his forthcoming book *Artisans of Glory: Historical Thinking and Politics in Seventeenth-Century France*.

There was, however, some continuing learned attention to the people's speech. Not because it was wise: if anything, it needed to be corrected. Not because it was beautiful: peasant speech had long ago been declared unsuitable for pastorals and eclogues, lest they (in Fontenelle's phrase) "smack too much of the countryside." Neither the preromantic movement in France nor the active scholarly research on the Middle Ages had yet turned taste toward the beauty of the contemporary folk song or poem* (the Comte de Caylus could praise the "natural grace" and "naiveté" of some old fabliaux, but they were a different matter from folk art). But for some scholars, the people's speech was useful. Thus, clerics brought out new Breton-French and Provençal-French dictionaries because they needed to talk to peasants and city folk ("the best Breton [dialect] for me is the one I need," said a vicar of Vannes, "for each one of us must be attached to the language of his People . . . [and] must make a point of talking as one talks in the Parish").[59]

In addition, students of the development of the French tongue —whether they stressed its Celtic, Frankish, or Latin roots—found increasingly that present-day dialects and peasant usage could help them understand the language and vocabulary of the past. Already in 1581 Claude Fauchet had argued in his *Origin of the French Language* that the "rustic Romaine" of Charles the Bald's time was rather like contemporary Provençal. By the eighteenth century, La Curne de Sainte-Palaye was keeping extensive notes on dialects and drawing upon them and other features of rural speech to help him define words in his important glossary of Old French.[60]

Reflection on the history of language as well as on the history of religion also produced a theory that had consequences for learned concepts of popular life—the theory of primitive culture. Notions of the primitive, whether idyllic or brutish, had, of course, a very long history behind them, stretching back to antiquity. At

* Herder's collection of German folk songs first appeared in 1778, but the publication of Ossian had turned his attention to the beauty of folk art well before then.

the end of the sixteenth century, the historian La Popelinière was already proposing a theory of cultural stages for mankind, the first of which described illiterate peoples "*presque ruraux et non civilisez*." Preserving their culture through song, verse, sign, statue, and dance, they were exemplified by the contemporary "savage" peoples in the New World and by the early inhabitants of Greece and of Europe, such as the Celts. The theory, not exclusive to La Popelinière, was modified and elaborated in the next centuries at the hands of Locke and Vico abroad and of French thinkers such as Fontenelle, Charles de Brosses, Rousseau, and Court de Gèbelin, to mention but a few.[61]

What is important for us here in their varied and conflicting views are two common features. First, primitive peoples were not simply without certain tools, techniques, or information; their psychological and mental processes were different from those of civilized peoples. This was reflected in their language, which was concrete and sensory: at worst, incapable of abstraction; at best, mythic and emblematic. Second, evidence for primitive mentality was found not only among "savages" and ancient Greeks and Celts, but among children and the lower classes of their own day, both rural and urban. Similarities between Indians and European peasants had been noted before (in the mid-sixteenth century, Jean de Léry, hearing the funeral laments of the women of Brazil, thought of the laments of the women of Béarn), but by the eighteenth century such comparisons were more frequent. Vico's Age of the Gods evidently owed quite a bit to the people of Naples.[62]

Did this theory of the "primitive" really change anything substantial in learned thought about the people? In the evaluation of popular culture it did not, for one could approve of or dislike the primitive as one wished. In the definition of popular culture it did. What kind of concept of *culture* had been implied or expressed in the work of proverb collectors? None, really. Either the collectors were in such close exchange with popular culture that they did not think about whether it involved a different ordering of experience and values, or they perceived it as a jumble of isolated attributes. The people's customs and speech were old, naive, and uninventive,* to be characterized by what they lacked (proper education, letters, right doctrine) rather than by what they had. The theory of the "primitive" hardened these alleged characteristics and added a few more. But, whatever interpretive drawbacks it had, the "primitive" was at least an ordering principle, and thus a small step toward an anthropological concept of culture.[63]

In any case, this was a concept that came into play in the one fresh work on proverbs that appeared in eighteenth-century France—the *Matinées Sénonoises*, published in 1789 by Jean-Charles-François Tuet, professor of letters and a canon at Sens. Tuet's preliminary essay tried to put proverbs in a long historical perspective. They were the product of an earlier stage of human culture. They were not "the remains of the ancient philosophy," as Aristotle had claimed, but were produced in an age when people were unable to reflect, took things on face value, spoke little, and expressed themselves in short sentences "imprinted with the seal of truth." In later but still not fully civilized periods, such as that of Homer, the moral and social distance between the lettered and the people was still close: "One could utter proverbs before the great, which one would blush to say in honest society today." Indeed, in France itself up to the reign of Henri IV, proverbs had been freely used by poets and writers. But then as the language perfected itself, it pulled away from the proverbial style and rejected with disdain all words that were lowered by passing too often through the mouth of the people. As for the people, they still talked in proverbs, as one could tell any day by listening to their women gossiping. This was because the people still remained in a primitive state.

Why then did Tuet have the taste for collecting proverbs which

---

* Pasquier had stressed the fact of change in popular speech and customs, though he had not considered the question of creativity. As learned interest grew in finding traces of the distant past in popular speech and customs, so the "oldness" of popular culture and its unchanging quality were emphasized all the more, and inventiveness within it seemed all the less likely.

(if reflective skills would just pass down to the people) would surely disappear? Because, on the eve of a revolution he was soon to support, Tuet thought the learned had pushed their delicacy too far. He regretted those earlier days "when what was well thought and said had an absolute beauty, independent of popular usage, and when there had existed a kind of community of language, for which [proverbs] were a source of riches."[64]

And finally, we come back to the Académie Celtique and its questionnaire of 1805. If the events of the past fifteen years had restored "a kind of community of language," it was not readily apparent in the pages of the Academy's *Mémoires*. The Revolution and its settlement had indeed strengthened the bond between national sentiment and the study of the popular. The "ancient Celtic splendor" of France was talked about with feeling. Celtic traces in popular speech, proverbs, customs, and monuments were described with fullness and local detail.[65] The people themselves were approached with stony sobriety.*

Sometime during 1806–7, Jacques-Antoine Du Laure, former Girondin in the Convention, serious scholar of phallic cults and fertility rites, and major author of the Academy's questionnaire, went to visit two hamlets in the *département* of the Seine-et-Marne in search of a "sepulchral monument worthy of mark."[66] He inquired about local customs, recorded part of a mocking female marriage chant, noted the commonest local insult (*loup garou*), talked to the *curé*, found an ancient burial mound, and promised to pay a peasant if he found any more jewels in his digging there. He ended his thorough report with the fervent wish that every member would take similar trips to collect the monuments of the past and "bring to light those shadowy centuries." And what were the thoughts of the masked *femmes folles* whose song he had caught? And of the digging peasant, who had sold a Gallic jewel to a merchant for almost nothing and given another to his son for a plaything? We are not told.

---

* In contrast not only with Herder but with Michelet's approach later in *Le peuple* (1846).

[IV]

About the time that the Académie Celtique was entering its fifth year, a physiologist, university-trained surgeon, and professor at the Paris Medical Faculty named Anthelme Richerand published his *Erreurs populaires relatives à la médecine.*[67] It was part of a significant, though sparse, line of books on "Popular Errors" about medicine and health—a line that had been originated in 1578 by Laurent Joubert, Chancellor of the Faculty of Medicine at the University of Montpellier. Whereas learned proverb collectors had initially been appreciative of their popular material, the collectors of vulgar errors were critical of the people to begin with. Whereas proverb collectors envisaged only learned or upper-class use of their work (either use of proverbs, suitably altered, in speech, writing, and reflection, or their use as a means of studying regional or national history and culture), collectors of vulgar errors (like collectors of religious "superstition") were trying to change things about the people. They hoped to correct the beliefs and behavior of medical practitioners down to the midwives and of as wide a segment of the "people" as they could reach. In fact, the circulation of the books of popular errors seems to have been limited to physicians and educated surgeons, and to learned readers generally.[68] The point is the intention of the collectors: however wrong the people were, they were at least worth lecturing to.

Did these differences affect the quality of either the reporting or the interpreting of popular culture? Let us take a look at the major examples of this medical genre and see whether they add anything to our understanding of learned collectors.

Though clearly anticipated by theological writing against religious error, the *Erreurs populaires* had no medieval precedent in medicine. To be sure, the fourteenth-century physician Guy de Chauliac included among the surgical practitioners of his day the Teutonic Knights, who cured by charms, and "women and idiots," who handed over all sicknesses to the saints; but he did not detail their errors. The manuscript tradition was, however, amply supplied with regimens for health, plague remedies, and books of medical secrets in Latin and the vernacular, which passed into print with titles like *Le régime de santé*, *The Treasure of the Poor*, and *The Secrets of Women*, attributed to Albertus Magnus.[69] New vernacular works then appeared in a like vein, some by physicians and some not. The most frequently printed was *The Secrets of Alexis of Piedmont* (first French edition, 1557), with remedies and recipes that the aged "Don Alexis" had collected not only from learned and noble men but also from "poore women, Artificers, and Pesants."[70]

Here then was part of the Error. The rest—the major part—was dispersed throughout society, especially in the medical proverbs and practices of the peasants and the *menu peuple*. The most erroneous proverb of all was "every man his own physician."[71]

The situation that led to Joubert's *Erreurs populaires* of 1578 had in it the same ingredients that gave rise to the spurt of proverb-collecting in the sixteenth century, but they acted to different effect. First, Joubert and other humanist physicians were convinced that they had an improved method for the study and practice of medicine, based on the purification of Greek texts (especially those of Galen) and on the new study of anatomy. Thus, the medieval tradition had to be purged of errors, both those handed down by the School of Salerno and those embodied in vulgar sayings. The assault on it was a more vigorous one than the remaking of the general corpus of medieval proverbs.[72]

Second, the fluidity of social boundaries within the upper levels of the social structure in the sixteenth century was found also in the field of medicine, but was there a source of more conscious conflict. As a university-trained group (almost all of them laymen since the fifteenth century), the physicians feared competition in the cities from an increasingly literate and educated elite among the surgeons, not to mention encroachment from apothecaries and even presumptuous midwives (Joubert described with indignation the day he and one of the other leading physicians of France went to visit a woman suffering from hysteria only to be barred admit-

tance by an old midwife, who insisted that the woman was pregnant and that that was not their province).[73] The conflict was further exacerbated by enemies within—Paracelsus and his followers,
who rejected Greek medicine, purified or unpurified, in favor of
"experience" and who chided physicians for their inordinate
greed.[74]

Third, as we have seen in an earlier chapter, printing had complicated the relationship of the physician to the public. Not only
were false remedies being disseminated throughout Europe; worse,
some physicians had the poor judgment to publish medical books
in the vernacular, addressed to the untrained and on subjects that
they could not fail to misunderstand. As the standards of vernacular speech had to be safeguarded, so did those of medicine.
The answer, as Joubert saw it, was to use the press and the vernacular as a means of control over medical practice and over the
people—"to contain the people within the limits of its vocation,"
as one of his supporters said.[75]

Joubert planned to collect and correct popular errors about
health and medicine from conception to the grave, though he
never completed the entire life cycle in the published volumes.
His book was a kind of dialogue like that between Simplician and
Cosimo, with each chapter beginning with a popular saying or
custom, which he then documented and discussed from his years
of practice. He was an attentive collector; how could he persuade
people to change their ways if he was not precise about what they
were doing wrong? Nor was he fussy about matters of style or
purity of speech. Thus, some of his "errors" had been submitted
to him by readers. Thus, some of his sayings were quoted in dialect
or were on particular subjects that make them unlikely to have
been recorded in other circumstances: *"Apres la figue un verre
d'eau: apres la melon un verre de vin,"* *"Qui boit verjus, pisse
vinaigre,"* *"Bien venant, bien getant: Il vaud mieux fourmage
[fromage] que boullie."* Is it a good idea to sit a woman in labor
on a hot caldron, or to put her husband's hat on her stomach, as
do the good women of the villages around Montpellier? The hat

probably will not help much, unless perhaps to serve as a compress and aid expulsion. He thinks it originated as a way to represent the husband at the delivery.[76]

What then were the characteristics that Joubert assigned to popular culture? It was shot through with error and ignorance. The village goodwives and midwives—dexterous and practiced yet illiterate, working only with memorized recipes and routines, unable ever to find anything new—were its perfect expression.* When the people did or said something right from a medical point of view—such as putting a male child to wet-nurse with a woman who had given birth to a female child, and vice versa; or such as the old Gascon adage "A man can beget as long as he can lift a sheaf of straw"—it was always for the wrong reasons. Like the proverb collectors, Joubert saw the people as lacking in consciousness; the learned had to explain to them the meaning of their behavior.[77]

Joubert's work had considerable impact within the learned community, though there were those who thought he had been too frank about sexual errors. It was translated into Italian within a few years; the term *"erreurs populaires"* or "vulgar errors" was widely used; and the book had several imitators in the seventeenth and eighteenth centuries.[78] Some, such as Sir Thomas Browne, extended the inquiry into the area of natural philosophy more gener-

---

* Joubert did not consider that all female medical practice was worthless. He dedicated his *Grande Chirurgie de M. Guy de Chauliac* to his mother Catherine de Genas, praising her work bandaging the poor and the sick, her ointment for *mal des tetins* (which had helped so many poor women, and was now known throughout the Dauphiné, the Lyonnais, and Provence), her herbed wine, and her jellies. (Dedication of August 1, 1578. The work was first published in 1580 at Lyon.)

On the other hand, Joubert was totally out of sympathy with the view expressed by the jurist René Choppin in the course of describing a suit brought by the Faculty of Medicine at Paris against a peasant woman practicing medicine. Choppin commented "how many savants in Medicine have been outdone by a simple old peasant woman, who with a single plant or herb has found a remedy for illnesses despaired of by physicians." *Traité de Privileges des Personnes Vivans aux Champs (1575)* in *Oeuvres* (Paris, 1662), 3: 57.

ally; others stayed close to medicine and health. James Primerose's *Popular Errours, or the Errours of the People in Physick* (1651), based in part on his medical practice in France, was translated into French in 1689 and expanded by the physician Jean de Rostagny, member of a short-lived Société Royale de Médecine.* Luc d'Iharce's *Erreurs populaires sur la médecine* of 1783 was inspired by the reforming zeal of the new Société Royale de Médecine, which had undertaken a major investigation throughout France into epidemics and their treatment. Richerand placed his *Erreurs populaires* of 1810 in the same reforming tradition—he wanted to persuade the people that medicine was not a domestic art—though he pointed out that a true philosophy of science had not been born in the days of Joubert and Primerose.[79]

Many of the elements in the situation had persisted, though. The traditional literature of popular remedies and recipes was being printed in abundance in the seventeenth and eighteenth centuries. With such titles as *The Charitable Remedies of Madame Fouquet, Collection of the Most Beautiful Secrets of Medicine,* and *Medicine and Surgery of the Poor,* it addressed itself to charitable ladies, to rural *curés,* and even to the "poor who were languishing and dying in the countryside."[80] Enlightened physicians simply could not put a stop to them. The "charlatans" and Empiricks, whom Joubert had censured briefly, also loomed large in the works of the later "correctors": Quacksalvers, Mountebanks,

---

* Jean de Rostagny identifies himself on the title page of the *Traité de Primerose sur les erreurs vulgaires de la medecine* (Lyon, 1689) as *Medecin de la Société Royale.* The year before another book in the "correcting" tradition had been published, which also referred to a Royal Society of Medicine: *Secrets concernant la beauté et la santé. Recueillis et publiez par ordre de Monsieur Daquin, Conseiller du Roy ... et Premier Medecine de sa Majesté. Par M. de Blegny, Conseiller, Medecin ordinaire de Monsieur, et Directeur de la Société Royale de Medecine* (Paris, 1688). Nicolas de Blégny (1652-1722), a surgeon, physician, and medical journalist, here organized selected traditional remedies by topics and tried to assess for each one whether it would work or not. Evidently, the Société, which has not been discussed in the scholarly literature, did not last long. The later Société Royale de Médecine was founded in 1776-77.

Paracelsists—they were hawking their balms, unguents, bezoar stones, and chemical poisons in the streets and at the crossroads and, worse yet, dispensing them in secret. Just anyone had the presumption to think he or she could meddle in medicine—from theologians and the domestic servants of physicians and barbers down to certain little women who drew their remedies from hearsay or from vernacular books and who even practiced surgery. The clearest example of the credulity of the people was their trust in such impostors.[81]

Indeed, for Primerose, Rostagny, Iharce, and Richerand, the people were, if anything, more caught in the web of error than they had been for Joubert.* Theirs was a culture thick with false sayings: "the comet presages plague"; "who goes to bed thirsty arises healthy" (said in the seventeenth century in the Languedoc and Provence); "a sick person's bedclothes should never be changed"; "what pleases the mouth is soft on the stomach." Theirs was a culture saturated with women's bouillons, infusions, and hot drinks, which did not help and might even harm the invalid or parturient mother.[82] Theirs was a world where peasants, who knew a few simples and many superstitions, promised to protect their fellow villagers from the sicknesses allegedly caused by sorcerers, or else founded their cures on "nature"—the changes in the stars, the seasons, or the size of herds. And the populace flocked to them, so eager were they to recover their health without interrupting their work (Iharce told how in 1780 a peasant near Versailles, who claimed to have received medical knowledge at his first communion, dispensed a remedy of *eau de vie*, sugar, and salt to huge crowds, some of whom later died from their ailments).[83]

These features of popular culture the medical collectors had

* The medical correctors did not think that popular errors were found exclusively among peasants and the *menu peuple*. Young physicians might be troubled by them, said Joubert. When persons of high rank hold "*Erreurs populaires*," said Iharce, they are nevertheless "*peuple*" in this regard. Richerand wanted to correct the "vulgar errors" of physicians as well as those of the people.

explained up to the eighteenth century in terms similar to those used by proverb collectors. The people were naive, mostly illiterate (Iharce mentioned a few peasants who could read and write, but it did not improve things), and ignorant. Their culture changed only very slowly; and, however much it made use of practical experience, it was incapable of innovation on its own. Then in the eighteenth century, the concept of the people as still in a primitive stage of development appeared in regard to medicine just as it did in regard to language, religion, and proverbs. As the Protestant physician Daniel Le Clerc pointed out in 1702 in his *Histoire de la Medecine*, the very earliest stages of medicine—pre-Aesculapian and even Aesculapian medicine—were all primitive in character. They involved little more than mere observations; charms, amulets, and other priestly magic; and simple surgical operations. When cures took place, it was because the force of imagination and the faith in oracles of these early people were so strong. The medicine of the ancient Celts and of contemporary savages had similar characteristics. And, indeed, Le Clerc went on, "We must envisage these Ancients as like our peasants of today." Subsequent historians of medicine made the same argument, and Iharce referred to it in passing.[84]

It was this character in popular culture that the Celtic Academy wished to record before it was too late, and that the physicians of progress wanted to describe and destroy. Iharce saw a ray of hope in a recent episode at Montpellier—the charivari of a charlatan. The people put him on a skinny ass, his head turned toward the tail, and promenaded him through the streets with shouts while bystanders threw garbage.[85] The charivari was, of course, part of that whole world of Error. But Iharce did not notice the irony, nor did he stop to ask whether there were resources in the people's culture that could help them make corrections on their own.

When I first began this enterprise on proverbs and errors, I was sanguine about my results, thinking "I have two strings to my bow." After a while I feared rather that I might be *"entre deux selles, le cul à terre."* In fact, we have noted that the controlling assumptions about the nature of popular culture were the same in both genres and that the social and cultural distance between the learned and the people widened at the same time, whether the savants were literary men or physicians.

So, too, I think we can fit the data together and draw some conclusions about whether these learned sources leave us traces of the people's life. This essay has stressed why and how collectors were likely to alter their material. Some change occurred simply in recording it in French and ordering it in print for other learned persons to read. On the whole, modifications were greatest when collectors wanted to integrate popular material immediately into the speech and life of the upper classes. Criticism of the present behavior of peasants and curiosity about the historical past usually prompted fuller, more particular reporting. Once we have become aware of the likelihood and character of such distortions or omissions, however, we have some chance of getting back to the snatches of conversation and series of acts to which the collectors were referring. Historians employ such a technique all the time, of course, when they are studying kings and scholars. It is just especially difficult to use our sources when the culture under study is oral or partially literate (the kind familiar to anthropologists), instead of the literate one whose rules historians understand.

With this said, we can be grateful for the printed collections. We cannot always have a Christofle Sauvageon leaving his manuscript memoirs on the special character of speech in the Sologne in the eighteenth century ("They speak little . . . but express themselves in highly significant and forceful words which they have invented. . . . When it's smoky in a room, they say the thing and its cause at the same time . . . *'la cheminée est engornée'* ")[86] but we still have Bouelles or Moisant de Brieux assisting us toward that insight. We cannot always have the notebook of a village healer (to stop colic "put the big finger of the left hand on the navel and say . . ."),[87] but we can still have Joubert and Iharce reporting what they know from their practice. Moreover, their critical observations are at least as useful as the recipes and remedies printed on the popular genres, *The Secrets of Alexis* and the *Charitable Remedies*: the former are pretending to tell us what the peasants actually do, whereas the latter are making recommendations to peasants and others about what they might do.

This essay has further suggested that however rich the concrete data in some collections, they were *all* very poor in interpreting popular culture. If collectors sometimes gave local context to a proverb or custom, they still "disembedded" it from its culture, not thinking about how it was used or what it meant locally. They assigned to peasants or city folk conventional traits unsupported even by their own findings (some of them part of our definitions of folk culture and popular culture today).

The key to this failure in interpretation, I think, lay not in whether the collectors loved or hated the people, approved or disapproved of them, were close to or distant from them, but in the fact that their work was not mixed with two qualities: some interest in popular culture for its own sake, along with whatever other uses it had for the learned; and some respect for popular culture, whatever arguments they had with it.

We, current historians of popular culture in preindustrial Europe, have a strong streak of interest in the people. But I am not sure we really respect their ways very much; and this makes it hard for us to understand their lives, just as it was for our learned forebears. Maybe Solomon and Marcolf can serve as a model for us and provide a device for engendering respect. Let us not imagine just that we are watching our subjects with their differences in symbols, social intercourse, and technical apparatus. Let us imagine that they are in some sense equivalent to us, in some kind of exchange with us while we look them over, able to answer us back if we should go astray. What might I say to one of my learned subjects?

NZD: Laurent Joubert, you had contempt for the midwives you knew and did not think about how they served the village women. Your *Popular Errors* was just an effort to keep the physicians on top.

LJ: That's not true. I praised the midwife Gervaise who came regularly to public dissections of female corpses at Montpellier. I was trying to give the people better health. You are incurably naïve.

Now that I think of it, I am not sure whether I want to be Solomon or Marcolf. It depends on who has the last word.

Notes

Notes

The following abbreviations and short forms are used in the Notes:

ACh Archives de la Charité de Lyon
ADR Archives Départementales du Rhône
AEG Archives d'Etat de Genève
AEG, PC *Idem*, Procès criminels
AEG, RCon *Idem*, Registres du Consistoire
AHD Archives de l'Hôtel-Dieu de Lyon
AML Archives municipales de Lyon
Annales ESC *Annales. Economies, Sociétés, Civilisations*
BHR *Bibliothèque d'humanisme et renaissance*

BSHPF *Bulletin de la société de l'histoire du protestantisme français*
Crespin, *Martyrs* Jean Crespin, *Histoire des Martyrs persecutez et mis à mort pour la Verité de l'Evangile, depuis le temps des Apostres jusques à present (1619)*, ed. D. Benoît (Toulouse, 1885-89).
Hist. eccl. Histoire ecclésiastique des Eglises Réformées au Royaume de France, ed. G. Baum and E. Cunitz (Paris, 1883-89).

1. Strikes and Salvation at Lyon

1. To the older survey of sixteenth-century Lyon by Roger Doucet in *Histoire de Lyon* (ed. A. Kleinclausz [Lyon, 1939], 1: *Des origines à 1595*), one can now add the major study by Richard Gascon, *Grand commerce et vie urbaine au XVIe siècle. Lyon et ses marchands* (Paris, 1971).

2. The story of these labor conflicts was first told by Henri Hauser in his *Ouvriers du temps passé* (Paris, 1898), chap. 10. Marius Audin described the same material in the *Gutenberg-Jahrbuch*, 1935. Further printed sources were discovered by L. M. Michon and Paul Chauvet. They are described in the latter's book *Les ouvriers du Livre en France des origines à la Revolution de 1789* (Paris, 1959), pp. 35—40 and pp. 47—51. All the material given here on the organization and activity of the Company of the Griffarins is new and is based on archival research in Lyon and Geneva. The relationship of the strikes and labor organization to the Reformation in Lyon has not previously been considered.

3. Even Michel Jove, official publisher for the Jesuits of Lyon in the early 1560's, flirted with Protestantism around 1557.

4. "La Réforme et les classes populaires," *Revue d'histoire moderne et contemporaine* 1 (1899—1900): 24, 31.

5. For instance, Norman Cohn, *Pursuit of the Millennium* (2d. ed., New York, 1961), pp. 28—30. Harold Grimm, in his suggestive "Social Forces in the German Reformation," *Church History* 31 (1962): 11—12, distinguishes among journeymen, free laborers, and beggars, but then says "it was among these lower classes that the distinction between rich and poor was most advanced and that preachers of radical religious and social reform gained many followers who were willing to use violence in achieving their goals." Claus-Peter Clasen, however, found that whereas most urban Anabaptists in Württemberg were artisans, they were mostly "of the

middle class." "There is no evidence," he goes on, "that indigent journeymen and indebted small masters constituted the bulk even of the early Anabaptists in the cities." "The Sociology of Swabian Anabaptism," *Church History* 32 (1963): 155.

6. *Remonstrances, et Memoires, pour les Compagnons Imprimeurs, de Paris et Lyon: Opposans. Contre les Libraires, maistres Imprimeurs desdits lieux: Et adiointz* (n.p., n.d. [Lyon, 1572]). Internal evidence shows this to have been drawn up by the Lyon journeymen. It is also based to a considerable extent on arguments and even phrases from journeymen briefs in Lyon in 1539—40 (AML, AA151, ff. 68ᵛ—70ʳ; Bibl. nat., nouv. acq. fr. 8014, pp. 690—710).

7. Bibl. nat., nouv. acq. fr. 8014, pp. 692—94; *Remonstrances*, ff. A iʳ—ᵛ, B iiʳ.

8. AML, CC684 (1520), f. 3ʳ, showing a printers' journeyman still among the officers of the Confraternity of the Printers, but BB33 (1514), ff. 153ʳ, 158ʳ, showing the two groups already forming. I have traced the early development of the Company partly through the urban militia records (such as EE20 and EE21), where strike leaders of 1539 (AA151, f. 68ᵛ) appear as *dixainiers* for groups of journeymen. The name "Captain of the Printers" (the leader of the journeymen's group) first appears in a public document in 1524 (BB42, f. 215ʳ).

9. On Pagnini's work, see Timoteo Centi, "L'attività letteraria di Santi Pagnini (1470—1536)," *Archivum fratrum praedicatorum* 15 (1945): 5—51. Another cleric who supported Pagnini's program was the humanist Jean de Vauzelles; see N. Z. Davis, "Holbein's *Pictures of Death* and the Reformation at Lyons," *Studies in the Renaissance* 3 (1956): 111—18, and Chapter 2 below. The term "nonchalant" was actually used by canon-count Gabriel de Saconay to describe the clergy of Lyon in these years; *Discours catholique, sur les causes et remedes des malheurs intentés au Roy et escheus à son peuple par les rebelles Calvinistes* (Lyon: Michel Jove, 1568), p. 30.

10. Jean Janin, alias Le Collonier. These are actually the phrases he used talking back to Catholic authorities in prison; but since he had just been proselytizing among printers and other artisans, I here assume that he said much the same thing to them. *Procès de Baudichon de La Maison Neuve, accusé d'hérésie à Lyon* (Geneva, 1873), pp. 3, 20—21, 52—54, 58—59, 61.

11. Jean Guéraud, *La chronique lyonnaise de Jean Guéraud, 1536—1562*, ed. Jean Tricou (Lyon, 1929), pp. 54—55; Jean Calvin, *Ioannis Calvini opera quae supersunt omnia*, ed. G. Baum, E. Cunitz, and E. Reuss (Brunswick, 1863—80), 14: 147—49, 140 (hereafter cited as *Calvini opera*).

12. Etienne Dolet, *Commentariorum Linguae Latinae Tomus Primus* (Lyon, 1536), 2: col. 266. In 1580, out of 115 printers' journeymen assembled to give power of attorney, 43 (about one-third) could not sign their names. On physical work: Bibl. nat., nouv. acq. fr. 8014, pp. 696—97; *Remonstrances*, f. A iʳ.

13. *Recueil faict au vray de la chevaucheè de l'asne faicte en la ville de Lyon . . . mil cinq cens soixante six . . .* , in *Archives historiques et statistiques du Département du Rhône* 9 (1828—29): 418.

14. *Remonstrances*, ff. A iʳ, B iiʳ—ᵛ.

15. *Ibid.*, f. A iʳ. Also, the same point in Bibl. nat., nouv. acq. fr. 8014, p. 649.

16. AEG, PC 1397: "maintenir l'ordre de l'imprimerie," "maintenir le droict de l'imprimerie," "les ordonnances de l'imprimerie." These documents are described fully in my forthcoming book on Lyon in the Reformation.

17. *Epistre en latin de maistre Aime Meigret . . . Plus un sermon en Francois*, ed. Henry Guy, in *Annales de l'Université de Grenoble. Section lettres-droit* 5 (1928): 210. The sermon was given in both Grenoble and Lyon.

18. Antoine de Marcourt, *A Declaration of the Masse, the fruyte thereof* (Wittenberg, 1547), ff. A ivʳ, B iv—B iiʳ, C iiiʳ. This is a translation of Marcourt's *Declaration de la messe*, printed first in 1534 in Switzerland, where he had fled from Lyon.

19. *Monologue de messire Jean Tantost, lequel recite une dispute il ha eue contre une dame Lyonnoise* (Lyon, 1562). This work was written before the death of the Inquisitor Mathieu Orry in 1557, as he is mentioned in the play.

20. Claude Baduel to Calvin (letter of 1551), in *Calvini opera*, 14: 147—49. "Celestial bread" from Pierre de Vingle's edition of the Bible in French in 1529 (E. Droz, "Pierre de Vingle, l'imprimeur de Farel," in *Aspects de la propagande religieuse* [Geneva, 1957], p. 45).

21. These remarks are based on a social and vocational analysis of several thousand male Protestants in Lyon that will be published in my forthcoming book.

The social distribution of urban Protestantism in the mid-sixteenth century is also described—on the basis of smaller samples of males—for Montpellier by E. Le Roy Ladurie (*Les paysans de Languedoc* [Paris, 1966], pp. 342—44) and by Philip Benedict in his interesting current doctoral dissertation for Princeton University, "Rouen During the Wars of Religion." Though neither study has considered the significance of the vocational distribution of urban Protestantism in detail, both confirm the "cross-class" character of the urban Protestant movement—drawing in significant numbers (as at Lyon) from all levels of the urban population, except for the unskilled at the bottom. Le Roy Ladurie insists on the importance of literacy as a characteristic of the male adherents to Protestantism, and this is found in Lyon as well. See also the important article by Pierre Chaunu, "Niveaux de culture et Réforme," BSHPF 118 (1972): 205—26.

22. So many heretical editions came out of Lyon in the 1550's, despite periodic investigations of the printing shops by Catholic authorities, that the canon-counts feared that "all Christianity is going to think that Lyon lives like Geneva" (ADR, B, travée 355 [1551—1685] "les Protestants," ff. 1r—3r). For the persistence of economic conflict in the same years, ADR, B, Sénéchaussée, Registres de l'Audience, Feb.—Oct. 1556.

23. *Histoire des triomphes de l'Eglise lyonnaise* (Lyon, 1562), reprinted in *Archives historiques et statistiques du Département du Rhône* 13 (1830—31): 233.

24. AEG, PC1397.

25. The Collège de la Trinité was founded by a lay confraternity and then taken over by the Consulate in the late 1520's. The Aumône-Générale was founded in 1534, an impressive organization involving aid to poor families, aid to the unemployed, and an orphanage, administered by the city government. See Chapter 2 below.

26. Bibl. nat., nouv. acq. fr. 8014, p. 691; *Remonstrances*, f. A ir—v.

27. AEG, PC 1397, 1307.

28. For instance, Jullien Mouchet, leader of the Griffarins in the 1560's, was the son and nephew of leaders of the 1530's and 1540's; Guillaume Testefort, another leader of the 1560's and 1570's, was the son of a notary and rather well off. On the other hand, this group did periodically consult with the members in "assemblies" (AEG, PC 1306, 1307).

29. *Remonstrances*, f. C iv.

30. AML, BB49, ff. 203v—204v, 210r—211r. On cooperation with other labor groups: AEG, PC 1397.

31. The list of the 74 *surveillants* and the 21 deacons has been compiled primarily from AML, GG87, Liasse 1, pièce 2, and ACh, E171, E170, and E10 *passim*. The term *surveillant* is definitely used instead of "elder" in Lyon. Antoine du Pinet confirms the archival evidence: "*De ces Surveillans, accompagnez des ministres, est composez le Consistoire.*" (*La Conformité des Eglises Reformees de France et de l'Eglise primitive* [n.p., 1564], p. 78; dedication from Lyon, 1564).

32. *Instruction Chrestienne* (Geneva, 1564), 2: 721—22. According to du Pinet, new members of the Consistory were chosen by the Consistory and named to the people on one Sunday. If no one had anything to report against them after three or four Sundays, they were declared elected (*Conformité*, p. 46). Though these "elections" were to have occurred every year, many of the *surveillants* held their posts from year to year. For a view on church organization published in Lyon, which printers' journeymen undoubtedly sympathized with, see R. M. Kingdon, "Calvinism and Democracy," *American Historical Review* 69 (1964): 394—96.

33. Gabriel de Saconay, *Genealogie et la Fin des Huguenaux, et descouverte du Calvinisme* (Lyon: Benoît Rigaud, 1573), p. 54a; see also his *Discours catholique*, p. 68.

34. Crespin, *Martyrs*, 1: 712—13, 553, on the transformation of one of the men in the conventicles, Mathieu Dymonet, from a dissolute young man to a sober Protestant.

35. Baduel to Calvin (1551), *Calvini opera*, 14: 147—49. Since, as Baduel said, there were no journeymen in the conventicles, it was not until the Consistory was set up that they could know how they were judged and by what standards. See also Pierre Viret, *L'Interim, Fait par Dialogues* (Lyon, 1565), pp. 197—98.

36. AEG, RCon, 23 (1567): 160vff. The registers of the Consistory of Lyon have all been

lost or destroyed. I have pieced together a picture of the cases and individuals who came before it by finding many specific references in the Registers of the Consistory of Geneva. Also, ministers, men, and letters moved back and forth from Geneva to Lyon frequently in the 1560's.

37. AEG, PC 1307. This was said by Colladon and Spifame (who had been a leading figure in Lyon during the 1562—63 regime) as an opinion in the trial of Griffarin Galiot Thibout. Though the trial took place in Geneva, where Thibout had taken refuge, the whole prosecution was instituted and engineered from Lyon. The Lyon pastor Salluard gave information on the case, and all details were quickly known among the Lyon journeymen. The response of the Griffarins to the execution of Thibout was "Messieurs of Geneva are bloodthirsty" (AEG, RCon, 24: 13ʳ). Pastor Salluard was married to Barbe Vincent, daughter of one of the leading merchant publishers of Lyon.

38. *Instruction Chrestienne* 1: 607; the same kind of thing is found in the work of the Franciscan Jean Benedicti, who preached in Lyon (*La Somme des Pechez* [Paris, 1595], p. 100). Raymond de Roover, "La doctrine scolastique en matière de monopole et son application à la politique économique des communes italiennes," in *Studi in onore di Amintore Fanfani* (Milan, 1962), pp. 158—66.

39. A. Sachet, *Le Pardon annuel de la Saint Jean et de la Saint Pierre à Saint-Jean de Lyon* (Lyon, 1914—18), 2: 68—75, with lengthy quotes from the chapter minutes.

40. In regard to the use of apprentice labor, for instance, the Geneva ordinances on printing of 1560 were favorable to the workers. The influence of pastors Beza and Des Gallars on these ordinances was important; Paul Chaix, *Recherches'sur l'imprimerie à Genève de 1550 à 1564* (Geneva, 1954), pp. 21, 26.

41. Compromise urged by Charles de Sainte-Marthe; "To the Masters and Journeymen of the Printing Industry of Lyon," *Poésie françoise*, in C. Ruutz-Rees, *Charles de Sainte-Marthe* (New York, 1910), p. 734.

42. All of the Griffarins tried in Geneva were denied the Holy Supper; and Pierre de Lexert and Jullien Mouchet, questioned by the Lyon Consistory, surely had the same thing happen to them.

43. Du Pinet, *Conformité*, pp. 87—88; Pierre Viret, *Exposition familiere des principaux poincts du Catechisme* (n.p., 1562), pp. 271—72.

44. AEG, PC 1397, 1306, 1307; the Geneva inquiries received much aid and testimony and many letters against the Griffarins from Lyon Protestants.

45. AEG, PC 1397, and RCon, 24 (1567): "le serment faict en ceste secte," f. 10ᵛ. This is not, of course, the first time the term "sect" is used in this connection. It is employed, for instance, in fourteenth-century Florence in regulations prohibiting artisanal organizations in the silk industry; N. Rodolico, "The Struggle for the Right of Association in 14th Century Florence," *History*, 2d. ser. 7 (1922): 181, n. 2. The hostility to divisiveness per se is greater in a Protestant society, which finds this an additional objection against monastic orders; Pierre Viret, *De l'Authorité et Perfection de la Doctrine'des Sainctes Escritures . . .* (Lyon, 1564), pp. 22—23.

46. For instance, see G. Lenski, *The Religious Factor* (New York, 1963), p. 11.

47. See E. Troeltsch, *Social Teachings of the Christian Churches* (London, 1950), p. 339.

48. Full evidence for these statements will be given in my forthcoming book on Lyon in the Reformation. Spiritual Libertinism, as well as varieties of Unitarianism, found a number of individual supporters in Lyon (Guillaume Guéroult, the Bauhin family, various Italians, etc.), but no movement could crystallize around their views. Printers' journeymen might help Guéroult print his unorthodox attacks on Calvin (such as his *Epitre du Seigneur de Brusquet*) and laugh along with him, but he offered them no practical religious alternative. See E. Balmas, "Tra Umanesimo e Riforma: Guillaume Guéroult," in *Montaigne a Padova e altri studi* (Padua, 1962); and H. Meylan, "Bèze et les Italiens de Lyon," BHR 14 (1952): 234—49.

49. Emond Auger, *De la vraye, reale et corporelle presence de Iesus Christ* (Paris, 1566), pp. 14, 18.

50. Only thirteen printers' journeymen removed to Geneva after 1572, and several of these (such as Claude Lescuyer, who testified against the Griffarins in the 1565 trial of Thibout) were Forfants. The names of the refugees have been compiled from the *Livre des habitants de Genève*, ed. P. Geisendorf (Geneva, 1957—63), 2. In addition, several Protestant journey-

men, such as Pierre Coritain, Pierre Sermigny, and Michel Blanchier, returned to Lyon and Catholicism in the late 1560's or in the 1570's. The support given to the *politiques* is clear from the *Plaisans devis* recited by the journeymen's recreational leader, the Seigneur de la Coquille and his Suppôts, in the 1580's and 1590's; *Recueil des plaisants devis* (Lyon, 1857).

2. *Poor Relief, Humanism, and Heresy*

1. Vives to Cranvelt, August 16, 1527, in Juan Luis Vives, *De l'assistance aux pauvres,* trans. R. A. Casanova and L. Caby (Brussels, 1943), p. 42. A new translation of Vives' work into English, with introduction, has been made by Sister Alice Tobriner, under the title *A Sixteenth-Century Urban Report* (Social Service Monographs, 2d ser., School of Social Service Administration, University of Chicago), Chicago, 1971.

2. J. Nolf, *La réforme de la bienfaisance publique à Ypres au XVIe siècle* (Ghent, 1915), pp. 51, 69; Charles du Plessis d'Argentré, *Collectio Judiciorum de novibus erroribus* (Paris, 1728), 2: 84—85: "pia ac salutare"; "Id quod non Catholicorum est, et vivorum fidelium, sed impiorum Haereticorum Valdensium Wiclefisiarum et Lutheranorum."

3. [Jean de Vauzelles] *Police subsidaire a celle quasi infinie multitude des povres survenus a Lyon lan Mil cinq cens trente Ung/Avec les Graces que les povres en rendent tant a messieurs de leglise que aux notables de la ville. Le tout fort exemplaire pour toutes aultres citez* (Lyon: Claude Nourry, dit le Prince, n.d. [1531]).

4. *Tractatus Catholice eruditionis ad testimonium et legem recurrens, confutansque libellum perniciosum velamine elemosine pauperibus Lugduni impense propalatum* [sic], *Editione exaratus Fratris Nicolai Morini Blesensis Ordinis fratrum predicatorum doctoris theologi ac heretice pravitatis inquisitoris . . .* (Lyon: Guillaume Boulle); Colophon: printed for Boulle by Jean Crespin, dit du Carré, September 4, 1532; ff. 74ᵛ, 66ᵛ.

5. R. H. Tawney, *Religion and the Rise of Capitalism* (Holland Memorial Lectures, 1922; Harmondsworth, Engl., 1964), pp. 262—64. W. Cunningham, in his *Christianity and Economic Science* of 1914, had already attributed the stern Scotch treatment of children and unemployed adults to Calvinism.

6. Christopher Hill, "Puritans and the Poor," *Past and Present* 2 (Nov. 1952): 32—50. Hill has treated the subject at greater length in chap. 7 of *Society and Puritanism in Pre-Revolutionary England* (London, 1964). For a critique of Hill's article see V. Kiernan, "Puritanism and the Poor," *Past and Present* 3 (Feb. 1953): 45—51.

7. Nolf, *Réforme,* pp. 69, 51.

8. Brian Tierney, *Medieval Poor Law. A Sketch of Canonical Theory and Its Application in England* (Berkeley and Los Angeles, 1959), chaps. 1 and 3.

9. Hans Baron, "Franciscan Poverty and Civic Wealth as Factors in the Rise of Humanistic Thought," *Speculum* 13 (1938): 1—37. Charles Trinkaus has stressed in his "Humanist Treatises on the Status of the Religious: Petrarch, Salutati, Valla" (*Studies in the Renaissance* 11 [1964]: 23—27) how serious Salutati was in praising the vow of poverty to a friend who was a religious But Salutati was able to resist the attractions of that status, and his justification for poverty, as Trinkaus points out, is very different from that of the twelfth century. Salutati talked of the socially useful actions of the moderately poor; the twelfth century, of meeting Christ among the poor. See Michel Mollat, "Pauvres et pauvreté à la fin du XIIe siècle," *Revue d'ascétique et de mystique* 41 (1965): 305—23, and also his report given at the Thirteenth International Congress of Historical Sciences (Moscow, 1970), "Les pauvres et la société médiévale." On Northern thinkers, see F. Rapp, "L'église et la pauvreté en Alsace à la fin du moyen age," in "Résumés des travaux présentés à la Conférence de Recherches dirigés par M. Mollat" (mimeographed, Faculté des Lettres et Sciences Humaines de l'Université de Paris, 1964—65).

A major new collection, edited by Michel Mollat, has numerous important essays on attitudes toward poverty in the late Middle Ages: *Etudes sur l'histoire de la pauvreté (Moyen Age—XVIe siècle)* (Paris, 1974).

10. D. C. Coleman, "Labour in the English Economy of the Seventeenth Century," *Economic History Review,* 2d ser., 8 (1956): 286.

11. Emanuel Chill, "Religion and Mendicity in Seventeenth-Century France," *International Review of Social History* 7 (1962): 400—425. Enclosing the poor was also supported by

mercantilist thinkers irrespective of religion: J.-P. Gutton, "A l'aube du XVIIe siècle: Idées nouvelles sur les pauvres," *Cahiers d'Histoire* 10 (1965): 87—97. See also Marc Venard, "Les oeuvres de charité en Avignon à l'aube du XVIIe siècle," *XVIIe Siècle* 90—91 (1971): 144—46 especially; Wilma Pugh, "Social Welfare and the Edict of Nantes," *French Historical Studies* 8 (1974): 349—76.

12. Georg Ratzinger, *Geschichte der Kirchlichen Armenpflege* (Freiburg im Breisgau, 1884); Franz Ehrle, *Beiträge zur Geschichte und Reform der Armenpflege* (Freiburg im Breisgau, 1881).

13. W. J. Ashley, *An Introduction to English Economic History and Theory*, 4th ed. (London, 1906), 2: 340—46. Sidney and Beatrice Webb, *English Local Government: English Poor Law History*, Part I: *The Old Poor Law* (London, 1927), pp. 1—60. Also see F. Salter, *Some Early Tracts on Poor Relief* (London, 1926), with an introduction by S. Webb.

14. Pierre Bonenfant, "Les origines et le caractère de la Réforme de la bienfaisance publique aux Pays-Bas sous le règne de Charles-Quint," *Revue belge de philologie et d'histoire* 6 (1927): 230. Italics mine. Jean Imbert seems to be following Bonenfant in talking of Vives' project as a "programme protestant" in *Les hôpitaux en France* (Paris, 1966), p. 24. In all other respects these works are immensely valuable.

15. G. R. Elton, "An Early Tudor Poor Law," *Economic History Review*, 2d ser., 6 (1953): 65 and 65, n. 2, where he quotes the Sorbonne decision on Ypres. Whether or not the real author was a Protestant is not at issue here. The point is the assumption underlying Elton's inference.

16. Basic printed sources on the Aumône-Générale are the following: *Inventaire-sommaire des archives hospitalières antérieures à 1790, Ville de Lyon. La Charité ou Aumône-Générale*, ed. M. A. Steyert and F. Rolle (Lyon, 1874); E. Richard, "Les origines de l'Aumône-Générale à Lyon," *Revue du lyonnais*, 5th ser., 50 (1886): 329—39; Henri de Boissieu, "L'aumône-générale de 1534 à 1562," *Revue d'histoire de Lyon* 8 (1909): 43—57, 81—105, 205—23, 255—76; *idem*, "L'Aumône-Générale sous la domination protestante," *Bulletin de la société littéraire historique et archéologique de Lyon* 3 (1908—9): 1—32; A. Croze, "Statuts et règlements primitifs de l'Aumône-Générale de Lyon," *Revue d'histoire de Lyon* 13 (1914): 363ff. An interesting popular study of the Aumône-Générale through the eighteenth century is Gabriel Arminjon, *Banquier des pauvres* (n.p., 1957). Further, since the initial publication of this article, Jean-Pierre Gutton has published his useful *La société et les pauvres: l'exemple de la généralité de Lyon, 1534—1789* (Paris, 1971).

For Spain, Maria Jimenez Salas, *Historia de la Asistencia Social en España en la edad moderna* (Madrid, 1958); Antonio Rumeu de Armas, *Historia de la Prevision Social en España* (Madrid, 1944); Jean Sarrailh, "Note sur la réforme de la bienfaisance en Espagne à la fin du XVIIIe siècle," *Eventail de l'histoire vivante . . . Hommage à Lucien Febvre* (Paris, 1953), 2: 371—80. The best data on sixteenth-century urban experiments in Spain come from Juan de Medina, *De la orden que en algunos pueblos de Espanse ha puesto en la limosna* (Salamanca, 1545).

17. On the population of Lyon in the sixteenth century, see Richard Gascon, *Grand commerce et vie urbaine au XVIe siècle. Lyon et ses marchands* (Paris, 1971), pp. 341—50. The figures here are based on my calculations from remaining birth and militia records in Lyon, as well as from other sources, to be given in my forthcoming book *Strikes and Salvation at Lyon*. On city growth, see A. Kleinclausz et al., *Lyon des origines à nos jours* (Paris, 1925), pp. 22—30, 160, 166.

18. The Norwich census of the poor in 1570 also shows a majority of the poor from skilled trades (J. F. Pound, "An Elizabethan Census of the Poor," *University of Birmingham Historical Journal* 8 [1962]: 139, 152—53). In addition, on the place of artisans among the poor and on the problem of poverty more generally at Lyon, see Gascon, *Grand commerce*, pp. 392—404; *idem*, "Economie et pauvreté aux XVIe et XVIIe siècles: Lyon, ville exemplaire et prophétique," in *Etudes sur l'histoire de la pauvreté* (cited in n. 9), pp. 747—60.

19. J. F. Pound found in Norwich in 1570 that the average number of children in poor families where both parents were alive was 2.34 ("An Elizabethan Census," p. 142), whereas my figures from Lyon in the 1530's for such families give three children as both the median and the average. This could be the result of a difference in sample, his being 351 families described in a census, mine being 33 families mentioned at random by the rectors among many more poor

families. Yet there may be a real difference in standard of living between the two cities at the different periods: only 4 of his total 351 families have 7 children, whereas 3 of the 33 families found in Lyon have 7 children (see Table 2).

20. ACh, E4, ff. 1^v, 172^r; E5, p. 296.

21. ACh, E4, f. 1^r. The epidemics of these years were mild, however. In the spring of 1531 there were only twelve victims at the plague hospital (E138, f. 90^v). The Consulate began to become alarmed in March 1532, when there were 32 victims (AML, B51, f.92^v). It was not until 1564 that there was a plague with a very high death toll and with large numbers of inhabitants fleeing the city. For an excellent discussion of disease in a sixteenth-century city, see Brian Pullan, "The Famine in Venice and the New Poor Law, 1527–1529," *Bollettino dell' Istituto di Storia della Società e dello Stato Veneziano* 5–6 (1963–64): 159–68.

22. *Générale description de l'antique et célèbre Cité de Lyon . . . par N. de Nicolay . . . cosmographe du Roy* (1573 MSS; Lyon, 1881), p. 17. *Remonstrances et Memoires pour les Compagnons Imprimeurs de Paris et Lyon . . .* (n.p. [Lyon], n.d. [1572]), A, f. i^r.

23. Numerous women asked the Aumône-Générale for special aid until they were up after childbirth (ACh, E4, ff. 59^r, 94^v, 172^r). In 1556, the cost of the lying-in of a baker's daughter was estimated at 3 livres (ADR, 3E347, ff.137^r–138^v); at this period 3 livres roughly equaled twelve days' salary of an unskilled urban worker. In many cases in the Norwich census the wives of poor men worked (Pound, "An Elizabethan Census," p. 137).

24. The placard of the 1529 grain riot in Lyon blamed the high price on "false usurers" hoarding grain until they got their price. The weather was good, said the placard, and there had been no military requisition of grain (AML, BB46, f. 101^{r-v}). On the impact of speculation on grain prices, see C. Verlinden,J. Craeybeckx, E. Scholliers, "Mouvements des prix et des salaires en Belgique au XVIe siècle," *Annales ESC* 10 (1955): 179–89. On grain prices at Lyon, see Gascon, *Grand commerce*, pp. 538–48, 920–21.

25. AHD, E1, f. 3^r.

26. ACh, E4, ff. 1^r, 100^v, 118^v, 120^v, 122^r, 150^r, 158^r.

27. The statute of the Ypres poor-relief system also shows special concern for child-beggars (Salter, *Some Early Tracts*, pp. 47, 53). During the later Middle Ages hospitals for foundlings were established, which kept the youngsters until they were seven or eight, and there were also a small number of hospitals for orphans (as one in Douai: F. Leclère, "Recherches sur la charité . . . au XIVe siècle à Douai," *Revue du Nord* 48 [1966]: 145). But in the North, the great period for the foundation of establishments for children *separate* from other hospitals is the late fifteenth and sixteenth centuries. See L. Lallemand, *Histoire de la Charité* (Paris, 1906), 3: 139, 148; W. J. Marx, *The Development of Charity in Medieval Louvain* (Yonkers, N.Y., 1936), pp. 74–75; Jean Imbert, *Les hôpitaux en droit canonique* (Paris, 1947), p. 127; Jean Delumeau, *Vie économique et sociale de Rome dans la seconde moitié du XVIe siècle*, Bibliothèque des écoles françaises d'Athènes et de Rome, fasc. 184 (Paris, 1957), p. 410.

28. C. Paultré, *De la repression de la mendicité et du vagabondage sous l'ancien régime* (Paris, 1906), pp. 17 ff. Lallemand, *Histoire de la Charité*, 3: 346–47. Manuel Colmeira, *Historia de la economia politica en España* (Madrid, 1965), pp. 599–600.

For the punishment of vagabonds at Paris from 1351 on, see Bronislaw Geremek, "La lutte contre le vagabondage à Paris aux XIVe et XVe siècles," in *Ricerche storiche ed economiche in memoria di Corrado Barbagallo* (Naples, 1970), 2: 213–36.

29. Paultré, *Repression*, pp. 29, 34–35, 51–53. The *Liber vagatorum* of the late fifteenth century was based on the listing of the Senate of Basel made in the early fifteenth century. Also see Sebastian Brant's chapter on beggars in the *Narrenschiff* (1494) and Erasmus' colloquy "Beggar Talk" in *The Colloquies of Erasmus*, trans. Craig R. Thompson (Chicago, 1965), especially p. 251. This colloquy appeared for the first time in 1524.

30. Erasmus, "Beggar Talk," in *The Colloquies of Erasmus*, p. 252; see also Frank Aydelotte's delightful *Elizabethan Rogues and Vagabonds* (Oxford, 1913).

31. A. Sachet, *Le pardon annuel de la Saint Jean et de la Saint Pierre à Saint Jean de Lyon* (Lyon, 1918), 1: 491–92.

32. Guillaume Paradin, *Memoires de l'histoire de Lyon* (Lyon: Antoine Gryphius, 1573), p. 281. *La Police de l'Aulmosne de Lyon* (Lyon: Sébastien Gryphius, 1539), p. 7. The coming

of countryfolk to the city in time of famine was an old and widespread custom in Europe (Paultré, *Repression,* pp. 64—65; Pullan, "The Famine in Venice").

33.   Charles Mullett, *The Bubonic Plague and England* (Lexington, Ky., 1956), pp. 22—23, 44—46. Sachet, *Le pardon annuel,* 1: 493: in 1468 beggars were chased from the cloister of Saint Jean because of the danger of infection.

34.   ACh, E4, f. 6ᵛ; A1, letter of Henri de Gabiano. Vives, *De l'assistance aux pauvres,* pp. 186—87. Pullan, "The Famine in Venice," pp. 159, 167—68. Venard, "Oeuvres de charité en Avignon," p. 139.

35.   Morin, *Tractatus,* f. 31ʳ, estimated a total of 8,000 poor fed by the temporary organization, whereas the *Police de l'Aulmosne* estimated 7,000 to 8,000 (pp. 11—12). The figures I present are based on the actual accounts for the distribution of 1531 (ACh, E138, ff. 89ʳ, 90ᵛ).

36.   Vauzelles, *Police subsidaire,* f. A iiiʳ; *Police de l'Aulmosne,* p. 7. Rabelais had carried on public dissections in Lyon in 1537, and the author of the *Police de l'Aulmosne,* who may have been Vauzelles himself, had evidently been reminded of the 1531 famine while watching Rabelais' dissections. Morin, *Tractatus,* ff. 24ᵛ—25ʳ. The 1528 famine in Vicenza and Venice had a similar impact on witnesses (Pullan, "The Famine in Venice," pp. 153, 157).

37.   Vauzelles, *Police subsidaire,* ff. A iiᵛ— A iiiᵛ, B iiiiʳ⁻ᵛ, C iiᵛ.

38.   AML, BB48, ff. 275ʳ, 276ᵛ; Vauzelles, *Police subsidaire,* f. B iᵛ.

39.   The full archival sources for the *rebeine* have been printed by M. G. and G. Guigue in *Bibliothèque historique du Lyonnais* (Lyon, 1886). Symphorien Champier's eyewitness account is also essential, but must be used with caution because of his false and unsubstantiated theory on the relation of Protestant heresy to the *rebeine: Sensuyt ung petit traicte de la noblesse et anciennete de la ville de lyon. Ensemble de la rebeine ou rebellion du populaire de la dicte ville contre les conseillers de la cyte et notables marchans a cause des bledz . . .* (Paris: Jean Saint Denis, 1529); *Cy commence ung petit livre de lantiquite, origine et noblesse . . . de Lyon: Ensemble de la rebeine et coniuration ou rebellion du populaire . . .* (Lyon, January 1529/30). P. Allut has reproduced the second edition in his *Etude biographique et bibliographique sur Symphorien Champier* (Lyon, 1859), pp. 333—82. Henri Hauser followed Champier's account in his article "Etude critique sur la 'Rebeine' de Lyon," *Revue historique* 61 (1896): 265—307.

40.   "Vidimus des lettres patentes de François Iᵉʳ, 1529," ed. N. Weiss, BSHPF 59 (1910): 501—4.

41.   Nicolas Volcyr, *L'histoire et Recueil de la triumphant et glorieuse victoire obtenue contre les seduyctz et abusez Lutheriens du pays Daulsays . . .* (Paris, 1526), in the library of lawyer Claude Bellièvre, who was a Consul in 1523—24 and also at the time of the *rebeine* (Lucien Auvray, "La bibliothèque de Claude Bellièvre, 1530," *Mélanges offerts à M. Emile Picot* [Paris, 1913], 2: 356). Volcyr and Champier had both been in the service of the Duke of Lorraine and Volcyr wrote a poem for one of Champier's works (Allut, *Etude biographique,* p. 173). Volcyr's history stresses the connection of the Peasants' Revolt with Lutheran heresy.

42.   Champier, *Rebeine* (1529), f. xviᵛ.

43.   See Chapter 1 above and N. Z. Davis, "A Trade Union in Sixteenth-Century France," *Economic History Review,* 2d ser., 19 (1966): 66. The *Memoires* of the moderate Catholic Guillaume Paradin do not give heresy as the background to the *rebeine,* though Paradin followed Champier's account in other ways. The arch-opponent of Protestants, Claude de Rubys, described the *rebeine* as a simple grain revolt (*Histoire veritable de la ville de Lyon . . .* [Lyon, 1604]). In Paris, a citizen described it in his diary as a grain revolt: *"y eust à Lyon grande mutinerie, à cause de la charté des bleds . . ."* (*Journal d'un Bourgeois de Paris,* ed. V. Bourrilly [Paris, 1910], p. 322).

44.   Vauzelles, *Police subsidaire,* f. C iiᵛ. AML, BB49, ff.203ᵛ—4ᵛ, 210ʳ—11ʳ.

45.   AML, BB49, f. 216ᵛ.

46.   *Ibid.,* ff.269ʳ—73ᵛ, 275ʳ—76ʳ; BB51, ff.92ᵛ, 100ᵛ; BB52, 6ʳ, 9ʳ, 56ʳ—57ᵛ, 77ᵛ, 80ᵛ, 133ᵛ. See also *La Police de l'Aulmosne,* p. 17; Paradin, *Memoires,* p. 290.

47.   Vives, *De l'assistance aux pauvres,* p. 53.

48.   On Vauzelles, see Ludovic de Vauzelles, "Notice sur Jean de Vauzelles," *Revue du Lyonnais,* 3d ser., 13 (1872): 52—73; Emile Picot, *Les français italianisants au XVIe siècle*

(Paris, 1906), 1: 118ff.; and N. Z. Davis, "Holbein's *Pictures of Death* and the Reformation at Lyons," *Studies in the Renaissance* 3 (1956): 111—18.

49. Vauzelles, *Police subsidaire*, f. C ii^v. *L'entree de la . . . Reyne Eleonor en la Cité de Lyon L'an mil cinq cens trente trois . . .*, in T. Godefroy, *Le Ceremonial François* (Paris, 1649), 1: 804—16.

50. *Hystoire evangelique des quatre evangelistes en ung fidelement abregee . . .* (Lyon: Gilbert de Villiers, 1526), dedicated to Marguerite de France: Vauzelles wanted those who could not read Latin to be able to participate in the "riches" of the Gospel. *La Passion de Iesu Christ, vifvement descripte, par le Divin engin de Pierre Aretin . . .* (Lyon: Melchior and Gaspard Trechsel, March 1539/40), dedication to the princess Jeanne de Navarre stressing the moral lessons to be learned from meditating on the Crucifixion. *La Genese de M. Pierre Aretin, Avec la vision de Noë . . .* (Lyon: Sébastien Gryphius, 1542), dedication to François Ier, "Monarque d'Eloquence," presenting to him the "divine eloquence" of Aretino. *Les Simulachres et Histories Faces de la Mort . . .* (Lyon: Melchior and Gaspard Trechsel, 1538), dedication to the Abbess de Saint Pierre in Lyon. "The Pictures of Death . . . are the mirror by which one can correct the deformities of sin and embellish the soul."

Vauzelles was not a great stylist, but his writing in these works aimed at a wide audience is direct, colorful, and effective, in contrast to the many precious turns of phrase in his letters to Aretino and his poems for the Queen's Entry.

51. Vauzelles, *Police subsidaire*, f. C iv^v; idem, *Simulachres*, f. A iii^{r-v}. He said in the *Hystoire evangelique*, in justifying his departure from the exact text of Scripture, that the words were not magical but rather that faith in the words was what counted. "*Toutes choses ou la foy nest la principalle ouvriere sont supersticieuses et damnables*"(f. iii^v). This is an Erasmian view rather than the Lutheran "faith alone." He is also like Erasmus in criticizing ceremonialism but accepting the merit of true works.

52. T. M. Centi, "L'attività letteraria di Santi Pagnini (1470—1536)," *Archivum fratrum praedicatorum* 15 (1945): 5—51.

53. Pagnini to Clement VII in *In Utriusque Instrumenti nova translatio* (Lyon: Antoine du Ry, 1528); quoted in Centi, "L'attività letteraria," p. 20: "*rogatus . . . a civibus illis florentinis concionari statui in proxima quadragesima, quum multos audierim Lutheriana infectos haeresi.*"

54. *Habes Hoc in libro candide Lector Hebraicas Institutiones . . .* (Lyon: Antoine du Ry for François de Clermont, bishop of Avignon, 1526); dedication to Federico Fregoso, archbishop of Salerno, defending the usefulness of Hebrew letters in studying the Bible and the support of Saint Jerome for this view. *Hoc est, Thesaurus Linguae Sanctae. Sic enim inscribere placuit Lexicon hoc Hebraicum* (Lyon: Sébastien Gryphius, 1529), dedication to Fregoso, saying among other things that a pure life is expressed in pure language. *Santis Pagnini . . . Isagogae ad sacras literas, Liber unicus . . . Isagogae ad mysticos sacrae scripturae sensus, Libre XVIII . . .* (Lyon: François Juste at expense of Thomas de Gadagne and Hugues de La Porte, 1536/37). Printed posthumously with Pagnini's dedication to Cardinal Jean du Bellay, saying he is writing against heresies on the Virgin and the Sacrament, and with a letter from Champier praising Pagnini. It was Gadagne, the financer of this work, whom Pagnini persuaded to subsidize additions to the plague hospital. His wife was a relative of Pagnini.

55. Centi, "L'attività letteraria," p. 26 n. 78, p. 46.

56. The dating of the speech: since we have started the *aumône*, the price of grain has already fallen, "pour certain ung evident miracle, attendu que nous sommes en May" (Vauzelles, *Police subsidaire*, f.Aiiii^v). This sermon was presumably given at a meeting of Consuls and notables (perhaps outdoors in the Franciscan courtyard, where large meetings were sometimes held) rather than formally from a church pulpit. That it was intended for oral delivery is strikingly clear from its style: frequent direct address, apostrophes, rhetorically repeated phrases, etc. The sermon is *not* disposed in the "modern" style of the later Middle Ages (theme, protheme, etc.). Rather, Vauzelles seemed to be making gestures toward a Ciceronian disposition. Also, biblical events and personnages are applied directly and sometimes prophetically to events and persons in Lyon—a technique common in English pulpit oratory of the sixteenth century (see M. Maclure, *The Paul's Cross Sermons* [Toronto, 1958], pp. 151, 173). The learned preamble on the etymology of place names in Lyon (f. A ii^{r-v}) seems to be answering some etymological conjectures that Champier added to the 1530 edition of his *Rebeine*, ff.4^v—5^r; and Vauzelles may have added it to the printed edition.

57. Vauzelles' brother Mathieu and his friend Claude Bellièvre were both working unsuccessfully to have a *parlement* established in Lyon.

58. Vauzelles, *Police subsidaire*, f. B iii^v. Cf. Erasmus, *A Book Called in Latin Enchiridion Militis Christiani* . . . (London, 1905; based on the English translation: London, 1533), chap. 13, esp. pp. 171—72.

59. AML, BB52, ff. 57^r, 62^r, 77^v; *Inventaire-sommaire des archives communales antérieures à 1790. Ville de Lyon*, ed. F. Rolle (Paris, 1865), CC849: Consulate presents Burgundy wine to Brother Santo for his "daily preaching on behalf of the poor and the hospitals." Champier to Tournon in Pagnini, *Isagogae*, f. C ii^{r-v}.

60. Tierney, *Medieval Poor Law*, pp. 116—19.

61. John Durkan, "John Major: After 400 Years," *The Innes Review* 1 (1950): ·131—39; *idem*, "The Beginnings of Humanism in Scotland," *The Innes Review* 4 (1953): 5—24; J. H. Burns, "New Light on John Major," *The Innes Review* 5 (1954): 83—97; Francis Oakley, "On the Road from Constance to 1688: The Political Thought of John Major and George Buchanan," *Journal of British Studies* 2 (1962): 1—31; *idem*, "Almain and Major: Conciliar Theory on the Eve of the Reformation," *American Historical Review* 70 (1965): 673—90.

62. *Joannis Maioris doctoris theologi in Quartum Sententiarum quaestiones* . . . (Paris: Josse Bade, 1516), ff.lxx^v—lxxiiii^r.

63. Salter, *Some Early Tracts* (cited in n. 13), p. 62; Bonenfant, "Les origines" (cited in n. 14), p. 222.

64. Vauzelles, *Police subsidaire*, f. B iiii^v. No one has yet found any manuscripts or printed versions of Pagnini's poor-relief sermons, so it is at present impossible to know what kind of role he played in suggesting new institutions. He had been interested in poor relief already in Florence and Avignon (Champier to Tournon, in Pagnini, *Isagogae*, f. C ii^{r-v}). The great preacher and humanist Johann Geiler attempted to persuade the Strasbourg authorities to set up a new system of poor relief in a series of sermons in 1497—1501, though the reform itself was not made until 1523 (F. Rapp, "L'église et la pauvreté" [cited in n. 9], and letter of November 1966).

65. Nolf, *Réforme* (cited in n. 2), p. liv; Jimenez Salas, *Historia* (cited in n. 16), p. 92 n. 11. M. Bataillon, "J. L. Vives, réformateur de la bienfaisance," BHR 14 (1952): 151. Villavicenzo's book, written to attack Vives' *De subventione pauperum* and a later defense of welfare reform in Bruges by Gilles Wijts, was entitled *De oeconomia sacra circa pauperum curam a Christo instituto* (Antwerp: Plantin, 1564).

66. ACh, E4, f. 8^{r-v}.

67. Allut, *Etude biographique*, p. 252; Lallemand, *Histoire de la Charité*, 4.2: 480ff. G. D. Mansi, ed., *Sacrorum conciliorum nova et amplissima collectio* (Florence, 1759 — 98; reprint, ·Paris and Leipzig, 1901—27), 32, cols. 905—7. The first mention I have found of a "*mont-de-piété*" for Lyon is in 1571, and then it was the Consulate, not the Franciscans, who made the proposal (AML, BB89, ff.48^r—49^v). Nothing came of the project. M. Gutton discusses this subject for seventeenth-century Lyon in *La société et les pauvres*, cited in n. 16. See also Howard M. Solomon, *Public Welfare, Science, and Propaganda in Seventeenth-Century France: The Innovations of Théophraste Renaudot* (Princeton, N.J., 1972), pp. 48—53.

68. Vauzelles, *Police subsidaire*, f. C ii^{r-v}. On Erasmus' view of ·the laity, see James K. McConica, *English Humanists and Reformation Politics under Henry VIII and Edward VI* (Oxford, 1965), chap. 2.

69. L. de Vauzelles, "Notice sur Matthieu de Vauzelles," *Revue du lyonnais*, 3d ser., 9 (1870): 504—29; V. L. Saulnier, *Maurice Scève* (Paris, 1948), 1: 34. AHD, ff. 1^{r-v}, 2^v—3^v. AML, BB49, f. 215^v (M. de Vauzelles suggests that a roll be made of the wealthy who can provide grain to the town and that they be constrained to give). ACh, E4, ff.5^v—7^r, 12^{r-v}. Other lawyers from Consular families, such as Jean du Peyrat, Claude Bellièvre, and Eynard de Beaujeu, played important roles in forming the Aumône-Générale.

70. Auvray, "Bibliothèque" (cited in n. 41), p. 358.

71. Published by Melchior and Gaspard Treschel, who also printed works by Champier and later Jean de Vauzelles' edition of Holbein's *Pictures of Death*.

72. ADR, Fonds Frécon, Dossiers Rouges, II, B. AML, BB52, ff. 1^r, 57^{r-v}, 149^r. ACh, E138, f. 1^r.

73. ACh, E138, ff.2ʳ⁻ᵛ, 28ᵛ; E139, p. 24; E4, f.1ʳ—13ᵛ. Turquet was not merely used as a contact for money-raising among Italian residents in Lyon but was repeatedly present at the meetings to plan the Aumône-Générale in early 1534.

74. *Traicte des Péages, Composé par M. Mathieu de Vauzelles docteur es droits* . . . (Lyon: Jean de Tournes, 1545), p. 105. Vauzelles used the chapter on privileges and exemptions of the clergy as an excuse for outlining a whole series of reforms for the Catholic clergy.

75. Sometime before 1522, Broquin's mother Pernette Andreyet became a widow and married the banker and merchant Antoine Du Blet (ADR, Fonds Frécon, II, B). On this friend of Farel, see *Guillaume Farel, 1489—1565,* ed. Comité Farel (Neuchatel, 1930), pp. 120—29, and Henri Hours, "Procès d'hérésie contre Aimé Maigret," BHR 19 (1957): 16. After he died, Pernette must have decided she had had enough of such dangerous men and married a respectable Catholic lawyer, Maurice Poculot.

76. Eugène Vial, "Jean Cleberger," *Revue d'histoire de Lyon* 11 (1912): 81—102, 273—308, 321—40; 12 (1913): 146—54, 241—50, 364—86. N. Weiss, "Le réformateur Aimé Meigret. Le martyr Etienne de la Forge et Jean Kléberg," BSHPF 39 (1890): 245—69. ACh, E150, p. 12. *La Police de l'Aulmosne,* p. 10. Kleberger had given 500 livres during the famine of 1531, and by mid-1539 about 2,300 livres more. The archbishop's contribution by that date was well below 2,000 livres. In Kleberger's will of August 25, 1546, he gave a further 4,000 livres to the Aumône (ADR, 3E4494, f. 168ʳ).

77. The only example known to me of subsidized housing outside of hospitals is the Fuggerei, or cottages for elderly workers, built by Jacob Fugger in Augsburg. Professor Karl Helleiner has told me that individual Beguine houses could be "rented" by widows in the Netherlands in the late Middle Ages. Whether or not this constituted "subsidized low-cost housing" would depend on the amount of money given by the widows.

78. Woodrow Borah, "Social Welfare and Social Obligation in New Spain: A Tentative Assessment," in *XXXVI Congresso Internacional de Americanistas, Seville, 1964* (Seville, 1966), 4: 45—57. J. H. Elliott, *The Old World and the New, 1492—1650* (Cambridge, 1972), p. 27.

79. In 1492, Waldensian ministers from Italy were proselytizing in rural villages near Lyon. When they came to Lyon, it was only for a pilgrimage to Waldo's neighborhood, not to preach. In any case, the inquisition of these men later in Dauphiné shows that they were no longer stressing apostolic poverty. (Peter Allix, *Some Remarks upon the Ecclesiastical History of the Ancient Churches of Piedmont* [Oxford, 1821], pp. 335—45.) There is no reference in any Lyonnais literary source of the sixteenth century to a continuing tradition of Waldensianism *in* Lyon. Rather, Champier and other Catholics attack Lutheranism as a "rebirth" of that old heresy. The quote about Waldo's street comes from Barthelemy Bellièvre (ca. 1460—ca. 1529), in Claude Bellièvre, *Souvenirs de voyages . . . notes historiques . . . ,* ed. Ch. Perrat (Geneva, 1956), p. 74. See also René Fédou, "De Valdo à Luther: Les 'Pauvres de Lyon' vus par un humaniste lyonnais," in *Mélanges André Latreille* (Lyon, 1972), pp. 417—21. On *compagnonnages* in Lyon, see N. Z. Davis, "A Trade Union."

80. Vauzelles, *Police subsidaire,* ff. B iiᵛ, B iiiiᵛ.

81. J. Beyssac, *Les chanoines de l'église de Lyon* (Lyon, 1914), pp. xxii—xxv; J. Déniau, *La commune de Lyon et la guerre bourguignonne, 1417—1435* (Lyon, 1955), pp. 167—70; R. Fédou, *Les hommes de loi lyonnais à la fin du moyen age* (Paris, 1964), pp. 330—31.

82. Bonenfant, "Les origines" (cited in n. 14), pp. 208—10; Marx, *Development of Charity* (cited in n. 27), pp. 49—59; Jean Imbert, "La Bourse des pauvres d'Aire-sur-la-Lys à la fin de l'Ancien régime," *Revue du Nord* 34 (1952): 13—36; Leclère, "Recherches" (cited in n. 27), pp. 149, 152—53. These tables were also known as the *Tables du Saint-Esprit.*

83. J. Gerig, "Le Collège de la Trinité à Lyon avant 1540," *Revue de la Renaissance* 9 (1909): 75—77.

84. Déniau, "La commune," pp. 137—40. Kleinclausz (ed.), *Histoire de Lyon* (cited in n. 17), 1: 293—94.

85. M. C. Guigue, *Recherches sur Notre-Dame de Lyon* (Lyon, 1876), pp. 95—120. AHD, E1, ff.1ʳ—5ᵛ. Though the Consulate had concerned itself with repair of buildings and financing the hospital, it had not undertaken an effective reform until 1524, when the records begin. In Paris, too, the town council had taken over the administration of the Hôtel-Dieu from the

chapter of Notre Dame at the end of the fifteenth century. This process culminated in royal edicts of 1546 and 1561 placing all hospitals in France under the supervision of laymen (Roger Doucet, *Les Institutions de la France au XVIe siècle* [Paris, 1948], 2: 808; Jean Imbert, "L'Eglise et l'Etat face au problème hospitalier au XVIe siècle," in *Etudes du Droit Canonique dédiées à Gabriel Le Bras* [Paris, 1965], pp. 576−92).

86. E.g., 1546 will of Florentine merchant-publisher Jacques de Giunta: 50 livres tournois to Aumône-Générale, dowries of 10 écus each for thirty poor girls (to be administered by orphanage program of Aumône-Générale), clothing for twelve poor men who carried torches at his funeral (ADR, 3E4494, f. 190r); 1558 will of potter Jean Chermet: 5 livres tournois to Aumône-Générale, 20 livres tournois for dowries for poor girls (to be administered by Aumône-Générale), 5 livres tournois for Hôtel-Dieu, 2 sous each to four poor men who will carry his coffin (ADR, 3E5300,̓ ff. 153v−55r).

87. Guigue, *Bibliothèque* (cited in n. 39), p. 257; Allut, *Etude biographique*, p. 231; Bellièvre, *Souvenirs* (cited in n. 79), pp. 122, 129−30. For the limitations on confraternities made in 1528−29 by the provincial council of the church at Sens: Mansi, *Sacrorum conciliorum . . . collectio* (cited in n. 67), 32, col. 1196. In 1539, a royal ordinance forbade confraternities of artisans throughout the kingdom; but they were still functioning in Lyon as elsewhere in 1561, when the Edict of Orléans ordered that all their goods and revenues be turned over to governmental authorities to be used for poor relief and education.

88. ACh, E4, f. 12r-v, E7, p. 391; *Police de l'Aulmosne*, pp. 25−26; Boissieu, "L'aumône-générale de 1534 à 1562," p. 256. The institution of the Aumône as well as the prohibition of all begging was authorized by an ordinance of Jean du Peyrat, the king's lieutenant-general at Lyon (of a Consular family), March 3, 1533/34. Town cries were made on the provisions of the Aumône, including urgent requests not to give alms in public.

89. Boissieu, "L'aumône-générale," p. 97, for the exact wording of the early "tillets." In the early years, parchment tickets were granted to families where the aid was evidently needed for a very long time, paper tickets to others (ACh, E4, *passim*). Lead tokens̓had been used during the famine of 1531, but the personal ticket obviously made it easier to prevent abuses of the dole. Tickets were to be turned in if the recipient left town. *Police de l'Aulmosne*, pp. 37−38. On earlier use of token coinage for distributions, see William J. Courtenay, "Token Coinage and the Administration of Poor Relief During the Late Middle Ages," *Journal of Interdisciplinary History* 3 (1972−73): 275−95.

90. Bonenfant, "Les origines," p. 217. The Rouen census is described in Salter, *Some Early Tracts* (cited in n. 13), p. 115. The Lyon censuses have unfortunately disappeared, though J. F. Pound has found and described the Norwich census of 1570 ("An Elizabethan Census" [cited in n. 18], p. 138). Brian Pullan does not report a census in Venice, but given some of the provisions of its poor law of 1528/29−that poor of the city be distributed among parishes so that each has its quota according to its wealth−it is clear that there must have been some sort of list prepared, at least within each parish (Pullan, "The Famine in Venice," pp. 173−74, and *Rich and Poor in Renaissance Venice* [Cambridge, Mass., 1971], pp. 252−54).

91. Vauzelles, *Police subsidaire*, ff. B iiiiv, C iir-v.

92. ACh, E4, f. 1v. As Ambrose Raftis, C.S.B., has pointed out to me, monastic institutions had made similar calculations in the medieval period as a basis for aid to the poor. The chapter of Saint Jean, however, was not making such observations in the sixteenth century.

93. ACh, E4, f. 3r.

94. AHD, E1, ff. 3v, F18. ACh, E4, f. 14v. On the development of parish records in France, see M. Fleury and L. Henry, *Des registres paroissiaux à l'histoire de la population* (Paris, 1956), pp. 17−21.

95. The ordinances themselves came from the rectors of the Aumône. They are introduced by a review of the events of 1531, which uses the material from Vauzelles' *Police subsidaire*. There are also views expressed there on the merit of charity−"*nous pouvons acquerir le celeste heritage avec un payement terrien*"−with which Vauzelles would have agreed. On the other hand, the style of the introduction is different not only from the prophetic excitement of the May 1531 sermon−a difference to be expected−but also from the calmer exposition of Vauzelles' commentaries to the Holbein *Pictures of Death*. Yet Vauzelles undoubtedly had something

to do with the final form of the ordinances. He had wanted earlier to write on the subject, and was currently much concerned with the Hôtel-Dieu, which is also described in the *Police de l'Aulmosne*. Strongly interested in illustration—as shown by his work for the 1533 Entry and the Holbein *Pictures*—he could very well have programmed the woodcuts for the *Police de l'Aulmosne*. Finally, Vauzelles had Gryphius publish one of his Aretino translations the very next year.

96. I have looked through all entries in the Decimal Index to the Art of the Low Countries under Acts of Mercy and have benefited from the comments of W. McAllister Johnson of the Department of Fine Arts of the University of Toronto. E. Staley has reproduced a few late-fifteenth-century Florentine woodcuts and drawings of the traditional acts of mercy (*The Guilds of Florence* [London, 1906], pp. 538, 545, 553). The crowds are somewhat less grotesque and less frantic than in the Netherlandish scenes but the donations occur as usual in the street. Even the *mons pietatis* is shown as a literal pile of money in the middle of the road.

A late-fifteenth-century painting in the oratory of San Martino in Florence represents the recipients of the traditional acts of mercy as "solid individuals" rather than miserable poor. Richard Trexler interprets them to be "the shamefaced poor," that is, persons from genteel families who had fallen on hard times ("Charity and the Defense of Urban Elites in the Italian Communes," in *The Rich, the Well Born and the Powerful*, ed. F. Jaher [Urbana, Ill., 1974], pp. 90–91). A painting made for the cathedral of Antwerp about 1525—the Antwerp triptych of the Last Judgment and the Seven Acts of Mercy—depicted almoners in an official garb dispensing food and clothes to the poor outside the temple (M. J. Friedländer, *Early Netherlandish Painting* [Leyden, 1967–]8, no. 87; I am grateful to Larry Silver for this reference). Both of these examples are moving in the direction of the Lyon woodcut.

For seventeenth-century Dutch distribution scenes in the tradition of the Lyon illustration, see *Arm in de Gouden Eeuw* (Amsterdams Historisch Museum, October 23, 1965—January 31, 1966), nos. 17–19. Also see Pierre Deyon, "A propos du paupérisme du milieu du XVIIe siècle: Peinture et charité chrétienne," Annales ESC 22 (1967), fig. 1, for a painting in the medieval tradition.

97. N. Rondot, *L'ancien régime de travail à Lyon* (Lyon, 1897), p. 34.

98. The 493 wills made in fourteenth-century Douai and examined by Françoise Leclère, "Recherches" (cited in n. 27), do not have any rehabilitative or educational bequests. J. A. F. Thomson has looked at this question carefully in wills of fifteenth-century London and found a shift in the direction of education and rehabilitation, but only a very slight one. Only 3.5 percent of the wills studied had educational bequests and they were mostly for university studies in theology. This is in great contrast to the educational foundations of the later period, which W. K. Jordan has described in *Philanthropy in England, 1480–1660* (New York and London, 1959). In the earlier period there were no foundations for apprenticeship, and only 10 percent of the wills provided dowries for poor girls (J. A. F. Thomson, "Piety and Charity in Late Medieval London," *The Journal of Ecclesiastical History* 16 [1965]: 178–95).

99. Kleinclausz (ed.), *Histoire de Lyon* (cited in n. 17), 1: 136–37.

100. On this program, see Boissieu, "L'aumône-générale de 1534 à 1562," pp. 209–22; and Paul Gonnet, *L'adoption lyonnais des orphelins légitimes* (Paris, 1935).

101. *Police de l'Aulmosne*, pp. 19–20, 29–30; Paradin, *Memoires*, pp. 291–92: "*Une Maistresse, pour les filles, laquelle leur apprent à filler, à couldre en divers ouvrages, à aucunes à lire, selon ce à quoy elle iuge leur esprit estre enclin, & propre.*" This is not as good an educational program as that recommended by Vives for girls. He wanted them all to be taught to read, and the talented ones to be allowed to go somewhat further (Vives, *De l'assistance aux pauvres*, p. 214). Luther's ordinance for Leisnig provided that the girls be taught to read. In Lille, whose poor-relief system was reformed in 1527, a burgher founded a school for poor children in 1544, where both the boys and girls would be taught to read and write. Lyon was perhaps backward in regard to educating poor females, but see n. 166 below.

102. The admitting of qualified foundlings from the Hôtel-Dieu to the Collège de la Trinité had been anticipated by the Confraternity of the Trinity when the school was turned over to the municipality in 1527. In 1529, however, the Consulate was still discussing the question of free tuition at the college. (Gerig, "Collège" [cited in n. 83], pp. 77–78, 83). Not until the

Aumône-Générale provided elementary instruction for the foundlings and other orphan boys was there a real possibility of their going on to the college.

103. Turquet collected and distributed for the Aumône in its first year (ACh, E139, p. 24; E144), and attended the planning meetings in early 1534. In August and September 1536, Turquet and Mathieu de Vauzelles discussed the establishment of the silk industry with the Consulate, and the need for special privileges and exemptions to encourage the industry (AML, BB55, ff.193ʳ, 194ᵛ, 196ᵛ).

104. Turquet elected rector Feb. 1535/36 (ACh, E4, f. 209ʳ). "Le sire Estienne Turquet a Remonstré aud. Srs. quil est tous les jours apres Remonter sus la manufacture des veloux en ceste ville ce quil ne bonnement faire sans tousjours quelque petite aide de laulmosne" (E5, p. 271). Also, pp. 182, 272, 332, 368, 388, 398.

105. Boissieu, "L'aumône-générale" (cited in n. 16), p. 222.

106. Vauzelles, *Police subsidaire*, f. B iiiiᵛ.

107. ACh, E4, ff.6ʳ–7ʳ, 12ʳ, 124ʳ; Boissieu, "L'aumône-générale," p. 258.

108. *Documents concernant les pauvres de Rouen*, ed. G. Panel (Rouen, 1917), p. xxvi; M. Fosseyeux, "La taxe des pauvres au XVIe siècle," *Revue d'histoire de l'Eglise de France* 20 (1934): 418.

109. An interesting illustration of this is the change made by Paradin in the ordinances of the Aumône-Générale which he reproduced in his *Histoire*. In the 1539 ordinances, the tower is justified as follows: "*Pour conserver et entretenir de poinct en poinct l'ordre de l'aulmosne et affin que lesdictz Recteurs soyent bien et deument obeiz . . .*" (p. 21). In Paradin: "*Pour la conservation de l'ordre de ceste aumosne tant generale, il a esté besoing d'une coercion & terreur, pour tenir en cervelle & en bride aucuns des povres qui sont turbulents: & refractaires, & qui ne veulent prester obeissance aux recteurs . . .*" (p. 292).

110. "*Lors verrez vous plusiers maraulx maris . . . ,*" Vauzelles, *Police subsidaire*, f. C iiʳ. ACh, E4, ff.6ʳ–7ʳ.

111. Paultré, *Repression* (cited in n. 28), pp. 78–79; *Documents . . . de Rouen*, p. 50.

112. ACh, E4, f. 98ʳ.

113. The rectors unfortunately did not record all their reasons in granting or denying *aumônes*. Sometimes ill-health, pregnancy, age, or physical deficiency were recorded as the occasion for the alms. In many cases, married women or men are granted *aumônes*, sometimes for a specified period of time, with no explanation for the grant. The ordinances under which the rectors operated nowhere specify that the family of a temporarily unemployed man is to be refused aid. They simply say "there are some poor householders and craftsmen . . . heavily burdened with children and whose jobs are not sufficient to nourish them." The rectors will decide whether they deserve help on the basis of number of children, what their wives do, and the character of their jobs (ACh, E4, f. 1ᵛ). This certainly left the door open for aid for very poor families during slack seasons. Also the ordinances provided that the rectors especially scrutinize the rolls after Easter to remove any healthy persons who could find work in the summer (when employment opportunities increased), but they could readmit these same persons to distributions after Saint Martin's Day (Nov. 11) "*si la pitie et necessité le requiert.*" This, too, suggests aid to the temporarily unemployed so long as job opportunities appeared slim to the rectors.

114. Paultré, *Repression*, pp. 62–63; G. Montaigne, "La police des paouvres de Paris," ed. E. Coyecque, *Bulletin de la société de l'histoire de Paris et de l'Ile-de-France* 15 (1888): 117.

115. Colmeira, *Historia* (cited in n. 28), p. 603.

116. Elton, "Early Tudor Poor Law" (cited in n. 15), pp. 57–58. The English scheme involved a nationwide public works project, rather than urban projects, and the penalties for refusing to work or disobedience were prison and branding. The main improvement over the French urban projects was the suggestion of "reasonable wages." Vives proposed sending all healthy beggars who were not natives of the city back to their home town (whereas in Lyon they could remain as long as they did not beg and found a job or worked on the public projects). The remaining unemployed adults who were poor through their own fault (due to gambling, bad way of life, etc.) were to be given hard work and a small amount of food. They must not die of hunger, "but be constrained by frugality of food, hard labor, and austerity to tame their passions." The forced work suggested by Vives went, however, beyond ditch-digging and construction to assigned

work in textile shops (*De l'assistance aux pauvres*, pp. 200–204). In Geneva, "*mendicants qui peuvent travailler*" from the countryside were sent to the city to work digging ditches for the fortifications (the chronicler Michel Roset, quoted by A. Biéler, *La pensée économique et sociale de Calvin* [Geneva, 1961], p. 156). Because this work was also used for refugees who came to Geneva and could not find work right away, the workers were treated with more consideration than in Lyon. Beggars and people living as vagabonds were not allowed in the city (*ibid.*, p. 153).

117. Vauzelles, *Police subsidaire*, f. B iiiiᵛ.

118. On the English rogue literature, see Aydelotte (cited in n. 30), chap. 6. Bernardino de Sahagún, *General History of the Things of New Spain*, trans. A. J. O. Anderson and C. E. Dibble (Santa Fe, N.M., 1950–61); Alonso de Zorita, *The Brief and Summary Relation of the Lords of New Spain*, trans. B. Keen (New Brunswick, N. J., 1963). Zorita's account is slightly romanticized, while Sahagún's is often a verbatim account, without moral judgments, of what the Aztecs told him. The Franciscan Sahagún was interested in church policy toward the Indians; the judge Zorita in state policy.

Pantagruel plays all kinds of tricks, but he is not a beggar or vagabond like Lazarillo. Montaigne on beggars: in Book III, chap. 13, of the *Essais*, "De l'experience."

119. See the testimony of an Italian vagabond in Rome, 1595 (Delumeau, *Vie économique* [cited in n. 27], pp. 405–6) and the material from the ex-vagabond Pechon de Ruby's *La vie généreuse des mercelots, guez et boesmiens* (1596) described in Paultré, *Repression*, pp. 42ff. Also see the excellent study by M. Gongora, "Vagabondage et société pastorale en Amérique latine," *Annales ESC* 21 (1966): 159–77. On business arrangements and training programs among Venetian beggars, see Pullan, *Rich and Poor*, pp. 302–7.

120. See, for instance, the study *Nineteen Negro Men* by Gertrude Zemon Gass and Aaron Rutledge (San Francisco, 1967), an evaluation of the retraining of unemployed men in Detroit as practical nurses, and A. B. Hollingshead and F. C. Redlich, *Social Class and Mental Illness: A Community Study* (New York, 1958), pp. 115ff. Seventy-six percent of the families in the lowest class in the Hollingshead-Redlich study were "completely isolated" from any community group. Family life was also disrupted, which meant further isolation.

121. ACh, E5, pp. 407, 412.

122. *Ibid.*, p. 403.

123. N. Z. Davis, "A Trade Union in Sixteenth-Century France," p. 62; Archives Nationales, Χ¹ᵃ 4911, f. 80ʳ⁻ᵛ.

124. ACh, E5, p. 296; E4, ff.149ʳ, 112ᵛ–13ʳ, 12ᵛ. N. Z. Davis, "A Trade Union," pp. 64–65. Only at the end of the seventeenth century do a few mercantilist writers in England and religious thinkers in France begin to advocate higher wages (Coleman, "Labour in the English Economy" [cited in n. 10], p. 281; Pugh, "Social Welfare" [cited in n. 11], p. 374, citing a 1694 memoir found in the archives of the Company of the Holy Sacrament in Lyon). Richard A. Clowman and Richard M. Elman, "Poverty, Injustice and the Welfare State," *The Nation* (Feb. 28, 1966), pp. 230–32.

125. The basic *aumône* for an adult male in the 1530's was a twelve-pound loaf of wheat bread (thus somewhat more than the ten and a half pounds that the rectors estimated a male ate each week) and one sou. Since the rectors further estimated in 1534 that the food other than bread necessary for an adult male would cost him three deniers per day, the basic *aumône* would not cover all food expenses for the week. During periods of unemployment, there would still be problems unless the *aumône* was raised. Two or three times the basic *aumône* was given to a man with wife and children, and the rectors at their discretion made adjustments upward and downward. See ACh, E4, ff. 1ᵛ, 9ʳ; *Police de l'Aulmosne*, pp. 23–24. There is no certain evidence of whether the basic *aumône* had been raised by 1561, though not long after that date a certain blind man and his wife were being given six pounds of bread and five sous (ACh, E10, p. 565).

Here are the prices for a pound of beef paid by the Aumône-Générale for several years up to the First Religious War. Since most of them are special Lenten prices, they are probably slightly below the market price: April 1535, 4½ deniers; March 1539, 5 deniers; April 1549, 6 deniers; March 1550, 6 deniers; March 1561, 6 deniers; December 1561, 8 deniers. The real effects of inflation are seen later in the century. In February 1587, the Consulate ordered butchers to sell beef to the Aumône at 23 deniers per pound (AML, BB118, ff.24ᵛ–25ʳ). Mutton prices were usually two to three deniers above beef. Further on meat prices in Lyon in Gascon, *Grand commerce*, p. 922.

126. In March 1560, when there were about 215 sick people in the hospital, the ratio of deaths to entries was 0.20; in a four-week period in late fall 1560, when there were about 250 sick people in the hospital, the ratio was 0.38; in January 1561, with about 330 people in the hospital, the ratio was 0.30 (AHD, F21). Cf. the 0.30 ratio of deaths to entries in 1539–40, when the total number of sick in the hospital was usually under 200 (see Table 3).

127. The persistence of adult begging, against which cries had to be made periodically throughout the century, was due to the character of the economic system, the tenacity of old behavior patterns, and the inadequate police force of Lyon. The ordinances of 1539 specifically note the improvement in regard to child beggars, and they do not figure in later plaints by the rectors about begging. The 1539 ordinances also claim a disappearance of cases of "plague" since the institution of the Aumône. A description of the Paris welfare system in the 1550's does the same (*Police de l'Aulmosne*, p. 44; G. Montaigne [cited in n. 114], p. 106). If true, these claims presumably reflect an increase in resistance to the plague due to the decrease in other disease and the decrease in famine. On the drought of 1556: Paradin, *Memoires* [cited in n. 32], p. 357. Crises in provisioning did not end, of course, but they were dealt with slightly more efficiently in the years after 1534.

128. *Police de l'Aulmosne*, p. 24–27; Boissieu, "L'aumône-générale" (cited in n. 16), pp. 263–67. The changes from ACh, E138 (1534–35) to ACh, E150 (1537–39) already show the increase in sources of income. Simple administrative expenses for the Aumône were not high. Exemptions from the king kept the cost of certain necessities down. Rent to the Franciscan monastery for offices was low; a granary–grinding grain for the establishment–and a bakery on the large premises supplied the bread for the Aumône. The rectors and solicitors for the Aumône worked without pay; the beadles and schoolteachers had to be paid.

129. ACh, E5, p. 215, E7, p. 470; *Police de l'Aulmosne*, p. 35 (the clerk "*sollicitera les particuliers donataires de l'aumosne, comme les nations estranges, & autres bienfacteurs, de porter & envoyer les dons promis. Et s'il est besoing, d'en contraindre quelcun par proces, sera tenu d'en advertir le Secretaire . . .*").

130. Vauzelles, *Police subsidaire*, f. B iiiiᵛ.

131. Morin (cited in n. 4), ff. 65ʳ–66ᵛ.

132. Nolf, *Réforme* (cited in n. 2), p. 64. Jimenez Salas, *Historia* (cited in n. 16), p. 90.

133. *Police de l'Aulmosne*, p. 44.

134. Non-French rectors of the Aumône-Générale include Etienne Turquet, Girardin Panse, Albisse d'Elbene, Andrea Cenami, Georges Obrecht. Among non-natives of Lyon on weekly rolls: Jacques Perrier, shoemaker from Chambéry (ACh, E4, f. 119ᵛ); Mathieu du Boys, barber from Valence (f. 177ᵛ); widow Jane Mole from the Velay (f. 55ᵛ); a girl from Quirieu in Dauphiné (f. 63ᵛ); wife of Mathieu Vulpa (E7, p. 237), an Italian name; Estienne Harestonny (p. 270), probably German; Jeanne de Sarragosse, "paovre femme espagnole" (E18).

135. *Police de l'Aulmosne*, pp. 36–37. Almost all the *passades* were given in money. If we can assume that the standard *passade* was one sou, then approximately 4,100 people were thus aided from August 10, 1538, to June 30, 1539 (ACh, E150), and about 4,450 people from March 1550 through December 1550 (E162). In case of an emergency, the funds for the *passades* were cut, and a few times these distributions stopped.

136. In March 1537/38, the rectors refused to admit a widow to the rolls because she was not living in Lyon when the Aumône began (E5, f. 132ᵛ). This requirement was stated as such in the 1539 printed ordinances. From what can be seen of people who were later received at distributions, the requirement cannot have been stated as "being in Lyon in 1534" for very long after the printing of the ordinances in 1539. In 1588, the Consulate speaks of a three-year residence requirement for "pauvres valides" (AML, BB120, f. 198ʳ). Boissieu states that it was seven years, but does not give his source ("L'aumône-générale," p. 98).

137. G. Montaigne (cited in n. 114), p. 111; AEG, Archives hospitalières, Kg 12; H. Grandjean, "La bourse française de Genève," *Etrennes genevoises* (1927), pp. 46–60. See the valuable

discussion of this problem in Pullan, "The Famine in Venice," pp. 165–76, and *Rich and Poor*, Part II, chap. 4.

138. Tierney, *Medieval Poor Law* (cited in n. 8), p. 57. Vives pointed out that civil law allowed such preferences (*De l'assistance aux pauvres*, p. 201). See also Trexler, "Charity and the Defense of Urban Elites" (cited in n. 96).

139. It is also possible that inhabitants of Lyon who had properties or seigniories in rural areas aided them by direct contributions. W. K. Jordan has pointed out that Londoners founded rural charities (*Philanthropy in England* [cited in n. 98]); and Brian Pullan has speculated that this might be the case for Venice ("The Famine in Venice," p. 176). The chapter of Saint Jean, with substantial properties in the Lyonnais, gave an annual *aumône* in grain to the poor of various villages (ADR, 10G113, ff. 100ʳ, 256ʳ⁻ᵛ; 10G115, ff. 55ᵛ–56ʳ).

140. ACh, E4, ff. 4ᵛ, 32ʳ.

141. The Lyon edition was purchased in 1535 in Montpellier by the Spaniard Fernand Colomb (son of the explorer), which indicates something of the circulation of Vauzelles' sermon (L. Galle, "Les livres lyonnais de la bibliothèque du Baron Pichon," *Revue du lyonnais*, 5th ser. [1897]: 431).

Irene Brown, who is working on sixteenth-century Toulouse, has kindly provided me with information about Jean Barril. This wine merchant subsidized the publication of several works in Toulouse in the 1530's, including a book of moral instruction for women of high rank, dedicated to Marguerite de Navarre; a description of Catholic victories by the Count Palatine Frederick; and an interesting report of Franciscan conversion and education of Indians in Mexico. Possibly Vauzelles' connection with Barril was through Marguerite. The Toulouse title of Vauzelles' sermon is the same as in n. 3 above, with the following phrase added: *Dirigee a honneste homme Jehan Barril marchant de Tholoze pour la communiquer aulx habitans dicelle. Dung vray zelle* [Vauzelles' device].

142. *Police de l'Aulmosne*, p. 17. There are several typographical differences between the title page of *La Police de l'aulmosne de Lyon*, which is call-number 355969 at the Bibliothèque municipale de Lyon, and *La Police de L'Aulmosne de Lyon*, which is located in AML, GG140; though a different woodcut was used, the emblem is the same. At the request of the Consuls and rectors of the Aumône, the Sénéchaussée granted Gryphius a *privilège* for two years, Jan. 11, 1538/39.

143. Vives' editions given by Casanova and Caby, *De l'assistance aux pauvres*, pp. 265–88; the Ypres editions in Salter, *Some Early Tracts* (cited in n. 13), pp. 32–33. The preface to the Latin edition of the Ypres ordinances says that many learned men are debating what to do about the multitude of paupers. The plan of Ypres is offered as a solution for others throughout the Christian republic (*Forma subventionis pauperum quae apud Hyperas Flandorum urbem viget, universae Reipublicae Christianae longe utilissima* [Antwerp: Martin Lempereur, 1531], vᵒ of title page). Nuremberg editions: O. Winckelmann, "Die Armenordnungen von Nurnberg (1522) . . . ," *Archiv für Reformationsgeschichte* 10 (1912–13): 243–46. I know of no copy of the printed version of the Paris ordinances, but G. Montaigne says in the manuscript he sent to the Cardinal de Tournon that there was a printed edition (G. Montaigne [cited in n. 114], p. 106). The Chartres project is described in a 1557 Latin work by the jurist Vincent de la Loupe (E. Armstrong, "Robert II Estienne à Paris," *Bibliothèque d'humanisme et renaissance* 20 [1958]: 353). The Bruges system was defended by Gilles Wijts, *De continendis et alendis domi pauperibus* (Antwerp, 1562). Juan de Medina, abbot of Saint Vincent in Salamanca, dedicated his work to Prince Philip, with whom he had already discussed the project (Medina [cited in n. 16], ff.A iiʳ–A ivᵛ).

144. On Morin, ADR, 3 H 1, *passim*; and J. Beyssac, *Les prieurs de Notre-Dame de Confort* (Lyon, 1909), p. 43.

145. "Dung vray zelle," it appeared on the Toulouse edition. If Morin had had any doubts about the authorship of the work, he could easily have checked with the printer, Claude Nourry, whose name is on the title page and who lived across the street from the Dominican convent.

146. Morin, *Tractatus* (cited in n. 4), f. 26ʳ. The quote is from Joel 2: 16.

147. Morin, ff.65ʳ–66ʳ. The discussion of the Consuls and notables about obligation toward foreigners: AML, BB49, ff. 269ᵛ–73ᵛ; BB52, ff. 56ᵛ–57ʳ.

148. Morin, f. 31ᵛ; AML, BB46, f. 76ᵛ.
149. Morin, f. 6ᵛ ("ydiomate vulgari"), f. 77ʳ. Morin took his mandate to attack this book from the provisions of a recent provincial church council at Sens (f. 6ʳ; Mansi, *Sacrorum conciliorum . . . collectio*, 32, col. 1198). For the Sorbonne attack on Hebrew letters and on Erasmus: D'Argentré (cited in n. 2), p. 34; M. Mann [Phillips], *Erasme et les débuts de la réforme française* (Paris, 1934), pp. 75—77, 118—20, 140.
150. Morin, ff.20ʳ, 31ᵛ, 55ᵛ, 22ʳ—23ᵛ, 30ᵛ, 6ᵛ. Vauzelles' careful handling of biblical examples with exact citations in his 1538 commentaries on Holbein's *Pictures of Death* was probably a response to Morin's criticism. Vauzelles' quote on the Waldensians or Poor Men of Lyon, as they had been called: "*Je me tais aussi dung aultre temps auquel Lyon fust par sa simplicite trop charitable: si grand aulmosnier que de celuy en redonda ung non petit reproche.*" (*Police subsidaire*, f. A iiiᵛ). His criticism of Luther: *ibid.*, ff. B iiiʳ, C iᵛ.
151. *Police subsidaire*, f. B iiiiᵛ. A. J. Krailsheimer, *Rabelais and Franciscans* (Oxford, 1963), pp. 290—91; Lucien Febvre, *Le problème de l'incroyance au XVIe siècle* (Paris, 1947), pp. 303—6. Michael Screech, *L'évangélisme de Rabelais. Aspects de la satire religieuse au XVIe siècle* (*Etudes rabelaisiennes* 2, Geneva, 1959), pp. 30—34. Morin, ff.64ʳ—65ʳ.
152. Vauzelles, *Police subsidaire*, f. B iiiᵛ; Morin, ff.38ʳ—55ʳ, 63ʳ-ᵛ. Mansi, *Sacrorum conciliorum . . . collectio*, 32, cols. 1102, 1127.
153. I have looked through the registers of the chapter of Saint Jean for the years 1531, 1532, and 1533 and found no sign of trouble for Vauzelles, who held the judicial post of "chevalier." He came periodically to meetings to perform his regular duties (ADR, 10G114, ff.37ʳ, 73ᵛ; 10G115, ff.36ʳ, 57ʳ). His comment on theology degrees: *La Passion de Iesu Christ* (cited in n. 50), p. 3.
154. Merle d'Aubigné, "La Réforme à Lyon. Procès inquisitionnel contre Baudichon de la Maisonneuve . . . ," BSHPF 15 (1866): 121.
155. ACh, E4, ff.54ᵛ—55ʳ, 59ᵛ—60ʳ, 79ʳ, 128ʳ—29ᵛ (the abbot of Ainay, a Benedictine establishment, agrees to the conversion of their annual grain distribution to the Aumône, provided that its officers prevent begging in the quarter), 139ᵛ—40ʳ, 158ᵛ—59ʳ, 174ʳ, 194ʳ, 203ʳ; E5, f. 133ʳ, pp. 215, 219 (the suit against the archbishopric for failure to pay its pledge after the death of Archbishop François de Rohan and while the see was being administered by the bishop of Autun, who had been granted the "régale" by François Iᵉʳ), f.121ʳ (two Poor Clares forbidden to beg publicly in town), p. 467 (a mendicant from Montpellier forbidden to beg in Lyon). *Police de l'Aulmosne*, p. 43.
156. See W. K. Jordan, *Philanthropy in England* (cited in n. 98), on the switch in philanthropic uses in Protestant England. The criticism of this work, based on its neglect of inflation, has not undermined Jordan's basic conclusions: "The statistics document the swing away from religion to poor relief as the major object to benefactions" (review by D. C. Coleman, *Economic History Review*, 2d ser. 13 [1960—61]: 113—15).
157. Boissieu, "L'aumône-générale," p. 267. The translation and publication of the sermon by Gregory Nazianzen, a project that combines the interests of Christian humanism and welfare reform, I have treated more fully in an article that appeared in *Renaissance Quarterly* (20 [1967]: 455—64).
158. Allut, *Etude biographique* (cited in n. 39), p. 241. Champier made helpful suggestions about welfare reform at meetings of the notables in 1531 and 1532 (AML, ββ49, ff. 216ᵛ, 273ʳ), but he resigned his post on the Consulate in December 1533 (BB52, f. 168ᵛ) and was not present at any of the meetings that planned the Aumône in early 1534. His bitterness about the *rebeine* and a streak of xenophobia and nostalgia for Lyon's past ("*mieulx vault ung escu entre les siens, que ung noble avec les estranges et differens de meurs et conditions,*" Allut, p. 226) may have made him unsuited for planning an organization that depended heavily on foreign participation. Champier was a personal friend of Pagnini, but he was probably feuding with Vauzelles.
159. E.g., *La Chirurgie de Paulus Aegineta . . . Le Tout traduict de Latin—Francoys par Maistre Pierre Tolet Medecin de l'Hospital* (Lyon: Etienne Dolet, 1540): he has translated this for the necessity and use of surgeons' journeymen (p. 3). On the translations of Tolet and Jean Canape and on medical activities in the 1530's: V. L. Saulnier, "Lyon et la medecine aux temps de la renaissance," and H. Joly and J. Lacassagne, "Médecins et imprimeurs lyonnais au XVIe siècle,"

both in *Revue lyonnaise de médecine*, 1958. Though Rabelais did no translating of medical works, his public dissections in Lyon were part of this same teaching effort.
160. Nolf, *Réforme* (cited in n. 2), pp. 54—55.
161. *Police de l'Aulmosne*, pp. 42—44. The poor who did not appear at the procession without legitimate excuse could be deprived of their alms. Catholics occasionally provided in their wills that poor orphan girls from Saint Catherine's hospital be part of their funeral service. For similar processions of the poor at Paris and Orléans, see G. Montaigne (cited in n. 114), p. 117, and Fosseyeux, "La taxe des pauvres" (cited in n. 108), p. 423.
162. These canisters can still be seen at the Musée des Hospices Civils de Lyon.
163. Guy de Tervarent, *Attributs et symboles dans l'art profane, 1450—1600* (Geneva, 1958—59), cols. 302—3. V. G. Graham, "The Pelican as Image and Symbol," *Revue de litterature comparée* 36 (1962): 235—43. Emile Mâle, *L'art religieux de la fin du Moyen Age en France* (Paris, 1925), pp. 317—22. R. Freyhan, "The Evolution of the Caritas Figure in the Thirteenth and Fourteenth Centuries," *Journal of the Warburg and Courtald Institute* 11 (1948): 68—86. Edgar Wind, "Charity. The Case History of a Pattern," *Journal of the Warburg and Courtald Institute* (1937—38): 322—25. *Idem*, "Sante Pagnini and Michelangelo," *Gazette des Beaux Arts* 26 (1944): 211—35. A large painting of a seated charity figure with children was done by Andrea del Sarto for François Ier around 1518 (Louvre; I am grateful to Larry Silver for calling this to my attention). A marble statue of a seated charity figure with children, made in France in the sixteenth century, can be seen at the City Art Museum in St. Louis.
164. Letter of Claude Monier from prison to the conventicles of Lyon, 1551, in Crespin, *Martyrs*, f. 205^v.
165. Among numerous rectors who held office after they were committed to the Protestant cause were the publisher Jean Frellon; the merchant-publisher Antoine Vincent; the important German banker and friend of Théodore de Bèze, Georges Obrecht.
166. The records and accounts of the Protestant regime are in ACh, E10, E170, E171. The confiscation of confraternity funds for the sake of poor relief, begun in 1561, was concluded energetically by the Protestant regime. A hundred books of religious instruction were bought for the orphan girls of Saint Catherine's (E10, p. 508), which indicates either a new policy toward educating the girls or that the Aumône's policy had already turned in that direction after the 1539 ordinances were published. The mechanism of the orphanages was also used to apprentice novices from the monasteries (p. 453).
167. Pierre Viret, *Metamorphose chretienne, faite par dialogues* (Geneva: Jacques Brès, 1561), p. 229. For perceptive remarks on Calvinist reaction to poverty, see R. Stauffenegger, "Réforme, richesse et pauvreté," *Revue d'histoire de l'Eglise de France* 52 (1966): 52—58.
168. A biting and witty satire by a doctor of theology who had converted to Protestantism and left Lyon in 1530, though he was in close touch with the city in the next years. The work was printed in Neuchâtel in 1533 by Pierre de Vingle, also a refugee from Lyon and the son-in-law of Nourry, the printer of Vauzelles' sermon. On Marcourt, see Gabrielle Berthoud, *Antoine Marcourt, réformateur et pamphlétaire* (Geneva, 1973).
169. Monier in Crespin, *Martyrs*, f. 205^v.
170. ACh, E5, f. 147^r; E10, pp. 367, 398, 430, 584; E170, f. 1^r; E171, ff. 6^v—7^v.
171. E.g., Claudine Perrussin, wife of a merchant draper, 100 livres tournois to poor of Reformed Church of Lyon, October 1571; Charles Sartoris, Piedmontese merchant in Lyon, 4 écus d'or soleil to poor in the Reformed Church of Lyon who come from Piedmont, 1571 (AEG, Notaires, Jovenon, II, 92^v—96^r, 89^r—92^v); Jean Chamarier, butcher and hotelkeeper of Lyon, 10 livres tournois to Aumône-Générale, 5 livres for building temples of Reformed Church, 1564 (ADR, 3E7185, August 28, 1564); Regnaud Chollet, master dyer, 25 livres tournois to the Aumône-Générale, 12 livres tournois 10 sous to the Bourse des Pauvres Etrangers at Geneva, 1567 (AEG, Notaires, Rageau, IX, 336—39); Jean Bezines, merchant and Consul of Lyon, 100 livres tournois to the Aumône-Générale, 50 livres tournois to the Hôtel-Dieu, 200 livres tournois to one of the elders of the Consistory of the Reformed Church of Lyon (to distribute to poor Protestants). If the latter was prevented from making this distribution, Bezines revokes the bequests to the Aumône and the Hôtel-Dieu, and gives 350 livres tournois to the Reformed Church (ADR, B, Insinuations, A, ff. 58^v—60^v, Sept. 13, 1564). Note also the testament of the Catholic merchant Gérardin Panse: 1,000 livres tournois to the Aumône-Générale,

but only on condition that it is governed by Catholics. If not, he gives 500 livres tournois to the Hôtel-Dieu and 500 livres tournois for dowries for poor Catholic girls (*ibid.*, f. 44ʳ, August 9, 1564).

172. In *Strasbourg and the Reform* (New Haven, Conn., 1967), Miriam Chrisman points out that the reform of welfare there in 1522 predated the arrival of Capito and Bucer. If some members of the town government were already drawn to Lutheran teachings, others were not. The initial reform of welfare grew out of earlier developments and was "not linked directly to the Reformation" (p. 277). Here too an examination of the welfare reformers might reveal a coalition.

173. On Venice, see Pullan, *Rich and Poor*, Part II. On the "sacralization" of *procureurs* and *hospitaliers* of the Hôpital Général of Geneva by Calvin, who amalgamated them with the Deacons of the Reformed Church, see R. W. Henderson, "Sixteenth Century Community Benevolence: An Attempt to Resacralize the Secular," *Church History* 38 (1969): 421; and Robert Kingdon, "Social Welfare in Calvin's Geneva," *American Historical Review* 76 (1971): 61. For the role of canons in the Bureau des Pauvres of Amiens, created in 1573, see Pierre Deyon, *Amiens, capitale provinciale* (Paris, 1967), pp. 348–49; at Avignon, Venard, "Oeuvres de charité" (cited in n. 11), p. 144.

174. Jean Imbert, "Les prescriptions hospitalières du Concile de Trente et leur diffusion en France," *Revue d'histoire de l'Eglise de France* 42 (1956): 5–28. Archives Nationales, X¹ᵃ 4911, 78ʳ. The attitude of the French church toward urban welfare schemes is suggested by its *cahier* at the Estates of 1560. The church accepts these projects, but requests that its contributions be voluntary not obligatory.

175. See, for instance, Jerrold E. Seigel, "Civic Humanism or Ciceronian Rhetoric? The Culture of Petrarch and Bruni," *Past and Present* 34 (July 1966): 3–48; and Hans Baron, "Leonardo Bruni: 'Professional Rhetorician' or 'Civic Humanist'?" in *Past and Present* 36 (April 1967): 21–37.

176. Erasmus, *Enchiridion*, letter to Volzius: "*Quid aliud est civitas quam magnum monasterium?*" (*Opera Omnia* [Cologne, 1555], 3, col. 346). Vauzelles had used a similar metaphor in the *Police subsidaire*—Lyon is a "*vray cloistre de vertu*" (f. B ivʳ); *La Police de l'Aulmosne*, p. 44.

177. ACh, E4, f. 79ʳ; *La chronique lyonnaise de Jean Guéraud, 1536–1562*, ed. Jean Tricou (Lyon, 1929), p. 113.

178. Pound, "An Elizabethan Census," p. 144; Wallace T. MacCaffrey, *Exeter, 1540–1660* (Cambridge, Mass., 1958), pp. 12, 113.

3. City Women and Religious Change

1. Florimond de Raemond, *L'histoire de la naissance, progrez et decadence de l'hérésie de ce siècle* (Rouen, 1623), pp. 847–48, 874–77. Raemond's work first appeared in 1605—four years after his death—and had many subsequent editions.

2. Gabriel de Saconay, "Preface," in Henry VIII, *Assertio Septem Sacramentorum adversus Martinum Lutherum* (Lyon, 1561), p. xlvi. Claude de Rubys, *Histoire veritable de la ville de Lyon* (Lyon, 1604), p. 84. Crespin, *Martyrs*, 1: 385–87; 3: 203–4, 392.

3. Anderson's book was printed in 1857 and came out in French in 1865–69. Roland K. Bainton, *Women of the Reformation in Germany and Italy* (Minneapolis, Minn., 1971), *Women of the Reformation in France and England* (Minneapolis, Minn., 1973); Lucien Febvre, *Amour sacré, amour profane, Autour de l'Heptaméron* (Paris, 1944); Henry Heller, "Marguerite of Navarre and the Reformers of Meaux," BHR 33 (1971): 271–310; Nancy L. Roelker, *Queen of Navarre: Jeanne d'Albret, 1528–1572* (Cambridge, Mass., 1968); Charmarie Jenkins Blaisdell, "Renée de France between Reform and Counter-Reform," *Archiv für Reformationsgeschichte* 63 (1972): 196–225.

4. Once we turn to Catholic religious life, however, or to the radical Protestant sects, we find that much more consideration has been given to the role of women in religious change. See, for instance, R. W. Southern, *Western Society and the Church in the Middle Ages* (Harmondsworth, Engl., 1970); Robert E. Lerner, *The Heresy of the Free Spirit in the Later Middle Ages* (Berkeley and Los Angeles, 1972); Henri Brémond *Histoire littéraire du sentiment religieux en France depuis les Guerres de Religion* (Paris, 1916–62); Keith Thomas, "Women and the Civil

War Sects," *Past and Present* 13 (April 1958): 42—62; and R. F. Wearmouth, *Methodism and the Common People of the Eighteenth Century* (London, 1945), pp. 217—38.

5. Max Weber, *The Sociology of Religion*, trans. Ephraim Fischoff (Boston, 1964), pp. 104—6; Robert A. Lowie, who suggested greater variation in female styles of religious sensibility in chapter 10 of his *Primitive Religion*, which appeared in 1924 (two years after Weber's work); and Keith Thomas, "Women and the Civil War Sects."

6. Lawrence Stone, *The Crisis of the Aristocracy* (Oxford, 1965), p. 739; Robert Mandrou, *Introduction à la France moderne* (Paris, 1961), p. 117.

7. Nancy L. Roelker, "The Appeal of Calvinism to French Noblewomen in the Sixteenth Century," *The Journal of Interdisciplinary History* 2 (1972): 391—418; Patrick Collinson, "The Role of Women in the English Reformation Illustrated by the Life and Friendships of Anne Locke," *Studies in Church History* 2 (1965): 258—72.

8. Roland H. Bainton, *The Reformation of the Sixteenth Century* (Boston, 1952), pp. 256—60; Bainton, *Women* (1971), pp. 9—10; André Biéler, *L'Homme et la femme dans la morale calviniste* (Geneva, 1963).

9. Guy E. Swanson, "To Live in Concern with a Society: Two Empirical Studies of Primary Relations," in A. J. Reiss, Jr., ed., *Cooley and Sociological Analysis* (Ann Arbor, Mich., 1968), pp. 102—4, 111—16; Erik Erikson, *Young Man Luther. A Study on Psychoanalysis and History* (New York, 1958), pp. 71—72.

10. Marie Dentière, *La Guerre et deslivrance de la ville de Genesve*, in A. Rilliet, ed., *Mémoires et documents publiées par la société d'histoire et d'archéologie de Genève* 20 (1881): 342.

11. Pierre Goubert, *Beauvais et le Beauvaisis de 1600 à 1730* (Paris, 1960), p. 38 and p. 38, n. 6; David Herlihy, "The Tuscan Town in the Quattrocento. A Demographic Profile," *Medievalia et Humanistica*, n.s. 1 (1970): 99—100.

12. This description of patterns of immigration by sex is based on my analysis of all Lyon marriage contracts extant in the notarial records at the Archives départementales du Rhône (Series 3E and B) for Easter 1557 — Easter 1558 and Easter 1560 — Easter 1561. A similar differential between male and female immigration to urban centers is noted by Richard Gascon, "Immigration et croissance urbaine au XVIe siècle: l'exemple de Lyon," *Annales ESC* 25 (1970): 994. (M. Gascon's conclusions are somewhat weakened by the fact that the hospital records used as his source include both travelers and inhabitants indiscriminately.) Herlihy, "Tuscan Town," 101—2; Marcel Lachiver, *La population de Meulan au 17e siècle* (Paris, 1969), p. 94.

13. E.g., Bronislaw Geremek, *Le salariat dans l'artisanat parisien aux XIIIe—XVe siècles* (Paris, 1968), p. 55; Enea Balmas, *Montaigne a Padova e altri studi sulle letteratura francese del cinquecento* (Padua, 1962), p. 207; ADR, 3E3765, ff.179ᵛ, 289ᵛ—90ᵛ (master printer Etienne. Dolet and his wife Loyse Giraud together borrowed money to furnish a printing shop, 1539—41).

14. For instance, ADR, 3E7180, ff.988ᵛ—89ʳ; B, Insinuations, Donations, 25, ff.222ᵛ—24ʳ; Ernest Coyecque, *Recueil d'actes notariés relatifs à l'histoire de Paris et de ses environs au XVIe siècle* (Paris, 1923), no. 3998. See also Henri Hauser, *Ouvriers du temps passé* (5th ed.; Paris, 1927), chap. 8: "Le travail des femmes."

15. ACh, E9, shows many orphan girls being hired out as chambermaids to simple artisanal families. J. J. Servais and J. P. Laurend, *Histoire et dossier de la prostitution* (Paris, 1965), pp. 139—209. Felix Platter, *Beloved Son Felix* (London, 1961), pp. 36—37. Jean Guéraud, *La chronique lyonnaise de Jean Guéraud, 1536—1562*, ed. Jean Tricou (Lyon, 1929), p. 76. ADR, 3E7179, ff.411ᵛ—21ʳ (female labor on construction sites, 1 s. 6 d. to 2 s. a day; unskilled male labor, up to 4 s. a day [July 1562]).

16. *Inventaire-sommaire des archives communales antérieures à 1790*, ed. M. F. Rolle, *Ville de Lyon* (Paris, 1865), CC152; AML, CC1174, f. 10ᵛ; Crespin, *Martyrs*, 1: 305; 3: 296, 702.

17. Hauser, *Ouvriers*, pp. 156—57. Women in the great grain riot or *grand rebeine* of Lyon in 1529: M. C. and G. Guigue, *Bibliothèque historique du Lyonnais* (Lyon, 1886), p. 258; P. Allut, *Etude sur Symphorien Champier* (Lyon, 1859), p. 358.

18. Guillaume Paradin, *Mémoires de l'histoire de Lyon* (Lyon, 1573), p. 356 (because she knew Latin, Pernette du Guillet was "*dessus et outre la capacité de son sexe*"). Père du Colonia, *Histoire littéraire de la ville de Lyon* (Lyon, 1730), 1: f. IIᵛ. Mme. Michel Jullien de Pommerol, *Albert de Gondi, Maréchal de Retz* (Geneva, 1953), pp. 13—17. George E. Diller, *Les Dames des*

Roches; étude sur la vie littéraire à Poitiers dans la deuxieme moitié du XVIe siècle (Paris, 1936).
L. Clark Keating, *Studies on the Literary Salon in France, 1550–1615* (Cambridge, Mass., 1941).
  19. Based on an analysis of hundreds of contracts in ADR, 3E.
  20. Further information on male literacy in the sixteenth century can be found in E. Le Roy Ladurie, *Les paysans de Languedoc* (Paris, 1966), 1: 345–48; 2: 882–83. On male-female literacy rates in seventeenth-century Amiens: P. Deyon, *Amiens, capitale provinciale* (Paris, 1967), p. 342; D. E. Smith, *History of Mathematics* (New York, 1953), 2: 199–202.
  21. Eileen Power, *Medieval English Nunneries* (Cambridge, 1922), pp. 264–70; Charles Jourdain, "Mémoire sur l'education des femmes au Moyen Age," *Excursions historiques et philosophiques* (Paris, 1888), pp. 505–7. Evidence for Lyon comes from archival material over several decades in the late fifteenth and sixteenth centuries.
  22. Foster Watson, *Vives and the Renascence Education of Women* (New York, 1912). Vives' Latin treatise on the education of women, published in late 1523, came out in English in 1529 and in French translation in the 1540's (*L'institution de la femme chrestienne . . . nouvellement traduict en langue Françoise par Pierre de Changy Escuier* [Lyon: Jean de Tournes, 1543], dedicated by Changy to his teenage daughter Marguerite). *Farce nouvelle fort joyeuse des femmes qui apprennent a escrire en grosse lettre*, listed in "Répertoire historique et bibliographique de l'ancien théâtre" (Bibl.´ nat., Mss., nouv. acq. fr. 12646, XV, f. 363ʳ).
  23. Georges Tricou, "Louise Labé et sa famille," BHR 5 (1944): 67–74. *Oeuvres de Louise Labé*, ed. P. Blanchemain (Paris, 1875), pp. 3–4, 80. Labé's poems were first published in Lyon by Jean de Tournes in 1555.
  24. Jacques Toussaert, *Le sentiment religieux en Flandre à la fin du Moyen Age* (Paris, 1963), pp. 89–243. On numerous godmothers: baptismal records at Lyon, AML, GG528 (1568), passim; GG2 ff. 89ᵛ, 93ʳ, 109ʳ, and throughout. The *relevailles* are discussed in Keith Thomas, *Religion and the Decline of Magic* (London, 1971), p. 38.
  25. Toussaert, *Sentiment religieux*, pp. 204–24; Allen N. Galpern, "Change without Reformation: Religious Practice and Belief in Sixteenth-century Champagne" (Ph.D. diss., University of California at Berkeley, 1971), pp. 23–40. Sample wills at Lyon: A chambermaid leaves 8 livres (this could be one or two years' salary, depending on her age) for funeral expenses and subsequent masses for her soul, 1543 (ADR, 3E336, ff.132ʳ–33ᵛ); a pewterer's wife sets up elaborate processions and funds thirty masses in the thirty days following her funeral, 1545 (3E337, f. 20ʳ); a spice merchant's wife funds three high and twenty-five low masses on the day of her death and on its anniversary, and a low mass daily for one year, 1552 (3E344, ff. 31ᵛ–37ʳ); a male shearer of woolen cloth funds one high mass and thirty low masses (3E5297, June 3, 1542); a male packer funds masses for his soul, funding three high masses at 15 sous each (3E7183, Aug. 8, 1555; each high mass cost about five days' wages).
  26. On the importance of confraternities, see Toussaert, *Sentiment religieux*, pp. 478–93; John Bossy, "The Counter-Reformation and the People of Catholic Europe," *Past and Present* 47 (May 1970): 58–59; and Galpern, "Change without Reformation," pp. 75–105. *Répertoire des anciennes confréries et charités du Diocèse de Rouen*, ed. Louis Martin (Rouen, 1936), pp. 143–60. Writing about Rouen in 1587, N. Taillepied added a confraternity of spinning women (*filassières*) under the patronage of Saint Anne (*Recueil des Antiquitez et Singularitz de la Ville de Rouen* [Rouen, 1587], p. 66).
  L. Petit de Julleville, *Histoire du théâtre en France: Les mystères* (Paris, 1880), 1: 413. Organizations among unmarried males are discussed in Chapter 4 below.
  In an interesting article on the new Confraternity of the Rosary, founded by the Dominicans at Colmar in 1484, J.-C. Schmitt points out that somewhat more than half the membership was female. He specifically relates this to the exclusion of women from other confraternities and to the privateness of the devotions (no common masses, no processions, no banquets – only prayers): "Apostolat mendiant et société. Une confrérie dominicaine à la veille de la Réforme," *Annales ESC* 26 (1971): 100–102. One may add that the founder of the order in Colmar was none other than Jacob Sprenger, celebrated inquisitor and judge of witches and author of a chapter on "Why women are more prone to superstition than men" in the *Malleus Maleficarum*. Sprenger clearly preferred to have women at home saying their rosaries. The Confraternity of the Rosary spread in France primarily in the seventeenth century.

Some other Counter-Reformation confraternities may have seen some increase in the percentage of female members. See, however, the interesting picture given by Michel Vovelle for Provence in the eighteenth century: confraternities were primarily masculine organizations, whereas women dominated in acts of private devotion (*Piété baroque et déchristianisation en Provence au XVIIIe siècle* [Paris, 1973], pp. 297—98).

27. Imbart de La Tour, *Les origines de la Réforme* (Melun, 1944), 2: 515—18. Adrien Montalembert, *La merveilleuse hystoire de lesperit de Lyon* (Lyon, 1887): a work of 1528 describing the spectacular reform of a Lyon convent. The rich possibilities for communication back and forth between nuns and the women of their quarter are suggested in Jeanne de Jussie, *Le levain du Calvinisme ou commencement de l'hérésie de Genève*, ed. A. C. Grivel (Geneva, 1865). The high percentage of female religious in Florence in the first half of the sixteenth century (R. C. Trexler, "Le célibat à la fin du Moyen Age: Les religieuses de Florence," Annales ESC 27 [1972]: 1329—50) is in great contrast with the picture in France and is a product of the unusual conditions in the marriage market in that city.

28. Special editions of the life of Saint Margaret and prayers to her on behalf of pregnant women were frequent in the early sixteenth century. The following two both date from around 1515: *La vie de Madame Saincte Marguerite, vierge et martyre avec son oraison* (n.p., n.d.; copy in the Folger Library, Washington, D.C.); *La vie de Ma Dame Saincte Marguerite, vierge et martyre, Avec son Antienne et Oraison* (n.p., n.d.; copy in the Academy of Medicine, Toronto).

29. A. J. Krailsheimer, *Rabelais and the Franciscans* (Oxford, 1963), pp. 31—32; De Rubys, *Histoire veritable* (cited in n. 2), p. 355. However, a tract with editions up to 1530, written by a nun for secular women (*Cy commence une petite instruction et maniere de vivre pour une femme seculiere*), urges women to read holy books and to think about what they read. It also includes a chapter describing the visit of a virtuous woman to a doctor of theology from whom she seeks advice (Alice Hentsch, *De la littérature didactique du Moyen Age, s'adressant spécialement aux femmes* [Cahors, 1903], pp. 223—25).

30. Jean Bouchet, *Le panegyric de Loys de la Trimouille*, chap. 20; "Des moeurs, vertus, gouvernement et forme de vivre de Madame Gabrielle de Bourbon," quoted by Charles de Ribbe, *Les familles et la société en France avant la Révolution d'après des documents originaux* (2d ed.; Paris, 1874), 2: 88—89.

31. Desiderius Erasmus, *The Colloquies of Erasmus*, trans. Craig R. Thompson (Chicago, 1965), pp. 217—23.

32. *Monologue de Messire Iean Tantost lequel recite une dispute qu'il ha eue contre une dame Lyonnoise* (n.p. [Lyon], 1562). Compare also the play performed at La Rochelle in 1558 before the king and queen of Navarre, Antoine de Bourbon and Jeanne d'Albret: a dying woman tries to get help from the useless remedies (relics, indulgences, etc.) of priests and monks but is made healthy and joyous only after a simple stranger quietly leaves her "a book of recipes." The book is the New Testament; the "physician," a heretic burned at the stake (BSHPF 8 [1859]: 278—79).

33. *Le moyen de parvenir a la congnoissance de Dieu et consequemment à salut* (Lyon: Robert Granjon, 1562), ff.a iiii^r, c iiii^r—c v^r, d ii^{r-v}, e ii^{r-v}. This work had an earlier edition in 1557.

34. *Cantique des fidelles des Eglises de France qui ont vaillamment sousteuu pour la parole de Dieu, auquel ils en rendent graces* (Lyon, 1564), f. A iv^v.

35. [Gabriel de Saconay], *Discours catholique, sur les causes et remedes des malheurs intentés au Roy et escheus à son peuple par les rebelles Calvinistes* (Lyon: Michel Jove, 1568), pp. 65—66. Crespin, *Martyrs*, 1: 306; 2: 668—69; 3: 318—19.

36. Emond Auger, *Continuation de l'Institution, Verite et Utilite du Sacrifice de la Messe, Avec Les Responses aux Obiections des Calvinistes . . . Par M. Emond Auger, de la Compagnie de Iesus* (Paris: Pierre l'Huillier, 1566), pp. 115—16. Gabriel de Saconay, *Genealogie et la Fin des Huguenaux, et descouverte du Calvinisme* (Lyon: Benoît Rigaud, 1573), p. 60a. An anti-Lutheran play of 1533 makes the opposite point of the Protestant play cited in n. 32 above. Put on at the Collège de Navarre in Paris, it portrayed a woman tranquilly sewing until she begins to read the Bible. She then loses control of herself and behaves violently toward others. Marguerite de Navarre was the target for this play. (N. Wiess and V. L. Bourrilly, "Jean du Bellay, les

protestants et la Sorbonne," BSHPF 52 [1903]: 209. I am grateful to James Farge for this reference.) On later Catholic Bibles, see Eugenie Droz, "Bibles françaises d'après le Concile de Trente," *Journal of the Warburg and Courtauld Institutes* (1965): 209–22.

37. The social distribution of Protestant males and females here is based on an analysis of some 4,000 males and about 750 females known to have been Protestants in Lyon in the mid-sixteenth century. (The disparity between male and female figures is due in part to the kinds of documents available. For instance, while Reformed marriage contracts provide the names of both spouses, lists of Protestants whose property is to be confiscated ordinarily give only the male heads of households.) Further, an analysis has been made of all the female martyrs from France and Flanders (over 250) mentioned by name in Crespin's *Martyrs*.

On the continued illiteracy of some Reformed women in the 1570's see, for instance, ADR, 3E2810, *passim*.

38. E.g., Crespin *Martyrs*, 1: 668–69; 2: 35–36; 3: 259–60. No pattern of superior constancy by the city women emerges clearly in the lists of abjured and nonabjuring heretics compiled by the militia in Lyon in the late 1560's.

39. The data concerning several hundred women from Lyon are too extensive to present here. In a sample of about 175 Protestant city women listed in Crespin as prisoners or victims of riots, 43 were either widows or unmarried, 17 others were identified by their own occupations (very unusual in sixteenth-century documents not directly concerned with economic matters and thus suggesting some identification of these women with their work), and one other was a former nun. In listings of Protestant suspects in Toulouse in 1568–69, out of 37 women, 20 were either widows or unmarried (Paul Romane-Musculus, "Les protestants de Toulouse en 1568," BSHPF 107 [1961]: 69–94).

40. On the Catholic loyalties of Magdeleine and Catherine des Roches in Poitiers, see Keating, *The Literary Salon in France* (cited in n. 18), pp. 59–61. Louise Labé's maternal aunt Marguerite Roybet, widow of a barber and a *barbière* in her own right, was part of the Protestant movement by the late 1550's.

41. Saconay, *Genealogie*, p. 60a: "*Catechiseurs des femmes.*" [Pierre Viret], *Exposition familiere des principaux poincts du Catechisme et de la doctrine Chrestienne* (n.p. [Lyon], 1562), pp. 277–78. See n. 166 to Chapter 2, above.

42. Dentière, *La guerre et deslivrance* (cited in n. 10), Introduction and pp. 378–80. Dentière was still concerned enough about having been criticized as a woman for the publication of the *Deslivrance* that she left her name off the work. Her *Epistre tres utile, faict et composée par une femme chrestienne de Tornay, envoyee a la Royne de Navarre* was published in 1539 with the false address of Antwerp.

43. Crespin, *Martyrs*, 3: 318; Raemond, *Histoire* (cited in n. 1), pp. 875–76; Noel Taillepied, *Histoire de l'Estat et Republique des Druides* (Paris, 1585), f. 33^{r-v}. Robert Kingdon, *Geneva and the Consolidation of the French Protestant Movement* (Madison, 1967), pp. 106–9. See also the proselytizing of women in Montélimar in 1555–57 described in Jean-Jacques Hemardinquer, "Les femmes dans la Réforme en Dauphiné," *Bulletin philologique et historique, 1959* (Paris, 1960), pp. 388–89.

44. *Moyen de parvenir* (cited in n. 33), ff. C v^v, C vii^{r-v}, D iii^{r-v}; Pierre Viret, *Instruction Crestienne en la doctrine de la Loy et de l'Eglise* (Geneva: Jean Rivery, 1564), 2: 721–28.

45. Jean Calvin, *Ioannis Calvini opera quae supersunt omnia*, ed. G. Baum, E. Cunitz, E. Reuss (Brunswick, 1863–1900), 20: col. 208 (hereafter cited as *Calvini opera*). I am grateful to Charmarie Blaisdell for calling this letter to my attention. Jeanne d'Albret, queen of Navarre, was allowed to be present at the National Synod of the Reformed Church held at La Rochelle in 1571 but was given no vote (Samuel Mours, *Le protestantisme en France au seizième siècle* [Paris, 1959], p. 213).

46. Robert Kingdon, *Geneva and the Coming of the Wars of Religion* (Geneva, 1956), pp. 139, 143. The Consistory of Lyon in the early 1560's included a publisher-printer, a master barber-surgeon, wealthy innkeepers, and even a merchant-shoemaker.

47. The publication of Marie Dentière's *Epistre* caused a major scandal in Geneva, including the arrest of its printer, because of the criticism in it of the Genevan ministers as cowardly and opportunistic and its implied support for the banished Calvin (Gabrielle Berthoud, *Antoine*

Marcourt, réformateur et pamphlétaire [Geneva, 1973], pp. 65–70). That its author was a female did not help matters.

On books published in Geneva in the sixteenth century, see Paul Chaix, Alain Dufour, and Gustave Moeckli, *Les livres imprimés à Genève de 1550 à 1600* (Geneva, 1966), and J. A. Tedeschi, "Genevan Books of the Sixteenth Century," BHR 31 (1969): 173–80.

The only Protestant females I know of who published poetry are the noblewoman Georgette de Montaney (1540–1581), whose *Emblemes ou Devises Chrestiennes* appeared at Lyon in 1571, and the queen of Navarre, Jeanne d'Albret, whose song "Jesus est mon esperance" appeared in a *chansonnier* at Lyon in 1564 (Jacques Pineaux, *La poésie des protestants de langue française, 1559–1598* [Paris, 1971], pp. 297–98). An edition of Jeanne's letters to important personages was also published in 1568. In contrast, several female poets — some of them from non-noble families — are listed in the *Dictionnaire des lettres françaises:* Pernette du Guillet, Helisenne de Crenne, Marie de Romieu, Madeleine and Catherine Des Roches, Nicole Estienne (in the Catholic branch of the Estienne family), and Anne de Marquets (*Dictionnaire des lettres françaises, publié sous la direction de G. Grente* [Paris, 1951]: *Le seizième siècle*).

48. N. Z. Davis, "Peletier and Beza Part Company," *Studies in the Renaissance,* 11 (1964): 188–222.

49. E. Gaullieur, *Etudes sur la typographie genevoise du XVe au XIXe siècle* (Geneva, 1855), p. 131, n. 1; AEG, PC, 2d ser., no. 620 (investigation of Antoinette Rosset, wife of barbersurgeon Jean Yvard of Lyon); *Le blason des basquines et vertugalles* (Lyon: Benoît Rigaud, 1563), reprinted in A. de Montaiglon, ed., *Recueil de poésies françoises des XVe et XVIe siècles* (Paris, 1885), 1: 293–303. (For another Protestant attack on hoop skirts see Viret, *Instruction Crestienne,* 1: 562ff.) Paradin, *Memoires,* p. 355. Calvin, *Gratulatio ad . . . Dominum Gabrielem de Saconay* (1561) in *Calvini opera,* 9: 428: "*plebeia meretrix.*" V. L. Saulnier, *Maurice Scève* (Paris, 1948), 1: 386.

50. Claude Haton, *Mémoires de Claude Haton,* ed. F. Bourquelot (*Collection des documents inédits sur l'histoire de France;* Paris, 1857), 1: 49–50; Guéraud, *Chronique* (cited in n. 15), p. 147; Raemond, *Histoire* (cited in n. 1), p. 1010.

51. *Calvini opera,* 10: 12. N. Z. Davis, "The Protestant Printing Workers of Lyons in 1551," *Aspects de la propagande religieuse* (Geneva, 1957), p. 257. Hemardinquer, "Les femmes dans la Réforme," pp. 393–94.

52. *Calvini opera,* 21: 595; Guéraud, *Chronique,* p. 148; Thomas Platter, *Journal of a Younger Brother. The Life of Thomas Platter,* trans. S. Jennett (London, 1940), p. 40.

53. *Hist. eccl.,* 1: 614, 913; Crespin, *Martyrs,* 3: 522.

54. Marie le Jars de Gournay, *Egalité des hommes et des femmes* (1622), reprinted in M. Schiff, *La fille d'alliance de Montaigne, Marie de Gournay* (Paris, 1910), pp. 75–76.

55. Biéler, *L'Homme et la femme* (cited in n. 8), pp. 90–91.

56. Ilza Veith, *Hysteria, The History of a Disease* (Chicago, 1965), chaps. 2, 4, 6, 7; Michael Screech, *The Rabelaisian Marriage* (London, 1958), chap. 6.

57. D. B. Miller, "The Nuns of Hesse," a talk given at the Sixteenth-Century Studies Conference, Concordia University, St. Louis, August 1971; Jussie, *Le levain du calvinisme* (cited in n. 27), pp. 91–93; Miriam Chrisman, "Women and the Reformation in Strasbourg, 1490–1530," *Archive for Reformation History* 63 (1972): 150–51. Some nuns followed Marie Dentière's example and became Protestant (Hemardinquer, "Les femmes dans la Réforme," pp. 388–90, 390 n. 2), but the major base of urban Calvinism among women was not in the nunnery.

58. Chrisman, pp. 155–57. B. Klaus, "Soziale Herkunft und Theologische Bildung lutherischer Pfarrer der reformatorischen Frühzeit," *Zeitschrift für Kirchengeschichte* 80 (1969): 22–49; B. Vogler, "Recrutement et carrière des pasteurs Strasbourgeois au 16e siècle," *Revue d'histoire et de philosophie religieuse* (1968), pp. 151–74. See Erikson, *Young Man Luther,* p. 71.

59. W. and M. Haller, "The Puritan Art of Love," *Huntington Library Quarterly* 5 (1941–42): 235–72; P. N. Siegel, "Milton and the Humanist Attitude toward Women," *Journal of the History of Ideas* 11 (1950): 42–53; John G. Halkett, *Milton and the Idea of Matrimony* (New Haven, Conn., 1970). E. V. Telle, *Erasme de Rotterdam et le septième sacrament. Etude d'évan-*

gelisme matrimoniale (Geneva, 1954); M. M. de la Garanderie, "Le féminisme de Thomas More et Erasme," *Moreana* 10 (1966).

60. *Hist. eccl.* 3: 518. *La Polymachie des Marmitons, ou la gendarmerie du Pape* (1563), in Montaiglon, *Recueil* (cited in n. 49), 7: 51—65. Jean Calvin, *Commentary on the Epistles of Paul the Apostle to the Corinthians*, trans. John Pringle (Edinburgh, 1848), 1: 361 (1 Cor. 11:12). R. Stauffenegger, "Le mariage à Genève vers 1600," *Mémoires de la société pour l'histoire du droit et des institutions des anciens pays bourguignons* 27 (1966): 319—29. AEG, RCon, 19 (1562), f. 188ᵛ.

61. Calvin, *Commentary on the Epistles of Paul*, 1: 353, 357—61 (1 Cor. 11:3, 8—12); Calvin, *Commentaries on Genesis*, trans. John King (Edinburgh, 1847), 1: 171—72 (chap. 3, par. 16). Crespin, *Martyrs*, 1: 438—39, 675, 706—7; 2: 232 (for especially affectionate letters, see 2: 331, 471—73). AEG, PC, 1st ser., no. 1202; 2d ser., no. 1535.

62. Indeed, it is interesting to note how Charlotte d'Arbaleste, wife of Philippe du Plessis de Mornay, used the theory of the subjection of the wife to her husband to defend her independence against Pastor Bérault and the Consistory of Montauban, who in 1584 had denied her the Holy Supper, ostensibly for her hairdo. In the course of the dispute she argued that in the absence of her husband, *"sans le commandement duquel il ne m'estoit loisible de faire aucun changement,"* she could not comply with their wishes. *Mémoires de Madame de Mornay*, ed. Madame de Witt (Paris, 1869), 2: 283, 297.

63. Jussie, *Le levain du calvinisme*, p. 94. G. Bosquet, *Histoire de M. G. Bosquet sur les troubles Advenus en la ville de Tolose l'an 1562* (Toulouse, 1595), chap. 13, p. 150. Guéraud, *Chronique*, p. 54. De Rubys, *Histoire*, p. 402; Crespin, *Martyrs*, 1: 306, 465, 518—19; 2: 407—15; and *passim*. In December 1561, Claudine Dumas, hostess of the Chariot at Lyon and widow of the humanist school rector Barthélemy Aneau, opened her inn to the Protestants for worship (Guéraud, *Chronique*, p. 146; ADR, 3E5018, June 9, 1562; AML, CC1174, f. 25ʳ).

64. Crespin, *Martyrs*, 3: 392.

65. Alice S. Rossi, "Sex Equality: The Beginnings of Ideology," reprinted from *The Humanist*, Sept.—Oct. 1969, in *The Radical Teacher*, ed. F. Howe and F. Lauter (Dec. 30, 1969), pp. 24—28.

66. This approach to Protestantism derives in part from Weber and is found in the work of Guy E. Swanson, *Religion and Regime, A Sociological Account of the Reformation* (Ann Arbor, Mich., 1967), esp. chap. 10 and pp. 261—62 on "secularization," and "To Live in Concern"; S. N. Eisenstadt, *The Protestant Ethic and Modernization*, ed. S. N. Eisenstadt (New York and London, 1968), chap. 21; and Robert N. Bellah, *Beyond Belief* (New York, 1970), chap. 2: "Religious Evolution." Bellah's brilliant and influential article first appeared in 1964; for some of his recent thoughts, which moderate his earlier position, see n. 68. The sociologist Janet Zollinger Giele has applied Bellah's scheme to sex roles, arguing that, although Protestant marriage sermons emphasize "the proper role of women," "they signify an actual increase in freedom to carry on many activities without regard for sex" ("Centuries of Childhood and Centuries of Womanhood, An Evolutionary Perspective on the Feminine Role," *Women's Studies* 1 [1972]: 97—110).

67. See, for instance, the very limited role allowed to women in Genevan crafts of the early eighteenth century described by Liliane Mottu-Weber, "Apprentissages et économie genevoise au début du XVIIIe siècle," *Schweizerische Zeitschrift für Geschichte* 20 (1970): 340—47. I am grateful to E. W. Monter for this reference.

68. Keith Thomas in "Women and the Civil War Sects" has similar reservations about the relationship between Protestantism and social change. See also Bellah's "No Direction Home. Religious Aspects of the American Crisis" (in *Search for the Sacred: The New Spiritual Quest*, ed. Myron Bloy, Jr. [New York, 1972]), in which he points out how earth, or mother, religions can correct some of the legalistic and ascetic features of sky, or father, religions. (He urges here a spiritual solution moving beyond both.) The economist Ester Boserup has also shown that assimilationist social patterns sometimes lead to less power for women in modern economic and political life than pluralistic ones (*Woman's Role in Economic Development* [London, 1970], esp. pp. 153—54). Boserup does not use the terms *assimilationist* and *pluralistic*, but the patterns she describes are similar to those thus labeled by Rossi.).

4. The Reasons of Misrule

1. Claude de Rubys, *Histoire veritable de la ville de Lyon . . . par Maistre Claude de Rubys*,

Conseillier du Roy en la Seneschaussee et siege Presidial de Lyon, et Procureur general de la communauté de ladicte ville (Lyon: Bonaventure Nugo, 1604), pp. 499–500, 501, also p. 370. Dedication from de Rubys to Chancellor Pomponne de Bellièvre, dated Dec. 31, 1600 (f. * 3ᵛ). De Rubys (1533–1613) was twice Consul of Lyon and had been town lawyer since 1569.

2. M. Du Tilliot, *Mémoires pour servir à l'histoire de la fêtes des Foux* (Lausanne and Geneva, 1751), pp. 1–76. L. Petit de Julleville, *Les comédiens en France au Moyen Age* (Paris, 1885), pp. 29–41; E. K. Chambers, *The Medieval Stage*, 1st ed. 1903 (Oxford, 1948), 1: 274–335. Enid Welsford, *The Fool, His Social and Literary History* (London, 1935), pp. 199–202. Paul Adam, *La vie paroissiale en France au XIVe siècle* (Paris, 1964), p. 274: at Arles, the Evêque Fol pretended to administer sacraments to the spectators, especially confession, with ridiculous gestures. See Roger Vaultier, *Le Folklore pendant la guerre de Cent Ans d'après les Lettres de Rémission du Trésor des Chartes* (Paris, 1965), p. 88, on the Feast of Fools at Lille. Also on Lille, L. Lefebvre, *L'évêque des fous et la fête des Innocents à Lille du XIVe au XVIe siècles* (Lille, 1902). The Feast was suppressed there sometime between 1526 and 1531. (I am grateful to Robert DuPlessis for this reference.)

L. Dacheux, *Un réformateur catholique à la fin du quinzième siècle. Jean Geiler De Kayserberg* (Paris, 1876), pp. 58–59, on the Feast of Fools at the cathedral of Strasbourg. *Histoire de Bordeaux*, ed. C. Higounet (Bordeaux, 1962–66), 4: 216, on the Feast of Fools and its suppression in 1544 at Bordeaux. In a treatise of 1608, the lawyer Jean Savaron listed some of the fifteenth-century church edicts against the Feast of Fools: *Traitté contre les masques. Par M. Iean Savaron sieur de Villars, Conseiller du Roy, President et Lieutenant general en la Seneschaulcee d'Auvergne et Siege Presidial de Clairmont, Maistre des Requestes de la Royne Marguerite* (Paris, 1608), p. 12.

3. The range of organizational possibilities is suggested by the festivities for the Fêtes des Rois, or Twelfth Night. Philippe Ariès describes celebrations primarily within the family: *Centuries of Childhood, A Social History of Family Life*, trans. R. Baldick (New York, 1962), pp. 73–74. An illustration of the Fête des Rois in a 1584 Book of Hours also depicts a small family celebration, here in the street: *Heures de Nostre Dame A l'usage de Rome en latin et francois. Reveues Corrigees et enrichies de devotes Oraisons et belles Figures* (Paris: Abel Langelier, 1584), f. A iiᵛ. Vaultier gives examples both of festivities organized by the youth and of more informal celebrations: *Le Folklore*, pp. 97–102. The journals of Felix and Thomas Platter are rich sources for urban festivities and the range of formality and informality involved: see *Beloved Son Felix. The Journal of Felix Platter*, trans. S. Jennett (London, 1961), pp. 48–49, 52, 80, 85, 112, 128; and *Journal of a Younger Brother. The Life of Thomas Platter*, trans. S. Jennett (London, 1963), pp. 76–79, 94–95, 118–24, 172–73.

4. Petit de Julleville, *Les comédiens*, pp. 192–256; Chambers, *Medieval Stage*, 1: 373–89; Welsford, *The Fool*, pp. 203–7; Howard M. Brown, *Music in the French Secular Theatre* (Cambridge, Mass., 1963), pp. 26–36.

5. Lists of these and officers from other cities can be found in *Recueil des chevauchées de l'asne faites à Lyon en 1566 et 1578 augmenté d'une complainte inédite du temps sur les maris battus par leurs femmes, précédé d'un avant-propos sur les fêtes populaires en France* (Lyon, 1862), pp. vii–xiii. Petit de Julleville, *Les comédiens*, pp. 232–56; Arnold Van Gennep, *Manuel de folklore français* (Paris, 1943–49), 1: 203–6; P. Sadron, "Les associations permanentes d'acteurs en France au Moyen-Age," *Revue d'histoire de théâtre* 4 (1952): 222–31; Brown, *Music*, pp. 26–29. Further on Bordeaux: P. Harlé, "Notes sur la Basoche et ses 'farces' au XVIe siècle," *Revue d'histoire de Bordeaux*, 1912, pp. 349–51 (I am grateful to Robert Wheaton for this reference). Further on Lyon: Jean Tricou, "Les confréries joyeuses de Lyon au XVIe siècle et leur numismatique," *Revue du numismatique*, 5th ser., 1 (1937): 293–317. Further on Amiens: Vaultier, *Le Folklore*, pp. 90–91. Further on Rouen: F. N. Taillepied, *Recueil des Antiquitez et singularitez de la ville de Rouen . . . par F. N. Taillepied, lecteur en theologie* (Rouen: Martin le Megissier, 1589), pp. 61–62; A. Floquet, "Histoire des Conards de Rouen," *Bibliothèque de l'Ecole des Chartes* 1 (1839): 105–23; R. Lebègue, "La vie dramatique à Rouen de François Iᵉʳ à Louis XIII," *Bulletin philologique et historique, 1955–56* (Paris, 1957), pp. 399–427. Further on Dijon and other "Folly societies" in Burgundy: Du Tilliot, *Mémoires*, pp. 81ff.

6. Le Prince de Mal-espargne, le Cardinal de Maucomble, l'Evêque de Plattebourse, le Duc

de Frappecul, and le Grand Patriarche des Verollez. See *Les triomphes de l'Abbaye des Conards avec une notice sur la fête des fous,* ed. Marc de Montifaud [Mme de Quivogne] (Paris, 1874), pp. 35–38. This is a reprint of a collection of the Abbey's festivals that originally appeared in Rouen in 1587.

7. *Recueil de la chevauchee faicte en la ville de Lyon, le dix septiesme de novembre 1578. Avec tout l'ordre tenu en icelle* (Lyon, 1578), reprinted in *Collection des meilleurs dissertations, notices et traités particuliers relatifs à l'histoire de France,* ed. C. Leber (Paris, 1838), 9: 154. Tricou, "Les confréries joyeuses," pp. 309–13 and plates. The coin of "le Baron de rue Neufve et ses supos," reproduced in Plate 5, has a motto suggesting jurisdiction: "Nostre iustice regnera en tous temps." Mock coins thrown in Lille, Vaultier, *Le Folklore,* p. 89; mock coins in Abbeville, in J. de Wailly et Maurice Crampon, *Le folklore de Picardie* (Amiens, 1968), pp. 255–56.

8. "Les Advocats, Conseillers et Iuges des . . . Abbayes de Malgouvert," in *L'ordre tenu en la chevauchee, faicte en la ville de Lyon,* ed. G. Guigue in *Archives historiques et statistiques du département du Rhône* 9 (1828–29): 420–21. The "bancq de Malconseil" was maintained by the festive organization of the printers' journeymen: *La chronique lyonnaise de Jean Guéraud, 1536–1562,* ed. Jean Tricou (Lyon, 1929), p. 61.

9. Du Tilliot, *Mémoires,* pp. 108, 114; Bibliothèque municipale de Dijon, Ms. 911, pp. 42–43; *Les triomphes de l'Abbaye des Conards,* p. 76. On the *causes grasses* of the societies of the Basoche, see below, n. 55.

10. "Letres [sic] Nouvelles contenantes le Privilege et Auctorite davoir deux Femmes: Concede et ottroye iusques a cent et ung ans a tous ceulx qui desirent estre mariez deux fois: datees du penultieme iour dapvril mil cinq centz trente six," in *Les Ioyeusetez Facecies et Folastres Imaginacions de Caresme Prenant, Gauthier Garguille, Guillot Gorice, Roger Bontemps* (Paris: Techener, 1830–31), 5. The letters are issued in the name of the Abbé des Conardz and other dignitaries in his court and dated April 29, 1536. The secret alliance of François Ier with the Turks was made in February 1536.

11. Claude Noirot, *L'Origine des masques, mommeries, bernez, et revennez es iours gras de caresme prenant, menez sur l'asne à rebours et charivary. Le Iugement des anciens Peres et philosophes sur le subiect des masquarades, le tout extrait du livre de la Mommerie de Claude Noirot, Iuge en mairarie de Lengres* (Langres, Jean Chauveau, 1609), reprinted and edited by C. Leber, *Collection des meilleurs dissertations . . . relatifs à l'histoire de France* (Paris, 1838), 9: 50–53. Vaultier, *Le Folklore,* p. 91. Henri Lalou, "Des charivaris et de leur repression dans le midi de la France," *Revue des Pyrénées* 16 (1904): 497.

12. *L'ordre tenu en la chevauchee* (cited in n. 8), pp. 406–9, 412. It was customary in Lyon to announce the name of the beaten husbands as well as their quarter and occupation, but this time the "martyrs" prevailed upon the Abbeys to suppress their names (p. 405).

13. De Rubys, *Histoire veritable,* p. 501. Noirot, *Origine des masques,* pp. 53–55, 64–65. P. Saintyves, "Le charivari de l'Adultère et les courses à corps nus," *L'Ethnographie,* new ser., 31 (1935): 7–36. According to Saintyves, a charivari parade on an ass against an adulterous couple is characteristic of northern France and Belgium and has.a Germanic origin. The harsher penalty of being forced to parade naked through the town, he says, is found in southern France and goes back to the more severe penalties of Greece and Rome.

A Dijon charivari against a man who beat his wife in the month of May in 1583, reported in "Livre de souvenance ou Journal de M. Pépin, Chanoine musicale de la Sainte Chapelle de Dijon," *Analecta Divionensia* (Dijon, 1866), 1: 31. Chambers, *Medieval Stage,* 1: 170. Further on the women's "revenge" during the month of May, see Van Gennep, *Manuel,* 1: 1693–94, and Chapter 5 below.

14. Guillaume Paradin (ca. 1510–1590), *Le Blason des Danses* (Beaujeu, 1556), reprinted in *Ioyeusetez,* 15: 53, 81. Polydore Vergil had discussed various ancient festivals and *ludi* in *De rerum inventoribus Libri Octo* (1502), which had many subsequent editions in France.

15. Noirot, *Origine des masques,* pp. 56–84. The *Traitté contre les masques* of the lawyer Savaron (cited in n. 2) discusses the ancient origin of masking, but in addition stresses the role of the devil as author of mummeries (p. 3). A recent study of riding backward as a penalty is Ruth Mellinkoff, "Riding Backwards: Theme of Humiliation and Symbol of Evil," *Viator* 4: 153–76.

16. Chambers, *Medieval Stage*, 1: 94ff., 134–44, 323–35. Also see Welsford, *The Fool*, chap. 3.

17. Chambers, *Medieval Stage*, 1: 372–74. This theory was first suggested by M. du Tilliot in the eighteenth century and then developed by Petit de Julleville (*Les comédiens*, pp. 37–38, 144–46, 194–95), from whom Chambers has adopted it. Welsford (pp. 202–3) and Brown (*Music*, p. 26) accept this view on the whole, though Brown admits that the "exact relationship of the secular fools to their sacred models can probably never be known." Luc Verhaeghe, in a recent critical edition of one of the plays of the Infanterie Dijonnoise, gives a sophisticated version of the older theory: "thus integrated into the general tradition of the Feast of Fools, the company of Mère Folle could be the offspring of a purely sacred festival in honour of the Virgin, who after her miraculous Assumption, keeps watch over fools" ("Vers composés pour les enfants de la Mère-Folle de Dijon vers le fin du XVIe siècle," Mémoire de license [dactylographié], Faculty of Letters, University of Ghent, p. 36; translation mine). Though the image and cult of the Virgin may well have contributed to the use of "Mother" as a festive title in Dijon and elsewhere (see p. 99 above), Verhaeghe's theory is unsubstantiated and unconvincing.

18. Vaultier, *Le Folklore*, pp. 29, 31. The Abbeys were carrying out a local popular justice (village or neighborhood, as we shall see), sometimes in areas not covered by law, at other times in areas where the law had long since been changed. But they cannot be looked on as acting "in place of" or "by delegation of" the seigneur. See pp. 117–18 and n. 80 below on the relation of city Abbeys to the authorities.

19. Maurice Agulhon, *Pénitents et Francs-Maçons de l'ancienne Provence* (Paris, 1968), pp. 59–60. This work is an excellent and important study of "sociabilité" in southern France in the late eighteenth century, including the organization of youth. For information on the earlier period, however, M. Agulhon relied almost entirely on a little study of 1879 by Octave Teissier, which described festive activities and officers among wealthy young men in Provençal cities in the late fifteenth and sixteenth centuries, especially the "Prince of Love" in Marseille. This led M. Agulhon to talk of the festive Abbeys "at their origin, at the time of declining chivalry, an aristocratic affair." An accurate picture of the origin of the Abbeys must rest, however, on studying them in both city *and* countryside and in several parts of France. The name "Prince of Love" does suggest the customs of courtly love, but it is quite exceptional as a festive title among the Abbeys.

20. For instance, at Lille the Roi de l'Epinette was elected each year at Mardi Gras from 1220 on (Van Gennep, *Manuel*, 1: 923; Sadron, "Les associations," p. 227), whereas the first reference to the Evêque des Fous at the Lille cathedral is 1301 (Vaultier, *Le Folklore*, p. 88). The impression that Misrule Abbeys *originated* in the fifteenth century seems to me a reflection of the bias of our sources: one would expect the Feast of Fools to be mentioned more frequently in the earlier centuries simply because there were clergy involved. Also see n. 35 below.

21. Quoted by Welsford, *The Fool*, p. 202, and by M. Bakhtin, *Rabelais and His World*, trans. H. Iswolsky (Cambridge, Mass., 1968), p. 75. The quotation is from a 1444 discussion at the Faculty of Theology of the University of Paris: "But, they [the defenders of the Feast of Fools] say, we act thus in jest and not seriously, as has been the custom of old, so that the foolishness innate in us can flow out once a year and evaporate. Do not wineskins and barrels burst if their bungs are not loosened once in a while? Even so, we are old wineskins and worn barrels; the wine of wisdom fermenting within us, which we hold in tightly all year in the service of God, might flow out uselessly, if we did not discharge it ourselves now and then with games and foolishness. Emptied through play, we may become stronger afterwards to retain wisdom" (J. P. Migne, *Patrologia Latina*, 207: 1171, translation mine).

22. Roger Caillois, *Les jeux et les hommes*, rev. ed. (Paris, 1967), pp. 171–72. J. Huizinga's great *Homo Ludens*, first published in 1944, gave the major impetus to studies like that of Caillois. Huizinga concentrates, however, on the play element in "high" culture rather than examining the popular forms of play and justice discussed in this paper. Also see "Games, Play and Literature," *Yale French Studies* 41 (1969).

23. Keith Thomas, "Work and Leisure in Pre-Industrial Society," *Past and Present* 29 (Dec. 1964): 53–54.

24. Written in 1940 and published in Russian in Moscow in 1965, Bakhtin's *Rabelais and His*

World was brought out by the M.I.T. Press in 1968. See chap. 1, especially pp. 4–12, and chap. 2. For Bakhtin, the "bourgeois" period seems to date from the seventeenth century. Rabelais is interpreted in his relation to "popular" cultural forms, not in relation to the specific values of the bourgeoisie. For other studies that argue for the multivalence of symbolic inversion in ritual or in carnivalesque play, see Victor Turner, *The Ritual Process. Structure and Anti-Structure* (Chicago, 1968), chaps. 3–5; William Willeford, *The Fool and His Scepter* (Evanston, Ill., 1969); and Laura Makarius, "Ritual Clowns and Symbolical Behaviour," *Diogenes* (1970), pp. 44–73.

25. I have used Van Gennep's *Manuel de folklore français* and *Le folklore des Hautes-Alpes* (Paris, 1946) as well as André Varagnac, *Civilisation traditionnelle et genres de vie* (Paris, 1948). Van Gennep's work is based both on twentieth-century surveys in several parts of France and on a wide search of regional and historical literature. No customs are referred to in my text, however, unless they have a documented date from the late medieval period or the sixteenth century, or unless they are found also in the archival materials from the fourteenth and fifteenth centuries reported by Vaultier or in some other historical source.

26. Vaultier, *Le Folklore*, pp. 9–10, 17, 24, 32, 94, 111. For a use of *compagnons à marier* in the village of Vanves in 1540/41, see E. Coyecque, *Recueil d'actes notariés relatifs à l'histoire de Paris et de ses environs au XVIe siècle* (Histoire Générale de Paris, Collection de documents; Paris, 1923), no. 3690; Van Gennep, *Manuel*, 1: 196–205; Varagnac, *Civilisation*, pp. 142–43, 151. Another term used is *garçon du village* (Vaultier, *Le Folklore*, p. 65; *Ioyeusetez*, 1: 68 [cited in n. 10]). Varagnac cites an Albigensian charter of 1136, which talks of Roi des Jouvenceaux and his activities as well established (*Civilisation*, p. 172). See also Claude Gauvard and Altan Gokalp, "Les conduites de bruit et leur signification à la fin du Moyen Age: le Charivari," Annales ESC 29 (1974): 700 and n. 27.

27. Pierre Goubert, *Beauvais et le Beauvaisis de 1600 à 1730* (Paris, 1960), p. 32, n. 33; U. M. Cowgill, "The People of York: 1538–1815," *Scientific American* 233 (Jan. 1970): 108–9.

28. Van Gennep, *Manuel*, 1: 205, 1075; Du Tilliot, *Mémoires*, p. 181 (prohibition of the annual election of a Prince, Abbot, or Captain by the "Enfants de Cuisery" in Burgundy); R. Mandrou, *Introduction à la France moderne* (Paris, 1961), p. 185; L. Celier, "Les moeurs rurales au XVe siècle d'après les lettres de rémission," *Bulletin philologique et historique, 1958* (Paris, 1959), p. 416; Lucienne Roubin, *Chambrettes des Provençaux* (Paris, 1970), pp. 169–79.

29. Vaultier, *Le Folklore*, pp. 52–54, 103–5 (other examples from Normandy, the Auvergne); Ariès, *Centuries*, pp. 76–77 (examples from the Auvergne); Van Gennep, *Manuel*, 1: 169–70, 202–3. A boxing match between married and nonmarried men at Carnival, 1554, is described in *Le journal du Sire de Gouberville*, ed. l'Abbé Tollemer and E. de Robiliard de Beaurepaire (Mémoires de la Société des antiquaires de Normandie, 31 [1892]), p. 72. Some of the rural sports, such as Shrovetide football, described by Dennis Brailsford in Elizabethan England (*Sport and Society, Elizabeth to Anne* [London, 1969], pp. 54–58) may also have been between different parishes or age groups. See n. 41 below.

30. Vaultier, *Le Folklore*, pp. 46–48, 80; Varagnac, *Civilisation*, pp. 71–81. Cf. Varagnac, pp. 241–42, 251, on the special connections of young men and young women with the village dead. Van Gennep's discussion of the fires of St. Jean in *Manuel*, 1: 1727–1928, with references to the late medieval period or the sixteenth century on pp. 1737–41 (Jumièges and Montreuil), p. 1746 (Alsace), p. 1762 (Ile-de-France and Brie), p. 1767 (La Cordelle in the Lyonnais), p. 1794, pp. 1816–17, and *passim*. Van Gennep gives, p. 1793, a text from medieval England about *pueri* who make firebrands on Saint John's Day.

31. Vaultier, *Le Folklore*, p. 65. Van Gennep on May bushes and branches: *Manuel*, 1: 202, 1516–75, including some historical references.

32. Vaultier, *Le Folklore*, pp. 10–11, 111–12.

33. *Ibid.*, pp. 17–20; a lengthy description of the marriage scenario in Van Gennep, *Manuel*, 1: 385–613.

34. For instance, Vaultier, pp. 9–10: ducking is the penalty given by the *compagnons de la bachellerie* for adultery in the village of Laleu, near La Rochelle in the late fourteenth century. On ducking as a penalty, see J. W. Spargo, *Juridical Folklore in England Illustrated by the Cucking Stool* (Durham, N.C., 1944), with some material on the Continent as well. On riding backward as a penalty, see Mellinkoff, "Riding Backwards," cited in n. 15. Parades backward

on an ass for husbands beaten by their wives in Senlis (1376), parade by the neighbor of the beaten husband at Sainte Marie des Champs (1393): Vaultier, *Le Folklore*, p. 41. See also Plate 7. At a village near Avesnes, the Fête des Durmenés, that is of beaten husbands, was always held on Saint Lawrence's Day; the man was led on an ass conducted by his wife, the young men preceding him with music: Vaultier, p. 42. Van Gennep, *Manuel*, 1: 202, 602–13. Also see Varagnac, *Civilisation*, pp. 168–75. The relations between the young unmarried men and the newly married ones are complex, with the latter sometimes having jurisdiction over the former: Varagnac, p. 162.

An amusing village charivari in the sixteenth century against a newly wed husband who failed to consummate his marriage until the third night is recounted in *Ioyeusetez*, 1: 64–68 (cited in n. 10). This is interesting because there was ecclesiastical legislation in the Middle Ages in some parts of France prohibiting intercourse between newlyweds for three nights, or the Nights of Tobias (Van Gennep, *Manuel*, 1: 554–55).

35. Vaultier, *Le Folklore*, pp. 23, 30–35; Van Gennep, *Manuel*, 1: 614–28. See the article by Lalou (cited in n. 11), who also discusses the origin of the word. Also see Noirot's etymologies, pp. 71–84. Du Cange's definition of charivari centers on the question of remarriage: "*Ludus turpis tinnitibus et clamoribus variis quibus illudunt, iis qui ad secundas convolant nuptiis*" (A shameful game which is played with ringing and various kinds of clamor against those who are marrying a second time); "*Secundo nubentibus fit charavaritum . . . nisi se redimant et componant cum abbate juvenum*" (A charivari is made against those marrying a second time . . . unless they redeem themselves and settle with the abbey of youth): *Glossarium*, 2: 284, 290. Also see Charles V. Langlois, *La Vie en France au moyen age* (Paris, 1925), 2: 250, n. 1; and P. Fortier-Beaulieu, "Le charivari dans le Roman de Fauvel," *Revue de folklore française et de folklore coloniale* 11 (1940): 1–16, on a charivari in the Roman de Fauvel, composed around 1310. See illustration, Plate 8.

36. André Rosambert, *La veuve en droit canonique jusqu'au XIVe siècle* (Paris, 1923), pp. 96–145; A. Esmein, *Le mariage en droit canonique*, ed. R. Génestal, 2d ed. (Paris, 1929), pp. 236–39. Men who had been married twice or more could not receive holy orders. *Dictionnaire de droit canonique* 6: 780–81. Rabelais has Pantagruel and Panurge talk of sermons against second marriages (*Le Tiers Livre des Faicts et dicts héroïques du bon Pantagruel*, chap. 6, in *Oeuvres complètes*, ed. J. Boulenger and L. Scheler [Paris, 1955], pp. 349–50), but the church repeatedly condemned charivaris against remarriages (see n. 90).

37. Lalou, "Des charivaris," pp. 495–98; Van Gennep, *Manuel*, 1: 618, 625–27. Varagnac, *Civilisation*, pp. 199–200, 253. Lalou, Varagnac, and P. Fortier-Beaulieu all consider that the charivari expresses to some extent a concern with the dead spouse. A summary of Fortier-Beaulieu's work is given in "Le veuvage et le remariage," *Revue de folklore française et de folklore coloniale* 11 (1940): 67–69.

38. Rosambert, *La veuve*, p. 145. Also *Edict de Roy defendant a tous et a tous venans a secondes nopces de n'avancer leur secondes parties ou leurs enfants l'un plus que l'autre* (Lyon: B. Rigaud, 1560). This edict was prompted by a "scandalous" second marriage of a noblewoman, but the problem might still come up even in the modest peasant estate.

39. Van Gennep, *Manuel*, 1: 247, 614; Varagnac, *Civilisation*, pp. 196–97; Claude Lévi-Strauss, *Mythologiques, Le cru et le cuit* (Paris, 1964), pp. 292–95. Edmé de la Poix de Fréminville, *Dictionnaire ou traité de la police générale des villes, bourgs, paroisses et seigneuries de la campagne* (Paris, 1758), pp. 92–93 on the actions of "*jeunes gens de village*" when a "foreign" male marries a girl in their parish. Gauvard and Gokalp, "Charivari" (cited in n. 26), pp. 693–99.

40. In the village of Auneuil in rural Beauvais in the late seventeenth century, only 48.9 percent of those born survived to age twenty: Goubert, *Beauvais*, (cited in n. 27), p. 39. In Meulan about the same time, the percentage of survivors at age twenty was even lower (M. Lachiver, *La population de Meulan du 17e au 19 siècle* [Paris, 1969], pp. 202, 206. In the town of York, England, in the sixteenth century, only about eleven percent of the men and women lived to age 40, a very high death rate: Cowgill, "People of York," p. 108. In Colyton, England, for both sexes combined, life expectancy from 1538 to 1624 was age 43: E. A. Wrigley, *Population and History* (New York, 1969), p. 87. Past the age of 40, men were more likely to find a spouse

and remarry than women: Goubert, *Beauvais*, p. 38 and p. 38, n. 46. On the old man marrying a young woman, see, for instance, "Ung esbatement vulgairment nommé Chalivary d'omme viel qui se marie en femme ou fille jeune," Bibl. nat., Mss., nouv. acq. fr. 12646, ff.508^r—512^r ("his member is as loose as an eel," etc.).

Charivari chants in Van Gennep, *Manuel*, 1: 626, and *Folklore des Hautes-Alpes*, p. 168. The image of the "Vieille-folle d'amour" in J. Nailbé, "Le thème de la vieille femme dans la poésie satirique du 16e et du début du 17e siècles," BHR 26 (1964): 109—10.

41. S. Eisenstadt considers games and competitions between married and unmarried men a typical feature of *rites de passage*, "the dramatization of the encounter between the several generations": "Archetypal Patterns of Youth," *The Challenge of Youth*, ed. E. Erikson (New York, 1965), p. 33; *From Generation to Generation* (New York, 1964), pp. 31—32.

42. Ariès, *Centuries*, pp. 25, 29; French editions: *L'enfant et la vie familiale sous l'ancien régime* (Paris, 1960 and 1973), pp. 14, 18—19. The importance of this pioneering work is undisputed, but there is a lack of clarity in its description and analysis of youth and the nuclear family, sometimes based on inadequate evidence and other times drawing wrong inferences from the evidence. At one point Ariès touches on a few of the festivities discussed here, though he says nothing of the organization of the youth, or of charivaris. His incorrect conclusion: "One has the feeling here of dealing with *the last traces* of a very old structure, in which society had been organized by categories of age. [The earlier work of Van Gennep had already made clear the importance of age categories in rural areas on into the nineteenth century.] Now there existed only *a mere memory* of all this, which reserved for the young an essential function in certain great collective celebrations. It should be noted, moreover, that *the ceremony made little distinction between the children and the young people. . . .*" *L'enfant et la vie familiale*, p. 76. (Italics and translation mine.)

Two studies that are valuable for our understanding of modern concepts of adolescence, but that accept Ariès' view of the earlier period, are Kenneth Keniston, "Social Change and Youth in America," in *Challenge of Youth* (cited in n. 41), pp. 191—222, and John and Virginia Demos, "Adolescence in Historical Perspective," *Journal of Marriage and the Family* 31 (Nov. 1969): 632—38.

43. See, for instance, Eduard Hoffman-Krayer, *Feste und Brauche des Schweizervolkes* (Zurich, 1940), which describes the various *knabenschaften* and their *katzenmusiken*. Also Louis Junod, "Le charivari au pays de Vaud dans le premier tiers du 19e siècle," *Schweizerisches Archiv für Volkskunde*, 46 (1950): 114—28. Junod gives examples of charivaris and the Abbayes des Enfants from the sixteenth and seventeenth centuries. Also see n. 45.

44. E. Hoffman-Krayer and H. Bächtold-Staubli, *Handwörterbuch des Deutschen Aberglaubens* (Berlin, 1931/32), 4: 1125—31, article on "Katzenmusiken," especially p. 1131, which mentions the *Burschenverbanden* and the *Knabenschaften*.

45. Giuseppe C. Pola Falletti-Villafalletto, *Associazioni Giovanili e Feste Antiche, Loro Origini* (Milan, 1939). Vol. 1 deals with urban and rural youth groups in Italy with many historical examples. They are called *Badie, Abbazie,* and other names similar to those in France. Vol. 2 deals with France and gives further information on youth groups in Switzerland. Vols. 3 and 4 describe the role of youth groups in the year's festivals; pp. 449ff. in 4 concentrate on "Le Scampanate" or charivaris.

See also the discussion of the organization of youth in Florence in Richard Trexler, "Ritual in Florence: Adolescence and Salvation in the Renaissance," in *The Pursuit of Holiness in Late Medieval and Renaissance Religion*, ed. C. Trinkaus with H. A. Oberman (Leiden, 1974); and N. Z. Davis, "Some Tasks and Themes in the Study of Popular Religion," in the same work, pp. 318—26.

46. Tekla Dömötör, "Erscheinungsformen des Charivari im Ungarischen Sprachgebiet," *Acta Ethnographica Academiae Scientiarum Hungaricae* 6 (1958): 73—89. The organization of young men is discussed on pp. 79—80.

47. The major new study of the English charivari or rough music is Edward P. Thompson, " 'Rough Music': Le Charivari anglais,"*Annales* ESC 27 (1972): 285—312, which provides rich data and analysis especially for the eighteenth and nineteenth centuries. An earlier introductory study is Violet Alford, "Rough Music or Charivari," *Folklore* 70 (1959): 505—18.

There are references to charivaris and to rural youth groups in England, but it is still uncertain whether the former activity was regularly undertaken by the latter during the fifteenth through the seventeenth century. Chambers (*Medieval Stage*, 1: 152—54) describes "riding the stang" and "skimmington riding," both accompanied by a noisy din, and also ducking as forms of village punishment against sexual and other offenders in the late medieval period and sixteenth century. C. Hole in *English Folklore*, 2d ed. (London, 1944—45), adds "the staghunt," "kettling," and "low-belling" as words for charivaris. Enid Porter describes "rough music" (variously called "tin kettling," "tinning," and "tin-panning") for marital infidelity in twentieth-century Cambridgeshire: *Cambridgeshire, Customs and Folklore* (London, 1969), pp. 8—9. In the earlier period, ducking was a common village punishment for taming the shrewish wife. Branking was seen in sixteenth-century Scotland and spread to England as another punishment for the domineering wife: she was placed in an iron muzzle and led through the streets by a cord.

I have found no discussion of the organization of age categories in the English village. The Lords of Misrule, however, seem to be an example of youth officers — not the Lords of Misrule elected at the Christmas revels at Gray's Inn or at court, but the "wildheads of the parish" (described in 1585 by Philipp Stubbs in his *Anatomie of Abuses*), who elect a captain of mischief called "my Lord of Misrule" and who go about with hobby-horses (a hobby-horse was sometimes used in "riding the stang") and with pipers and drummers. See Joseph Strutt, *The Sports and Pastimes of the People of England* (London, 1904), pp. 267—68; E. Barber, *Shakespeare's Festive Comedy* (Cleveland, 1968), pp. 27—28. Finally, a charivari against a domineering wife described by Andrew Marvell in "The Last Instructions to a Painter" (lines 373—89) underlines the educational function of the action for the young: "From Greenwich . . . / Comes News of pastime martiall and old: / A Punishment invented first to aw / Masculine Wives, transgressing Natures Law, / Where, when the brawny Female disobeys, / And beats the Husband till for peace he prays, / No concern'd Jury for him damage finds, / Nor partiall Justice ner Behavior binds, / But the just Street does the next House invade, / Mounting the Neighbor Couple of lean Jade; / The Distaffe knocks, the Grains from Kettle fly, / And boys and Girls in Troops run hooting by. / Prudent Antiquity, that knew by Shame, / Better than Law, domestick Crimes to tame, / And taught Youth by Spectacle innocent!" (I am grateful to the late Rosalie Colie for this reference.)

48. J. A. Pitt-Rivers, *The People of the Sierra*, 1st ed. 1954 (Chicago, 1961) on the Andalusian *cencerrada* and the *Vito*, or humiliating nickname; also his essay "Honour and Social Status," in J. G. Peristany (ed.), *Honour and Shame. The Values of Mediterranean Society* (London, 1965), pp. 46—48. On the movement in the eighteenth century to prohibit young farm laborers from putting on *cencerradas*, see [Gaspar Melchor de Jovellanos], *Informe de la sociedad Economica de Madrid . . . en el expediente de Ley Agraria* (1795), in *Biblioteca de Autores Espanoles*, 50: 134. (I am grateful to Richard Herr for this reference.)

49. Eisenstadt, "Archetypal Patterns" (cited in n. 41), p. 40. And see Noel du Fail's image of a peasant community on a Feast Day, where he found that "most of the old and young people were out, though separated from each other, because (as the old proverb has it) 'like seeks like.' The young were practising archery, boxing, gymnastics, racing and other games." The old watched them "refreshing the memory of their adolescence, taking a singular pleasure in watching the frolicking of this capricious youth" (*rafraichissans la memoire de leur adolescence, prenans un singulier plaisir à voir folastrer cette inconstante jeunesse*). *Propos rustiques* (Lyon, 1547—49), chap. 1, translation mine.

50. It may well be that the sons of *laboureurs* were more likely to be elected Abbot of Youth than the sons of poor peasants or of newcomers to the village. But the evidence from Vaultier gives no support to Agulhon's view (based, as we have seen in n. 19, on a study of Marseille) that the Abbeys were aristocratic to begin with and became popular only in the eighteenth century. Nor is there any evidence of the splitting of the Abbeys along economic lines in the village in the earlier period. This happens only in urban centers, as we will see.

Varagnac, on the other hand, underplays the influence of economic differentiation on *other* features of rural life and also exaggerates the role of youth as *the* custodians of the festive life (see especially chap. 8). Agulhon shares these reservations about Varagnac: *Pénitents*, pp. 380—81, n. 59.

51. Agulhon, *Pénitents*, pp. 43—54. I do not think that any of the shooting-societies and archery-societies that developed in the countryside (and in the city, too) in the fourteenth and (for artillery) fifteenth centuries were *confined* to young unmarried men. The annual "King" was the man who won the shooting or archery contest. For continued conflicts and ritualized contests between the *garçons* of different parishes in the eighteenth century, see H. Hours, "Emeutes et émotions populaires dans les campagnes du Lyonnais au XVIIIe siècle," *Cahiers d'histoire* 9 (1964): 144—48.

52. Vaultier, *Le Folklore*, p. 106. Cf. the 1566 parade of the ass in Lyon, with the Count de la Fontaine (a quarter in the city) and his Abbey dressed as "Egyptians,"the Judge of Misrule and his men dressed as lawyers, the Judge himself in violet robes on a float, and the Admiral du Griffon and his men in a "galley" on wheels: *L'ordre tenu en la chevauchee* (cited in n. 8), pp. 406, 419, 412. See Plate 3.

53. Listing of some of the printed editions for the Abbeys of Rouen (begin 1537), Lyon (begin 1566), and Dijon (begin 1604) in Petit de Julleville, *Les comédiens* (cited in n. 2), pp. 256—61.

54. *L'ordre tenu en la chevauchee*, pp. 345—53. Some of the officers listed in the 1540/41 Mardi Gras *fêtes* at Rouen appear to come from different streets or sections of town: *Les triomphes de l'Abbaye de Conards*, p. 35. On Abbeys elected by quarters in Draguignan in the seventeenth century, see Roubin, *Chambrettes*, pp. 169—70.

55. Petit de Julleville, *Les comédiens*, pp. 88—142. Adolphe Fabre, *Les Clercs du Palais. Recherches historiques sur les Bazoches des Parlements et les Sociétés dramatiques des Bazochiens et des Enfants-sans-souci* (Lyon, 1875). H. G. Harvey, *The Theatre of the Basoche* (Cambridge, Mass., 1941). *Journal d'un bourgeois de Paris sous le règne de François Ier (1515—1536)*, ed. L. Lalanne (Paris, 1854), pp. 44, 268—69. P. Harlé, "Notes sur la Basoche" (cited in n. 5). Mlle. Huard, "Les clercs de la Basoche à Château-Thierry," *Revue de folklore français et de folklore colonial*, 5 (1934): 53—68.

That the Basoche developed from the basic form of the youth-abbey is suggested not only by structural similarities, but also by historical connections. At an unspecified date in Burgundy, the Roi de la Basoche was also the Roi de la Jeunesse (Petit de Julleville, *Les comédiens*, p. 141). In some places, the patron saint of the Basochiens was Saint Nicolas, who was also the patron saint of students and some youth-groups: Jean Savaron, *Traitté des confrairies* (Paris: Pierre Chevalier, 1604), ff.10v—11r; Van Gennep, *Manuel*, 1: 207—8. In Lyon in 1518, the Basochiens participated in dramatic activities with some of the Misrule Abbeys: AML, BB37, f. 183r-v. Further in the 1566 Misrule parade against husband-beaters, the Basoche was invited to join the parade: *L'ordre tenu en la chevauchee*, pp. 346—47. According to Fabre (*Les Clercs*, p. 34), the Basochiens had to be unmarried, though I do not know whether this was in fact the case in the sixteenth century.

On Abbeys organized or elected by occupational categories in Nice and Draguignan, see Roubin, *Chambrettes*, pp. 170—71.

56. *L'ordre tenu en la chevauchee*, pp. 413—14, 410—11; ACh, E4, f. 103r; *La chronique lyonnaise de Jean Guéraud* (cited in n. 8), p. 93.

57. *Les triomphes de L'Abbaye des Conards*, p. 23; Du Tilliot, *Mémoires*, p. 116. Also the 1566 parade on the ass at Lyon ended with the baptism of a baby born to one of the festive officers: *L'ordre tenu en la chevauchee*, p. 422.

As literary historians have ignored the rural youth-abbeys, so those social historians who have known about the youth-abbeys have failed to notice how in many cases the urban festive organizations lost their age-specificity. The important Abbazia degli Stulti of Turin seems an example of a one-time youth-abbey which by the end of the fifteenth century included men of different ages: see the statutes of the Abbey in Pola Falletti-Villafalletto, *Associazioni* (cited in n. 45), 1: 35—36; and the discussion in F. Cognasso, *L'Italia nel Rinascimento* (Turin, 1960), 1: 601ff. The carnival organizations in Nuremberg in the fifteenth and sixteenth centuries were also made up of people of different age categories: S. L. Sumberg, *The Nuremberg Schembart Carnival* (New York, 1941), pp. 54—60.

58. Du Tilliot, *Mémoires*, pp. 179—80.

59. I have done little with sixteenth-century Paris in this study. Its festive life had distinctive

traits due to the great importance of the University (see n. 62) and the Parlement, and to the increasing role of the city as capital and residence for the court. Thus the Basoche and the festive activities of the students dominated over more popular neighborhood groupings and activities. The Enfants-sans-souci, headed by the Mère Sotte, were by 1500 a semiprofessional group of players and poets. Pierre Gringoire, Mère Sotte in the opening decades of the century, had many collections of his poems printed. The company lost its importance in the latter half of the century, due to change in literary taste. A Confrérie des Sots, which put on plays in Paris in the middle of the sixteenth century, had as its officers in 1548 two master masons, a master paver, and a currier, and included merchants among its members. Marcel Poete, *Une vie de cité. Paris de sa naissance à nos jours* (Paris, 1927), p. 269.

Reference to charivaris in Paris from an early-sixteenth-century poem: "du bruit seigneurial / que dames ont par leurs charivaris / En tous quartiers" ("L'advocat des dames de Paris," *Mémoires de la société de l'histoire de Paris et de l'Ile-de-France* 44 [1917]: 115).

60. On Rouen, F. N. Taillepied, *Recueil des Antiquitez et singularitez de la ville de Rouen* (Rouen, 1589), p. 59. The Enfants de la Ville were separate from the Conards, with a confraternity at a different church. Other examples of an urban youth group being confined in the sixteenth century to the children of the "best" families: Marseille with its Prince of Love, elected by "the youth from the noble and bourgeois families and other adolescents of the town" (Agulhon, *Pénitents*, pp. 59–60, citing a text from Teissier); the "noble" Abbaye des Enfants at Lausanne (H. Meylan and M. Guex, "Viret et MM. de Lausanne, La Procédure de 1557," *Revue historique vaudoise* 3 [1961]: p. 114); the Compagnie della Calza at Venice (Pola Falletti-Villafalletto, *Associazioni*, 1, chapter on Venice; Cognasso, *L'Italia*, 1: 604ff.).

61. This is the account given in the sixteenth century by François Bonivard of Geneva. See Pola Falletti-Villafalletto, *Associazioni*, 2: 47–48, and H. Naef, *Les origines de la Réforme à Genève* (Geneva, 1936), pp. 113–15. After the establishment of the militia, however, there were still Sots and a Dame Folie in Geneva.

62. The organization, rituals, and activities of student groups are outside the scope of this study. Ariès' material on this is very useful: *Centuries*, pp. 242–46. M. Crévier, *Histoire de l'Université de Paris depuis son origine jusqu'en l'année 1600* (Paris, 1761), pp. 147–48, 191, has references to the banning of student plays in the sixteenth century because (as we might guess) real persons were being criticized and attacked.

63. Ariès' argument rests primarily on the imprecision in the language used to describe categories of age: *adolescens* and *puer* are used indiscriminately, *jeune* is used for a long span of years, etc.: *Centuries*, pp. 25–26; *L'enfant et la vie familiale*, pp. 13–16. These are interesting facts, but without further evidence and analysis, one cannot infer that a period of adolescence was not recognized, any more than one can infer from the imprecision of contemporary North American usage ("kids" used familiarly for people from age 5 to 35; "I'm going bowling with the boys" used by 40-year-olds; "Hey, boy," to a black adult) that we do not recognize a period of adolescence. M. Ariès leans very heavily on Jean Corbichon, "the 1556 translator" (*"le traducteur de 1556,"* p. 13) of a thirteenth-century encyclopedia by Bartholomew the Englishman: Corbichon says there are only three ages in French, "childhood, youth, and old age." In fact, Corbichon was chaplain to Charles V, king from 1364 to 1380.

Note that while Robert I Estienne was imprecise in the use of *adolescent, jeune,* and *garçon,* he did have a clear idea of a stage that was different from boyhood: *"Un Ieune garson, Iuvenis: Ung ieune filz depuis douze ans iusques a vingt et ung. Adolescens"* (*Dictionaire Francoislatin* [Paris: Robert I Estienne, 1549], p. 320, and see pp. 15 and 214 on *adolescence* and *enfant*).

64. Eisenstadt, "Archetypal Patterns," pp. 32, 34–35.

65. B. Geremek, *Le salariat dans l'artisanat parisien aux XIIIe–XVe siècles* (Paris, 1968), pp. 31, 54; Henri Hauser, *Les ouvriers du temps passé*, 5th ed. (Paris, 1927), p. 22; R. Mousnier, *Paris au XVIIe siècle* (Paris, 1962), p. 235. And see Chapter 6 below, "The Rites of Violence," part 4.

66. See N. Z. Davis, "A Trade Union in Sixteenth-Century France," *Economic History Review*, 2d ser., 19 (1966): pp. 46–68.

Steven R. Smith finds not only a clear-cut identity, a "sub-culture," among London apprentices of the seventeenth century, but mentions "informal gatherings" among them, as at breakfasts on Sunday, and "more formal meetings of apprentices, such as religious services" ("The London Apprentices as Seventeenth-Century Adolescents," *Past and Present* 61 [Nov. 1973]: 149–61, especially p. 156). The latter, of course, would place them under the direction of an adult rather than in an *independent* organization of their age category. Insofar as English apprentices did have a stronger independent organizational life than apprentices in French cities in the seventeenth century, it may be connected with the relative strength of journeymen's organizations in France.

67. I have worked through the series EE for the sixteenth century in the Archives municipales de Lyon. On the 1536 list, for instance, we find François Rabelais, then about age 42, the printer Thibaud Payen, then about age 30, and printers' journeymen, young and old: EE21, ff. 7ᵛ, 12ʳ, 42ʳ. The geographical position of Lyon necessitated a militia that utilized all available manpower. For Paris, see G. Picot, "Recherches sur les quartiniers, cinquanteniers et dixainiers de la ville de Paris," *Mémoires de la société de l'histoire de Paris et de l'Ile-de-France* 1 (1875): 132–66.

68. Jean Tricou, *Les Enfants de la Ville* (Lyon, 1938): Tricou calls them "cette jeunesse dorée" (this golden youth). *La chronique lyonnaise de Jean Guéraud*, ed. Tricou (cited in n. 8), pp. 31, 43–44, 51, 63, 93–94, 97–98, 117–18. *La magnificence de la . . . triumphante entree de la noble et antique Cité de Lyon faicte au Treschrestien Roy . . . Henry deuxiesme . . . MDLXVIII*, ed. G. Guigue (Lyon, 1927), pp. 149–50.

69. Roubin, *Chambrettes*, p. 170.

70. In 1529, Jean Neyron, a merchant not of a Consular family, was Abbot of Misrule of the quarter of Saint Vincent: *Inventaire sommaire des archives communales antérieures à 1790. Ville de Lyon*, ed. F. Rolle (Paris, 1865), CC139; ACh, E4, f. 103ʳ, "Jean Rameau paintre . . . apelle le Juge des Sotz." Of 42 members of the Abbey of Misrule of the rue Mercière meeting in 1517 (AML, EE9, pièce 1), I have been able to identify the occupations of 21: two merchants, three apothecaries, a potter, four booksellers, a mirrormaker, a shoemaker, two leather-workers, a goldbeater, two furriers, a painter, two metalworkers, and one weaver. None of these men were members of the Consular elite, though a few were well-off and had property in the neighborhood.

71. *Les triomphes de l'Abbaye des Conards*, p. 14: Jacques Syreulde, formerly "huissier" in the Parlement of Rouen; the Baron de Moulineaux was in fact a miller (pp. 6–11).

72. "*En mai 1583, l'Infanterie s'est remuée par l'avis de Pocard, le tailleur . . .*," "Livre de souvenance ou Journal de M. Pépin," p. 31. In the May 1579 charivari against Du Tillet there was a dialogue between two *vignerons*, who spoke of "*notre infanterie*" (Petit de Julleville, *Les comédiens*, p. 210). Cf. G. Roupnel, *La ville et la campagne au 17e siècle. Etude sur les populations du Pays Dijonnais* (Paris, 1922), pp. 153–54.

73. AML, EE9, pièce 1, May 16, 1517.

74. Cognasso, *L'Italia*, 1: 601ff.

75. "Thus children . . . / To avoid quarrels and fights, / I forbid you to curse each other . . . / Put yourselves in peace . . .": *Querelles de Marot et Sagon*, pièce no. 1. Also note the "edict" of the Abbot of Conards in 1541 abolishing long court cases and all errors "in order to keep our agents in peace, friendship and repose": *Les triomphes*, p. 19.

76. Document printed by M. Carrand in the *Archives historiques et statistiques du département du Rhône*, 11 (1830): 189–91.

77. De Rubys, *Histoire veritable*, p. 501. In 1598 Thomas Platter describes a kind of "stinkbomb" that the young people of Uzès let off during charivaris against widows or widowers remarrying people of an inappropriate age: *Journal*, p. 172.

78. Rosambert, *La veuve*, p. 145. P. C. Timbal, "L'esprit du droit privé," *XVIIe siècle* 58–59 (1963): 38. Interestingly enough, an important feature of the decline in the female legal position was the limitations placed on the widows who remarried, especially in regard to their handling of property. These women were remarrying "follement" (Rosambert, p. 145). Thus one of the community concerns that had nourished charivaris against remarriages was now directed in the city (as well as among the nobility) only against the "headstrong" woman. This reinforced the tendency to bring social pressure to bear against her through charivaris.

On the contrasting independence of widows in town and country in fifteenth-century Tuscany, see C. Klapisch, "Fiscalité et démographie en Toscane (1427–1430)," *Annales ESC* 24 (1969): 1333.

79. Du Tilliot, *Mémoires*, pp. 12—13; Vaultier, *Le Folklore*, p. 91; F. N. Taillepied, *Recueil des Antiquitez . . . de la ville de Rouen*, pp. 61—62. Also note the motto on the coin on Plate 5.

80. Charivaris permitted by the Parlement of Grenoble at the time of jurisconsult Guy Pape, ca. 1402—ca. 1487: De Rubys, *Histoire veritable*, p. 501. Youth-abbeys prohibited in the Dauphiné by the Conseil d'Etat in 1671: A. Van Gennep, *Le folklore du Dauphiné* (Paris, 1932), 1: 67. Prohibitions of charivaris by the Parlement of Toulouse in 1537, 1542, 1545, 1549, 1551: Lalou, "Des charivaris," pp. 502—4; by Parlement of Dijon in 1606: Vaultier, *Le Folklore*, p. 35, and Bibl. nat., Mss. Coll. Dupuy 630, f.83. Prohibitions of "Abbeys" and charivaris in Lyon by the *temporal* justice of the archbishop of Lyon in 1483 and 1484: Claude Bellièvre, *Souvenirs . . . Notes historiques* (Geneva, 1956), pp. 108—9. Judicial attack on the Abbey of the rue Mercière in AML, BB37, ff. 8ᵛ, 80ʳ, 111ᵛ; *Archives historiques et statistiques du Rhône* 11: 189—91. Town of Gap prohibits charivaris and "debauchery" of the Abbey of Misrule in 1601: Van Gennep, *Folklore des Hautes-Alpes*, p. 70, n. 3. The permit of the Orange city council in 1511—12 in Vaultier, *Le Folklore*, p. 243. Royal action against satirical political farces by the Basoche in Paris, in *Journal d'un bourgeois de Paris . . . (1515—1536)*, pp. 44, 268—69. Royal edicts against masking in 1539, 1561, 1578—80 and edicts of the Parlement of Paris in 1509 and 1514 against the sale of masks in Paris given in Savaron, p. 13, and Noirot, pp. 126—27.

Similarly complex relations between Abbeys and governments are suggested in Cognasso's material on Italy, where charivaris or "*scampanate*" are forbidden and barriers placed across the road to coerce widows or widowers remarrying to pay a forfeit, but where some Abbeys, as in Turin, are granted statutes by the authorities: Cognasso, *L'Italia*, 1: 45, 601ff.

81. *Les triomphes de l'Abbaye des Conards*, pp. 11—15; Floquet, "Histoire des Conards" (cited in n. 5), p. 107; René Herval, *Histoire de Rouen* (Rouen, 1947), 2: 45.

82. Herval, *Histoire de Rouen*, 2: 45.

83. *Les triomphes de l'Abbaye des Conards*, pp. 11—13, 30—74.

84. *Journal d'un bourgeois de Paris . . . (1515—1536)*, p. 44. The king tried to use the professional society of the Enfants-sans-souci on one occasion for his own propaganda: in 1512 he commissioned Mère Sotte (Pierre Gringoire) to write a play against the Fifth Lateran Council, convoked by Pope Julius II (Brown, *Music*, pp. 8—9). On the *Anerie* of Dijon, see Verhaege, "Vers composés pour les enfants de la Mère-Folle," pp. 52—53.

85. *Recueil des plaisants devis recites par les suppots du Seigneur de la Coquille* (Lyon, 1857), pp. 8, 27—31, 57—62. Sixteenth-century editions of the *Plaisans devis* discussed in J. Baudrier, *Bibliographie lyonnaise* (Lyon, 1895—1921), 6: 2 ff.

86. C. A. Beerli, "Quelques aspects des jeux, fêtes et danses à Berne pendant la première moitié du XVIe siècle," *Les fêtes de la Renaissance*, ed. Jean Jacquot (Paris, 1956), p. 351. According to B. Bax, one of the first events of the German Peasants War was the assembling of peasants at Waldshut in August 1524 under cover of church ale: B. Bax, *The Peasants War in Germany* (London, 1899), p. 36. See also the discussion by Peter Weidkuhn of the connections between masked carnivals and uprisings among the *Knabenschaften* in Germany and German Switzerland ("Fastnacht, Revolte, Revolution," *Zeitschrift für Religions-und Geistegeschichte* 21 (1969): 289—305 (I am grateful to Gerald Strauss for calling this article to my attention).

87. Sadron, "Les associations," p. 224, and Petit de Julleville, *Les comédiens*, p. 236, for the list of Abbeys in Cambrai. Du Tilliot, *Mémoires*, p. 108 and n. Of course, masks were practical equipment for conspirators; they were used in the attempted Protestant seizure of Besançon in 1575 (*Histoire de Besançon. Des Origines à la fin du XVIe siècle*, ed. C. Fohlen [Paris, 1964], p. 631). But in the Cambrai uprising, the whole apparatus of carnival was used.

88. E. Le Roy Ladurie, *Les paysans de Languedoc* (Paris, 1966), 1: 395—99. L. Scott Van Doren, "Revolt and Reaction in the City of Romans, Dauphiné, 1579—1580," *The Sixteenth Century Journal* 5 (1974): 91—100. On uprisings of males in female dress, see Chapter 5 below, "Women on Top."

89. Du Tilliot, *Mémoires*, pp. 181—83; Petit de Julleville, *Les comédiens*, pp. 218—22. The royal edict played on the word *mère* and *merde*. As usual, the Abbey survived the royal prohibition against it. The insurrection is described in B. Porchnev, *Les soulèvements populaires en France de 1623 à 1648* (Paris, 1963), pp. 135—42.

90. H. Lalou, "Des charivaris," pp. 499—501 mentions prohibitions from the council of

Angers (1269), the synod of Avignon (1337), and the council of Tours (1445). Adam, *La vie paroissiale*, p. 272, gives fourteenth-century statutes from the church at Avignon, Meaux, Bourges, Tréguier, Reims, and Troyes. Noirot, *Origine des masques*, p. 84, gives statutory prohibitions by the bishop of Langres, 1404 and 1481. Prohibitions against charivaris were made in Lyon by Archbishop Charles de Bourbon in 1466 and repeated in the synodal statutes published by Archbishop Pierre d'Epinac in 1577: A. Pericaud, *Notes et documents pour servir à l'histoire de Lyon, 1574-1589* (Lyon, 1843), p. 39. Synodal statutes of the church of Nevers prohibited charivaris under pain of excommunication and a fine of 100 sous: G. D. Mansi (ed.), *Sacrorum conciliorum . . . collectio* (Paris, 1903-27), Vol. 32, col. 340.

91.   Paradin, *Blason* (cited in n. 14); he criticizes not only carnival license to mock authorities, but all dances, "royaumes," and diversions on saints' days. Savaron, *Traitté* (cited in n. 2), pp. 8-9.

92.   Floquet, "Histoire des Conards," pp. 111-12 and 112, n. 1.

93.   Mandrou, *Introduction*, p. 187; A. L. Herminjard, *Correspondance des réformateurs dans les pays de langue française* (Geneva, 1878-98), 4: 31-34, and 34, n. 10; H. Hauser, "Lettres closes de François Ier sur les protestants de Savoie (1538)," BSHPF 42 (1894): pp. 594-97. Beerli, p. 361, on Protestant religious themes in the carnival of 1523 at Berne. H. Naef, pp. 441-62, on Geneva. H. Patry, "La réforme et le théâtre en Guyenne au XVIe siècle," BSHPF 50 (1901): 523-28; 51 (1902): 141-51.

94.   H. Meylan, "Viret et MM. de Lausanne," p. 114. Similarly, the Schembart carnival at Nuremberg was used to mock the Lutheran preacher Andreas Osiander: Sumberg, pp. 178-79.

95.   *Histoire ecclésiastique des églises Réformées au Royaume de France* (Antwerp, 1580), 2: 610-11. P. F. Geisendorf, *La vie quotidienne au temps de l'Escalade* (Geneva, 1952), p. 79: opposition to the fires of Saint Jean, wedding barriers, and charivaris in rural canton of Geneva. Le Roy Ladurie, p. 344: opposition of urban Huguenots of Montpellier to masquerades and festivals of Catholic peasants. A. Péricaud, *Notes et documents pour servir à l'histoire de Lyon, 1560-1574* (Lyon, 1842), p. 46: a Protestant minister and elder of the church assault a group of Catholics dancing in front of a parish church. A. Borrel, "Recueil de pièces," BSHPF 6 (1858): 13-14: Consistory of Nîmes forbids a member of the church to participate in fête of the Basoche in 1592. Ann Guggenheim, who has been working on the Reformation in sixteenth-century Nîmes, has found many cases of the Consistory summoning people for dancing and masking in the 1580's.

The *Histoire de la Mappemonde papistique*, an anti-papist piece appearing at Geneva in 1566, includes a festival scene with "Seigneur Caresme-Prenant avec des Inquisiteurs ses compagnons."

Perhaps the fierce hostility of the *"compagnacci*, voyous de bonne famille," to Savonarola is a pre-Reformation example of the kind of tension being examined here: R. Klein, "La dernière méditation de Savonarola," BHR 23 (1961): 442.

96.   For another example of Calvinist hostility to life lived "on two levels," see the Puritan attitude toward sport and physical recreation discussed by Brailsford, *Sport and Society*, pp. 127-33. As Baxter said, the proper way to physical fitness was exercise in the ordinary course of one's work.

97.   R. Stauffenegger, "Le mariage à Genève vers 1600," *Mémoires de la société pour l'histoire du droit* 27 (1966); AEG, RCon, 19 (1562), f. 188^v.

98.   *Calvini opera*, 19: 409-11; R. Kingdon, *Geneva and the Coming of the Wars of Religion in France, 1555-1563* (Geneva, 1956), p. 110. Popular looting and parades with relics took place the first days of the Reformed seizure of Lyon in 1562. Then the Consistory and Huguenot Consulate made strong efforts to regain all seized material and the rest of the confiscation proceeded in an "orderly" way. L. Niepce, *Monuments d'art de la Primatiale de Lyon détruits ou aliénés pendant l'occupation protestante en 1562* (Lyon, 1881).

99.   Geisendorf, p. 79 (charivaris and other customs persist in the canton of Geneva in the late sixteenth century despite opposition). Felix and Thomas Platter, though good Protestants from Basel, participated in masking and dancing during their student days in France, though Thomas did not like the charivaris he heard and smelled in Uzès: *Journal*, p. 172.

On charivaris, Misrule Abbeys, and parades backward on a horse in the canton of Geneva in 1626, 1632, and 1669, all in connection with men beaten by their wives: AEG, PC, 1st ser.,

2704, 2883; 2d ser., 2712 (I am grateful to E. W. Monter for calling these trials to my attention). Junod, pp. 117ff. (cited in n. 43), on charivaris in the Pays du Vaud in the nineteenth century despite the opposition of the Consistory for three centuries. Van Gennep found traces of youth-abbeys in Protestant Montbéliard in the twentieth century: *Manuel*, 1: 199.

100. The Conards of Rouen had an office for their confraternity at Notre Dame de Bonnes Nouvelles, where they assembled to talk of the Abbey's business (Taillepied, *Recueil*, p. 61). The theologian Taillepied was quite tolerant of various "popular customs" of the ancient Gauls still current in France, including New Year's celebrations, which he thought did not "prejudice the salvation of souls" (*Histoire de l'Estat et Republicque des Druides* [Paris, 1585], f. 120^r). The Confrérie des Sots at Paris (see n. 59) also had a chapel.

101. Gabriel de Saconay, *Genealogie et la Fin des Huguenaux* (Lyon: Benoît Rigaud, 1573), p. 602; Gabriel de Saconay, *Discours catholique, sur les causes et remedes des Malheurs intentés au Roy ... par les rebelles Calvinistes* (Lyon: M. Jove, 1568), p. 66.

102. For instance, in the 1566 parade on the ass in Lyon, the Lord of Misprint bore a sword with the words "The King will put the impious to flight" written on it, referring to Charles IX's earlier visit to Lyon during which Reformed services could not be held in the city. The anchor worn by the Lord of Misprint and his band was to represent those "good Printers' Journeymen" who had not left town (that is, to go to Geneva) and not changed in their religion. The night of the parade, the wife of the Abbot gave birth to a son, and the next day the whole procession was repeated, without floats, and ended up at a Catholic church for baptism. Thus this "pastime and recreation of the Mind" ended "without scandal," "having baptized a beautiful baby" (*L'ordre tenu en la chevauchee*, pp. 417–22). The Parade was retimed at the last minute to coincide with the arrival in Lyon of the duke and duchess of Nemours, who were much associated with a strong Catholic position. De Rubys especially praised this affair and its inventor: *Histoire veritable*, p. 409. Though other *chevauchées* had Catholic features to them, in the 1580's and 1590's the Lord of Misprint and his band were opposed to the League and supported a "Politique" position.

In Rouen, the Conards resumed operations by 1569, after the Protestant domination of Rouen was over. Though the Conards were a Catholic group, the 1587 edition of their past "Triumphs" included the 1540 verse which had criticized both "papelardise" and "schisme." Just before the League seizure of Paris, the Conards mounted a float in which a royal scepter was being pulled in all directions by the Guises. The booksellers who sold the 1587 *Triomphes* were condemned to pay fines and their copies were confiscated. Floquet, pp. 118–19; Herval, p. 47; Ch. Ouin-Lacroix, *Histoire des anciennes corporations d'arts et métiers et des confréries religieuses de la capitale de la Normandie* (Rouen, 1850), p. 338.

In Dijon, on the other hand, the Infanterie may have supported the League position. In 1579 it paraded in honor of the duke of Mayenne and the whole house of Guise. "Livre de souvenance ... de M. Pépin," p. 26.

103. Eisenstadt, "Archetypal Patterns," pp. 38–48. On the changing characteristics and organization of "youth" in the latter period, see the valuable new book by John R. Gillis, *Youth and History* (New York, 1974), chaps. 2–3.

104. Davis, "A Trade Union in Sixteenth-Century France."

105. Eric Hobsbawm, *Primitive Rebels* (Norton Library ed., 1965), pp. 6, 57–65. Also see the excellent discussion of the interpenetration of an old millenarian structure and a new historical situation in Nathan Wachtel, "Structuralisme et histoire: à propos de l'organisation sociale de Cuzco," Annales ESC 21 (1966): 92–93.

106. The Abbey in Rouen decayed in the early seventeenth century, in Dijon in the late seventeenth century. On the decay of urban Abbeys and the persistence of rural ones in Picardy, see Wailly and Crampon, p. 258. Political charivaris in the eighteenth and early nineteenth centuries, Junod, p. 127; Charles Tilly, "Collective Violence in Nineteenth-Century French Cities" (Public lecture, Reed College, Feb. 1968); P. Larousse, *Grand dictionnaire universel du XIXe siècle* (Paris, 1865), 3: 995–96. Also, see Agulhon, *Pénitents*, pp. 62–63. For political charivaris in French Canada in 1837–38, R.-L. Séguin, *Les Divertissements en Nouvelle-France* (Ottawa, 1968), pp. 73–74.

107. This suggestion has also been made by Mandrou, *Introduction* (cited in n. 28), p. 186, n. l.

5. Women on Top

1. Pierre Grosnet, *Les motz dorez De Cathon en francoys et en latin . . . Proverbes, Adages, Auctoritez et ditz moraulx des Saiges* (Paris, 1530/31), f. F. vii^r. Claude de Rubys, *Les privileges franchises et immunitez octroyees par les roys . . . aux consuls . . . et habitans de la ville de Lyon* (Lyon, 1574), p. 74. Christopher Hill, "The Many-Headed Monster in Late Tudor and Early Stuart Political Thinking," in C. H. Carter, ed., *From the Renaissance to the Counter-Reformation, Essays in Honour of Garrett Mattingly* (London, 1966), pp. 298–324.

2. Laurent Joubert, *Erreurs populaires au fait de la medecine* (Bordeaux, 1578), pp. 161ff. François Poullain de La Barre, *De l'excellence des hommes contre l'egalité des sexes* (Paris, 1675), pp. 136ff., 156ff. Ilza Veith, *Hysteria, The History of a Disease* (Chicago, 1965). Michael Screech, *The Rabelaisian Marriage* (London, 1958), chap. 6. Thomas Sydenham, in his important *Epistolary Dissertation to Dr. Cole* (1681), connects the delicate constitution of the woman with the irregular motions of her "animal spirits" and hence explains her special susceptibility to hysteria. Winthrop Jordan, *White over Black. American Attitudes toward the Negro, 1550–1812* (Chapel Hill, N.C., 1968), pp. 11–20, 187–90.

3. Heinrich Institoris and Jacob Sprenger, *Malleus Maleficarum* (ca. 1487), trans. M. Summers (London, 1928), Part I, question 6: "Why it is that Women are chiefly addicted to Evil Superstitions." Florimond de Raemond, *L'histoire de la naissance, progrez et decadence de l'hérésie de ce siècle* (Rouen, 1623), pp. 847–48, 874–77. Fleury de Bellingen, *L'Etymologie ou Explication des Proverbes françois* (La Haye, 1656), p. 311ff. James E. Phillips, Jr., "The Background of Spenser's Attitude toward Women Rulers," *Huntington Library Quarterly* 5 (1941–42): 9–10. [John Aylmer], *An Harborowe for Faithfull and Trewe Subiectes, agaynst the late blowne Blaste, concerninge the Government of Wemen* (London, 1559). J. Simon, *Le gouvernement admirable ou la République des Abeilles* (Paris, 1742), pp. 23ff. John Thorley, in *The Female Monarchy. Being an Enquiry into the Nature, Order and Government of Bees* (London, 1744), still finds it necessary to argue against those who cannot believe in a queen bee (pp. 75–86).

4. See, for instance, Juan Luis Vives, *The Instruction of a Christian Woman* (London, 1524), and François de Salignac de la Mothe Fénelon, *Fénelon on Education*, trans. H. C. Barnard (Cambridge, 1966).

5. P. C. Timbal, "L'esprit du droit privé," *XVIIe siècle* 58–59 (1963): 38–39. P. Ourliac and J. de Malafosse, *Histoire du droit privé* (Paris, 1968), 3: 145–52, 264–68. L. Abensour, *La femme et le féminisme avant le Révolution* (Paris, 1923), Part 1, chap. 9. Alice Clark, *The Working Life of Women in the Seventeenth Century* (London, 1919; reprint 1968). E. Le Roy Ladurie, *Les paysans de Languedoc* (Paris, 1966), pp. 271–80 and *Annexe* 32, p. 859.

6. Christine de Pisan, *The Boke of the Cyte of Ladyes* (a translation of *Le Tresor de la Cité des Dames*, 1405; London, 1521), f. Ee iv. Henry Cornelius Aggripa of Nettesheim, *Of the Nobilitie and Excellencie of Womankynde* (translation from the Latin edition of 1509; London, 1542), f. B iv^r-v.

7. Jean Calvin, *Commentaries on the Epistles of Paul The Apostle to the Corinthians*, trans. J. Pringle (Edinburgh, 1848), 1: 353–61 (1 Cor. 11:3–12). William Gouge, *Domesticall Duties*, quoted in W. and M. Haller, "The Puritan Art of Love," *Huntington Library Quarterly* 5 (1941–42): 246. John G. Halkett, *Milton and the Idea of Matrimony* (New Haven, 1970), pp. 20–24. Gordon J. Schochet, "Patriarchalism, Politics and Mass Attitudes in Stuart England," *Historical Journal* 12 (1969): 413–41. Catherine E. Holmes, *L'éloquence judiciaire de 1620 à 1660* (Paris, 1967), p. 76. Ourliac and de Malafosse, *Droit privé*, 3: 66 ("*L'époque des rois absolus est aussi celle des pères absolus.*"). John Locke, *The Second Treatise of Government*, ed. T. P. Peardon (Indianapolis, Ind., 1952), chap. 7, par. 82; chap. 9, pars. 128–31.

8. [Gabriel de Foigny], *Les avantures de Jacques Sadeur dans la découverte et le voyage de la terre australe* (Amsterdam, 1732), chap. 5, especially pp. 128–39.

9. Robert Delevoy, *Bruegel* (Lausanne, 1959), pp. 70–75.

10. Deut. 22:5; 1 Cor. 11:14–15. Saint Jerome, *The Letters of Saint Jerome*, trans. C. C. Mierow (London, 1963), 1: 161–62 (Letter 22 to Eustochium). Robert of Flamborough, *Liber Penitentialis*, ed. J. F. Firth (Toronto, 1971), Book 5, p. 264. (I am grateful to Carolly Erickson

and Stephen Horowitz for the last two references.) Jean Calvin, "Sermons sur le Deuteronome," in *Ioannis Calvini, opera quae supersunt omnia*, ed. G. Baum, E. Cunitz, and E. Reuss (Brunswick, 1863–80), 28: 17–19, 234 (hereafter cited as *Calvini opera*). Vern Bullough, "Transvestites in the Middle Ages," *American Journal of Sociology* 79 (1974): 1381–94.

11. Pierre de l'Estoile, *Mémoires-journaux*, ed. Brunet et al. (Paris, 1888–96), 1: 142–43, 157, 180. François-Timoléon de Choisy, *Mémoires*, ed. G. Mongrédien (Paris, 1966), pp. 286–360. Bullough's "Transvestites in the Middle Ages," which I have read as this essay goes to press, also discusses male cross-dressing in social rather than in psychopathological terms, that is, in terms of the higher and lower qualities assigned to male and female traits: males who dress as women have a temporary or permanent desire for status loss (p. 1393). I think this is accurate as a very preliminary formulation. My essay shows the *varied* functions of role inversion and transvestism as well as the gains in power and the options they brought to males.

12. Max Gluckman, *Order and Rebellion in Tribal Africa* (New York, 1963), Introduction and chap. 3. Victor Turner, *The Forest of Symbols, Aspects of Ndembu Ritual* (Ithaca, N.Y., 1967), chap. 4. *Idem, The Ritual Process. Structure and Anti-Structure* (Chicago, 1968), chaps. 3–5. Gregory Bateson, "Culture Contact and Schismogenesis," *Man* 35 (Dec. 1935): 199. J. C. Flügel, *The Psychology of Clothes* (London, 1930), pp. 120–21. Marie Delcourt, *Hermaphrodite. Myths and Rites of the Bisexual Figure in Classical Antiquity* (London, 1956), chap. 1. James Peacock, "Symbolic Reversal and Social History: Transvestites and Clowns of Java," in Barbara Babcock-Abrahams, ed., *Forms of Symbolic Inversion* (forthcoming). See also Rodney Needham's discussion of symbolic reversal and its relation to classification in his introduction to E. Durkheim and M. Mauss, *Primitive Classifications*, trans. R. Needham (Chicago, 1972), pp. xxxviii–xl.

13. William Willeford, *The Fool and His Scepter* (Evanston, Ill., 1969), especially pp. 97–98.

14. Ian Donaldson, *The World Upside-Down, Comedy from Jonson to Fielding* (Oxford, 1970), p. 14.

15. Stith Thompson, *Motif-Index of Folk Literature* (rev. ed.; Bloomington, Ind., 1955–58), K310, K514, K1321, K1836, K2357.8. Sir Philip Sidney, *The New Arcadia*, Book I, chap. 12. Honore d'Urfé, *Astrée* (1609–19). John Marston, *The History of Antonio and Mellida* (1602). Willeford, *The Fool*, pp. 58–62.

16. Delcourt, *Hermaphrodite*, pp. 84–102. John Anson, "Female Monks: The Transvestite Motif in Early Christian Literature," forthcoming in *Viator* (I am grateful to Mr. Anson for several bibliographic suggestions). The transvestite saints appearing in Voragine's *Golden Legend* are St. Margaret, alias Brother Pelagius (Oct. 8); Saint Pelagia, alias Pelagius (Oct. 8); Saint Theodora, alias Brother Theodore (Sept. 11); Saint Eugenia (Sept. 11); and Saint Marina, alias Brother Marinus (June 18). See also Bullough, "Transvestites," pp. 1385–87.

17. Thompson, *Motif-Index*, K3.3, K1837. A. Aarne and Stith Thompson, *The Types of the Folktale* (2d rev. ed.; Helsinki, 1964), 88A, 890, 891A. Giovanni Boccaccio, *Decameron*, Second Day, Story 9. William Shakespeare, *The Merchant of Venice*, Act II, scenes 4–6; Act IV, scene 1. M. J. L'Héritier de Villandon, *Les caprices du destin ou Recueil d'histoires singulieres et amusantes. Arrivées de nos jours* (Paris, 1718), *Avertissement* and tale "L'Amazone Françoise." Celeste T. Wright, "The Amazons in Elizabethan Literature," *Studies in Philology* 37 (1940): 433–45. Edmund Spenser, *The Faerie Queen*, Book III, Canto 1.

18. Spenser, *Faerie Queene*, Book V, Cantos 4–5; Wright, "Amazons," pp. 449–54. "The Lady Who Was Castrated," in Paul Brians, ed. and trans., *Bawdy Tales from the Courts of Medieval France* (New York, 1972), pp. 24–36. David Kunzle, *The Early Comic Strip. Narrative Strips and Picture Stories in the European Broadsheet from 1450 to 1825* (Berkeley and Los Angeles, 1973), pp. 224–25. Giovanni Boccaccio, *Concerning Famous Women*, trans. G. G. Guarino (New Brunswick, N.J., 1963), pp. 231–34.

19. Chaucer, *The Canterbury Tales*, "The Wife of Bath's Prologue." François Rabelais, *La vie très horrifique du Grand Gargantua, père de Pantagruel*, chaps. 3–6. Mikhail Bakhtin, *Rabelais and His World* (Cambridge, Mass., 1968), pp. 240–41. *Les quinze joies de mariage*, ed. J. Rychner (Geneva, 1963). Harry Baxter, "The Waning of Misogyny: Changing Attitudes Reflected in *Les Quinze Joyes de Mariage*," Lecture given to the Sixth Conference on Medieval Studies, Western Michigan University, Kalamazoo, Michigan, 1971. H. J. C. von Grimmelshausen, *Courage*,

The Adventuress and the False Messiah, trans. Hans Speier (Princeton, 1964). Johannes Janssen, *History of the German People at the Close of the Middle Ages*, trans. A. M. Christie (London, 1896–1925), 12: 206, n. 1. Kunzle, *Early Comic Strip*, p. 225. *Mari et femme dans la France rurale* (catalogue of the exhibition at the Musée national des arts et traditions populaires, Paris, September 22–November 19, 1973), pp. 68–69.

20. Ben Jonson, *Epicoene*, Act IV. See Donaldson, *World Upside-Down*, chap. 2, and Edward B. Partridge, *The Broken Compass* (New York, 1958), chap. 7. Thomas Shadwell, *The Woman-Captain* (London, 1680). William Shakespeare, *As You Like It*, Act IV, scene 1. For an interesting view of Shakespeare's treatment of Katharina in *The Taming of the Shrew*, see Hugh Richmond, *Shakespeare's Sexual Comedy* (Indianapolis, Ind., 1971), pp. 83–101. Henri d'Andeli, *Le Lai d'Aristote de Henri d'Andeli*, ed. M. Delboville (Bibliothèque de la Faculté de Philosophie et Lettres de l'Université de Liège, 123; Paris, 1951). Hermann Schmitz, *Hans Baldung gen. Grien* (Bielefeld and Leipzig, 1922), Plate 66 (reproduced here as Plate 11). K. Oettinger and K.-A. Knappe, *Hans Baldung Grien und Albrecht Dürer in Nürnberg* (Nuremberg, 1963), Plate 66. Kunzle, *Early Comic Strip*, p. 224.

21. *Erasmus en zijn tijd* (Catalogue of the exhibition at the Museum Boymans–van Beuningen, Rotterdam, October-November 1969), nos. 151–52. See also no. 150, *The Fools' Tree* (ca. 1526), by the "Petrarch-Master" of Augsburg, reproduced here as Plate 10. Willeford, *The Fool*, Plate 30, drawing by Urs Graf. Erasmus, *The Praise of Folly*. See also Dame Folly leading apes and fools in H. W. Janson, *Apes and Ape Lore in the Middle Ages and Renaissance* (London, 1952), pp. 204–8 and Plate 36.

22. See, for instance, John Ashton, ed., *Humour, Wit and Satire in the Seventeenth Century* (New York, 1968; republication of the 1883 ed.), pp. 82ff. John Wardroper, ed., *Jest upon Jest* (London, 1970), chap. 1. Aarne and Thompson, *Folktale*, 1375, 1366A. Kunzle, *Early Comic Strip*, pp. 222–23.

23. S. L. Sumberg, *The Nuremberg Schembart Carnival* (New York, 1941), especially pp. 83–84, 104–5. Maria Leach, ed., *Funk and Wagnalls Standard Dictionary of Folklore, Mythology and Legend* (New York, 1949–50), "Schemen." Jean Savaron, *Traitté contre les masques* (Paris, 1608), p. 10. M. du Tilliot, *Mémoires pour servir à l'histoire de la Fête des Foux* (Lausanne and Geneva, 1751), pp. 8, 11–12. Arnold Van Gennep, *Manuel du folklore français* (Paris, 1943–49), 1.3: 908–18. Violet Alford, *Pyrenean Festivals* (London, 1937), pp. 16–25. Compare the Pyrénées Bear and Rosetta with the Gyro or grotesque giant woman, played by young men on Old Candlemas Day in the Orkney Islands (F. M. McNeill, *The Silver Bough* [Glasgow, 1961], 3: 28–29). Curt Sachs, *World History of the Dance* (New York, 1963), pp. 335–39.

24. Joseph Strutt, *The Sports and Pastimes of the People of England* (new ed.; London, 1878), pp. 449–51, 310–11, 456. C. L. Barber, *Shakespeare's Festive Comedy* (Princeton, 1951), p. 28. Leach, *Dictionary of Folklore*, "Fool Plough," "Morris."

25. Leach, *Dictionary of Folklore*, "Transvestism." Willeford, *The Fool*, p. 86. Van Gennep, *Manuel*, 1.8: 910. Alford, *Festivals*, pp. 19–22. Sachs, *Dance*, pp. 335–39.

26. Henry Bourne, *Antiquitates Vulgares; or the Antiquities of the Common People* (Newcastle, 1725), pp. 147–48. McNeill, *Silver Bough*, 4: 82. Roger Vaultier, *Le Folklore pendant la guerre de Cent Ans* (Paris, 1965), pp. 93–100. J. Lefebvre, *Les fols et la folie* (Paris, 1968), p. 46, n. 66. A. Holtmont, *Die Hosenrolle* (Munich, 1925), pp. 54–55. Donaldson, *World Upside-Down*, p. 15. Van Gennep, *Manuel*, 1.3: 884. Strutt, *Sports*, p. 125.

27. For full documentation and bibliography on this material, see Chap. 4, "The Reasons of Misrule," and E. P. Thompson, " 'Rough Music': Le Charivari anglais," *Annales ESC* 27 (1972): 285–312.

28. P. Sadron, "Les associations permanentes d'acteurs en France au moyen-age," *Revue d'histoire de théâtre* 4 (1952): 222–31. Du Tilliot, *Mémoires*, pp. 179–82. David Williams, *The Rebecca Riots* (Cardiff, 1955), pp. 53–54. Willeford, *The Fool*, pp. 175–79.

29. See Chapter 4, "The Reasons of Misrule," n. 34. J. W. Spargo, *Juridical Folklore in England Illustrated by the Cucking-Stool* (Durham, N.C., 1944). McNeill, *Silver Bough*, 4: 67.

30. In addition to the sources given in n. 28, see Hogarth's illustration of a Skimmington Ride made about 1726 for Samuel Butler's *Hudibras* ("Hudibras encounters the Skimmington"), reproduced here as Plate 13.

31. Enid Welsford, *The Fool, His Social and Literary History* (London, 1935), pp. 153–54.

Van Gennep, *Manuel*, 1.4: 1452—72, 1693—94. Lucienne A. Roubin, *Chambrettes des Provençaux* (Paris, 1970), pp. 178—79. Chap. 4, "The Reasons of Misrule," n. 13. Jean Vostet, *Almanach ou Prognostication des Laboureurs* (Paris, 1588), f. 12^{r-v}. Erasmus, *Adagiorum Chiliades* (Geneva, 1558), col. 135, "Mense Maio nubunt malae." Gabriel Le Bras, *Etudes de sociologie religieuse* (Paris, 1955), 1: 44. On the women's revenge at Saint Agatha's day in the Savoie, see A. Van Gennep, "Le culte populaire de Sainte Agathe en Savoie," *Revue d'ethnographie* 17 (1924): 32.

32. Kunzle, *Early Comic Strip*, pp. 225, 236.

33. Poullain de La Barre, *De l'excellence des hommes*, Preface, especially his discussion of Saint Paul. *Idem, De l'égalité des deux sexes* (Paris, 1676), pp. 16—22. Mary Astell, *Some Reflections upon Marriage* (4th ed.; London, 1730), pp. 99—107. An early example of the primitive golden age theory and male usurpation is found in Agrippa, *Nobilitie and Excellencie*, f. G i^{r-v}. Turner, *Ritual Process*, chap. 5 (cited in n. 12).

34. Jean Calvin, *Commentaries on Genesis*, trans. J. King (Edinburgh, 1847), 1: 172 (Gen. 3: 16). Giambattista Vico, *The New Science*, trans. T. G. Bergin and M. H. Fisch (Ithaca, New York, 1968), nos. 369, 504—7, 582—84, 671, 985—94. Vico describes changes in the father's authority over his sons and in the character of the wife's dowry, but monogamous marriage and paternal power remain throughout. J. F. Lafitau, S.J., *Moeurs des sauvages ameriquains, comparees aux moeurs des premiers temps* (Paris, 1724), 1: 49—90. Anticipating Bachofen's work on matriarchy of a century later, Lafitau's theory of "ginecocratie" does not develop fully the notion of a matriarchal stage for all societies. He speculates that the Iroquois may have originated in Greece and the Mediterranean islands. On the uses of the New World for Old World thought, see Margaret Hodgen, *Early Anthropology in the Sixteenth and Seventeenth Centuries* (Philadelphia, Pa., 1964), and J. H. Elliott, *The Old World and the New* (Cambridge, 1970), chaps. 1—2.

35. Christine de Pisan, *Cyte of Ladyes*, ff.Ff v^r—Hh ii^r. Thomas Heywood, *Gynaikeion, or Nine Bookes of Various History, concerning Women* (London, 1624). Discussion of the Amazons by Pierre Petit in *De Amazonibus Dissertatio* (2d ed.; Amsterdam, 1687) and by Claude Guyon in *Histoire des Amazones anciennes et modernes* (Paris, 1740) tries to find plausible arguments to account for their bravery and successful rule. Both men insist they really existed. The Cartesian Poullain de La Barre did not use them in his arguments for women's entering the magistracy (*De l'égalité*, pp. 166 ff.). By the time Condorcet and Olympe de Gouges make a plea for the full citizenship of women in the early years of the French Revolution, the argument is being waged in terms of rights.

36. Delcourt, *Hermaphrodite*, pp. 93—96. Salomon Reinach, *Cultes, mythes et religions* (Paris, 1905), 1: 430, 453—56. M. C. E. Chambers, *The Life of Mary Ward, 1585—1645* (London, 1882). Mademoiselle de Montpensier, one of the leaders of the Fronde and victor in the siege of Orléans, may have drawn some inspiration from Jeanne d'Arc.

37. On the husband's power of correction over the wife, see William Blackstone, *Commentaries on the Laws of England* (Oxford, 1770), Book I, chap. 15; and Ourliac and de Malafosse, *Droit privé*, 3: 133, 140 (cited in n. 5). Evidence here comes from examination of diaries, criminal cases, and the records of the Geneva Consistory. See, for instance, Nicolas Pasquier's letter to his daughter describing the maneuvers within his own marriage in Charles de Ribbe, *Les familles et la société en France avant la Révolution* (Paris, 1874), 2: 85—87. On wives being beaten, *Journal de Gilles de Gouberville pour les années 1549-1552*, ed. A. de Blangy (Rouen, 1892), 32: 195 (tavernkeeper's wife sends two women over to the Sire de Gouberville for help as her husband has almost killed her through beating). On women telling off their husbands, AEG, PC, 1st ser., no. 1202; 2d ser., no. 1535. For women beating their husbands, in addition to charivaris against them, see a case of 1712, ultimately brought to the Parlement of Paris, against the wife of a merchant gold-beater, who insulted and beat her husband (E. de la Poix de Fréminville, *Traité de la police generale des villes, bourgs, paroisses et seigneuries de la campagne* [Paris, 1758]).

Alison Klairmont has described the woman's privileges during lying-in in an unpublished seminar paper at the University of California. Italian birth-salvers (that is, trays used to bring women drinks during labor and the lying-in) dating from the late fifteenth and sixteenth centuries were decorated with classical and Biblical scenes showing women dominating men (Victoria and Albert Museum; the Louvre). (I am grateful to Elizabeth S. Cohen and Susan Smith for this information.)

38. On women in different kinds of riots see Chapter 2 above. E. P. Thompson, "The Moral Economy of the English Crowd in the Eighteenth Century," *Past and Present* 50 (Feb. 1971): 115–17. Olwen Hufton, "Women in Revolution, 1789–96," *Past and Present* 73 (Nov. 1971): 39 ff. My colleague Thomas Barnes has kindly shown me several cases involving women tearing down enclosures, which he has examined in connection with his study of the Star Chamber. See also the excellent article by Patricia Higgins, "The Reactions of Women," in Brian Manning, ed., *Politics, Religion and the English Civil War* (London, 1973), pp. 179–222. John Spalding, *The History of the Troubles and Memorable Transactions in Scotland and England from 1624 to 1648* (Edinburgh, 1828), 2: 47–48. S. R. Gardiner, *The Fall of the Monarchy of Charles I, 1637–1649* (London, 1882), 1: 105–12. Le Roy Ladurie, *Les paysans*, p. 497. J. Beauroy, "The Pre-Revolutionary Crises in Bergerac, 1770–1789" (paper presented to the Western Society for the Study of French History, Flagstaff, Arizona, March 14–15, 1974), describes the important role of women in the May 1773 grain riots in Bergerac.

39. Margaret Ruth Kittel, "Married Women in Thirteenth-Century England: A Study of Common Law" (unpublished Ph.D. dissertation, University of California at Berkeley, 1973), pp. 226–33. Blackstone, *Commentaries* (1770), Book IV, chap. 2; Book I, chap. 15. Ourliac and de Malafosse, *Droit privé*, 3: 135–36. For advice on this matter, I am grateful to John M. Beattie of the University of Toronto, author of a forthcoming essay on "The Criminality of Women in Eighteenth-Century England," to appear in the *Journal of Social History*. Carol Z. Wiener discusses the ambiguities in the responsibility of married women for certain felonies and trespasses in England in the late sixteenth and early seventeenth centuries in an interesting article entitled "Is a Spinster an Unmarried Woman?" (forthcoming in the *American Journal of Legal History*). She speculates that the description of certain married women indicted for riot and other crimes in the Hertfordshire Quarter Sessions as "spinsters" may have been a legal fiction in order to require the women to accept responsibility for their acts.

On how husbands and wives jointly manipulated their diverse roles for their mutual benefit, see N. Castan, "La criminalité familiale dans le ressort de Parlement de Toulouse, 1690–1730," in A. Abbiateci *et al.*, *Crimes et criminalité en France, 17e–18e siècles* (Cahier des Annales, 33; Paris, 1971), pp. 91–107. Harvard Law School, Ms. 1128, no. 334, *Page vs. Page*, Nov. 13, 1605 (communicated by Thomas Barnes).

40. Roland Bainton, "Katherine Zell," *Medievalia et Humanistica*, n.s., 1 (1970): 3.

41. Henri Hours. "Les fayettes de Saint Just d'Avray. Puissance et limites de solidarité dans une communauté rural en 1774," prepared for a forthcoming issue of the *Bulletin de l'Académie de Villefranche* (manuscript kindly shown me by M. Hours).

On the background to the economic difficulties of the peasants in the Ariège and their relation to forest use, see Michel Chevalier, *La vie humaine dans les pyrénées ariégeoises* (Paris, 1956), pp. 500–517. Sources on the uprising: *Gazette des Tribunaux* 5, nos. 1432–1433, March 14–16, 1830, pp. 446–47, 450–51; M. Dubédat, "Le procès des Demoiselles: Resistance à l'application du code forestier dans les montagnes de l'Ariège, 1828–1830," *Bulletin périodique de la société ariégeoise des sciences, lettres et arts* 7, no. 6 (1900); L. Clarenc, "Le code de 1827 et les troubles forestiers dans les Pyrénées centrales au milieu du XIXe siècle," *Annales du Midi* 77 (1965): 293–317. A new study of this uprising by John Merriman is soon to appear: "The Demoiselles of the Ariège, 1829–1830," in John M. Merriman, ed., *1830 in France* (forthcoming).

42. The grain riot near Maldon is discussed more fully by William A. Hunt of the University of Michigan in his doctoral dissertation "The Godly and the Vulgar: Religion, Rebellion and Social Change in Essex, England, 1570–1688" (Harvard University, 1974). Eric Kerridge, "The Revolts in Wiltshire Against Charles I," *The Wiltshire Archaeological and Natural History Magazine* 57 (1958–60): 68–71. Historical Manuscripts Commission, *Report on the Manuscripts of . . . the Duke of Portland* (London, 1901), 7: 237–38 (reference kindly communicated by Lawrence Stone). Surrey Quarter Sessions, sessions roll 241, Oct. 1721 (kindly communicated by John M. Beattie of the University of Toronto). *Ipswich Journal*, Aug. 5, 1749 (kindly communicated by Robert Malcolmson, Queen's University, Kingston, Ont.). A. W. Smith, "Some Folklore Elements in Movements of Social Protest," *Folklore* 77 (1967), 244–45. "Memorial of the Inhabitants of Stockport and Vicinity" (Public Record Office, HO 42/128). I am grateful for this reference to Robert Glen, who discusses this episode in his doctoral dissertation "The

Working Classes of Stockport During the Industrial Revolution" (University of California, Berkeley, in progress).

In an article written many decades ago, Ellen A. MacArthur said that men dressed as women formed part of a very large female demonstration in August 1643, beating on the doors of Parliament to present petitions asking for peace with Scotland and the settlement of the Reformed Protestant religion ("Women Petitioners and the Long Parliament," *English Historical Review* 24 [1909]: 702–3). The recent work of Patricia Higgins, based on close study of many contemporary sources, does not take very seriously the contemporary claim that "some Men of the Rabble in Womens Clothes" mixed in the crowd. See "The Reactions of Women" (cited in n. 38), pp. 190–97.

43. Williams, *Rebecca Riots*. Thompson, " 'Rough Music,' " pp. 306–7. Daniel Wilson, *Memorials of Edinburgh in the Olden Time* (2d ed.; Edinburgh and London, 1891), 1: 143–45. Sir Walter Scott, *The Heart of Midlothian*, chap. 7.

44. G. F. Dalton, "The Ritual Killing of the Irish Kings," *Folklore* 81 (1970): 15–19. Vivian Mercier, *The Irish Comic Tradition* (Oxford, 1962), pp. 49–53. Arthur Young, *Arthur Young's Tour in Ireland, 1776–1779*, ed. A. W. Hutton (London, 1892), 1: 81–84; 2: 55–56. W. E. H. Lecky, *A History of Ireland in the Eighteenth Century* (New York, 1893), 2: 12–44. L. P. Curtis of Brown University and Robert Tracy of the University of California at Berkeley have given me assistance on these Irish matters. I am grateful to Professor Brendon Ohehir of the University of California at Berkeley for his deciphering of Lecky's reading of the Whiteboy signature and for his translation of it. The Irish personal name behind the English rendering "Sally" meant "Goodness" or "Wealth."

45. Thompson, " 'Rough Music,' " especially pp. 296–304. For examples of charivaris against wife-beaters in France in the early nineteenth century, see Cl. Xavier Girault, "Etymologie des usages des principales époques de l'année et de la vie," *Mémoires de l'Académie Celtique* 2 (1808): 104–6 (mentions charivari *only* against men who beat their wives in May; Girault lived in Auxonne, not far from Dijon, where the May prohibition was in effect in the sixteenth century); J. A. Du Laure, "Archeographe au lieu de La Tombe et des ses environs," *Mémoires de l'Académie Celtique* 2 (1808): 449 (mentions charivaris only against wife-beaters and against neighbors who do not go to the wife's aid; La Tombe is in the Seine-et-Marne); Van Gennep, *Manuel*, 1.3: 1073 (Van Gennep also gives examples of the older kind of charivari against the beaten husband, p. 1072).

An example from the American colonies is found in J. E. Culter, *Lynch-Law* (London, 1905), pp. 46–47: a group of men in Elizabethtown, New Jersey, in the 1750's called themselves Regulars and went about at night with painted faces and women's clothes, flogging men reported to have beaten their wives. I am grateful to Herbert Gutman for this reference.

6. The Rites of Violence

1. *Hist. eccl.*, 1: 537.

2. Claude Haton, *Mémoires de Claude Haton contenant le récit des événements accomplis de 1553 à 1592, principalement dans la Champagne et la Brie*, ed. Félix Bourquelot (Collection de documents inédits sur l'histoire de France; Paris, 1857), pp. 527–28.

3. V. A. Kolve, *The Play Called Corpus Christi* (Stanford, 1966), chap. 8. Also see L. Petit de Julleville, *Histoire du théâtre en France. Les mystères* (Paris, 1880), 2: 391, 408, 444–45. Bruegel's *Procession to Calvary* has some of this same gamelike, "orderly" quality.

4. Philipp Fehl, "Mass Murder, or Humanity in Death," *Theology Today* 28 (1971): 67–68; E. Panofsky, *The Life and Art of Albrecht Dürer* (Princeton, N.J., 1955), pp. 121–22. For the range of sixteenth-century explanations of human violence, see J. R. Hale, "Sixteenth-Century Explanations of War and Violence," *Past and Present* 51 (May 1971): 3–26.

5. Guillaume Paradin, *Memoires de l'Histoire de Lyon* (Lyon, 1573), p. 238; *Hist. eccl.*, 1: 192–93. See also Christopher Hill, "The Many-Headed Monster in Late Tudor and Early Stuart Political Thinking," in C. H. Carter, ed., *From the Renaissance to the Counter-Reformation. Essays in Honour of Garrett Mattingly* (London, 1966), pp. 296–324.

6. The literature on crowds and violence is vast. I list here only those works that have especially assisted the preparation of this paper: George Rudé, *The Crowd in History. A Study of Popular Disturbances in France and England, 1730–1848* (New York, 1964); E. J. Hobs-

bawm, *Primitive Rebels, Studies in Archaic Forms of Social Movement in the 19th and 20th Centuries* (Manchester, Eng., 1959); E. P. Thompson, "The Moral Economy of the English Crowd in the Eighteenth Century," *Past and Present* 50 (Feb. 1971): 76–136; Charles Tilly, "Collective Violence in Nineteenth-Century French Cities" (Public Lecture, Reed College, Feb. 1968); *idem,* "The Chaos of the Living City," in Charles Tilly, ed., *An Urban World* (Boston, 1974), pp. 86– 107; Charles Tilly and James Rule, *Measuring Political Upheaval* (Princeton, N.J., 1965) (I am grateful to Charles Tilly for his comments on this paper); Emmanuel Le Roy Ladurie, *Les paysans de Languedoc* (Paris, 1966), 1: 391–414, 495–508, 607–29; Roland Mousnier, *Fureurs paysannes* (Paris, 1967); M. Mollat and Philippe Wolff, *Ongles bleus, Jacques et Ciompi, Les révolutions populaires en Europe aux XIVe et XVe siècles* (Paris, 1970); J. R. Hale, "Violence in the Late Middle Ages: A Background," in Lauro Martines, ed., *Violence and Civil Disorder in Italian Cities, 1200–1500* (Berkeley, Calif., 1972), pp. 19–37; Neil J. Smelser, *Theory of Collective Behavior* (New York, 1971). There are also some helpful classifications of crowds in Elias Canetti, *Crowds and Power,* trans. Carol Stewart (German ed. 1960; New York, 1966), pp. 48–73.

7. As in, for instance, Philippe Wolff, "The 1391 Pogrom in Spain. Social Crisis or Not?," *Past and Present* 50 (Feb. 1971): 4–18; Norman Cohn, *The Pursuit of the Millennium* (2d ed., New York, 1961); Sylvia L. Thrupp, ed., *Millennial Dreams in Action. Studies in Revolutionary Religious Movements* (New York, 1970).

8. C. Verlinden, J. Craeybeckx, E. Scholliers, "Mouvements des prix et des salaires en Belgique au XVIe siècle," *Annales ESC* 10 (1955): 185–87. Janine Estèbe, *Tocsin pour un massacre. La saison des Saint-Barthélemy* (Paris, 1968), pp. 97–98, 196, 135–36, 189–98. Though I will take issue at several points in this paper with Estèbe's interpretation of the massacres, her valuable book is surely the most imaginative study we have had of the social psychology of that event. (Estèbe's comments on my essay, together with my rejoinder, will appear in a forthcoming number of *Past and Present.*) Wolff, "The 1391 Pogrom," p. 16; Rudé, *The Crowd in History,* pp. 62, 138. M. Wolff characterizes the pogrom at Valencia, where "violence directed against the Jews predominates, committed moreover by persons from the most diverse social backgrounds," as "pseudo-religious" (p. 16).

9. *Hist. eccl.,* 1: 248. Jean Guéraud, *La chronique lyonnaise de Jean Guéraud,* ed. Jean Tricou (Lyon, 1929), p. 151. Other examples: Geneva, Advent 1533, a young man interrupts a sermon of the Catholic theologian Guy Furbity, "Messieurs, listen . . . I will put myself in the fire to maintain that all he has said are lies and words of the Antichrist"; "Into the fire," shout some of the congregation (Jeanne de Jussie, *Le levain du Calvinisme ou commencement de l'hérésie de Genève* [Geneva, 1865], p. 74). In Rouen, a barber's journeyman denies at the end of a Franciscan's sermon that there are seven sacraments, insisting that there are only two: *Hist. eccl.,* 1: 335. Rouen, March 1562, in *Hist. eccl.,* 3: 713, n. 1. Toulouse, May 4, 1562, in Bosquet, *Histoire,* p. 38. Provins, 1560, Protestants disturb a Catholic sermon: Haton, *Mémoires,* pp. 136–37.

10. Crespin, *Martyrs,* 2: 307–8; 3: 515, for a similar episode in Flanders. *Hist. eccl.,* 1: 931.

11. Haton, *Mémoires,* p. 182. "Relations de l'émeute arrivée à Toulouse en 1562," in L. Cimber and F. Danjou, eds., *Archives curieuses de l'histoire de France* (hereafter cited as *Arch. cur.*) (Paris and Beauvais, 1834–40), 4: 347. *Hist. eccl.,* 3: 989. [Richard Verstegen], *Théâtre des cruautés des hérétiques au seizième siècle, contenant les cruautés des Schismatiques d'Angleterre . . . les cruautés des Huguenots en France, et les barbaries cruelles des Calvinistes Gueux aux Pays-Bas. Reproduction du texte . . . de 1588* (Lille, 1883), p. 38.

12. *Hist. eccl.,* 2: 650–51.

13. "Massacres de ceux de la Religion à Orléans," *Arch. cur.,* 7: 295. *Hist. eccl.,* 2: 839 (Valognes), 3: 315 (Orange).

14. From the memoirs of Canon Bruslart of Paris, quoted in *Arch. cur.,* 4: 57, n. 1.

15. Crespin, *Martyrs,* 2: 470.

16. Claude de Sainctes, *Discours sur le saccagement des Eglises Catholiques, par les Heretiques anciens et nouveaux Calvinistes en l'an 1562* (1563), in *Arch. cur.,* 4: 368; Haton, *Mémoires,* p. 375.

17. *Hist. eccl.,* 1: 308. The Catholic philologist Gilles Ménage still finds this explanation of

the term Huguenot in terms of ghosts plausible in the seventeenth century (*Les origines de la langue françoise* [Paris, 1650] , pp. 391—94).

On popular attitudes toward ghosts and the souls of the dead, see Arnold Van Gennep, *Manuel de Folklore Français* (Paris, 1943—58), 2: 791—803; André Varagnac, *Civilisation traditionnelle et genres de vie* (Paris, 1948), chap. 7; Roger Vaultier, *Le Folklore pendant la guerre de Cent Ans d'après les Lettres de Rémission du Trésor des Chartes* (Paris, 1965), p. 80; Keith Thomas, *Religion and the Decline of Magic* (London, 1971), pp. 587—606.

18. Haton, *Mémoires*, pp. 49—50, and p. 511 on "incest" among Huguenots, spurred on by reading the Bible in French. Crespin, *Martyrs*, 2: 546. Gabriel de Saconay, *Genealogie et la Fin des Huguenaux, et descouverte du Calvinisme* (Lyon, 1573), f. 68ᵛ, who cites a work by Antoine Mochi, alias De Mochares, *Apologie contre la Cene Calvinique*, printed in Paris in 1558. Guéraud, *Chronique*, p. 147. Also, note the reaction of the Catholics Florimond de Raemond and Claude de Rubys to male and female voices joining together in the Psalms: Florimond de Raemond, *L'histoire de la naissance, progrez et decadence de l'hérésie de ce siècle* (Rouen, 1623), p. 1,010; Claude de Rubys, *Histoire veritable de la ville de Lyon* (Lyon, 1604), pp. 390—91 ("Leurs chansons Androgynes," etc.).

19. Gentian Hervet, *Discours sur ce que les pilleurs, voleurs et brusleurs d'Eglises disent qu'ils n'en veulent qu'auz Prestres. Au Peuple de Rheims, et des environs* (Paris, 1563): "The execrable words of diabolic ministers," "pestilential little books full of poison." Haton, *Mémoires*, p. 150. Harangue of Canon Jean Quintin at Orléans, Dec. 1560, in *Hist. eccl.*, 1: 476. Another Catholic quotation expressing these attitudes and fears is "Nothing remains in the churches. The impious takes away everything. He destroys, he overturns, he pollutes all holy places" (from the manuscript "De tristibus Francorum," illustrated with pictures of the iconoclastic Protestants of Lyon with animal heads; Léopold Niepce, *Monuments d'art de la Primatiale de Lyon, détruits ou aliénés pendant l'occupation protestante en 1562* [Lyon, 1881] , pp. 16—17).

20. *Le Cabinet du Roi de France*, described in Jean-Jacques Servais and Jean-Pierre Laurend, *Histoire et dossier de la prostitution* (Paris, 1965), p. 170. Crespin, *Martyrs*, 3: 324; 1: 385—90. [Pierre Viret], *Le Manuel ou Instruction des Curez et Vicaires de l'Eglise Romaine* (Lyon, 1564), p. 137; for the identification of the author of this work see R. Linder, *The Political Ideas of Pierre Viret* (Geneva, 1964), p. 189. For other attacks on the sexual uncleanness of the Catholic clergy, see Jacques Pineaux, *La poésie des protestants de langue française (1559—1598)* (Paris, 1971), pp. 70—71.

21. *Hist. eccl.*, 1: 486; "Récit de l'oeuvre du Seigneur en la ville de Lyon pour action de grâce" and "Epigramme du Dieu des papistes," in Anatole de Montaiglon, ed., *Recueil de poésies françoises des XVe et XVIe siècles* (Paris, 1867), 7: 36—39, 42—45. On the loathsome and magical aspects of the Mass, Antoine de Marcourt, *Declaration de la messe* (Neuchâtel, 1534). *Les cauteles, canon et ceremonies de la messe* (Lyon, 1564) (see n. 82 below). Pineaux, *Poésie*, pp. 91—99. Thomas, *Religion*, pp. 33—35. Jean Calvin, *Institution de la religion chrétienne*, Book IV, para. 18, in *Calvini opera*, 4: col. 1,077 (*ces villaines ordures*).

Calvin's comments on the "mire" of his earlier life in the Preface to his Commentaries on the Psalms, *Commentaire sur le livre des Pseaumes* in *Calvini opera*, 31: col. 22. On the danger of "pollution" and "contamination" from Catholic religious life, Crespin, *Martyrs*, 1: 563; and Haton, *Mémoires*, pp. 407—8.

22. Haton, *Mémoires*, pp. 427—28; [Jean Ricaud] , *Discours du massacre de ceux de la Religion Reformée, fait à Lyon par les catholiques romains, le vingthuictieme de mois de août et jours ensuivant de l'an 1572* (1574) (Lyon, 1847), pp. 110—11; *De l'effroyable et merveilleux desbord de la rivière du Rhosne en 1570* (first published Lyon, 1576; Lyon, 1848 ed.), p. 6.

23. There were expiatory processions in Paris in the wake of "execrable crimes" against religious statues in 1528, 1547, 1550, 1551, 1554, and 1562, described in *Le Journal d'un bourgeois de Paris sous le règne de François Iᵉʳ (1515—1536)*, ed. V. L. Bourrilly (Paris, 1910), pp. 290—94; M. Félibien and G. A. Lobineau, *Histoire de la ville de Paris* (Paris, 1725), 4: 676—79, 728, 748, 755, 765, 804—5; *Arch. cur.*, 4: 99—102. Note also the expiatory procession in Lyon after an iconoclastic outrage in 1553 in Guéraud, *Chronique*, pp. 65—66.

24. "Et dirons tous d'une bonne unyon: /Vive la catholicque religion/ Vive le Roy et les bons parroyssiens,/ Vive fidelles Parisiens,/ Et jusques à tant n'ayons cesse/ Que chascun aille à la

messe/ Un Dieu, une Foy, un Roy": "Déluge des Huguenotz faict à Paris," in _Arch. cur._, 7: 259. See also the Parisian Catholic "Chanson de Marcel, prévôt des marchands" and other anti-Huguenot songs expressing hatred of disunity in M. Csécsy, "Poésie populaire de Paris avant la Saint-Barthélemy," BSHPF 118 (1972): 700—708. On Protestants as "vermin," Guéraud, _Chronique_, p. 141; Saconay, _Genealogie_, p. 64a; Claude de Rubys, _Histoire veritable_, p. 404.

25. "Lyon est bien changé . . ./ De Mercure le gain, & de Venus la dance/ Tout homme a delaissé, & toute outrecuidance": _Eglogue de deux Bergers, Demonstrant comme la ville de Lyon a esté reduite à la Religion vrayement Chrestienne, par la pure predication de l'Evangile_ (Lyon, 1564), f.A 4ʳ. "Quand ceste ville tant vaine/ Estoit pleine/ D'idolatrie et procès/ D'usure et de paillardise/ Clercs et marchans eut assès./ Mais si tost qu'en fut purgee/ Et changee/ Par la Parolle de Dieu:/ Cette engence de vipere/ Plus n'espere/ D'habiter en si sainct lieu": Antoine Du Plain, "De l'assistance que Dieu a Faite à son Eglise de Lyon" in H. L. Bordier, ed., _Le chansonnier huguenot au XVIe siècle_ (Paris, 1870), p. 221. On Catholic clergy as "vermin," see _Discours de la vermine et prestraille de Lyon, dechassé par le bras fort du Seigneur avec la retraicte des moines . . . Par E.P.C._ (1562) in Montaiglon, _Recueil_, 8: 24—45.

26. Thompson, "Moral Economy," pp. 91—115.

27. The essential documents on the _rebeine_ are reprinted in M. C. and G. Guigue, _Bibliothèque historique du lyonnais_ (Lyon, 1886); and on the Provins riot in Haton, _Mémoires_, pp. 714—25. For the relation of the food riot to governmental action in France in the late seventeenth and eighteenth centuries, see Louise Tilly, "The Food Riot as a Form of Political Conflict in France," _Journal of Interdisciplinary History_ 2 (1971): 23—57.

28. _Histoire veritable de la mutinerie, tumulte et sedition, faite par les Prestres Sainct Medard, contre les Fideles, le Samedy XXVII iour de December 1562_ [sic for 1561] in _Arch. cur._, 4: 55; memoirs of Canon Bruslart, _Arch. cur._, 4: 57, n. 1; Haton, _Mémoires_, p. 181. On Toulouse Catholic crowds leading Protestants to prison, see _Hist. eccl._, 3: 17—18.

29. Crespin, _Martyrs_, 1: 381—418, 494—500; 3: 639.

30. Samuel Y. Edgerton, Jr., "_Maniera_ and the _Mannaia_: Decorum and Decapitation in the Sixteenth Century," in F. W. Robinson and S. G. Nichols, Jr., eds., _The Meaning of Mannerism_ (Hanover, N.H., 1972), pp. 67—103. _Journal d'un bourgeois_, pp. 229, 373, 384—85. Claude Bellièvre, _Souvenirs de voyages en Italie et en Orient. Notes historiques_, ed. C. Perrat (Geneva, 1956), p. 26, n. 27. Haton, _Mémoires_, p. 375. Guéraud, _Chronique_, pp. 28—29. Pierre de L'Estoile, _Mémoires-journaux_, ed. Brunet et al. (Paris, 1888—96), 2: 323—24. F. A. Isambert et al., eds., _Recueil général des anciennes lois françaises_ (Paris, 1822), 12: nos. 115, 210; 13: nos. 18, 90. Edmé de la Poix de Fréminville, _Dictionnaire ou traité de la police générale des villes, bourgs, paroisses et seigneuries de la campagne_ (Paris, 1758), pp. 56, 171. Le Roy Ladurie, _Paysans_, p. 506; Roland Mousnier, _L'assassinat d'Henri IV_ (Paris, 1964), pp. 32—34. A. Allard, _Histoire de la justice criminelle au seizième siècle_ (Ghent, 1868), pp. 333—34.

31. _Hist. eccl._, 2: 175. For the Marché aux Pourceaux as a place of execution for heretics, see the _Journal d'un bourgeois_, pp. 384—85. Bosquet, _Histoire_, p. 38.

32. L'Estoile, _Mémoires-journaux_, 2: 85 (describing here the freeing by a Parisian crowd of a man condemned to death for impregnating a young woman).

33. Jean Philippi, _Mémoires_, in _Nouvelle Collection des Mémoires pour servir à l'histoire de France_, ed. Michaud and Poujoulat (Paris, 1838), 8: 634. Crespin, _Martyrs_, 2: 37; _Hist. eccl._, 1: 983. In Rouen, a Catholic crowd of 1563 pressured the Parlement to condemn Protestants to death; a Catholic crowd of 1571, having had some of its members arrested for killing Protestants, broke into the prison and freed them: _Hist. eccl._, 2: 792, n. 1; Crespin, _Martyrs_, 3: 662—63. For two examples of Catholic crowds seizing from the gallows female heretics who had been condemned merely to be hanged and burning them instead, see _Hist. eccl._, 3: 43—44, and L'Estoile, _Mémoires-journaux_, 3: 166.

34. Haton, _Mémoires_, pp. 704—6. The boys were aged twelve or younger, according to Haton.

35. _Hist. eccl._, 1: 970, 889.

36. Antoine de Marcourt, _The booke of Marchauntes_ (London, 1547), ff.C iᵛ–iiʳ. The _Livre des Marchands_ was first published in Neuchâtel in 1533. Antoine de Marcourt, _A declaration of the masse, the fruyte thereof, the cause and the meane, wherefore and howe it ought to be maynteyned_ (Wittenberg: Hans Luft [sic for London, John Day], 1547), f. D ivᵛ, conclusion written by Pierre Viret. This work by Marcourt first appeared in French at Neuchâtel in 1534.

37. Municipal schools in Toulouse, Lyon, and Nîmes among other places, and urban welfare systems in Paris, Rouen, Lyon, Troyes, Toulouse, and other cities. The municipal school at Toulouse has been the subject of a Harvard University Ph.D. dissertation by Irene Brown.

38. Emond Auger, *Le Pedagogue d'Armes. Pour instruire un Prince Chrestien à bien entreprendre et heureusement achever une bonne guerre, pour estre victorieux de tous les ennemis de son Estat, et de L'Eglise Catholique. Dedie au Roy. Par M. Emond, de la Compagnie de Iesus* (Paris, 1568), especially ff. 18ʳ–24ᵛ.

39. Letter from Pierre Viret to the *Colloque de Montpellier*, Jan. 15, 1562, in *Hist. eccl.*, 1: 975–77. Pierre Viret, *L'Interim, Fait par Dialogues* (Lyon, 1565), pp. 396–97. Linder, *Political Ideas*, pp. 137–38. Robert Kingdon, *Geneva and the Consolidation of the French Protestant Movement* (Madison, Wis., 1967), pp. 153–55.

40. See, for instance, the *Vindiciae contra Tyrannos* (trans. by J. H. Franklin) on this subject in J. H. Franklin, ed., *Constitutionalism and Resistance in the Sixteenth Century* (New York, 1969), pp. 154–56.

41. Crespin, *Martyrs*, 3: 694, 701, 711–12, and 717. The infrequency of these tales of remorse is all the more significant because they could be used so readily by Protestants to show the just punishment of God: cf. *Hist. eccl.*, 1: 357. Pastor Jean Ruffy, formally rebuked by Calvin for his role in an iconoclastic riot in Lyon in 1562 (Robert Kingdon, *Geneva and the Coming of the Wars of Religion in France, 1555–1563* [Geneva, 1956], p. 110), led a Protestant crowd against dancing Catholics in 1565 (De Rubys, *Histoire veritable*, p. 406). On ambivalence about disobedience and violent behavior that might be embedded deep in the feelings of rioters, I have no evidence one way or the other.

42. Guéraud, *Chronique*, p. 155; Charles Du Moulin, *Omnia . . . Opera* (Paris, 1681), 5: 618; Kingdon, *Geneva*, p. 110.

43. *Hist. eccl.*, 1: 352. There were other allegations that priests took part in Catholic riots: in Toulouse, 1562 (*Hist. eccl.*, 3: 4–5); in Lavaur, 1561 (1: 938–39); in Clermont in Auvergne, 1568 (Crespin, *Martyrs*, 3: 651). Also see the comments of the priest Claude Haton about brawling priests with swords in their hands, *Mémoires*, pp. 17–18.

44. For instance, priests at Nemours were said to have helped plan an attack on Protestants there in 1561, and Dominicans at Revel are alleged to have organized an attack on Psalm-singers the same year: *Hist. eccl.*, 1: 833–34, 959. The bishop of Autun was accused of organizing groups of artisans to exterminate Protestants in that city in 1562, and Cardinal Strozzi, the bishop of Albi, was supposed to have helped to organize a massacre in Gaillac in May 1562: *Hist. eccl.*, 3: 487–88, 80–81.

45. Crespin, *Martyrs*, 3: 390–91; Léopold Niepce, "Les trésors des Eglises de Lyon," *Revue lyonnaise* 8 (1884): 40, n. 1.

46. Haton, *Mémoires*, p. 182; *Histoire veritable de la mutinerie . . . faite par les Prestres Sainct Medard*, in *Arch. cur.*, 4: 56. On the position of the *chevalier du guet*, or chief officer of the watch, in Paris, see Isambert, *Recueil*, 12: no. 296. *Hist. eccl.*, 1: 889.

47. Estèbe, *Tocsin*, pp. 137–40. The orders given in the militia officers of Paris from Aug. 22 to Aug. 30, 1572, are printed in *Histoire Générale de Paris. Régistres des déliberations du Bureau de la ville de Paris*, ed. F. Bonnardot (Paris, 1883–1958), 7: 9–20. Also see the leadership of doctors of theology and militia captains in an unofficial burning of Protestant books by a Catholic crowd in Paris in 1568: Félibien and Lobineau, *Histoire*, 4: 828 (I am grateful to Alfred Soman for this reference).

48. Haton, *Mémoires*, p. 191. *Hist. eccl.*, 2: 537–38, 719–20.

49. Crespin, *Martyrs*, 3: 519–22; *Hist. eccl.*, 2: 719–20. Also, see Condé's letter to the king of May 1562, in which he argues that though "le peuple" were at fault for destroying images without waiting for an order from the magistrate, nevertheless, their action could be imputed to "a secret movement of God, inciting the people to detest and abhor idolatry, and not to any disobedience or rebellion": *Hist. eccl.*, 2: 74.

50. Ann H. Guggenheim, "Beza, Viret and the Church of Nîmes: National Leadership and Local Initiative in the Outbreak of the Wars of Religion," forthcoming in BHR.

51. Crespin, *Martyrs*, 2: 538, 546. *Hist. eccl.*, 1: 268–69.

52. Haton, *Mémoires*, pp. 527–29; *Hist. eccl.*, 1: 192–93, 481.

53. Crespin, *Martyrs*, 3: 727; Henri Hauser, "Le père Emond Auger et le massacre de Bor-

deaux, 1572," *Bulletin de la société d'histoire du protestantisme français*, 5th ser., 8 (1911): 289–306.

54. Haton, *Mémoires*, pp. 195–97, 681–82.

55. Fréminville, *Dictionnaire*, p. 400, citing edicts of 1536 and 1550. Isambert, *Recueil*, 12: no. 115 (Edict of Sept. 1523), p. 531 (Edict of Jan. 25, 1536), pp. 557–58 (Edict of May 9, 1539).

56. Jacques Toussaert, *Le sentiment religieux en Flandres à la fin du Moyen Age* (Paris, 1963), p. 90; T. J. Schmitt, *L'organisation ecclésiastique et la pratique religieuse dans la diocèse d'Autun de 1650 à 1750* (Autun, 1957), p. 166. Until the Council of Trent, canon law allowed that a marriage promised between two persons privately, without the presence of a priest, and consummated was a sacrament. Even after Trent, it took some time for the 1564 legislation requiring a priest's presence to be widely known and followed. See also Gabriel Le Bras, "L'excommunication des clercs par les laïques," in *Eventail de l'histoire vivante. Hommage à Lucien Febvre* (Paris, 1953), 1: 227–32.

57. *La Deffense civile et Militaire des Innocens et de l'Eglise de Christ* was published in Lyon in 1563, and was burned on June 12, 1563, after a condemnation by the pastors of Lyon and Governor Soubise: Du Moulin, *Opera*, 5: 17–22. On Old Testament precedents for private individuals killing tyrants, see Mousnier, *Assassinat*, p. 28.

58. These disturbances at Lyon included armed marches of hundreds of psalm-singing Protestant artisans and their wives in the spring of 1551; "assemblies and sedition" in the wake of heretical preaching by a Florentine at the St. Lawrence Hospital in August 1551; the theft of all the ornaments and the Sacrament from the Church of Fourvières in October 1551; the desecration of a crucifix and an image of Saint Anne in January 1553; etc. Guéraud, *Chronique*, pp. 54–55, 58, 65–66; ADR, B, Sénéchaussée, Sentences, 1551–52, Dec. 1551.

59. Georges and Geneviève Frêche, *Les prix des grains, des vins et des légumes à Toulouse (1485–1868)* (Paris, 1967), pp. 44–45. The famine and plague of 1557 were interpreted in Toulouse as the hand of God falling on the city for its iniquities. The local government then tried to purge the town of the "idle vagabonds," to feed the starving in Toulouse and from nearby villages, and to get rid of "infecting vapors" and other filth in the streets. Antoine Noguier, *Histoire Tolosaine* (Toulouse, n.d., royal privilege, 1559), pp. 126–33.

60. Micheline Baulant and Jean Meuvret, *Prix des céréales extraits de la Mercuriale de Paris (1520–1698)* (Paris, 1960), 1: 47, 49, 152–53. Maximum prices for wheat in December 1561 were something over five livres tournois per *sétier*, but a famine price would be thought of in Paris as something like the nine and a half livres tournois per *sétier* to which wheat rose in the summer of 1546.

61. G. and G. Frêche, *Prix*, p. 46; Baulant and Meuvret, *Prix*, 1: 56–57.

62. See n. 8 above. Crespin, *Martyrs*, 3: 518–19. A new study by Phyllis Mack Crew is forthcoming on the relation of preaching to iconoclasm in the Netherlands. Iconoclasm in the Netherlands is also being studied by the art historian David Freedberg of Westfield College, London.

63. As in the white processions in Lyon in the spring of 1504 and in the *grande rebeine* of Lyon in 1529: Paradin, *Mémoires*, p. 281; Chap. 2, "Poor Relief, Humanism, and Heresy." The assertion of the physician Symphorien Champier, whose granary was sacked in the *grande rebeine*, that the crowd also smashed religious statues in his house is surely false and was not taken seriously by contemporaries: see n. 43 to Chap. 2 above, and H. Hours, "Procès d'hérésie contre Aimé Meigret," BHR 19 (1957): 20–21. During the drought of spring 1556 in the Lyonnais, there were both penitential white processions of rural parishioners to Lyon and a crowd attack on boats removing grain from the city for the Order of Malta: Paradin, *Mémoires*, p. 357; Guéraud, *Chronique*, p. 95.

For famine prices and grain riots in Provins in 1573, see Haton, *Mémoires*, pp. 714ff.; for famine prices and a penitential procession in Paris in June 1521, see Baulant and Meuvret, *Prix*, 1: 94, and *Journal d'un bourgeois*, pp. 82–83; and for extraordinary prices and a bread riot in Paris in July 1587, see Baulant and Meuvret, *Prix*, 1: 223, and L'Estoile, *Mémoires-journaux*, 3:58.

64. As in Paris on the day after Pentecost 1528, when some heretics cut off the head of a

Virgin in a wall-niche at night: *Journal d'un bourgeois*, p. 291. Iconoclastic episodes in Lyon in January 1553 probably occurred at night: Guéraud, *Chronique*, p. 65. For iconoclastic riots in Annonay at night in 1561 see Achille Gamon, *Mémoires*, in *Nouvelle Collection des Mémoires pour servir à l'histoire de la France*, ed. Michaud and Poujoulat (Paris, 1838), 8: 611. For an iconoclastic riot by sailors of Dieppe at night in 1562, see *Hist. eccl.*, 2: 796.

65. Haton, *Mémoires*, pp. 340–41; *Hist. eccl.*, 1: 284.

66. *Hist. eccl.*, 1: 833–34; Crespin, *Martyrs*, 3: 210.

67. *Hist. eccl.*, 3: 4–5; Bosquet, *Histoire*, pp. 67–69. For an episode concerning a Reformed burial at Bordeaux on All Souls' Day 1561, see *Hist. eccl.*, 1: 870–71.

68. E.g., at the Vespers service on March 18, 1562, in Rouen (*Hist. eccl.*, 2: 713, n. 1); at Paris at the Sainte Chapelle in 1563 (Haton, *Mémoires*, p. 375); at Toulouse at the Eglise Saint Sernin while the Inquisitor della Lana was preaching, May 4, 1561 (Bosquet, *Histoire*, pp. 38–39). Bosquet claimed that a heretical merchant was killed by the zealous *menu peuple* after he shouted "You lie, hypocritical monk" and other blasphemous remarks. A Protestant account claims that the merchant was actually a Catholic, dissatisfied with the seditious remarks made by the preacher (*Hist. eccl.*, 1: 905). Protestant sources report other episodes in which jumpy Catholic worshipers killed persons as heretics who were in fact Catholics. The victims had been merely asking for more room or had laughed at a neighbor's remark (e.g., Angers in 1561, *Hist. eccl.*, 1: 837; Paris, Church of Saint Eustache, 1558, and at the Cimetière des Innocents, 1559, *Hist. eccl.*, 1: 193–94).

69. In addition to the well-known attack on the conventicle on the rue St. Jacques in Paris in 1557, there were four attacks on conventicles in Paris in April and May 1561: Félibien and Lobineau, *Histoire*, 4: 797–98; R. N. Sauvage, "Lettre de Jean Fernaga, procureur syndic de la ville de Caen, touchant les troubles survenus à Paris en avril 1561," BSHPF, 5th ser., 8 (1911): 809–12. Crowds in Lyon in Sept. 1561 were out to sack all houses in which "people were having certain assemblies," and threatened the house of the Protestant merchant Jérome Pellissari: ADR, B, Sénéchaussée, Audience, Sept.-Dec. 1561. For an attack on a conventicle in Auxerre on Oct. 9, 1561, see *Hist. eccl.*, 1: 852, and for one in Cahors on Nov. 16, 1561: Crespin, *Martyrs*, 3: 211.

70. *Histoire veritable . . .*, in *Arch. cur.*, 4:52; Haton, *Mémoires*, pp. 179–82, 147, 177–78; Félibien and Lobineau, *Histoire*, 4: 800. Also see the conflict between a Protestant service at a pastel mill at Castelnaudary and a Catholic procession for *Pâques fleuries* in 1562: *Hist. eccl.*, 3: 157.

71. E.g., at Geneva at the *Fête-Dieu*, see Jeanne de Jussie, *Le levain du calvinisme*, p. 94. At Le Croisic, Brittany, in 1558, and at Rouen in 1560, *Hist. eccl.*, 1: 179–80, 352. For the Lyon episode on Corpus Christi Day, 1560, see Guéraud, *Chronique*, pp. 133–34, and ADR, B, Sénéchaussée, Sentences, 1561–62, sentence of Sept. 12, 1561. At Clermont-Ferrand in 1568, Crespin, *Martyrs*, 3: 651.

72. The first big psalm-singing parades seem to have occurred in 1551 in Lyon, with artisans, and especially printers' journeymen, taking the initiative in organizing them: Guéraud, *Chronique*, pp. 54–55, letters of Claude Baduel to Calvin in 1551 in Jean Calvin, *Calvini opera*, 14: 16ff. See Guéraud on an episode in Lyon in Dec. 1561, *Chronique*, p. 145. Also see Haton, *Mémoires*, pp. 177–78, 190; Bosquet, *Histoire*, p. 60; and *Hist. eccl.*, 3: 2, on Toulouse in 1562. See L'Estoile, *Mémoires-journaux*, 1: 157, on the stoning of "Huguenot troops" returning from services into Paris in Sept. 1576, followed by a violent *mêlée*.

73. Haton, *Mémoires*, pp. 189–94.

74. De Rubys, *Histoire veritable*, p. 406; *Hist. eccl.*, 1: 969–70 and 970, n. 1. In Rouen in 1562, Protestant *menu peuple* stoned the members of the festive Abbey of Conards as they were about to begin their Mardi Gras activities: *Hist. eccl.*, 2: 713.

75. *Hist. eccl.*, 1: 844.

76. *Discours des troubles advenus en la Ville de Pamies le 5 Iuin 1566. Avec un brief recit des calamitez souffertes l'Annee precedente* (1567), in *Arch. cur.*, 6: 309–43. On the relation between carnival and masked festivities on the one hand and various kinds of disturbances on the other, see Le Roy Ladurie, *Paysans*, 1: 395–99; Chaps. 4 and 5 above; A. W. Smith, "Some Folklore Elements in Movements of Social Protest," *Folklore* 77 (1966): 241–51; Peter

Weidkuhn, "Fastnacht, Revolte, Revolution," *Zeitschrift für Religions-und Geistesgeschichte* 21 (1969): 289–305.

77. *Relation du massacre de la Saint-Barthélemy*, in *Arch. cur.*, 7: 88–89. Frances Yates, *The French Academies of the Sixteenth Century* (London, 1947), pp. 254–59. Marriage as a possible occasion for slaughter remained in the mind of Henri de Navarre. In 1588 he feared that the festivities an Armagnac nobleman was giving for his daughter's wedding were an occasion for a plot on his life. To prevent this, one of Navarre's supporters, a neighbor of the nobleman, entered the house with a band of men during the festivities and slaughtered about thirty-five gentlemen: L'Estoile, *Mémoires-journaux*, 3: 121.

78. *Hist. eccl.*, 1: 887.

79. *Histoire veritable de la mutinerie . . . faite par les Prestres Sainct Medard . . .*, p. 62; Crespin, *Martyrs*, 3: 205; *Hist. eccl.*, 2: 425, 433–35.

80. Crespin, *Martyrs*, 1: 495–98. *Discours de ce qui avint touchant la Croix de Gastines l'an 1571, vers Noel*, extracted from *Mémoires . . . de Charles IX*, in *Arch. cur.*, 6: 475–78. De Rubys, *Histoire veritable*, pp. 402, 412. [Jean Ricaud], *Discours du massacre de ceux de la Religion Reformée, fait à Lyon par les catholiques romains, le vingthuictieme du mois de août et jours ensuivant de l'an 1572* (1574) (Lyon, 1847), pp. 9–13.

81. Crespin, *Martyrs*, 3: 204. *Hist. eccl.*, 2: 650–51, 839, 883, 932–33; 3: 15, 315. Félibien and Lobinaux, *Histoire*, 4: 828. A variation in the destruction of books by authorities took place in August 1559 at Paris, when the Protestant peddler Marin Marie was burned. His Bibles and New Testaments were first hanged on a gallows next to him and then burned.

82. Bosquet, *Histoire*, pp. 22, 143–44. Haton, *Mémoires*, p. 181. De Sainctes, *Discours sur le saccagement . . .*, in *Arch. cur.*, 4: 384. *Hist. eccl.*, 1: 935; 2: 720, n. 1, and 925; 3: 515. A Catholic polemical piece from Toulouse describes the opening Protestant "crime" in that city as the sale by Protestant *libraires* of the *Canon de la Messe*, which the Calvinists had depraved. This is in all probability a Protestant edition of the Missal, with mocking and satirical footnotes throughout, which had various editions, including one in Lyon in 1564: *Les cauteles, canon et ceremonies de la messe. Ensemble la messe intitulé, Du corps de Iesuchrist. Le tout en Latin et en François: Le Latin fidelement extraict du Messel à l'usage de Rome imprimé à Lyon par Iean de Cambray l'an mil cinq cens vingt* (Lyon: Claude Ravot, 1564). In the comic tradition of Marcourt's *Livre des Marchands*, the work resembles in organization Pierre Viret's satirical *Manuel, ou Instruction des Curez et Vicaires* (Lyon: Claude Ravot, 1564). Also see Pineaux, *Poésie*, pp. 95–98.

As with statue-smashing, Protestant pastors much preferred that ecclesiastical libraries be confiscated and catalogued by the authorities (as in ADR, 3E566, Inventory of May 10, 1562) and not destroyed by the crowds. The *Histoire ecclésiastique*, 3: 515, expressed regret at the insolence of Huguenot soldiers who destroyed an enormous quantity of books at the Abbey of Cluny under the impression that they were all Missals.

83. Hervet, *Discours sur . . . les pilleurs; Hist. eccl.*, 1: 957. On the complexity of Catholic attitudes toward their statues, see Richard C. Trexler, "Florentine Religious Experience: The Sacred Image," *Studies in the Renaissance* 19 (1972): 25–29.

84. That priests and religious were the preferred (though not the exclusive) target for Protestant crowds is a fact emerging not only from an analysis of many crowd actions, but also from Catholic literature. The *Théâtre des Cruautés des hérétiques* gives few examples of lay persons murdered, but many of priests and religious. Claude de Sainctes' *Discours sur le saccagement* (1563) also stresses Protestant attacks on priests. Gentian Hervet's *Discours sur . . . les pilleurs* talks with horror of the Protestant war against unarmed priests and the Protestant claim that their grudge is against the priests only. He warns that once all the churches are destroyed, the Protestants will start on the common people.

85. *Discours des troubles advenus en la Ville de Pamies . . .*, p. 318; de Rubys, *Histoire veritable*, p. 406; Haton, *Mémoires*, p. 181.

86. Among the pastors killed or assaulted by Catholic crowds were Léonard Morel at Vassy, 1561; Pastors Richer and Marcil at Poitiers, 1562; Pastor Giscart at Castelnaudary, 1562; a pastor at Gaillac, 1562; and Pastor Bonnet at Mâcon, 1562. Martin Tachard, formerly pastor at

Val d'Angrogne and Montauban, was led in mockery through Foix in 1567. Among the pastors killed in the 1572 massacres were Bugnette, Le More, and Des Gorris at Paris; Jacques Langlois and N. Dives at Lyon; Pierre Loiseleur dit de Villiers and Louis Le Coq at Rouen; and a minister at Bordeaux.

87. Crespin, *Martyrs*, 3: 695, 721, 710ff., 678, 371—88. Haton, *Mémoires*, p. 181. *Relations de l'émeute de Toulouse*, p. 351. *Théâtre des cruautés*, p. 44. Bosquet, *Histoire*, chap. 2.

88. Estèbe, *Tocsin*, p. 196.

89. Tilly and Rule, *Political Upheaval*, pp. 59—60.

90. Crespin, *Martyrs*, 2: 545; 3: 676, 696.

91. *Hist. eccl.*, 3: 301—5. So also in Troyes, where a stockingmaker killed the merchant-provost of the town, who had formerly been a member of the Reformed Church, one expects that political grievances reinforced religious hatred: Crespin, *Martyrs*, 3: 685. At Meaux, Crespin reports that one Gilles Le Conte was killed in the 1572 massacres, less because of his Reformed Religion than because he was a tax-farmer for Catherine de Médicis and was sometimes hard on Catholics: *Martyrs*, 3: 682.

92. Though numerous other examples of "high isomorphy" can be found, the pages of Crespin are full of examples of artisans and merchants slaying people in their trade (3: 675) and of relatives slaying relatives (3: 676, 697). There are also individual cases of "high isomorphy," where the killing occurred "downward" — that is, the wealthy Catholic killed a poor Protestant. Indeed, the author of the *Tocsain contre les massacreurs* (in *Arch. cur.*, 7: 58—59) asked the following question: as for the little people who professed the Reformed Religion, what humanity could they expect after the illustrious families had been treated in such a fashion?

93. Figures compiled from *Première liste des chrétiens mis à mort et égorgés à Lyon par les catholiques romains à l'époque de la S. Barthélemi août 1572*, ed. P. M. Gonon (Lyon, 1847), and Crespin, *Martyrs*, 3: 707—18. Letters from Lyon to Paris in early September reported that between six and seven hundred people were killed in all: A. Puyroche, "Le Saint-Barthélemy à Lyon et le gouverneur Mandelot," BSHPF 18 (1869): 365; Jacques Pannier, *L'Eglise Reformée de Paris sous Henri IV* (Paris, 1911), p. 369, n. 1. These estimates seem high on the basis of all the available evidence from wills and burials.

94. *Rélation du massacre de la Saint-Barthélemy*, reprinted from *Mémoires de l'Etat de France sous Charles IX*, in *Arch. cur.*, 7: 151; Crespin, *Martyrs*, 3: 703.

95. Haton, *Mémoires*, pp. 190—93; *Hist. eccl.*, 1: 885—86. See also a religious riot with "high isomorphy" in Beaune, a small town with a very high percentage of winegrowers — that is, a large *rural* element — within its walls. In 1561 the winegrowers and others of the *menu peuple*, supported from above by one of the city councillors, attacked Protestants returning from services. The latter group included some of the wealthier families in Beaune. *Hist. eccl.*, 1: 864—65.

96. On Catholic rites of exorcism, see Thomas, *Religion and the Decline of Magic*, chaps. 2 and 15. For the Montpellier episode, see Philippi, *Mémoires*, p. 634. Cf. the somewhat different treatment by Estèbe of the Saint Bartholomew's Day massacre as a "ritual crime" and purification rite: *Tocsin*, p. 197. See also the interesting comment of Jacques Pineaux, "Poésie de cour et poésie de combat," BSHPF 118 (1972): 46.

97. Though Catholic writers such as the priest Claude Haton admit to various acts of desecration of corpses by *Catholic* crowds (e.g., *Mémoires*, pp. 704—6), they make remarkably few accusations against *Protestants* for the same kind of acts. Haton gives only one example — the dismemberment of a doctor of theology, killed in the Saint Médard massacre (*ibid.*, p. 181) — though he accuses the Huguenots of many other kinds of vicious actions. Bosquet's book on Toulouse gives one example of Protestants disemboweling a priest and displaying his entrails (*Histoire*, pp. 9—10, at Montauban), but stresses much more the Protestant humiliation and torture of living persons. The *Théâtre des cruautés des hérétiques*, which would surely have mentioned the Protestant acts of desecration of corpses if they had been common, talks only of the torture of living priests. In contrast, Protestant writings are full of descriptions of Catholic desecration of corpses, and Catholic sources describe these as well.

98. Calvin on Purgatory and the whereabouts of the soul between death and the Last Judgment in the *Institutes*, Book III, chap. 5, sections 6—10; Book III, chap. 25, section 6. See also

Keith Thomas' discussion of Protestant attitudes toward the dead in *Religion*, pp. 588—95, 602—6; Claude de Sainctes, *Discours sur le saccagement*, p. 381 (burning of "holy bones" at Orléans). Pineaux, *Poésie des protestants*, p. 91.

99. For the digging up and throwing around of saints' bones at Lyon, see Guéraud, *Chronique*, p. 156, and Niepce, *Monuments*, pp. 42—43.

100. Strange sounds in Paris at the Saint Bartholomew's Day massacres: Crespin, *Martyrs*, 3: 681. Bodies thrown to the dogs in Draguignan and in Fréjus in 1560 (*Hist. eccl.*, 1: 421, 429), and in Orléans (Crespin, *Martyrs*, 3: 693). Parts of corpses were sold at Villeneuve d'Avignon in 1561 ("Five pence for a Huguenot's liver!"); at Vire in 1562 ("who wants to buy the tripe of Huguenots?"); at Paris in 1572; at Lyon in 1572 (where an apothecary rendered fat from Protestant corpses and sold it at 3 blancs the pound): *Hist. eccl.*, 1: 978; 2: 846. *Le Tocsain contre les autheurs de Massacre de France*, in *Arch. cur.*, 7: 51. Crespin, *Martyrs*, 3: 713.

There are also a few reports of cannibalism by Catholics in the wake of crowd murder ("not for hunger," as Montaigne says of "Cannibals" in his *Essais*, "but to represent an extreme vengence"): at Carcassonne in 1561, Troyes in 1562, and Sens in 1562 (*Hist. eccl.*, 1: 94; 2: 478; 3: 419—20). Le Roy Ladurie reports a curious story of cannibalism among Protestants at Lodève in 1573: the body of Saint Fulcran, miraculously conserved, was shot and then eaten by order of the Huguenots in the wake of an uprising there (*Les paysans*, 1: 398, n. 5).

101. *Hist. eccl.*, 1: 931.

102. Haton, *Mémoires*, pp. 181—82; Guéraud, *Chronique*, p. 156; Bosquet, *Histoire*, p. 148; de Sainctes, *Discours*, p. 372. According to a Catholic witness, the Huguenots of Le Puy talked against the famous black Virgin of that city, saying that paper images of her were no better than toilet paper and that it would be a good idea to drag the statue through the sewage and mire of the city (Pineaux, *Poésie des protestants*, p. 89, n. 9).

103. For the muzzle at Toulouse in 1562, and the crowns of thorns at St. Martin de Castillan and Brignolles in 1562, see *Hist. eccl.*, 3: 43; Crespin, *Martyrs*, 3: 386—87. On punishments for the scold, see Chap. 4, notes 34 and 47. Prisoners were sometimes muzzled on the way to execution: L'Estoile, *Mémoires-journaux*, 3: 166.

104. Crespin, *Martyrs*, 3: 311—12; *Hist. eccl.*, 1: 935; Bosquet, *Histoire*, pp. 9—10; de Sainctes, *Discours*, p. 384. There were other charivari-like actions in religious riots. At Tours in 1562 Protestant women were taken back to mass on horseback "in derision" (probably facing backward on the horse): *Hist. eccl.*, 2: 695. At Mâcon in 1562, Pastor Bonnet was promenaded through the town with "mockery, a thousand raps on the nose and punches," the crowd crying, "Whoever wants to hear this pious and holy person preach, come to the Place de L'Escorcherie": *Hist. eccl.*, 3: 522. In 1567, Pastor Martin Tachart was led through Foix in triumph, in a "white bonnet, with a rosary round his neck": *Discours des troubles advenus en la Ville de Pamies*, p. 342. Bernard Palissy describes the humiliation of Protestant preachers in Saintes on their way to official execution, a humiliation perhaps as much at the hands of the *gens de justice* as at the hands of a crowd: they were dressed in green, like crazy people or fools, and were led through the streets bridled like horses (*Recepte véritable*, in *Oeuvres complètes* [Paris, 1961], p. 101). On charivaris, see Chap. 4, "The Reasons of Misrule."

105. Claude de Rubys, *Oraison prononcee a Lyon a la Creation des Conseillers et eschevins . . . le iour de la feste S. Thomas . . . 1567* (Lyon, 1568), f. Bb 2ᵛ; the journal of Canon Bruslart, reporting news from Rouen, quoted in *Hist. eccl.*, 2: 720, n. 1. Also mock prayers were said by the Catholics killing Protestants at Saintes (Palissy, *Recepte*, in *Oeuvres*, p. 112).

106. *Hist. eccl.*, 3: 518, 524, 158—59; 2: 963—64, 941—42; 3: 158—59. Philippi, *Mémoires*, p. 624. Crespin, *Martyrs*, 3: 721.

107. Troy Duster, "Conditions for Guilt-Free Massacre," in Nevitt Sanford and Craig Comstock, eds., *Sanctions for Evil* (San Francisco, 1971), chap. 3. Duster especially stresses the dehumanization of victims, and this volume contains several interesting essays on this matter.

108. Crespin, *Martyrs*, 3: 684; *Théâtres des cruautés des hérétiques*, p. 44.

109. Cohn, *Pursuit*, pp. 32, 137, 281.

110. Artisans in iconoclastic riots: *Hist. eccl.*, 1: 889, 702, 719. Analysis of Catholic crowds from Crespin, *Martyrs*, 3: 663—733. Catholic boatmen at Gaillac, *Martyrs*, 3: 82; Protestant sailors at Dieppe, *Martyrs*, 2: 796. Catholics arrested in the wake of the Corpus Christi day riot

at Lyon in 1561, during which Barthélemy Aneau, rector of the Collège de la Trinité, and others were killed: a boatman, a miller, a tavernkeeper, a shearer, a silkthrower (ADR, B, Sénéchaussée, Sentences, 1561–62, sentence of Aug. 14, 1561). Councillors from the Parlement of Toulouse in a violent Catholic crowd of May 1562 in *Hist. eccl.*, 3: 15.

In an interesting paper of May 1972, given at the Newberry Library Conference on the Massacre of Saint Bartholomew's Day, and to be published in a collection edited by Alfred Soman, John Tedeschi presented a hitherto unknown manuscript by Tomasso Sassetti, Newberry Lib., Castelvetro Mss. Cod. 78/2, describing the massacres at Lyon and especially in Paris: "Brieve Raccontamento del Gran Macello fatto nella città di Parigi." Sassetti reported that printers were active among the Lyon killers; but his assertion is not borne out by any other accounts by residents of Lyon, nor by the patterns of deaths (see n. 94 above). Only two merchant-publishers are known to have had a connection with the massacres – Guillaume Rouillé, who was a Consul at the time and thus bears some responsibility for what happened, and Alexandre Marsigli, a Luccan exile who killed a merchant Paolo Minutoli in the hope that he would be pardoned in Lucca and allowed to return. Sassetti had just arrived in Lyon when the Vespers occurred.

111. Crespin, *Martyrs*, 3: 692.

112. *Hist. eccl.*, 1: 227, 719; Crespin, *Martyrs*, 3: 522; *Discours des troubles advenus en la Ville de Pamies*, p. 325; Bosquet, *Histoire*, pp. 148–50. Also see Chap. 3, "City Women and Religious Change."

113. *Hist. eccl.*, 1: 913; Crespin, *Martyrs*, 3: 203–4, 392. At Lyon a woman was among those arrested for her actions in the Corpus Christi day riot of 1561: ADR, B, Sénéchaussée, Sentences, 1561–62, sentence of Aug. 14, 1561. Catholic women stoned a Protestant mercer at Vire in Normandy: *Hist. eccl.*, 2: 846.

114. Lyon: Guéraud, *Chronique*, p. 145. Castelnaudary: *Hist. eccl.*, 3: 157. Marseille, Toulon, Poignans, Forcalquier: *Hist. eccl.*, 3: 412–15. Provins and Sens: Haton, *Mémoires*, pp. 194, 315. In addition, the "petits enfans" ("children") of Auxerre start stoning the doors of a conventicle in 1561, and the "petits enfans" of Draguignan, egged on by priests and councillors in the Parlement of Aix, kill the important Protestant Antoine de Richier, Sieur de Mouvans, in 1560: *Hist. eccl.*, 1: 852, 421. The tug-of-war over a corpse by boys ten to twelve years old in Provins has already been described, as has the riot in Pamiers, provoked by the "jeunes hommes" ("young men") of the festive youth group. Already in Geneva in 1533, we see Catholic "enfants," twelve to fifteen years old, joining their mothers in Catholic crowds that stoned heretical women: Jeanne de Jussie, *Levain*, p. 47.

115. Toulouse: Bosquet, *Histoire*, p. 46; Crespin, *Martyrs*, 3: 726. (Students also participated in the 1572 massacres at Orléans, *ibid.*, 3: 695.) Poitiers: *Hist. eccl.*, 1: 227–28; 2: 703. Rouen: *Hist. eccl.*, 2: 719. Flanders: Crespin, *Martyrs*, 3: 519, n. 1; 522.

116. F. N. Taillepied, *Recueil des Antiquitez et Singularitez de la Ville de Rouen* (Rouen, 1587), pp. 195–97; L'Estoile, *Mémoires-journaux*, 3: 243–44, 247. Peter Ascoli also describes the role of children in the League procession of 1589 in "The Sixteen and the Paris League, 1589–1591" (University of California at Berkeley Ph.D. thesis, 1971). In a recent essay on fifteenth-century Florence, Richard Trexler has emphasized the role of male adolescents first in the processional life of the city and then as zealous and active supporters of Savonarola's war on the vanities: "Ritual in Florence: Adolescence and Salvation in the Renaissance," in *The Pursuit of Holiness in Late Medieval and Renaissance Religion*, ed. C. Trinkaus with H. A. Oberman (Leiden, 1974). Also cf. N. Z. Davis, "Some Tasks and Themes in the Study of Popular Religion," *ibid.*, pp. 318–26.

117. See n. 72 above. Philippi, *Mémoires*, p. 623.

118. For the role of Protestant targets in Nemours, see *Hist. eccl.*, 1: 834. For the white crosses in Mâcon, *ibid.*, 3: 518; and the red bonnets in Bordeaux, Crespin, *Martyrs*, 3: 729. For "Vive la Croix" in Toulouse, "Le Loup" (a Catholic password in Vire in Normandy), "Vive l'Evangile" in La Rochelle, see *Hist. eccl.*, 3: 33; 2: 845, 989.

119. *Hist. eccl.*, 1: 355, 844; *Discours des troubles advenus en la Ville de Pamies*, pp. 319–20.

120. *Hist. eccl.*, 3: 487; Crespin, *Martyrs*, 3: 287, 641; *Hist. eccl.*, 3: 158–59; 1: 913. Also see the "company" of horsemen of the draper Cosset of Meaux, founded in 1572 right after the massacres to round up and kill Huguenots who had escaped to nearby villages (Crespin, *Martyrs*,

3: 684), and the image-breaking band formed in 1562 in Mont-de-Marsan (*Hist. eccl.*, 2: 963–64).
121. Haton, *Mémoires*, p. 334. In Annonay in 1573, a young man, formerly head of the *Bazoche* or festive society of law clerks of Vismes, put himself at the head of eighty men "of his type" and lived off the countryside. This was evidently a Protestant band of young men. Achille Gamon, *Mémoires*, p. 615.
122. *Hist. eccl.*, 1: 983–86; Crespin, *Martyrs*, 3: 390–91.
123. Estèbe, *Tocsin*, pp. 194, 197.
124. The nonresistance of the Protestants is an extraordinary fact that emerges from all accounts of the 1572 massacres and that is in contrast with the militant high morale of the Protestants when they were attacked in, say, 1561–62. The Protestant martyrs described in Crespin in 1572 either try to run away – the males sometimes dressed in their wives' clothes (*Martyrs*, 3: 698) – or die bravely in their faith. When an individual does try to resist (such as Maistre Mamert, a schoolteacher and swordmaster in Orléans), it is the occasion of some notice by Crespin: *Martyrs*, 3: 697.

7. Printing and the People

1. *Euvres de Louize Labé Lionnoize. Revues et Corrigees par ladite Dame* (Lyon: Jean I de Tournes, 1556), Dedication. Trial of *meulquinier* Antoine Steppen, native of Cambrai, in C. L. Frossard, "La réforme dans le Cambrésis au XVIe siècle," BSHPF 3 (1854): 530. *Remonstrances, et Mémoires, pour les Compagnons Imprimeurs, de Paris et Lyon: Opposans. Contre les Libraires, maistres Imprimeurs desdits lieux: Et adiointz* (n.p., n.d. [Lyon, 1572]), f. A i^r (hereafter cited as *Remonstrances*). *Le Chirurgie de Paulus Aegineta . . . Ung Opuscule de Galien des Tumeurs . . . Le tout traduict de Latin en Francoys par Maistre Pierre Tolet Medecin de l'Hospital de Lyon* (Lyon: Etienne Dolet, 1540), p. 6.
2. Among many sources, see Robert I Estienne, *Dictionnaire Francoislatin, autrement dict Les Mots Francois, avec les manieres duser diceulx, tournez en Latin* (Paris: Robert I Estienne, 1549), pp. 454–55; Charles Du Moulin, *Summaire du livre analytique des contractz* (Paris, 1547), ff. A ii^v, 33^r; Guillaume de La Perrière, *Le miroir politique* (Paris, 1567), ff. 21^v, 58^v; Guillaume Paradin, *Memoires de l'histoire de Lyon* (Lyon, 1573), pp. 282–85; Claude de Seyssel, *La Grand' Monarchie de France* (Paris, 1557 [1st ed. 1519]), f. 16^r-v.
3. Robert Mandrou, *De la culture populaire aux 17e et 18e siècles. La bibliothèque bleue de Troyes* (Paris, 1964), pp. 9–10, 18, 22. Geneviève Bollème, "Littérature populaire et littérature de colportage au 18e siècle," in *Livre et société dans la France du XVIIIe siècle* (Paris, 1965), p. 65; idem, *Les almanachs populaires aux XVIIe et XVIIIe siècles. Essai d'histoire sociale* (Paris, 1969), "Avant-propos." See also Marc Soriano, *Les Contes de Perrault. Culture savante et traditions populaires* (Paris, 1968), pp. 480–81.
4. Louis B. Wright, *Middle-Class Culture in Elizabethan England* (Ithaca, New York, 1958 [1st ed. 1935]), p. 18; Mandrou, *Culture populaire*, pp. 19–20, 162. Bollème, however, has expressed some doubts about *whose* world view is revealed in almanacs and other popular literature.
5. *La decoration Dhumaine nature et aornement des dames. Compile . . . par Maistre Andre le Fournier docteur regent en la faculte de Medecine en Luniversite de Paris* (Lyon: Claude Veycellier, 1532).
6. A. H. Schutz, *Vernacular Books in Parisian Private Libraries of the Sixteenth Century, according to the Notarial Inventories* (University of North Carolina Studies in the Romance Languages and Literatures 25; Chapel Hill, 1955), pp. 39, 78, n. 85. Albert Labarre, *Le livre dans la vie amiénoise du seizième siècle. L'enseignement des inventaires après décès* (Paris, 1971), p. 274. *Le grand calendrier et compost des bergiers: Compose par le bergier de la grand [sic] montagne* (Lyon: Jean Cantarel, 1551), signature "Noel de Aloncourt, advocat pour le roy A Sens," copy in the Houghton Library, Harvard University.
Bollème admits to the wide range in the social background of readers of almanacs in the seventeenth and eighteenth centuries (*Almanachs*, p. 15).
7. Schutz, *Vernacular Books*, p. 34 (Arnauld de Villeneuve, to whom the *Tresor des povres* was attributed), p. 81, n. 137. E. Coyecque, *Recueil d'actes notariés relatifs à l'histoire de*

Paris et de ses environs au 16e siècle ("Histoire generale de Paris"; Paris, 1924), no. 106.

8. Mandrou, *Culture populaire*, pp. 162–63. Noel Taillepied, *Psichologie ou traité de l'apparition des esprits* (Paris, 1588), chap. 6. See also Chapter 5 above.

9. Jean-Paul Sartre, *Qu'est-ce que la littérature?* (1948), cited by Robert Escarpit in his valuable essay "Le littéraire et le social" (R. Escarpit, ed., *Le littéraire et le social. Eléments pour une sociologie de la littérature* [Paris, 1970], p. 18).

10. J. R. Goody, ed., *Literacy in Traditional Societies* (Cambridge, 1968). Elizabeth L. Eisenstein, "Some Conjectures About the Impact of Printing on Western Society and Thought: A Preliminary Report," *Journal of Modern History* 40 (1968): 1–56; *idem*, "The Advent of Printing and the Problem of the Renaissance," *Past and Present* 45 (Nov. 1969): 19–89; *idem* (with T. K. Rabb), "Debate. The Advent of Printing and the Problem of the Renaissance," *Past and Present* 52 (Aug. 1971): 134–44; *idem*, "L'avènement de l'imprimerie et la Réforme," *Annales ESC* 26 (1971): 1355–82. For a study of popular culture that uses a "relational" approach, see M. Agulhon, "Le problème de la culture populaire en France autour de 1848," Davis Center Seminar, Princeton University (May 1974).

For a critique of some of the techniques used by social historians in the study of books and literary culture in the eighteenth century, see R. Darnton, "Reading, Writing and Publishing in Eighteenth-Century France: A Case Study in the Sociology of Literature," in Felix Gilbert and S. R. Graubard, eds., *Historical Studies Today* (New York, 1972), pp. 238–50.

11. Lucien Febvre and Henri-Jean Martin, *L'apparition du livre* (Paris, 1958), pp. 285–86, 173–237; Henri-Jean Martin, *Livre, pouvoirs et société à Paris au XVIIe siècle (1598–1701)* (Geneva, 1969), pp. 319–26. N. Z. Davis, "Publisher Guillaume Rouillé, Businessman and Humanist," in R. J. Schoeck, ed., *Editing Sixteenth Century Texts* (Toronto, 1966), pp. 72–77. Schutz, *Vernacular Books*, pp. 31–73 (first appearance of craftsmen and small merchants among book-owners is in the 1520's); Coyecque, *Recueil*, nos. 270, 588. Roger Doucet, *Les bibliothèques parisiennes au XVIe siècle* (Paris, 1956), pp. 171–75 (lists names and occupations of book-owners in 194 Parisian inventories after death from 1493–1560). Out of 94 inventories from the years 1540–60, ten percent relate to persons below the level of the commercial and legal elite. Calculating from Martin's analysis of Parisian inventories after death in the seventeenth century (*Livre, pouvoirs et société*, p. 492), we get roughly ten percent of the book collections in the hands of lesser merchants, barber-surgeons, painters, and craftsmen.

12. Roger Vaultier, *Le folklore pendant la guerre de Cent Ans d'après les lettres de rémission du trésor des chartes* (Paris, 1965), p. 106. Bernard Guenée, *Tribunaux et gens de justice dans le bailliage de Senlis à la fin du moyen age (vers 1380–vers 1550)* (Paris, 1963), pp. 277–78, 317. Michel Devèze, *La vie de la forêt française au XVIe siècle* (Paris, 1961), 2: 112–13.

13. Emmanuel Le Roy Ladurie, *Les paysans de Languedoc* (Paris, 1966), pp. 345–47. Yvonne Bézard, *La vie rurale dans le sud de la région parisienne de 1450 à 1560* (Paris, 1929), pp. 249–52, 185–86. Guenée, *Tribunaux*, pp. 187–93. Jacques Toussaert, *Le sentiment religieux en Flandre à la fin du moyen age* (Paris, 1963), pp. 60–66. M. Gonon, *La vie quotidienne en Lyonnais d'après les testaments, XIVe–XVIe siècles* (Paris, 1968), p. 54 and p. 54, n. 2 (none of the testaments that prescribe the placing of children in school are from peasant parents). Bernard Bonnin, "L'éducation dans les classes populaires rurales en Dauphiné au XVIIe siècle," in *Le XVIIe siècle et l'éducation. Colloque de Marseille*, supplement to *Marseille* 88 (1972): 63–68 (I am grateful to Daniel Hickey for calling this article to my attention). A major new study of literacy in France from 1650 to the twentieth century is now under way by François Furet.

ADR, B, Insinuations, Donations, 14, ff.148^r–149^v. Isabelle Guérin, *La vie rurale en Sologne aux XIVe et XVe siècles* (Paris, 1960), p. 231, n. 5. Coyecque, *Recueil*, nos. 4078, 4806, 5380. The seventeenth and eighteenth centuries were periods when rural schools spread significantly.

14. Charles Estienne, *L'agriculture et maison rustique* (Paris: Jacques du Puys, 1564), chap. 7, f. 9^r. Paul Raveau, *L'agriculture et les classes paysannes. La transformation de la propriété dans le haut Poitou au 16e siècle* (Paris, 1926), p. 259. René Choppin, *Traité de Privileges des Personnes Vivans aux Champs* [1st ed. in Latin, 1575] in *Oeuvres* (Paris, 1662–63), 3: 16. René Fédou, *Les hommes de loi lyonnais à la fin du moyen age* (Paris, 1964), pp. 158–60.

15. E. Campardon and A. Tuetey, eds., *Inventaire des registres des insinuations du Châtelet*

de Paris pendant les règnes de François Ier et de Henri II (Paris, 1906), no. 735. ADR, B, Insinuations, Testaments, 1560—61, ff. 9^r—10^v; Henri and Julien Baudrier, *Bibliographie lyonnaise* (Lyon, 1895—1912), 9: 306.

16. Thomas Platter (1499—1582), *Autobiographie*, trans. M. Helmer *(Cahiers des Annales* 22 [Paris, 1964]), p. 42. Thomas taught one of his young cousins his ABC's in one day and that lad left the village soon after for a scholarly career (p. 50). When Platter returned much later to found a school for a short period, it was with a special evangelical mission.

No books are mentioned in the reviews of household possessions and wills made by Bézard, *Vie rurale;* Guérin, *Vie rurale;* Gonon, *Vie quotidienne;* and Raveau, *Agriculture.* Note the remarkably infrequent mention of books in notarial acts in the rural Mâconnais even in the seventeenth through nineteenth centuries (Suzanne Tardieu, *La vie domestique dans le mâconnais rural préindustriel* [Paris, 1964], p. 358 and p. 358, n. 2).

17. Prices taken from inventories after death in Labarre, *Livre*, p. 274, n. 20; Coyecque, *Recueil*, nos. 196, 96. The evaluation of Books of Hours varies considerably, depending on illustrations and bindings. The prices attributed to the same books when found in quantity in printers' stock are lower: the *Tresor des povres* at about eight deniers the volume (115s. 6d. for 165 copies) and the *Calendrier des bergers* at about six deniers the volume (69s. for 150 copies) in an inventory of 1522 (Doucet, *Bibliothèques*, p. 102, nos. 134, 150). Presumably these are wholesale prices for books that might not yet have been bound.

18. Martin, *Livre, pouvoirs et société*, pp. 319—20. When the Sire de Gouberville acquired books for his little library at the manor of Mesnil-au-Val in Normandy, they were purchased in Paris and Bayeux (A. Tollemer, *Un Sire de Gouberville, gentilhomme campagnard au cotentin de 1553 à 1562* [Paris, 1972], pp. 204—9). In the 1570's and early 1580's, the bibliophile François de La Croix du Maine found it much harder to acquire books in Le Mans and vicinity than in Paris *(Premier volume de la Bibliotheque du Sieur de la Croix-du-Maine* [Paris, 1584], Preface, f. a vii^r). A 1635 Paris edition of a book on surgery and health by H. Fierabras was purchased in July 1669 "a la foire de beaucaire" (written in the copy at the medical library of the University of California at San Francisco). It seems unlikely that books were sold at the Beaucaire fairs a century earlier.

19. On the variety of speech and dialect in sixteenth-century France and the growing separation between written and spoken language, see F. Brunot et al., *Histoire de la langue française des origines à 1900* (Paris, 1905—53), 1: xiii—xiv, 304ff; 2: 174—75.

Grégoire de Rostrenin, *Dictionnaire françois-celtique ou françois-Breton* (Rennes, 1732), preface; a Breton-French-Latin dictionary (Tréguier: Jean Calvet, 1499); a book of the Passion and Resurrection, the Death of the Virgin, and the Life of Man in Breton verse (Paris: Yves Quillevere, 1530); the Four Ends of Man in Breton verse (Morlaix, 1570); and two saints' lives in Breton.

G. Brunet, *Poésies basques de Bernard Dechepare . . . d'après l'édition de Bordeaux, 1545* (Bordeaux, 1847). Julien Vinson, *Essai d'une bibliographie de la langue basque* (Paris, 1891—98), 1, nos. 1—5 (only two of these entries were published in France; the others were printed in Pamplona or Bilbao). See n. 40 below.

20. *Chansons nouvelles en lengaige provensal* (black-letter; n.p., n.d.). Augier Gaillard, *Las Obras* (Bordeaux, 1574); L. Bellaud de la Bellaudière, *Obros et rimos provenssalos* (Marseille: P. Mascaron, 1595). La Croix du Maine lists four persons with manuscripts in Provençal (Jean de Nostredame, Guillaume Boyer, Olivier de Lorgues, and Pierre de Bonifaccis), but I cannot find any evidence of their being printed in that language.

21. *Cy est le compost et Kalendrier des bergeres . . . nouvellement compose sans contredire a celluy des bergiers* (Paris: "in the Hotel de Beauregart in the rue Cloppin at the Ensign of le Roy Prestre Iehan" [Guy Marchant and Jean Petit], n.d. [1499]). Signature in the copy at the University of Toronto Rare Book Library: "N. Chomat." The shepherdesses are named Sebille and Beatrix.

Bollème points out that the *Shepherds' Calendar* did not become part of the peddlers' literature, in a cheap edition, until the mid-seventeenth century *(Almanachs*, p. 40). Yet she sees the intended public for the work as always the peasants ("L'auteur qui, symboliquement, ne sait pas écrire donne au lecteur qui ne sait pas lire le moyen de se conduire mieux selon la sagesse naturelle. . . . Le Berger parle au berger, au laboureur, au paysan" – p. 16). I am suggesting, however, that the initial public for the work was not the peasants ("Who wants to have knowledge of the heavens . . . like the shepherds without letters [can here have it]. It is extracted and composed from their calendar and put into letters so that everyone can understand and know it like them. . . ." *Cy est le compost et kalendrier des bergiers nouvellement reffait* [Paris: Guy Marchant, 1493], f. h vii^v).

22. *Kalendrier des bergiers* (1493), f. h vii^v. Some of the verbal memory devices are recorded: ff. a v^r–a vi^r. Pierre Borel, *Tresor de Recherches et Antiquitez Gauloises et Françoises* (Paris, 1655), f. k iii^v.

23. *Kalendrier des bergiers* (1493), f. l iii^r; *Le grand Calendrier et compost des Bergers avec leur astrologie* (Troyes: Jean Lecoq, 154 [1]), ff. M i^r–M ii^r.

24. *Calendrier des Bergers* (1541), ff. O iiii^v–O v^v, J iv^v; *Kalendrier des bergiers* (1493), f. h iiii^v.

25. Jean Vostet, *Almanach, ou Prognostication des Laboureurs, reduite selon le Kalendrier Gregorien* (Paris: Jean Richer, 1588), f. 8^r.

26. Inventory after death of Jacques Nadreau, curé of Dampierre (Ile-de-France), includes the *Calendrier des bergers* and three other books (Jeanne Ferté, *La vie religieuse dans les campagnes parisiennes, 1622–1695* [Paris, 1962], p. 191 and p. 191, n. 147).

The religious section of the *Kalendrier* of 1493 goes from f. c iv^v–f. h i^r. The woodcut of the vices is a schematized layout. The 1541 *Calendrier* has two literal trees with branches showing the Fruits of the Flesh and Fruits of the Spirit.

27. "Chanson Nouvelle d'un compagnon nouveau marié qui n'a sceu iouyr de son espousee iusques à la troisieme nuict, sur le chant 'sus, mon amy, sus et la donc,' " in *Les Ioyeusetez Facecies et Folastres Imaginacions de Caresme Prenant . . .* (Paris, 1830–31), 1: 64–68.

28. L. Petit de Julleville, *Histoire du théâtre en France. Les mystères* (Paris, 1880), 1: 373–74. Arnold Van Gennep, *Manuel de folklore français contemporain* (Paris, 1943), 1.1: 209.

29. Petit de Julleville, *Théâtre*, 1: 384. Coyecque, *Recueil*, no. 4470. Perhaps the Saint Victor referred to here is Victorinus, the rhetorician and teacher of Jerome, who, while still a pagan, had a statue made to him in the Forum. The tale of the three-year-old martyr and his faithful martyred mother Julithe (d. 230) was well known in France, where numerous villages were named after him. He is included in the *Golden Legend*. See also G. Hérelle, *Les théâtres ruraux en France . . . depuis le XIVe siècle jusqu'à nos jours* (Paris, 1930).

30. F. Lesure, "Eléments populaires dans la chanson français au début du 16e siècle," in *Musique et poésie au XVIe siècle* (Colloques internationaux du CNRS, Sciences Humaines, 5; Paris, 1954), pp. 169–75. Patrice Coirault, *Recherches sur notre ancienne chanson populaire traditionnelle* (Paris, 1927–33), pp. 82–83; *Notre chanson folklorique*, p. 155–64.

31. Vaultier, *Folklore*, pp. 111–12; Mandrou, *Culture populaire*, p. 18; André Varangnac, *Civilisation traditionelle et genres de vie* (Paris, 1970), pp. 96–97, 209; Tardieu, *Vie domestique*, pp. 154–62. Maurice Agulhon, "Les Chambrées en Basse Provence: histoire et ethnologie," *Revue historique* 498 (1971): 359–60.

32. Noel du Fail, *Propos rustiques de Maistre Leon Ladulfi Champenois* (Lyon: Jean I de Tournes, 1547), ed. A. de La Borderie (Paris, 1878), pp. 36–37. The *veillée* at which these tales are told is supposed to have occurred not in 1547, but in the youth of one of the peasants. E. Le Roy Ladurie, "Mélusine ruralisée," Annales ESC 26 (1971): 604–6. On women as storytellers, see, for instance, Soriano, *Contes de Perrault*, p. 79.

33. Du Fail, *Propos*, pp. 15, 51. French editions of Aesop: Lyon, 1490 and 1499, prepared by the Augustinian Julien de Macho; new rhymed edition by Guillaume Corrozet, Paris 1542 and after. Greek and Latin editions: Elizabeth Armstrong, *Robert Estienne, Royal Printer* (Cambridge, 1954), p. 97; Germaine Warkentin, "Some Renaissance Schoolbooks in the Osborne Collection," *Renaissance and Reformation* 5, 3 (May 1969): 37. Urban ownership of Aesop: La-barre, *Livre*, p. 208; Schutz, *Vernacular Books*, pp. 72–73.

Editions of the *Roman de la Rose* in its "ancient language": fourteen between 1481 and 1528 in Paris and Lyon; three prose versions "moralised" by Jean de Molinet, 1500–1521; four editions between 1526 and 1538 in the translation attributed to Marot. No further editions until 1735! (Clearly the *Roman* did not become part of the peddlers' literature.) On these editions, on interest in the *Roman* among poets, and on Marot as probable translator, see Antonio Viscardi, "Introduction," in *Le Roman de la Rose, dans la version attribuée à Clément Marot*, ed. S. F. Baridon (Milan, 1954), pp. 11–90. Urban ownership of the *Roman*: Labarre, *Livre*, p. 210; Schutz, *Vernacular Books*, p. 67; Doucet, *Bibliothèques*, p. 87, n. 39.

34. I am grateful to E. Howard Bloch, Joseph Duggan, and John Benton for suggestions on this subject. Though many medieval manuscripts remain of the *Roman de la Rose* — some 300 — they are unlikely to have circulated among the peasants in this form. There is a short version of the *Roman* in manuscript, with much of the philosophical material omitted (E. Langlois, *Les manuscrits du roman de la Rose. Description et classement* [Lille, 1910], pp. 385–86). Here again there is no evidence that these excisions were made to prepare it for reading to peasants.

35. O. Douen, "La réforme en Picardie," BSHPF 8 (1859): 393. Crespin, *Martyrs*, 2: 468–69; P. Chaix, *Recherches sur l'imprimerie à Genève de 1550 à 1564* (Geneva, 1954), p. 194. Bernard Palissy, *Recepte véritable par laquelle tous les hommes de la France pourront apprendre à multiplier et augmenter leurs thrésors, in Oeuvres complètes* (Paris, 1961), pp. 104–5.

36. Crespin, *Martyrs*, 2: 423–25; 1: 335.

37. On the carter Barthélemy Hector: *Livre des habitants de Genève*, ed. P.-F. Geisendorf (Geneva, 1957), p. 55; H.-L. Schlaepfer, "Laurent de Normandie," in *Aspects de la propagande religieuse* (Geneva, 1957), p. 198; Crespin, *Martyrs*, 2: 437–38. On the peddlers in the Lyonnais, ADR, B, Sénéchaussée, Sentences, 1556–1559, Sentence of July 1559. Two of them, the dressmaker Girard Bernard, native of Champagne, and the shoemaker Antoine Tallencon or Tallenton, native of Gascony, purchased books from Laurent de Normandie a few months before their arrest (Schlaepfer, "Laurent de Normandie," p. 200).

38. See, for instance, Marcel Cauvin, "Le protestantisme dans le Contentin," BSHPF 112 (1966): 367–68; 115 (1960): 80–81. Le Roy Ladurie, *Paysans*, 348–51. For a picture of Protestant congregations in the seventeenth century in which individual *laboureurs* play their part, see P. H. Chaix, "Les protestants en Bresse en 1621," *Cahiers d'histoire* 14 (1969): 252–54.

39. Chaix, *Recherches sur l'imprimerie*, pp. 120–22; Eugénie Droz, "Le calendrier genevois, agent de la propagande" and "Le calendrier lyonnais," in *Chemins de l'hérésie* (Geneva, 1970–74), 2: 433–56; 3: 1–29. I have used the *Calendrier historial* printed at Lyon in 1563 by Jean I de Tournes and bound with the *Psalms* and *La forme des prieres ecclésiastiques*, printed by de Tournes for Antoine Vincent (Houghton Library; Droz no. 16); and *Calendrier Historial et Lunaire* (Lyon: printed by Symphorien Barbier, for Antoine Vincent, 1566), bound with the New Testament printed by Barbier for Vincent (Pacific School of Religion; Droz no. 19). See also Jean Delumeau, "Les réformateurs et la superstition," *Actes du colloque l'Amiral de Coligny et son temps (1972)* (Paris, 1974), pp. 451–87.

The Protestant *Calendriers* were not the first to use historical material. A 1550 *Heures de Nostre Dame a l'usaige de Romme*, published by Magdaleine Boursette, includes dates in its calendar: the death of the scholar Vatable, the Concordat of Leo X and François Ier, the birth of Henri II, etc. (Paris, 1550).

40. Vinson, *Essai*, nos. 3–4; L. Desgraves, *L'imprimerie à la Rochelle 2. Les Haultin* (Geneva, 1960): 1–3. The only other example I know of French Protestant publications in regional dialect is the catechism in "bernois," published by Pierre du Bois at Pau in 1564 at the request of Pastor Merlin for the "catechistes de ce pays de Bearn" (Schlaepfer, "Laurent de Normandie," p. 205, n. 1).

41. Crespin, *Martyrs*, 2: 438. The publisher of Protestant propaganda sometimes shared part of the risk with the peddler, contracting, for instance, that if the books were seized within a two-month period by the "enemies of the Gospel," the *libraire* would bear all the loss (Schlaepfer, "Laurent de Normandie," p. 199, n. 10; Chaix, *Recherches*, p. 59).

42. [Antoine Mizaud], *Les Ephemerides perpetuelles de l'air: autrement l'Astrologie des Rustiques* (Paris: Jacques Kerver, 1554), dedication. Signatures in the Houghton Library copy: "Claude Lorot, nimdunois [?], Claude Rinart son nepveu. Arte collude." On Mizaud's other works, see La Croix du Maine, *Bibliotheque*, pp. 17–18.

43. Jacques Guillemeau (1550–1613), *De la grossesse et accouchement des femmes . . . Par feu Jacques Guillemeau, Chirurgien ordinaire du Roy* (Paris, 1620; 1st ed. Paris, 1609), f. a iii^{r-v}.

44. Le Sieur L'Estoile, *Ephemerides ou Almanach iournalier pour l'an 1625* (Lyon, n.d.

[1625]), pp. 75—78. On gardens in the Languedoc, see Le Roy Ladurie, *Paysans*, pp. 60—68.
45. *Almanach, ou Prognostication des Laboureurs, reduite selon le Kalendrier Gregorien. Avec quelques observations particulieres sur l'Annee 1588 de si longtemps menacee. Par Iean Vostet Breton* (Paris: Jean Richer, 1588). The excerpts given by Bollème from *Le Messager boiteux* (pp. 77—78) include both the old verses and those made up by Vostet.
A German work with a similar rewriting of the year's sayings for the peasants appeared in 1590: Johann Rasch, *New Löstag. Nutzliche bedencken und unterscheidung der pöflischen alten Lösstag, die feldregel und Bauerenpractic angehend* (Rorschach, 1590). Archer Taylor, *The Proverb* (Cambridge, Mass., 1931), p. 117.
46. René Choppin (1537—1606), *De Privilegiis Rusticorum: Lib. III* (Paris: Nicolas Chesnau, 1575 [signature in the copy at the Bancroft Library: "Ex libris Calistriis"]). See further on Choppin and this work, N. Z. Davis, "René Choppin on More's Utopia," *Moreana* 19—20 (Nov. 1968): 91—96; and G. Marc'hadour, "Thomas More et René Choppin," *Moreana* 26 (June 1970), pp. 55—57.
47. Choppin, *Privilegiis*, Preface; poem to the "Diligenti Ruricolae." The French translation first appeared in 1622—23, in a posthumous edition of Choppin's works. There were two other Latin editions of the *Privileges* during Choppin's life (1582, 1590).
48. N. Weiss, "Vidimus des lettres patentes de François Ier, 1529," BSHPF 59 (1910), 501—4; Le Roy Ladurie, *Paysans*, 380—404; Bézard, *Vie rurale*, 289—90; V. Carrière, *Introduction aux études d'histoire ecclésiastique locale* (Paris, 1936), 3: 319—52. S. Gigon, *La révolte de la gabelle en Guyenne* (Paris, 1906); G. Procacci, *Classi sociali e monarchia assoluta nella Francia della prima metà del secolo XVI* (Turin, 1955), pp. 161—73, 213—30; Choppin, *Oeuvres* (1662—63), 3: 22 ("*la multitude des Rustiques de la Guyenne, qui alloient tumultueusement armée de villages en villages en l'an 1594*"). Jean Moreau, *Mémoires . . . sur les Guerres de la Ligue en Bretagne*, ed. H. Waquet (Archives historiques de Bretagne, 1; Quimper, 1960), pp. 11—14, 75—76. A. Le M. de La Borderie and B. Pocquet, *Histoire de Bretagne* (Rennes, 1906), 5: 173—81. Henri Drouot, *Mayenne et la Bourgogne, Etude sur la Ligue (1587—1596)* (Paris, 1937), 1: 39—55; 2: 291—92. Claude de Rubys, *Histoire veritable de la ville de Lyon* (Lyon, 1604), pp. 430—31; Daniel Hickey, "The Socio-Economic Context of the French Wars of Religion. A Case Study: Valentinois-Diois" (unpublished Ph.D. dissertation, Dept. of History, McGill University, 1973), chap. 4; L. S. Van Doren, "Revolt and Reaction in the City of Romans, Dauphiné, 1579—80," *Sixteenth Century Journal* 5 (1974): 72—77. See also Madeleine Foisil, *La révolte des Nu-Pieds et les révoltes normandes de 1639* (Paris, 1970), 178—83, on nicknames and organization of the Nu-Pieds.
49. ADR, 15G22, ff. 130r, 288r. Examples of schoolteachers and reckonmasters: ADR, 3E6942, ff. 315r—316v; 3E4984, June 20, 1564; 3E8029, Sept. 7, 1564; 3E336, f. 44r; 3E7184, ff. 238v—239r; 3E7170, Feb. 4, 1561/62; B, Insinuations, Donations, 25, f. 88r; AML, GG384, f. 43r, GG435, no. 415.
50. See Chapter 2 above. Jean-Pierre Seguin, *L'information en France de Louis XII à Henri II* (Geneva, 1961), p. 52.
51. ADR, 3E821, July 5, 1580; *Remonstrances . . . pour les Compagnons Imprimeurs* (cited in n. 1), f. A iv. Guenée, *Tribunaux*, pp. 213—14.
52. The Lyon analysis is based on a study of hundreds of contracts in ADR, 3E, for the decades of the 1560's and 1570's. Le Roy Ladurie, *Paysans*, pp. 333, 347, 882.
53. Le Roy Ladurie, *Paysans*, p. 333. According to André Bourde, in a lecture given at the University of California at Berkeley in December 1972, it was only in the course of the seventeenth century that French made important gains among the patriciate of Marseille, while the people continued to speak Provençal.
54. See note 11 above and Coyecque, *Recueil*, nos. 85—116; 241—270; 584—609; 3749—3791. The Amiens figures are calculated by me from the data given in Labarre, *Livre*, pp. 118—26 and 62—104. I have defined the "artisanal" group slightly differently from M. Labarre for purposes of this paper; that is, I have *excluded* from my count the unskilled workers included on pp. 124—26 and *added* some of the goldsmiths, butchers, etc. that Labarre has categorized with the "*classe marchande.*"
55. Labarre, *Livre*, pp. 260—63. Coyecque, *Recueil*, nos. 3768, 3791. A one-book library in

Lyon in 1563 in a room rented by a mason's helper from a miller's daughter: *"une bible en francois."* A five-book library in Lyon belonging to a merchant with a lot of paintings and furniture: *"Le livre des croniques, Les ordonnances des privileges des foyres de Lyon, Les troys miroirs du monde, La premiere partie de nouveau testament, Une Bible en francoys"* (ADR, 3E7179, ff. 467r—468r, 576r—577v).

56. The relation of prices to wages and purchases is, of course, rough:

Book	Price, place, date
Jean de Vauzelles, *Police subsidaire* . . .	
des povres	5 deniers, Montpellier, 1535
Livre d'arismetique	1½ deniers wholesale, Paris, 1522
Jacques de Bourbon, *Prinse . . . de Rodes*	3 sous, Paris, 1547/48
La bible des Noelz	2 sous, Paris, 1547/48
Philippe de Commines, *Les croniques du roy*	
Loys unze	5 sous, Paris, 1547/48

Sources: L. Galle, "Les livres lyonnais," *Revue du Lyonnais* 23 (5th ser., 1897): 431; Doucet, *Bibliothèques*, pp. 92, 119, 118, 126.

In the 1520's in "normal" years at Lyon, a loaf of *pain farain* cost 5 deniers. In the 1530's and 1540's, a pair of children's shoes might cost 4 s. 6 d.; a pound of candlewax, 2 s. Painters' journeymen and printers' journeymen had wages roughly equivalent to 8 s. per day in the 1540's; journeymen and workers in the building trades, about 5—6 s. per day.

57. Schlaepfer, "Laurent de Normandie," p. 207: 4 s. per copy of the New Testament, 16o. Presumably this is a wholesale price. Bibles and New Testaments varied enormously in price depending on format, illustration, etc. An illustrated New Testament in an Amiens Library in 1564 was estimated at 5 livres (Labarre, *Livre*, p. 311).

Le moyen de parvenir a la congnoissance de Dieu et consequemment à salut (Lyon: Robert Granjon, 1562; 1st ed. 1557), ff. g viiv—viiir.

58. Coyecque, *Recueil*, no. 588. Medieval university students often used manuscripts as security for loans. Crespin, *Martyrs*, 2: 430.

59. Bibl. Nat., Mss., Collection Dupuy, 630, f. 171r: *Memoire des livres que iay presté.* On book loans in the circle of the Sire de Gouberville, see Tollemer, *Gouberville*, p. 205.

60. Henri Hauser, *Ouvriers du temps passé* (5th ed.; Paris, 1927), pp. 82—85. Hauser points out how often regulations against night work were violated. Even when they existed, they prohibited work after 8, 9, or 10 P.M. In 1539, the Lyon printing ateliers ran till 10 P.M.; in 1572, they closed at 8 or 9 P.M.

61. For instance, *Patrons de diverses manieres Inventez tressubtilement Duysans a Brodeurs et Lingieres . . . A tous massons, menuisiers et verriers . . .* (Lyon: Pierre de Saint Lucie, n.d.). Vannoccio Biringuccio, *La Pyrotechnie ou Art du feu . . . traduite d'Italien en François par feu maistre Iacques Vincent* (Paris: Guillaume Iullian, 1572; 1st ed. 1556).

62. *Art et science de arismetique moult utille et profitable a toutes gens et facille a entendre par la plume et par le gect subtil pour ceulx qui ne scavent lyre ne escripre* (Paris: the widow Trepperel and Jehan Jehannot, n.d. [ca. 1520]). Under the title *L'Arithmetique et maniere de apprendre a Chiffrer et compter par la plume et par les gectz*, this work or slight variants thereof appeared many times throughout the century. A late version is *Arithmetique facile à Apprendre a Chiffrer et compter par la plume et par les gects* (Lyon: Benoît Rigaud, 1594). See David Eugene Smith, *Rara Arithmetica* (4th ed.; New York, 1970).

Guillaume de la Taissonnière, *Brieve Arithmetique fort facile a comprendre et necessaire à tous ceux qui font traffiq de marchandise . . . Ie te veux faire en quinze iours Sçavoir autant d'Arithmetique, qu'elle suffira pour tous iours Exercer ton art et practique* (Lyon: Benoît Rigaud, 1570; Pierre Rigaud, 1610).

63. Jean Visagier, *Epigrammatorum Libri IIII* (Lyon: printed by Jean Barbou for Michel Parmentier, 1537), p. 282 (poem to Cathelin Pellin and Michel Blanc, thanking them for work on the edition). Baudrier, *Bibliographie lyonnaise* 12: 468. Bernard de Girard du Haillan, *De l'Estat et succez des affaires de France* (Geneva: Antoine Blanc, 1596), last-page note from the printer: "nourrie en ieunesse, avec Dolet, Marot, etc."

64. *La vie de Ma Dame saincte Marguerite, vierge et martyr, Avec son Antienne et Oraison*

(n.p., n.d. [ca. 1520]).Gargamelle refers to this custom in the first edition of *Gargantua*. She would rather hear a quotation from John 16 during her delivery than "la vie de saincte Marguerite ou quelque autre capharderie" (François Rabelais, *Oeuvres complètes*, ed. J. Boulenger and L. Scheler [Paris, 1955], p. 22, n. 4).

65. Crespin, *Martyrs*, 2: 670–71; Palissy, *Recepte veritable*, in *Oeuvres*, pp. 106–7.

66. Jean Bullant, *Recueil d'Horlographie, contenant la description fabrication et usage des Horloges solaires* (Paris: Léon Cavellat for the widow Cavellat, 1598; 1st ed. 1561), f. Aa ii^r-v. (Bound with Bullant's *Geometrie et horlographie*, the Bancroft Library copy of the *Recueil* was purchased for 25 sous in 1606 by Charles Cocquerel.)

67. *Larithmetique de Milles Denorry gentilhomme chartrain, contenant la reduction tant de toutes especes de monnoyes . . . que des aulnes . . . poids et autres mesures d'un pais à l'autre: la forme de l'achat, vente et distribution de toute sorte de marchandise* (Paris: Gilles Gorbin, 1574), f. A i^v. AML, EE25, f. 13^v, GG87, piece 18. IAML, CC150, CC275. De Norry was almost certainly not of noble origin. For further information on de Norry and the commercial arithmetic, see N. Z. Davis, "Mathematicians in the Sixteenth-Century French Academies: Some Further Evidence," *Renaissance News* 11 (1958): pp. 3–10; and "Sixteenth-Century Arithmetics on the Business Life," *Journal of the History of Ideas* 21 (1960): 18–48.

The significance of the author portrait in the printed book was made known to me by Ruth Mortimer in a lecture given at the University of Toronto in November 1971, "A Portrait of the Author in Sixteenth-Century Italy," shortly to appear in expanded form as a book with the same title. The distinction between the manuscript and the printed book is not absolute: there are portraits stressing the author in the former (e.g., Christine de Pisan) and pictures stressing the dedicatee in the latter (e.g., La Croix du Maine's *Bibliotheque* has an engraving of Henri III, not of the author). Other examples of French portraits of authors of the new kind: the poet Louise Labé; the midwife Louise Bourgeois (see Plate 15); the surgeon Ambrose Paré in his 1561 *Methode curative des playes* and after; and the mathematical practitioners Lucas Tremblay *(Prediction merveilleuse sur les deux ecclypses* [Lyon: Benoît Rigaud, 1588]), Valentin Mennher, and Bartelemy de Renterghem (the latter two lived respectively in Antwerp and Aix-la-Chapelle, but published commercial arithmetics and books on accounting in French at Antwerp.

68. *Declaration des Abus et Ignorance des Medecins . . . Compose par Pierre Braillier, Marchand Apotiquaire de Lyon . . .* (Lyon: Michel Jove, n.d. [Jan. 1557/58], copy at British Museum owned by the Parisian surgeon and book-collector François Rasse des Neux, 1567). Braillier was an apothecary of only moderate wealth in Lyon from the 1540's to the 1560's (AML, CC41, f. 26^v, CC1174, f. 17^r). Nicolas Houel, *Advertissement, et declaration de l'institution de la Maison de la Charité Chrestienne establie es fauxbourgs Sainct Marcel . . . 1578* (Paris, 1580). On Houel, see La Croix du Maine, *Bibliotheque*, pp. 346–47 and *Dictionnaire des lettres françaises* (Paris, 1951), *Le seizième siècle*, p. 381. La Croix du Maine mentioned six other apothecaries who had composed works.

69. Paré's first work was *La methode de traicter les playes* (1545), published four years after he had been raised from journeyman to master at the Hôtel-Dieu of Paris. For Paré's presentation of himself, his training, and his intended public, see the "Au lecteur" in his *Oeuvres* (Paris, 1575 and after) and the "Apologie" accompanying the 1585 *Oeuvres*. Concerning the conflict about his status and authority, see Paré, *Des monstres et prodiges*, ed. J. Céard (Geneva, 1971), pp. xiv–xv.

Apart from Paré, La Croix du Maine lists 24 other surgeons, 23 of them with compositions, nineteen publishing works from the 1540's through the 1580's.

70. Jacques Cartier, "one of the most knowledgeable and experienced Pilots of his time" (La Croix du Maine, *Bibliotheque*, p. 180). Auger Gaillard, dit Le Charron; Jean Barril; Guillaume Poetou *(Dictionnaire des lettres françaises, 16e s.*, pp. 339, 84, 577 for details on their works). On Barril, also see Chapter 2 above and n. 141.

71. *Discours admirables, de la nature des eaux et fonteines . . . des metaux, des sels et salines . . . Avec plusieurs autres excellens secrets des choses naturelles . . . Le tout dresse par dialogues . . . Par M. Bernard Palissy* (Paris: Martin Le Jeune, 1580), Dedication, Advertissement aux Lecteurs, and afternote (f. * 8^r).

72. Eisenstein, "Advent of Printing," p. 68.

73. La Croix du Maine, *Bibliotheque*, pp. 348–51. Dumont was the proofreader for La

Croix's own book. Ph. Renouard, *Imprimeurs parisiens, libraires, fondeurs de caractères, et correcteurs d'imprimerie* (Paris, 1898), pp. 229–30. Of the pamphlets listed by La Croix, I have used *Extraict d'une lettre escritte par un Gentilhomme du Roy de Polonne, à Miezerich, le xxv Ianvier, 1574* (Newberry Library, no title page; La Croix says the printer was Denis du Pré). On the general characteristics of this literature, see Seguin, *L'information en France* (cited in n. 50), pp. 9–53.

74.   List compiled from La Croix du Maine, *Bibliotheque*; Antoine du Verdier, *La Bibliotheque d'Antoine Du Verdier, seigneur de Vauprivas* (Lyon: Barthélemy Honorat, 1585); and *Dictionnaire des lettres françaises, 16e s.*

75.   Dedications to women in works by Marie Dentière (*Epistre tres utile . . . composée par une femme chrestienne . . . envoyee a la Royne de Navarre,* 1538; see Chapter 3 above); Louise Labé (*Euvres;* cited in n. 1); and Louise Bourgeois ("Helisenne aux Lisantes," from *Les Oeuvres de Ma Dame Helisenne de Crenne* [Paris: Etienne Grouleau, 1551], and "Epistre aux dames," from *Les Oeuvres de Mes-Dames des Roches de Poetiers mere et Fille* [Paris: Abel L'Angelier, 1578]).

76.   Of the 40 female writers listed by La Croix du Maine, 23 kept their work in manuscript.

77.   La Croix du Maine, *Bibliotheque,* p. 358; *Dictionnaire des lettres françaises, 16e s.,* p. 315; *Les Misères de la Femme mariée . . . mis en forme de stances par Madame Liebault* (Paris: Pierre Menier, n.d.), reprinted by E. Fournier, *Variétés historiques et littéraires* (Paris, 1855), 3: 321–31. Nicole Estienne was the wife of the physician Jean Liébault.

Louise Bourgeois (1563–1636), *Observations diverses sur la sterilité, perte de fruct, foecondité, accouchements et maladies des Femmes et Enfants nouveaux naix . . . par L. Bourgeois dite Boursier, sage femme de Royne* (1st ed., Paris [Abraham Saugrain, 1609]; 2d ed., Rouen [widow of Thomas Daré, 1626]), Dedication to the Queen; author portrait at age 45, 1608; au lecteur. *Apologie de Loyse Bourgeois dite Bourcier sage femme de la Royne Mere du Roy et de feu Madame Contre le Rapport des Medecins* (Paris, 1627), p. 9.

78.   *Remonstrances . . . pour les Compagnons Imprimeurs* (cited in n. 1). *Plaidoyez pour la Reformation de l'imprimerie* (n.p., n.d. [Paris, 1572]), AML, BB120, f. 105ᵛ (printers submit to the Consulate a printed discourse of eight leaves with their complaints against the merchant publishers).

79.   *Les Triomphes de l'Abbaye des Conards, sous le Resveur en Decimes Fagot Abbé des Conards, Contenant les criees et proclamations faites, depuis son advenement iusques à l'An present . . .* (Rouen: Nicolas Dugord, 1587). This edition includes scenarios and poems from 1540 and from the 1580's. But the 1540 material was presumably first printed shortly after that date, for the 1587 work includes a permission to print from the lieutenant of the baillif of Rouen dated January 18, 1541.

Dictons Satyriques Iouez en la Ville de Lyon par les Trois Supposts de l'Imprimerie, avec le pauvre Monde et le Medecin. Accompagnez du Capitaine des Imprimeurs, ensemble des Compagnons, marchans en armes (Lyon: Nicolas Guerin, 1574). *Recueil des plaisants devis recites par les supposts du Seigneur de la Coquille* (Lyon, 1857) reprints the *Plaisans devis* of February 21, 1580; May 2, 1581; February 19, 1584; Carnival, 1589; March 8, 1593; and March 6, 1594. On the initial printing of the *Plaisans devis,* see Baudrier, *Bibliographie lyonnaise,* 6: 19–21. A detail of the title page of the 1594 *Plaisans Devis* appears in this book as Plate 1.

See further on the festive societies and their relation to politics in Chap. 4 above. The development of a new kind of national consciousness in pamphlet literature in the course of the sixteenth century has been studied by Myriam Yardeni in *La conscience nationale en France pendant les guerres de religion (1559–1598)* (Louvain, 1971).

80.   *Plaisans devis* of 1580 and of 1594.

81.   *Premier volume de la Bibliotheque du Sieur de la Croix-du-Maine Qui est un catalogue general de toutes sortes d'Autheurs, qui ont escrit en François depuis cinq cents ans et plus, iusques à ce iourd'huy* (Paris: Abel L'Angelier, 1584), p. 529. Signature in the Bancroft Library (Berkeley) copy: "Belin archdiacre de l'eglise du mans."

82.   *Euvres poetiques de Iaques Peletier du Mans, Intitulez Louanges* (Paris: Robert Coulombel, 1581), f. 14ᵛ. "Le profit qu'avons des lettres et livres et de la gloire de nos rimeurs," in *Discours non plus melancoliques que divers, de choses mesmement qui appartiennent a notre*

France (Poitiers: Enguilbert de Marnef, 1557), chap. 15. On the attribution of this work to Peletier, and for further bibliography on Peletier as well as discussion of the problems of popularization and right method, see N. Z. Davis, "Peletier and Beza Part Company," *Studies in the Renaissance* 11 (1964), especially pp. 196–201 and n. 39.

83. Crespin, *Martyrs*, 1: 527.

84. Emond Auger, *Continuation de l'Institution, Verite et Utilite du Sacrifice de la Messe* (Paris, 1566), pp. 53, 115. See also Chap. 3 above, and Eugénie Droz, "Bibles françaises après le Concile de Trente," *Journal of the Warburg and Courtauld Institutes* 18 (1965): 213.

85. Crespin, *Martyrs*, 1: 647.

86. E. Delaruelle et al., *L'Eglise au temps du grand schisme et de la crise conciliaire (1378–1449)* ("Histoire de l'Eglise depuis les origins jusqu'à nos jours," 14; Paris, 1964), 2: 712–21. Droz, "Bibles françaises," p. 222. *La Saincte Bible* (Lyon: Barthélemy Honorat, 1578), f. * 1ᵛ: "*Voyant, amy Lecteur, que la S. Bible en langue Francoise estoit de plusieurs requise, et qu'il ne s'en trouvoit plus de celles qui ont esté par le passé imprimees et mises en vente avec privilege du Roy: i'ay de l'advis et conseil de plusieurs scavans Docteurs et Predicateurs Catholiques, faict sortir en lumiere ceste-cy, sans gloses, additions ny distractions qui la puissent rendre suspecte. . . .*" This Bible, with illustrations used earlier in the Protestant editions at Lyon, is the one approved by the Faculty of Theology at Louvain; its publisher had been a Protestant until only a few years before. See also, Martin, *Livre, pouvoirs et société*, pp. 102–4.

87. *Paraphrase sur les Heures de nostre Dame, Selon l'usaige de Rome: traduictes de Latin en Francoys, par frere Gilles Cailleau* (Poitiers: Jean and Enguilbert de Marnef, 1542), f. A iiᵛ. See also the work of Benjamin Beausport in Droz, "Bibles françaises," pp. 218–20. Jean Guéraud, *La chronique lyonnaise de Jean Guéraud*, ed. J. Tricou (Lyon, 1929), p. 150.

88. On this process, see Brunot, *Histoire de la langue française*, 2: 36–55; Howard Stone, "The French Language in Renaissance Medicine," BHR 15 (1953): 315–43; V.-L. Saulnier, "Lyon et la médecine aux temps de la Renaissance," *Revue lyonnaise de médecine* (1958): 73–83; C. A. Wickersheimer, *La médecine et les médecins en France à l'époque de la Renaissance* (Paris, 1906), pp. 128–78. Alison Klairmont of the University of California at Berkeley is considering these subjects anew in her doctoral dissertation on the medical profession in sixteenth-century France.

Le troisieme Livre de la therapeutique ou Methode curatoire de Claude Galien (Lyon: printed by Jean Barbou for Guillaume de Guelques, January 1539/40), translated by "Philiatros" (that is, the physician Jean Canappe), "Philiatros au Lecteur," f. 29ʳ⁻ᵛ. Signature in the Houghton Library copy, f. 127ʳ: "faict par moy . . . compaignon sirurgien."

La Chirurgie de Paulus Aegineta . . . Ung Opuscule de Galien des Tumeurs contre nature . . . Le tout traduict de Latin en Francoys par Maistre Pierre Tolet Medecin de l'Hospital (Lyon: Etienne Dolet, 1540), p. 3: "*la continuelle priere (pour leur necessité et usage) des compaignons chyrurgiens de la ville de Lyon.*" Signature in the Houghton Library copy: "Jehan Derssert de Lyon."

Opuscules de divers autheurs medecins, Redigez ensemble pour le proufit et utilité des Chirurgiens (Lyon: Jean I de Tournes, 1552), translations by Canappe and Tolet.

De l'usage des parties du corps humain, Livres XVII. Escripts par Claude Galien et traduicts fidellement du grec en François (Lyon: Guillaume Rouillé, 1565), translated by Jacques Dalechamps. "*Et pource que la lecture de ce livre est non seulement utile mais aussi necessaire aus cheirurgiens . . .*" (f. 9ᵛ). Signature in the copy at the Université de Montréal: "Margueritte."

Chirurgie Francoise, Recueillie par M. Iaques Dalechamps, Docteur Medecin et Lecteur ordinaire de ceste profession à Lyon (Lyon: Guillaume Rouillé, 1570), f. † 7ᵛ: "*Le tout en nostre vulgaire Francoys, en faveur des compagnons et maistres Chirurgiens qui n'ont point este nourris aux lettres Greques et Latines.*"

89. *Raison de vivre pour toutes fievres . . . Par maistre Jean Lyege medecin* (Paris: M. Vascosan, 1557), dedication from Lyege to Antoinette de Bourbon, Duchesse de Guise. *Commentaire de la conservation de santé et prolongation de vie, Faict en Latin par noble homme Hierosme de Monteux . . . medecin ordinaire du Roy . . . traduict de Latin en François par maistre Claude Valgelas, docteur en Medecine* (Lyon: Jean I de Tournes, 1559), dedication from Valgelas to Louise Dansezune, dame de St. Chamond. *Cinq Livres De la maniere de nourrir et gouverner les*

enfans des leur naissance. Par M. Simon Vallembert, Medecin de Madame la Duchesse de Savoye . . . (Poitiers; 1565), dedication from Vallembert to Catherine de Médicis.

90. Vallembert, *Cinq Livres*, Preface. *The regiment of life* . . . *with the boke of children, newly corrected and enlarged by T. Phayre* (London, 1550), preface by Thomas Phayer to *The Boke of children. Seconde Partie des Erreurs populaires et propos vulgaires, touchant la Medecine et le regime de santé, refutés ou expliqués par M. Laurent Ioubert* (Paris: Lucas Breyer, 1580), f. B ii^v. *Annotations de M. Laurent Ioubert sur toutte la chirurgie de M. Gui de Chauliac* (Lyon: Etienne Michel, 1584), dedication from Isaac Joubert to Jean Bellièvre, January 1, 1580, pp. 4—18.

91. *Erreurs populaires au fait de la medecine et regime de santé corrigés par M. Laurent Joubert* . . . *la premiere partie* (Bordeaux: S. Millanges, 1578), Dedication, Book 2, chap. 4, pp. 380ff., *au lecteur. Seconde Partie des Erreurs populaires*: f. c i^v, "*Catalogue de plusieurs divers propos vulgaires et erreurs populaires colligez de plusieurs*" and given to Joubert by Barthélemy Cabrol (there follow 123 entries); pp. 159—87, "*Ramas de propos vulgaires et Erreurs populaires avec quelques problemes, anvoyes de plusieurs a M. Ioubert*" (there follow 333 entries).

92. *Chirurgie de Paulus Aegineta* (cited in n. 88), p. 6.

93. *Remonstrances* . . . *pour les Compagnons Imprimeurs* (cited in n. 1), f. C iii^r.

8. Proverbial Wisdom and Popular Errors

1. *Solomon et Marcolphus collocutores* (n.p., n.d.; Bibl. nat., Rés. mYc 289). Other editions at the Bibliothèque nationale: *Collationes quas dicunt fecisse mutuo rex Salomon sapientissimus et Marcolphus facie deformis et turpissimus* . . . (n.p., n.d.); *Les dictz de Salomon, Avecques les responces de Marcon fort ioyeuses* (n.p., n.d.); *Frag und antwort Salomonis unt Marcolf* (Nuremberg, 1487). At the Bibliothèque Méjanes in Aix-en-Provence: *Dits de Salomon* . . . (Paris: G. Eustace, n.d.). François Rabelais, *La vie* . . . *du grand Gargantua*, in *Oeuvres*, ed. J. Boulenger and L. Scheler (Paris, 1955), chap. 33, p. 101.

On this dialogue of sayings, see Robert J. Menner, ed., *The Poetical Dialogues of Solomon and Saturn* (New York, 1941); Walter Benary, ed., *Salomon et Marcolfus* (Sammlung mittellateinischer Texte, 8; Heidelberg, 1914); Enid Welsford, *The Fool, His Social and Literary History* (London, 1935), pp. 35—47; John Wardroper, *Jest upon Jest* (London, 1970), pp. 74—78; A. J. V. Le Roux de Lincy, *Le livre des proverbes français* (2d ed.; Paris, 1859), 1: viii—xi; Archer Taylor, *The Proverb* (Cambridge, Mass., 1931), pp. 177—78.

2. *Mémoires de l'Académie Celtique* 1 (1807): 1—5, 63—64, 72—86. The Académie Celtique was first called to my attention by Harry A. Senn: "The French School of Folklore to 1935" (unpublished Ph.D. dissertation, Dept. of French, University of California at Berkeley, 1972).

3. Noel Taillepied, *Histoire de l'Estat et Republique des Druides* . . . *Anciens François* (Paris, 1585); Jean Guénebauld, *Le Recueil de Chyndonax Prince des Vacies Druydes Celtiques Diionois* (Dijon, 1621); Antoine Gosselin, *Historia Gallorum Veterum* (Caen, 1636); M. Z. Boxhorn, *Originum Gallicarum Liber* (Amsterdam, 1654).

4. Hencricus de Gorinchem (d. 1431), *Tractatus de superstitiosis* (editions from the 1470's to the 1490's). Gorinchem was a professor at the University of Cologne. Jean-Baptiste Thiers, *Traité des superstitions* (Paris, 1679); *idem, Traité des superstitions qui regardent les sacraments* (Paris, 1692). Thiers is identified in his 1679 *Avocat des Pauvres* as *curé* of Champrond and in a later work as *curé* of Vibraie. Henry Bourne (1694—1733), *Antiquitates Vulgares; or the Antiquities of the Common People* (Newcastle, 1725). On Bourne, see Richard M. Dorson, *The British Folklorists. A History* (Chicago, Ill., 1968), pp. 10—13.

5. F. Lesure, "Eléments populaires dans la chanson française au debut du 16e siècle," in *Musique et poésie au XVIe siècle* (Colloques internationaux du CNRS, Sciences Humaines, 5; Paris, 1954), pp. 169—75. Patrice Coirault, *Recherches sur notre ancienne chanson populaire traditionnelle* (Paris, 1927—33), pp. 82—88; *idem, Notre chanson folklorique* (Paris, 1942), pp. 158—66. Both Lesure and Coirault doubt that these early song collections give accurate representation of rural or folk song. Curt Sachs, *World History of the Dance*, trans. B. Schönberg (New York, 1963), p. 344.

Jean d'Arras' version of Mélusine (late 14th century), which appeared in print in the late 15th century, gave as its sources "*de vrayes croniques*" obtained from the Duc de Berri and others

(*Melusine nouvellement imprimee a Paris* [Paris: Jean Petit, n.d.]). [Charles Perrault] , *Histoire ou contes du temps passé. Avec des Moralités* (Paris, 1697), ff. a iiᵛ–a ivᵛ. Mademoiselle Lhéritier, *La Tour Tenebreuse; et les jours lumineux, Contes Anglois* (Paris, 1705), "Préface," especially ff. e iiiᵛ–e ivᵛ.

6. Marc Soriano, *Les contes de Perrault. Culture savante et traditions populaires* (Paris, 1968). An important evaluation of the work of Mandrou, Bollème, and Soriano, and a statement of the problems involved in studying popular culture, can be found in Michel de Certeau, Dominique Revel, and Jacques Revel, "La beauté du mort: Le concept de 'culture populaire,' " *Politique aujourd'hui* (Dec. 1970): 3–23.

7. Le Roux de Lincy, *Proverbes*, 1: xxvii–xxxii; 2: 547–48. John Bednar has made a study of *Li proverbes au vilain* in his doctoral dissertation for the University of California at Berkeley; he has shown that the collection was composed by a cleric at the court of Philippe d'Alsace in Flanders sometime between 1170 and 1180. It was dedicated to the duke and probably sponsored by him. I am grateful to Mr. Bednar for this information. Some manuscripts attribute the collection to the Comte de Bretagne (Le Roux de Lincy, *Proverbes*, 2: 555). Mr. Bednar has forthcoming an English translation of these proverbs.

8. *Li proverbes au vilain*, ed. Adolf Tobler (Leipzig, 1895). Le Roux de Lincy, *Proverbes*, 2: 557.

9. *Li proverbes au vilain*, nos. 28, 230, 247, 293.

10. Chrétien de Troyes' use of proverbs from *Li proverbes au vilain* has been established by John Bednar (see n. 7 above).

11. W. G. Smith and J. E. Heseltine, comps., *The Oxford Dictionary of English Proverbs* (Oxford, 1935), p. 280; *Li proverbes au vilain*, no. 162. On the use of proverbs in Latin sermons, see Hans Walther, *Proverbia sententiaeque Latinitatis Medii Aevi* (*Carmina Medii Aevi posterioris latina*, 2; Göttingen, 1963), p. xv (I am grateful to John F. R. Coughlan for this reference). For proverbs in vernacular sermons, see G. R. Owst, *Literature and Pulpit in Medieval England* (Oxford, 1966), pp. 41–46.

12. *Li proverbes au vilain*, no. 175; Le Roux de Lincy, *Proverbes*, 2: 106. Antoine Loisel, *Institutes coutumières . . . ou manuel de plusieurs et diverses règles, sentences et proverbes, tant anciens que modernes du droit coutumier*, ed. T. Dupin and E. Laboulaye (Paris, 1846; 1st ed. 1607), 1: i, 31. On the slow spread of professional lawyers and *gens de justice* in the countryside in the late Middle Ages, see B. Guenée, *Tribunaux et gens de justice dans le bailliage de Senlis à la fin du Moyen Age* (Paris, 1963).

13. J. Truhlář, *Catalogus Codicum Manu Scriptorum Latinorum qui in C. R. Bibliotheca Publica atque Universitatis Pragensis Asserventur* (Prague, 1905–6), no. 2636 (14th century), no. 2655 (13th century). Le Roux de Lincy, *Proverbes*, 2: 547–57.

14. George Boas, *Vox Populi. Essays in the History of an Idea* (Baltimore, Md., 1969), pp. 8–25. *Li proverbes au vilain*, no. 280.

15. Etienne Pasquier, *Les recherches de la France* (Paris, 1633), Book 8, pp. 704–5..

16. Jacques Le Goff, "Culture cléricale et traditions folkloriques dans la civilisation mérovingienne," Annales ESC 22 (1967): 788–89, and 789, n. 1; *idem*, "Mélusine maternelle et défricheuse," Annales ESC 26 (1971): 601–2. P. Brians, trans. and ed., *Bawdy Tales from the Courts of Medieval France* (New York, 1972), pp. vii–ix. Per Nykrog, *Les Fabliaux: Etudes d'histoire littéraire et de stylistique médiévale* (Copenhagen, 1957). Loisel, *Institutes coutumières*, 1: i, 22.

17. John W. Baldwin, *Masters, Princes and Merchants. The Social Views of Peter Chanter and His Circle* (Baltimore, Md., 1970), 1: 37, 57.

18. Jacques Le Goff, *Les intellectuels au moyen age* (Paris, 1957), pp. 89–90. On the clerical Feast of Fools, see Chap. 4 above.

19. Philippus Beroaldus, *Oratio proverbiorum* (Bologna, 1499). Polydore Vergil, *Proverbiorum et adagiorum veterum . . . libellus* (Paris, 1498). Erasmus did not know of Vergil's earlier work when he published his *Adagia* in 1500.

Some persons simply published the medieval collections in traditional or slightly modified form. Thus we have from the poet and actor Pierre Gringoire *Les ditz et anctoritez* [*sic*] *des saiges philosophes* (n.p., n.d.), a version in couplets; and we have from Pierre Grosnet *Les motz dorez De Cathon en francoys et en latin* (Paris, 1530/31), with Latin sentences followed by French verse, among many editions attributed to Cato. A question about whether Cato the Elder was really the author of these "golden words" was finally raised by the humanist and educator Mathurin Cordier in his edition of *Disticha*, with Latin and French Commentary, "attributed to Cato" (seven editions printed by Robert I Estienne from 1534 to 1549; Elizabeth Armstrong, *Robert Estienne, Royal Printer* [Cambridge, 1954], pp. 105–6). An effort at a critical edition was made by the editor and poet Charles Fontaine in *Les dits des sept sages, Ensemble Plusieurs autres sentences Latines, extraites de divers, bons et anciens Auteurs* (Lyon, 1557). He put his translations into prose, claiming that the rhymed versions "added their young modern sense to the firm, brief, good old sense" and that their exposition "tweaked the nose of the poor guiltless sentences" (p. 4).

　　20.　Aristotle, *The Art of Rhetoric*, trans. and ed. J. H. Freese (London, 1926), 1: xv, 13–14; 2: xxi, 11–13. Also on Aristotle's views, see R. E. Habenicht's introduction to John Heywood, *A Dialogue of Proverbs* (Berkeley, Calif., 1963), p. 9; and Rudolf Pfeiffer, *History of Classical Scholarship* (Oxford, 1968), pp. 83–84, 208 (I am grateful to Elizabeth Eisenstein for this latter reference).

　　21.　Margaret Mann Phillips, *The "Adages" of Erasmus. A Study with Translations* (Cambridge, 1964), especially pp. 5–7, 27; *idem, Erasmus on His Times. A Shortened Version of the Adages of Erasmus* (Cambridge, 1967), pp. x–xi. Phillips sums up Erasmus' views from the Preface to *Adagiorum Collectanea* (1500) and *"Quid sic paroemia"* in *Adagiorum Chiliades* (Venice, 1508). See also Erasmus' discussion of *"Festina lente"* (Phillips, *Erasmus*, p. 3) and of *"Ollas ostentare"* (*ibid.*, pp. 142–43). Also see Erasmus' comment on vulgarity in style in his discussion of *"Herculei labores"* (*ibid.*, p. 27).

　　On Renaissance interest in the hieroglyphic, see among many sources *The Hieroglyphics of Horapollo*, trans. and introduction by George Boas (New York, 1950).

　　22.　Discussion of *"Herculei labores"* in Phillips, *Erasmus*, pp. 22–24. Phillips, *The "Adages,"* pp. 19–22.

　　23.　Bonaspes is listed as the editor and corrector of Polydore Vergil's work on the title of the Paris edition of 1508 (Lathrop C. Harper, Inc., Catalogue no. 212, #196). He also published a *Petit compost en francois* (Paris, 1516). *Proverbia communia tam gallico quam latino sermone per ordinem alphabeticum* (n.p. [Au Pellican], n.d.; copy in the Bernstein Collection, Jagiellonian Library, Cracow). *Proverbia communia noviter aucta revisa et emendata . . . a N.B.T. collectis* (n.p. [Paris]: Bernard Aubry, n.d.), f. d iiiᵛ: signed by Bonaspes from the College of Bayeux, 1513; ff.d viʳ–d viiᵛ: an oration by Joannis Egidius Nuceriensis (Jean Gilles de Noyers). Another edition with the same title but printed by Jean Merausse in Paris is in the Bernstein Collection in Cracow. Other editions were printed in Lyon by Claude Nourry (ca. 1525) and by Barnabé Chaussard.

　　Proverbia Gallicana secundum ordinem alphabeti reposita et ab Ioanne Aegidio Nuceriensi Latinis . . . traducta (Lyon: Jacques Maréschal, 1519–20). Includes a letter of Josse Bade to Nicolas Dorigny, councillor in the Parlement of Paris and editor of the work. Bade was the initial publisher of the work in Paris that year. Other editions: *Proverbia gallicana* (Lyon: Claude Nourry, n.d.); *Proverbia popularia* (Lyon: François Juste, 1539); *Proverbia gallicana . . . correcta et aucta per H. Sussannaeum* (Paris, 1552 and 1558; dedication by Sussanneau, dated 1549); *Proverbes communs et belles sentences . . . par I. Nucerin* (Lyon, 1558 and 1582). Gilles de Noyers was a fuller collector than Bonaspes, though he incorporated much of Bonaspes' work in his.

　　Thresor de la langue francoyse, tant ancienne que moderne . . . Reveu et augmente . . . par Iean Nicot . . . avec une grammaire francoyse et Latine et le recueil de vieux proverbes de la France (Paris: David Douceur, 1606).

　　24.　On Charles de Bouelles, see Colette Dumont-Demaizière, "Avant-propos" to her edition and translation of Bouelles, *Liber de differentia vulgarium linguarum et Gallici sermonis varietate* (Collection de la société de linguistique picarde, 14; Amiens, 1972), pp. 7–73; and Madame La Porte, "Charles de Bouelles (1479–1566)," *Moreana* 41 (1974): 37–47. Grietje Sloan is now completing a doctoral dissertation at the University of California at Berkeley on certain problems in the theology of Bouelles.

It is hard to understand why Madame Dumont-Demaizière says that after 1520 Bouelles was gradually forgotten by his contemporaries. He published numerous works after that date, some of them (such as his *Géometrie practique*) going through several editions. He was a close friend of the mathematician Oronce Finé of the Collège de France, the poet Sussanneau referring to them as "Oreste et Pylades" in a poem contributed to the 1542 edition of Bouelles' *Géometrie*. He evidently influenced Sussanneau to edit a new edition of Gilles de Noyers' *Proverbia* (see n. 23). Both François de La Croix du Maine and Antoine du Verdier devoted entries to him in their *Bibliothèques* in the 1580's (*Les bibliothèques françoises de La Croix du Maine et de Du Verdier Sieur de Vauprivas*, ed. Rigoley de Juvigny [Paris, 1773], 1: 104; 3: 294).

For Bouelles' views on language, see *De differentia vulgarium*, Dedication (dated September 1531); Book 1, chaps. 2, 18, 47–53. Bouelles thought the only archetypal language was that in which God had spoken to man at the creation. It would be spoken again by the blessed at the resurrection.

25. Charles de Bouelles, *Proverbiorum Vulgarium Libri tres* (Paris, 1531), Dedication to jurist Joachim Michon, February 16, 1527/28; also f. clxxi^r. Another edition was printed in Paris in 1558. *Paucula proverbia* of Bouelles were also included in editions of Erasmus' *Adagia* printed at Basel in 1574 and at Paris in 1579.

Proverbes et dicts sententieux, avec l'interpretation d'iceux, Par Charles de Bouelles Chanoine de Noyon (Paris, 1557), Carolus Bouillus benignis lectoribus S., f. * ii^r-v. Some scholars have doubted that Bouelles really wrote this edition (Dumont-Demaizière, "Avant-propos," pp. 37–38). They may have thought he was dead by that date (he would have been about 77), but Madame La Porte has proved he did not die until 1566. The *Proverbes* are right in the tradition of his earlier work; La Croix du Maine, Du Verdier, and others accepted him as the true author; and the *Proverbes* of 1557 were brought out by the same publisher — Sébastien Nivelle — who was responsible for the second edition of his *Proverbia* in 1558. In short, there is no reason to doubt the statement on the title page that the *Proverbes* were the work of Bouelles.

26. *Proverbiorum Vulgarium Libri tres*, Dedication; *Proverbes*, ff. 4^r, 15^r, 23^v, 17^v. For "*A longue voye . . .*" in a fifteenth-century manuscript by Jean Mielot, canon at Lille, see Le Roux de Lincy, *Proverbes*, 1: 81; 2: 548.

27. *De differentia vulgarium*, Book 1, chap. 17.

28. *Explications morales d'aucuns proverbes communs en la langue francoyse*, in the *Thresor de la langue francoyse* (cited in n. 23), separately paginated after Gilles de Noyers' *Proverbes*, pp. 17–23. The *Thresor* is a much expanded and improved version of the *Dictionnaire françois-latin*, originally published by Robert I Estienne. Jean Nicot (1530–1604) was responsible for the 1606 *Thresor*, published after his death, and for this reason it has been assumed that he was also the author of the *Explications morales*. I think this cannot have been the case. The three proverbs that have real reference to geographical localities all concern Troyes and the Champagne ("*De l'arbre d'un pressoir . . . ,*" "*Les cousteaux Iehan Colot, l'un vaut l'autre,*" "*Il ne craint ni les rez ni les tondus*"). Jean Nicot was born in Nîmes, died in Paris, and never lived in the Champagne. Further on Nicot and the *Thresor*, see *Dictionnaire des Lettres françaises, le seizième siècle* (Paris, 1951), pp. 227–30, 537.

29. Henri Estienne, *La précellence du langage françois* (1579), ed. E. Huguet (Paris, 1896), pp. 201–49. Pasquier, *Recherches* (cited in n. 15), Book 8, pp. 672–790. On Pasquier, see George Huppert, *The Idea of Perfect History* (Urbana, Ill., 1970), pp. 36–51; and D. R. Kelley, *Foundations of Modern Historical Scholarship* (New York, 1970), pp. 271–83, especially for his discussion of Pasquier's view of language and its mutations.

30. *Bonne Response a tous propos. Livre fort plaisant . . . auquel est contenu grand nombre de Proverbes, et sentences, ioyeuses . . . Traduict de la langue Italienne et reduyt en nostre vulgaire françoys par ordre d'Alphabet* (Paris, 1547). This work gives equivalents of French and Italian proverbs. "Aux lecteurs," ff. A iv–A iii^v, on enrichment of the language.

Gabriel Meurier, *Recueil de sentences notables, dicts et dictons communs, Adages, Proverbes et Refrains, traduits la pluspart de Latin, Italien et Espagnol, et reduits selon l'ordre Alphabetic* (Antwerp, 1568), "Au lecteur," p. 3^v. Editions of this work under the titles *Tresor des sentences dorees, proverbes et dits notables* and *Tresor de sentences dorees et dictons communs* also appeared at Rouen in 1579 and at Lyon in 1577 and 1582.

François Goedthals, *Les proverbes anciens flamengs et françois correspondants de sentences les uns aux autres* (Antwerp: Christophe Plantin, 1568). Goedthals was a citizen of Ghent. The Frenchman Plantin praises him for his work collecting *"les vrais proverbes accoustumés en Flameng"* and thinks the book will be *"aggreable à tous ceux qui se delectent de la naifveté des sententieuses manieres de parler des anciens"* (Dedication, pp. 3—6). On earlier collecting in the Netherlands, see R. Jente, ed., *Proverbia Communia, A Fifteenth Century Collection of Dutch Proverbs Together with the Low German Version* (University of Indiana Publications, Folklore Series, no. 4; Bloomington, 1947).

[Jean Le Bon], *Adages de Solon de Voge Par l'Hetropolitain, Premier livre, deux, trois et quatriesme. Reveuë par l'autheur* (Paris: Nicolas Bonfons, n.d.). On this curious writer, translator, and literary polemicist, see *Les Bibliothèques de La Croix du Maine et Du Verdier*, 1: 455—56; 4: 355. La Croix gives 1576 as the date for an edition of this work published by Bonfons. Le Bon was a native of Autremont near Chaumont en Bassigny and was physician to the Cardinal de Guise.

Cesar Oudin, *Refranes o Proverbios Castellanos. Traduzidos en lengua Francesa. Proverbes espagnols traduicts en françois* (2d ed.; Paris, 1609).

31. R. Doucet, *Les bibliothèques parisiennes au XVIe siècle* (Paris, 1956): library of Jean Ferron, lawyer in the Parlement of Paris, no. 628, the 1531 *Proverbiorum Vulgarium Libri tres* of Charles de Bouelles, valued at 2 sous. Ferron also had several collections of learned and Biblical proverbs (nos. 129, 273, 335, 480), including Erasmus' *Adagia*.

Bonne reponse a tous propos in the library of Pierre Dumas, Calvinist regent at Béziers; copy auctioned off for 10 deniers in 1577. He also had the *Adagia* of Erasmus (P. Jourda, "La bibliothèque d'un regent Calviniste," in *Mélanges d'histoire littéraire de la Renaissance offerts à Henri Chamard* [Paris, 1951], pp. 269—73; I am grateful to Michael Hackenberg for reference to this library).

Claude de Rubys, *Les privileges, franchises et immunitez octroyees par les roys . . . aux consuls, eschevins, manans et habitans . . . de Lyon* (Lyon, 1573), p. 45.

Pierre Pithou's collection in Bibl. Nat., Mss., Collection Dupuy, 630, ff. 183ʳ—201ᵛ. Loisel's manuscript collection of *Proverbes ruraux, vulgaires, anciens et modernes* mentioned in Loisel, *Institutes coutumières* (cited in n. 12), p. lxii. On Pithou and Loisel, see Kelley, *Foundations* (cited in n. 29), chap. 9.

32. Rabelais, *Le cinquiesme livre*, chap. 22, in *Oeuvres* (cited in n. 1), pp. 809—10. Translation of Urquhart, given by Rosalie Colie in her discussion of Rabelais in *Paradoxia Epidemica. The Renaissance Tradition of Paradox* (Princeton, N.J., 1966), pp. 45—47. Bruegel's *Netherlandish Proverbs* was signed and dated in 1559.

33. F. Brunot et al., *Histoire de la langue française des origines à 1900* (Paris, 1905—53), 2: 174—75. James B. Atkinson, "Naïveté and Modernity: The French Renaissance Battle for a Literary Vernacular," *Journal of the History of Ideas* 35 (1974): 179—98, discusses the various meanings of naive in the sixteenth century.

34. Curt Sachs, *World History of the Dance* (cited in n. 5), pp. 300, 346—52; Frances A. Yates, *The Valois Tapestries* (London, 1959), pp. 57—58.

35. Loisel, *Institutes coutumières*, pp. xxxv—xxxvi and *passim*. Atkinson, "Naïveté," n. 40. *Les Lettres d'Estienne Pasquier* (Lyon, 1597), ff. 1ʳ—4ʳ, 202ʳ—208ᵛ, 435ᵛ. On Pasquier and Loisel and their attitudes toward law, see Kelley, *Foundations*, chaps. 9—10.

36. Sources for the following paragraphs are as follows: Archer Taylor, *The Proverb* (cited in n. 1); Morris Palmer Tilley, *Elizabethan Proverb Lore* (New York, 1926), especially pp. 16—29; Charles G. Smith, *Shakespeare's Proverb Lore* (Cambridge, Mass., 1963), "Introduction"; R. E. Habenicht, "Introduction" to *John Heywood's "A Dialogue of Proverbs"* (Berkeley, Calif., 1963); Rosalie L. Colie, *The Resources of Kind. Genre-Theory in the Renaissance* (Berkeley, Calif., 1973), pp. 33—36.

Kenneth Burke, *The Philosophy of Literary Form* (Baton Rouge, La., 1941), pp. 293—304: "Literature as equipment for living," "Proverbs as strategies for dealing with situations"; G. B. Milner, "What is a proverb?," *New Society* 332 (Feb. 6, 1969): 199—202.

E. O. Arewa and Alan Dundes, "Proverbs and the Ethnography of Speaking Folklore," *American Anthropologist* 66, no. 6, part 2 (1964): 70—85 (I am grateful to Alan Dundes for bibliographical suggestions). John C. Messenger, Jr., "The Role of Proverbs in a Nigerian Judicial System," in Alan Dundes, ed., *The Study of Folklore* (Englewood Cliffs, N.J., 1965), pp. 299–307. Peter Seitel, "Proverbs: A Social Use of Metaphor," *Genre* 2 (June 1969): 143–61. Richard Priebe, "The Horses of Speech: A Structural Analysis of the Proverb," *Folklore Annual of the University Folklore Association* (Center for Intercultural Studies in Folklore and Oral History) 3 (1971): 26–32 (I am grateful to Samuel Kinser for this reference). Roger Abrahams, "Proverbs and Proverbial Expression," in Richard M. Dorson, ed., *Folklore and Folklife. An Introduction* (Chicago, 1972), pp. 117–27. V. R. Piskacek, "The Maasai," in *William Alanson White Newsletter* (Winter 1973–74), pp. 11–12; Elinor Keenan, "Norm-Makers, Norm-Breakers: Uses of Speech by Men and Women in a Malagasy Community," forthcoming in Richard Bauman and Joel Sherzer, eds., *The Ethnography of Speaking*. Peter Seitel, "Saying Haya Sayings: Two Categories of Proverb Use," forthcoming in Christopher Crocker and David Sapir, eds., *The Social Use of Metaphor*.

37. Seitel, "Saying Haya Sayings."

38. *"Auris Bâtava"* in Phillips, *Erasmus*, pp. 32–33 (see also *"Herculei labores,"* p. 18). *Explications morales*, p. 23.

39. Taylor, *Proverb*, p. 87. On peasants judging their own disputes, see René Choppin, *Traité de Privileges des Personnes Vivans aux Champs* (1575), in *Oeuvres* (Paris, 1662), 3: 70–71.

40. See note 31 above on lawyers' collections. Taylor, *Proverb*, pp. 86–97. Peter Stein, *Regulae Iuris, From Juristic Rules to Legal Maxims* (Edinburgh, 1966), chap. 9. Paul Kocher, "Francis Bacon on the Science of Jurisprudence," *Journal of the History of Ideas* 18 (1957): 3–26. W.R. Prest, *The Inns of Court under Elizabeth I and the Early Stuarts, 1590–1640* (London, 1972), pp. 116, 144ff. Albrecht Foth, *Gelehrtes römish-kanonisches Recht in deutschen Rechtssprichwörtern* (Tübingen, 1971). Aristotle talked of the use of proverbs as an "ancient witness" in cases of law (*Art of Rhetoric*, 1: xv, 13–14).

41. Le Roux de Lincy, *Proverbes*, 2: 548 (alphabetical list of Jean Mielot). Most of the lists without commentaries were alphabetical. Bouelles sometimes grouped his 1531 proverbs by topic, sometimes left them at random. His 1557 collection with commentaries, like the anonymous *Explications morales*, were placed at random. Note Bacon's comment on why he ordered his *Maxims of the Law* randomly: "disjoined aphorisms doth leave the wit of man more free to turn and toss, and to make use of that which is so delivered to more several purposes and applications" (quoted in Stein, *Regulae Iuris*, p. 172).

42. Michel de Montaigne, *Essais*, Book I, chap. 54, in *Oeuvres complètes*, ed. A. Thibaudet and M. Rat (Paris, 1962), p. 300.

43. Olivier de Serres, *Theatre d'Agriculture et Mesnage des Champs* (Paris, 1600), "Preface."

44. Among many sources, see Le Roux de Lincy, *Proverbes*, 1: lxv–lxxx; A. Adam, *Les libertins au XVIIe siècle* (Paris, 1964), pp. 12–14; P. Hazard, *La crise de la conscience européenne, 1680–1715* (Paris, 1935), especially pp. 121–83; Robert Mandrou, *Des humanistes aux hommes de sciences (XVIe et XVIIe siècles)* (Paris, 1973), pp. 154–62; Erich Auerbach, "La Cour et la Ville," in *Scenes from the Drama of European Literature* (New York, 1959), pp. 133–79 [excellent]; Brunot, *Histoire de la langue*, 4.1, especially pp. 227–39, 312–24, 381–87; Claude Favre de Vaugelas, *Remarques sur la langue françoise utiles à ceux qui veulent bien parler et bien escrire* (Paris, 1647), "Preface."

45. Dominique Bouhours, *Remarques nouvelles sur la langue françoise* (2d ed.; Paris, 1676), p. 564. *Ballet des Proverbes. Dansé par le Roy, le 17 Fevrier 1654* (Paris, 1654).

46. Le Roux de Lincy, *Proverbes*, 1: lxxx; [Jacques Lagniet], *Recueil des plus illustres proverbes, divisés en trois livres* (Paris: Jacques Lagniet, n.d. [Catalogue of the Bibliothèque Nationale says 1657; catalogue of the Bernstein Collection, Jagiellonian Library, Cracow, says 1667]).

47. Antoine Oudin, *Curiositez françoises, pour supplément aux Dictionnaires . . . avec une infinité de Proverbes* (Paris, 1656), "Preface," p. 23. *Les illustres proverbes historiques, ou recueil de diverses questions curieuses, pour se divertir agreablement dans les Compagnies* (Paris: Pierre David, 1655), "Au lecteur." This edition, unknown to Le Roux de Lincy (1: xliv; 2: 574), is at the Jagiellonian Library, Cracow, in the Bernstein Collection. Fleury de Bellingen, *L'Etymologie ou Explication des Proverbes françois . . . en forme de Dialogue* (La Haye, 1656).

Nouveaux proverbes espagnols et françois. Disposes selon l'ordre de l'Alphabet. Pour apprendre avec facilité à parler et escrire en ces langues (Paris, 1660). *Les illustres proverbes nouveaux et historiques* (Paris, 1665) [the preface differs from the 1655 edition]. *Proverbes choises. Explications etymologique, prose et vers* (Paris, 1703).

48. *Les Proverbes Basques recueillis par le S^r D'Oihenart, plus les poesies Basques du mesme Auteur* (Paris, 1657), "Preface." Oihenart was a lawyer in the Parlement of Navarre and had earlier published *Declaration historique de l'injuste usurpation et retention de la Navarre, faite par Espagne* (n.p., 1625) and *Notitia utriusque Vasconiae tum ibericae, tum aquitanicae qua, praeter situm regionis et alia scitu digna* (Paris, 1638).

49. Jacques Moisant de Brieux (1614–74), *Les origines de quelques coutumes anciennes, et de plusieurs façons de parler triviales. Avec un vieux manuscrit en vers, touchant l'Origine des Chevaliers Bannerets* (Caen, 1672), Dedication to the Duc de Montausier; pp. 3–5, 21–24. Moisant de Brieux mentions, pp. 3–5, that he had been a lawyer in the Parlement of Rouen. Examples of reference to Norman sayings or customs: pp. 38, 53, 56, 95–96, 115, 142. Also on Moisant de Brieux, see Nathan Edelman, *Attitudes of Seventeenth Century France Toward the Middle Ages* (New York, 1946), pp. 83; 83, n. 58; and 96, n. 5.

50. Jean-Baptiste Thiers, *Traité des superstitions qui regardent les sacramens* (5th ed., Paris, 1741; 1st ed. was 1692), 1: f. a iiii^{r-v}.

51. Moisant de Brieux, *Origines*, p. 15, discusses *Enfans de la Mate* (cut-purses, etc.): "*La mate etoit autrefois une place a Paris ou ces sortes de gens avoient de coutume de s'assembler.*" *Ibid.*, pp. 54, 140–41, discusses the "superstition" "*Faire les Rois avec quelqu'un*" and "*Bailler les Innocents . . . une coutume badine et ridicule.*" Fleury de Bellingen's *Etymologie* also benefits somewhat from the antiquarian spirit, though it is by no means as serious a piece of observation and discussion as that of Moisant de Brieux. See for instance pp. 56–57, the section on "*monter sur l'ours.*" On historical antiquarianism in the seventeenth century see George Huppert, "*La liberté du cerveau*: Notes on the psychology of Historical Erudition," in *Méthodologie de l'histoire et des sciences humaines: Mélanges en honneur de Fernand Braudel* (Toulouse, 1973), pp. 267–77.

52. Gilles Ménage, *Les origines de la langue françoise* (Paris, 1650), dedicatory epistle to M. du Puy and pp. 18, 652, 546–47. Pierre Borel, *Tresor de Recherches et Antiquitez Gauloises et Françoises, Reduites en ordre alphabetique* (Paris, 1655), f. k iii^{r-v}.

A 1694 edition of Ménage's work, now entitled *Dictionaire* [sic] *etymologique*, includes the *Origines de la langue française* of Pierre de Caseneuve and a *Vocabulaire Hagiologique* of *l'abbé* Claude Chastelain. Caseneuve (1591–1652), a native of Toulouse, was very much interested in the local history of the Languedoc as well as in Provençal. His treatise on *La Catalogne Françoise*, like Oihenart's on the Spanish Basque country, supports French claims to the area – that is, he combined regional loyalty with loyalty to France. Chastelain's work on the saints gives the Latin name for each saint followed ordinarily by variations on the name in different parts of France.

53. James Howell (1594?–1666),*Proverbs or Old Sayed Sawes and Adages in English (or the Saxon Toung), Italian, French and Spanish whereunto the British, for their great Antiquity and weight are added* (London, 1659).

54. On Howell's career, see the *Dictionary of National Biography*, 10: 109–14. James Howell, *A Survay of the Signorie of Venice* (London, 1651), p. 3. Royalist Maypoles in Christopher Hill, *Society and Puritanism in Pre-Revolutionary England* (London, 1964), p. 186.

55. Soriano, *Contes de Perrault* (cited in n. 6), Part 3, chaps. 5–6; Part 5, chap. 1.

56. *Ibid.*, pp. 292, 490.

57. *Dictionnaire des proverbes françois . . . Par G. D. B.* (Brussels: George de Backer, 1710). Joseph Le Roux, *Dictionnaire comique, satirique, critique, burlesque, libre et proverbial* (Amsterdam, 1718); *Dictionnaire du sieur Dubois* (Amsterdam, 1728); Joseph Panckoucke, *Dictionnaire des proverbes françois et des façons de parler comiques, burlesques et familières . . .* (Paris, 1748, and Frankfurt-am-Main, 1750).

58. *Encyclopédie ou Dictionnaire raisonné des sciences, des arts et des métiers* (Neuchâtel, 1765), 13: 510; 5: 910–12.

59. Bernard Le Bovier de Fontenelle, *Poesies pastorales . . . Avec un traité sur la Nature de L'Eglogue* (Paris, 1688), pp. 151–54. P. Van Tieghem, *Le sentiment de la Nature dans le*

Notes to Pages 254-57 343

Préromantisme européen (Paris, 1960), especially pp. 218—21; *idem, Le romantisme dans la littérature européenne* (Paris, 1969), chap. 1. Lionel Gossman, *Medievalism and the Ideologies of the Enlightenment. The World and Work of La Curne de Sainte-Palaye* (Baltimore, Md., 1968), especially pp. 332—48, and Part 3, chap. 7. Anne Claude, Comte de Caylus (1692—1765), "Mémoire sur les fabliaux," *Mémoires de l'Académie des Inscriptions*, 20: 358—59. Saveur-André Pellas (member of the order of Minimes), *Dictionnaire provençal et françois dans lequel on trouvera les mots Provençaux . . . et Proverbes expliquez en François* (Avignon, 1723). Grégoire de Rostrenin, *Dictionnaire françois-celtique ou françois-breton. Necessaire à tous ceux qui veulent apprendre à traduire le François en Celtique ou en langue Breton, pour Prêcher, Catechiser et Confesser, selon les differens Dialectes de chaque Diocèse* (Rennes, 1732). Rostrenin, a priest, mentions an earlier dictionary by the Jesuit Julien Maunoir, dated Quimper, 1659. M. de Châlons, *Dictionnaire Breton-François du Diocèse de Vannes . . .* (Vannes, 1723), "Avertissement."

60. Claude Fauchet, *Recueil de l'origine de la langue et poesie françoise, ryme et romans* (Paris, 1581), p. 28. Gossman, *Medievalism*, Part 3, chap. 1, pp. 191 and 191, n. 54; 211 and 211, n. 127.

Also see A. F. Jault's Introduction to his edition of the *Dictionnaire etymologique de la langue française* (Paris, 1750), in which he talks about the importance of "*les divers idiomes de nos Provinces*," the regional dialects, and "*le Langage même des habitans de la campagne et du bas peuple des villes*," all as sources for the earlier history of French. Antoine Court de Gébelin, *Le Monde primitif analysé et comparé avec le monde moderne consideré dans l'histoire naturelle de la Parole* (*Le Monde primitif*, 3; Paris, 1775), pp. 12—14. L. M. C. de La Tour d'Auvergne, *Nouvelles recherches sur la Langue d'origine et les Antiquités des Bretons pour servir à l'histoire du Peuple* (Bayonne, 1792).

61. Among many studies on this major question are George Boas, *Essays on Primitivism and Related Ideas in the Middle Ages* (New York, 1966; 1st ed., 1948); Gilbert Chinard, *L'Amérique et le rêve exotique dans la littérature française au XVIIe et au XVIIIe siècles* (Paris, 1913); George Boas, *Vox Populi* (cited in n. 14), pp. 112—42; Frank E. Manuel, *The Eighteenth Century Confronts the Gods* (New York, 1967; 1st ed., 1959), especially pp. 41—46, 141—42, 149—61, 184—209, 250—58; Margaret Hodgen, *Early Anthropology in the Sixteenth and Seventeenth Centuries* (Philadelphia, 1964), especially chaps. 8 and 12.

Lancelot Voisin de La Popelinière, *L'Histoire des histoires, avec l'Idee de l'Histoire accomplie* (Paris, 1599), pp. 25—34.

62. In addition to the sources in n. 61, Claude Guichard, *Funerailles et diverses manieres d'ensevelir des Rommains, Grecs et autres nations, tant anciennes que modernes* (Lyon, 1581), p. 463, quoting Jean de Léry's *Histoire d'un voyage faict en la terre du Bresil* (1578). Jean-Jacques Rousseau, *Essai sur l'origine des langues*, in *Oeuvres complètes* (Paris, 1825), 1: 469—564, chaps. 2—4.

Vico did not, however, discuss proverbs specifically in relation to one of his three kinds of society or culture (divine, heroic, human). Used by peoples "ancient and modern," they were evidence of "a mental language common to all nations." They contained similar meanings everywhere, but had widely diverse expression and style according to nation. Giambattista Vico, *La Scienza Nuova Prima*, ed. F. Nicolini (Bari, 1931), no. 385; *The New Science of Giambattista Vico*, trans. T. G. Bergin and M. H. Fisch (Ithaca, N.Y., 1968), nos. 161, 445. I am grateful to Stephen Greenblatt for calling this matter to my attention.

63. On the concept of "culture" and its relation to eighteenth-century scholarship and thought, see Gossman, *Medievalism*, pp. 176, 353; and Clifford Geertz, *The Interpretation of Cultures. Selected Essays* (New York, 1973), chaps. 2—3.

64. Jean-Charles-François Tuet, *Matinées Senonoises, ou proverbes françois, suivis de leur origine; de leur rapport avec ceux des langues anciennes et modernes* (Paris, 1789). Born in Ham in 1742, Tuet taught humanities at the Collège de Sens and died at Sens in 1797. Among his other works are *Eléments de poésie latine* (1778) and *Projet sur l'usage qui l'on peut faire des biens nationaux* (1790). *Dictionnaire des lettres françaises, Dix-huitième siècle* (Paris, 1960), L-Z, pp. 598—99.

For a very interesting discussion of "obscenity" and its history see Charles de Brosses, *Traité de la formation méchaniques des langues et des principes physiques de l'étymologie* (Paris, 1765), 2: 143—57. De Brosses, too, thought that the banning of so many words was regrettable.

65. See the introductory essays in Volumes 1 and 2 of the *Mémoires de l'Académie Celtique* (1807—8) for their statements of purpose and methodology. "*Ce que nous méprisons aujourd'hui comme des contes populaires, comme des monumens grossiers, sont des vestiges précieux de la sagesse [des] anciens legislateurs*" (1: 62—63). The Académie became the Société des Antiquaires in 1813.

66. Jacques-Antoine Dulaure (1755—1835), "Archéographe du lieu de la Tombe, et de ses environs," *Mémoires de l'Académie Celtique*, 2 (1808): 446—57. See also his *Des divinités génératrices chez les anciens et les modernes* (1825) (Paris, 1905), with an introductory notice on his life. Also see *Dictionnaire des lettres françaises. Le dix-neuvième siècle* (1971), A-K, pp. 339—40.

67. Anthelme Richerand (1779—1840), *Des erreurs populaires relatives à la médecine* (1st ed., 1810; 2d ed. revised, Paris, 1812).

68. The various works of *Erreurs populaires* went through fewer editions than the books of remedies and recipes (see notes 70 and 80 below). Signature in the copy of Laurent Joubert's *Erreurs populaires* (1578) at the Academy of Medicine, Toronto: "Urbain hemard." Noel Becquart, "Inventaire des effets d'un chirurgien de Périgueux en 1671," *Bulletin de la société historique et archéologique du Périgord* 95 (1968): 290—93: this surgeon owned Joubert's *Erreurs populaires* and another book with a similar. title.

69. *La grande chirurgie de M. Guy de Chauliac, medecin tres fameux de l'université de Montpelier, composée l'an de grace mil trois cens soixante trois. Restituée par M. Laurens Ioubert* (Lyon, 1580).

Le régime de santé is based on the Regimen of Health of the medieval School of Salerno, and had numerous editions in French and Latin in the sixteenth century. The *Tresor des povres* was attributed to the medieval physician Arnault de Villeneuve. The work and its editions are discussed in *Histoire littéraire de la France* (Paris, 1733—1941), 28: 96—98. Among numerous editions: *Le tresor des povres selon Arnoult de Villenove . . . et plusieurs autres docteurs en medecine de Montpellier* (Lyon: Claude Nourry, 1512). There were also editions at Paris (1512) and at Lyon (Benoît Rigaud, 1590). Among editions of "Albertus Magnus," *De secretis mulierum libellus . . .* (Lyon: Barthélemy Vincent, 1571); *Albertus Magnus de Secretis Mulierum . . .* (Amsterdam, 1665).

70. See on this work John Ferguson, *Bibliographical Notes on Histories of Inventions and Books of Secrets* (London, 1959). The work first appeared in Italian in Bologna in 1555; the first French edition was printed by Christophe Plantin in Antwerp in 1557 and was followed by several more by Guillaume Rouillé and others. I quote here the English translation, which first appeared in 1558: *The Secrets of Alexis: Containing Many Excellent Remedies against Divers Diseases . . .* (London, 1615), f. A 5^r.

Among books by sixteenth-century physicians in the "secrets" tradition: *La decoration Dhumaine nature et aornement des dames. Compile . . . par Maistre Andre le Fournier docteur regent en la faculte de Medecine en Luniversite de Paris* (Lyon, 1532); Jean Liébault, *Thrésor des remedes secrets pour les maladies des femmes* (Paris, 1587), as well as the medical material he contributed to the later editions of Charles Estienne's agricultural manual *La Maison Rustique; Les secrets et merveilles de nature. Recueillis de divers Autheurs . . . par Iean Iacques Wecker de Basle, Medecin de Colmer. Traduicts en Francois . . .* (Lyon, 1586).

71. Discussed by Laurent Joubert, *Erreurs populaires au fait de la medecine et regime de la santé* (Bordeaux, 1578), Book 1; and by Luc d'Iharce, *Erreurs populaires sur la médecine* (Paris, 1783), p. 494.

72. W. Wightman, *Science and the Renaissance* (Edinburgh, 1962), 1: 211—13; Owsei Temkin, *Galenism. Rise and Decline of a Medical Philosophy* (Ithaca, N.Y., 1973), pp. 125—28. In his *Précellence* of 1579 (cited in n. 29), Henri Estienne was responding to this work of purification (Joubert called it "a cleansing of the Augean stables"): physicians are finding much to criticize in the precepts of the School of Salerno. Many of them which were accepted some thirty years ago are now all contradicted (pp. 213—15).

73. Paul Delaunay, *La médecine et l'église* (Paris, 1948), pp. 81—83. C. A. E. Wickersheimer,

La *médecine et les médecins en France à l'époque de la Renaissance* (Paris, 1906), chap. 3.
J. Céard, "Introduction" to Ambrose Paré, *Des monstres et prodiges,* ed.
Jean Céard (Geneva, 1971), pp. xiv—xvi. Laurent Joubert, *Erreurs populaires et propos vulgaires touchant la medecine et le regime de santé . . . Reveuë corrigée et augmentée* (Bordeaux, 1579), p. 411.
74. Temkin, *Galenism,* pp. 128—33. Allen G. Debus, *The English Paracelsians* (New York, 1966), chap. 1. Paracelsus was not without professional standards himself: in the preface to his *Chirurgia minor,* he distinguished charlatans from true physicians; the former were *religieux,* who tried to cure through prayers, and butchers, and others who tried to practice on the basis of a little reading.
75. Laurent Joubert, *Segonde* [*sic*] *Partie des Erreurs populaires et propos vulgaires, touchant le Medecine et le regime de santé* (Paris, 1580), quotation from the introduction by the master surgeon Barthelemy Cabrol, f. B iᵛ.
76. On Joubert's career, see L. Dulieu, "Laurent Joubert, chancelier de Montpellier," BHR 31 (1969): 139—67; Joubert, *Erreurs* (1579), 1: 412—36; 2: c iᵛ—viᵛ. Idem, *Erreurs* (1580), pp. 159—87.
77. Joubert, *Erreurs* (1579), 1: 408—12, 528, 196—97.
78. On the attack on Joubert's work for its language in treating sexual matters, see Dulieu, "Joubert," pp. 148—49; and Joubert, *Erreurs* (1579), 1: 3—11. De Gli Errori populari dell'Eccellentiss. sign. Lorenzo Gioberti (Florence, 1592). Sir Thomas Browne, *Pseudoxia Epidemica or Enquiries into very many received tenents and commonly presumed truths* (4th ed., London, 1658; a French translation was published in 1735 and 1742); M. L. Castilhon, *Essai sur les erreurs et les superstitions anciennes et modernes* (Frankfurt, 1766).
79. James Primerose was born in Bordeaux, the son of a Scottish minister, and was later associated with Montpellier. His *De vulgi erroribus in Medicina Libri IV* appeared in Amsterdam in 1639 and in Rotterdam in 1658. First English translation: *Popular Errours, or the Errours of the People in Physick . . . translated into English by Robert Wittie* (London, 1651). Traité de Primerose sur les erreurs vulgaires de la medicine, avec des additions très curieuses par M. de Rostagny, medecin de la Société royale et de S.A.R. Madame de Guise (Lyon, 1689), dedication of Jean de Rostagny to the Bishop of Marseille, saying he has translated this from the English edition. Rostagny earlier published a work against Calvinism and in 1689 also published a translation of a work by Robert Boyle.
Iharce, *Erreurs populaires,* p. 387 (mention of the edicts of the Société Royale de Médecine). Richerand, *Erreurs* (1812), pp. v—viii.
On the medical profession and its institutions in the eighteenth century, see Roger Hahn, *The Anatomy of a Scientific Institution. The Paris Academy of Sciences, 1666—1803* (Berkeley, Calif., 1971), pp. 102—3; Jean Meyer, "Une enquête de l'Académie de Médecine sur les épidémies (1774—1794)," Annales ESC 21 (1966): 729—49; Jean-Pierre Peter, "Une enquête de la Société Royale de Médecine (1774—1794): Malades et maladies à la fin du XVIIIe siècle," Annales ESC 22 (1967): 711—51.
80. Among editions of Madame Fouquet's work: *Recueil de Receptes, Choisies, Experimentées et Approuvées . . . Reveuë et Corrigee de Nouveau* (Montauban, 1676); *Les remedes charitables de Madame Fouquet. Pour guerir a peu de frais toute sorte de Maux . . . Experimentez par la Dame* (Lyon, 1681), including a dedication, dated April 1680, to priests and clerics of the *Séminaires,* urging them to concern themselves with the sick; *Recueil des Remedes faciles et domestiques . . . Recueillis par les Ordres Charitables de . . . Madame Fouquet, pour soulager les Pauvres Malades* (Dijon, 1690), dedication from publisher "to pious and charitable ladies."
Recueil des plus beaux secrets de medecine, pour la guerison de toutes les maladies . . . Et la maniere de preparer facilement dans les Familles les remédes et medicamens (Paris, 1695).
La Medecine et la Chirurgie des Pauvres Qui contiennent Des remèdes choisis, faciles à preparer et sans dépense (Paris, 1749; and new edition, Paris, 1766). This work is *not* the same as Philippe Hecquet's *La Medecine, la chirurgie et la Pharmacie des Pauvres,* which, despite its title, was an attempt to remake the "secrets" book over in a way more satisfactory to enlightened physicians.
81. Rostagny, *Erreurs,* Book 1, chaps. 5—9; Iharce, *Erreurs,* pp. 382—415; Richerand, *Erreurs* (1812), pp. 312—15.

82. Rostagny, *Erreurs*, p. 296, Book 3, chaps. 3—4; Richerand, *Erreurs* (1812), p. 275.

83. Iharce, *Erreurs*, pp. 421—26. On "popular medicine" in the late eighteenth and nineteenth centuries, see M. Bouteillier, *Médecine populaire d'hier et d'aujourd'hui* (Paris, 1966), pp. 11—107. A doctoral dissertation by Matthew Ramsey of Harvard University is also under way on this subject.

84. Daniel Le Clerc, *Histoire de la Medecine, Où l'on voit l'Origine et les Progrès de cet, de Siecle en Siecle* (Amsterdam, 1702), Part 1, and pp. 25—46; François Dujardin, *Histoire de la Chirurgie, Depuis son origine jusqu'à nos jours* (Paris, 1774), pp. 2—29. Writing in 1804, Etienne Tourtelle thought the peasants were losing contact with the old ancestral traditions of herbal medicine because of "the facility with which they could run to a physician." Thus they were beginning to distinguish themselves from the medicine of *"les peuplades de sauvages"* (*Histoire philosophique de la médecine* [Paris, 1804], p. 3). Iharce, *Erreurs*, pp. 456—57.

85. Iharce, *Erreurs*, pp. 386—87.

86. Gerard Bouchard, *Le village immobile: Sennely-en-Sologne au XVIIIe siècle* (Paris, 1972), p. 365.

87. *Ibid.*, p. 120.

Index

Index

This book is set in Sabon, a typeface based
on designs by the sixteenth-century masters
Claude Garamond and Robert Granjon and named
for their contemporary Jacques Sabon,
a typefounder from Lyon